Politics 1968

Tom Furnanz #625
6850 El Colegio
Goleta, CA.
968-7925

WADSWORTH CONTINUING EDUCATION SERIES
Leonard Freedman, General Editor

Armament and Disarmament: The Continuing Dispute
edited by Walter R. Fisher and Richard D. Burns
Los Angeles State College

Contemporary Communism: Theory and Practice
edited by Howard R. Swearer and Richard P. Longaker
University of California, Los Angeles

Contemporary Labor Issues
edited by Walter Fogel and Archie Kleingartner
University of California, Los Angeles

Contemporary Moral Issues
edited by Harry K. Girvetz
University of California, Santa Barbara

Issues of the Sixties, Second Edition: 1965–1970
edited by Leonard Freedman
University Extension
University of California, Los Angeles

Metropolis: Values in Conflict
edited by C. E. Elias, Jr.,
James Gillies, York University, and Svend Riemer
University of California, Los Angeles

The New Technology and Human Values
edited by John G. Burke
University of California, Los Angeles

Politics 1968
edited by Francis M. Carney and H. Frank Way, Jr.
University of California, Riverside

Poverty: American Style
edited by Herman P. Miller
U.S. Bureau of the Census

Problems and Prospects of the Negro Movement
edited by Raymond J. Murphy and Howard Elinson
University of California, Los Angeles

Tension Areas in World Affairs
edited by Arthur C. Turner
University of California, Riverside
and Leonard Freedman
University Extension
University of California, Los Angeles

Politics 1968

FRANCIS M. CARNEY

H. FRANK WAY, JR.

University of California, Riverside

Wadsworth Publishing Company, Inc.
Belmont, California

L. C. Cat. Card No.: 67–30776

Printed in the United States of America

Preface

Politics 1968 presents the major economic, social, and international issues confronting both the nation and the voter in a presidential election year. This collection from the writings of the leading statesmen and political analysts in recent and current American politics has been prepared for the use of every responsible citizen who is—or should be— vitally concerned with the national and international politics that will play such a decisive part in choosing the next President of the United States. Even more than in recent presidential elections, the 1968 Republican and Democratic candidates, as well as the public, must be aware of their increasing responsibilities. The voter cannot analyze a candidate's awareness of his responsibilities without knowing what is going to be demanded of the next President. It has, therefore, been our objective to present various views of these responsibilities for the information and guidance of the voter, who will, of course, choose the next President.

Part One, "The Processes," presents a many-faceted analysis of our political system, especially as it operates in a presidential year and as it will influence and persuade the voter. Accordingly, the articles in this part focus attention on political parties and the electorate; the Presidency is examined in some of its dimensions with particular emphasis on the personal "style" of two Presidents. The emphasis changes in Part Two, "The Issues," to a presentation of conflicting views of the most important issues confronting the public and the government today. Regardless of which party the next President represents, he must have made his position on these vital issues sufficiently clear to have won the confidence of the majority of the American voters. Certainly, other important issues, such as agriculture, the re-examination of NATO, and the federal role in elementary and secondary education, will confront the voter in 1968. We feel, however, that the issues presented are major ones; whether they are debated in the campaign on a partisan basis or not, they are part of the political climate of our time and thus deserve thoughtful consideration.

Since many of the selections included in this collection have been excerpted, we have taken the liberty of giving some of them titles to indicate the nature of their content as presented in this book. We have transcribed the articles as faithfully as possible—correcting only obvious misprints, eliminating footnotes where feasible, and renumbering footnotes that remain.

We wish to extend our appreciation to the numerous individuals and organizations that have contributed to this publication. In particular, we thank the various authors whose articles appear here. We would also like to express our special gratitude to Leonard Freedman, University Extension, University of California, for his thoughtful comments and assistance.

Francis M. Carney
H. Frank Way, Jr.

Contents

Part One
The Processes

Everybody interprets everything in his own way. That's the problem with the world.

GEORGE HARRISON, O.B.E.

1
The Retreat from Politics

Thomas Carlyle was surely wrong when, in his rage against the bleak orthodox economics of his day, he labeled it "the dismal science." It is the "respectable professors" of politics who are the real practitioners of dismal science. "... for how we live is so far removed from how we ought to live," said Machiavelli, "that he who abandons what is done for what ought to be done, will rather learn to bring about his own ruin than his preservation." Max Weber not only characterized power and violence as the means specific to politics, but went on to insist that to have the "calling for politics" is to live with the fact that one's soul may be lost. For Paine, government was a "badge of lost innocence," and Madison called it the greatest of all reflections on man's nature.

One need not subscribe to some sweeping theory of an ineradicably sinful, corrupt, or bestial human nature to understand that a task of the political theorist is to explain away or make an accommodation with the fact that men can behave and often do behave wickedly or foolishly. One needn't think of politics as devoid of ethical content to understand that from time to time the politician, if he is responsible, must not shrink from using odious means. One knows that, if he is to adopt the political frame of reference, he must seem to be muttering a sour and crabbed negative to some of the loftiest, most generous aspirations of man. One enters politics as the gentle teacher and leaves as the strident martinet, if not as the hangman. Men in politics dream of justice, liberty, community, peace, truth, and the good life. But they find themselves in a world of power, struggle, interest, calculation, and obduracy. At best, politics is, as Weber said, a "strong and slow boring of hard boards."

It is no wonder, then, that men have almost always sought some substitute for politics, some rule or formula for ordering the myriad, messy affairs of men and societies. Wisdom, scripture, the teachings of Jesus, natural law, the absolute sovereign, the General Will, unregulated competition, no competition, class struggle, scientific planning, direct democracy, unlimited instinct gratification, universal love, and the eroticization of every relationship have all been offered as The One True Way which, if followed, would relieve men of the need for politics.

Why should it be so? What is the "dismal" element of politics? We think that there are two conditions essential to politics and that these conditions singly or in combination have the potential for estranging people from politics. In the first place, to be in politics is to be inextricably enmeshed in rule, power, authority, and conflict. The very words can be harsh and threatening, especially to men of humane and generous impulses. Rule, or authority, and the power behind it are external to their objects, alien to them, and implicitly coercive. No amount of flummery about the Real Will, the Rational Self, or the Social Compact can wholly obscure the alien and coercive character of authority. Today's unquiet Flower Children offer us but the most recent and flamboyant expression of the sense that politics and love have an antipodal relationship. The old men who comprise the intellectual paternity of the Flower Children— Herbert Marcuse, Erich Fromm, N. O. Brown are among the more notable—have brilliantly and seductively juxtaposed Eros Vanquished and Politics Triumphant. The crucial metaphors of politics also indicate the antithesis of politics and love; politics is almost unimaginable without contest, conflict, power, struggle, campaign, opposition, force, pressure, victory, and defeat. Under such metaphors, Eros cannot reign. Rue and melancholy will be the sometime companions of the thoughtful man in politics.

Here we would simply note that to be for politics is not to oppose Eros. If man were merely *homo homine lupus*, politics would not be possible. But so long as man has the potential to be wolfish, politics is necessary.

A second "dismal" element of politics is its moral ambiguity. We have just acknowledged that politics is not love. We have suggested that if men could always love one another, politics would not be necessary. But we also suggest that if men only hated, if they never loved one another, politics would not be possible. To speak of the moral ambiguity of politics is to pile paradox on top of paradox. To think of politics as no more than means, as no more than a vehicle for resolving disputes, as no more than a more or less mechanical calculation of material interests, as subsumable under the rubric of *Realpolitik,* is to vulgarize the thought of those who, like Weber, have stressed the elements of prudence, civility, restraint, and responsibility in politics. For politics is surely invested by our passionate attachment to our values. If politics is unimaginable without conflict and calculation, it is also unimaginable without the attachment of men to liberty, equality, justice, and fraternity. The paradox lies in the fact that, despite its inherent moral element, politics functions most effectively when it serves to reduce or transform its own ethical components. This is, of course, unsatisfying to the pure moralist. It is frustrating to one who views politics solely as the vehicle of expression or realization of a profound ethical commitment.

It is just this sense of politics—as serving to reduce moral tension—that such writers as Walter Lippmann and Hans J. Morgenthau have in mind when they urge the use of diplomacy as an alternative to using naked power or drawing sharp moral distinctions in international affairs. We would illustrate the point further by suggesting that our own Civil War was a consequence of the failure of our political system to reduce the sectional tension over the moral issue of human slavery. To say this, however, is not to make the crude error of thinking of politics as "the art of compromise." Politics involves compromise, of course, but it also involves the deepest commitment to moral ends. To politicize a moral end is not to abandon it, but to express it in another context. To politicize an end, one must frame it in a way that not only makes it a feasible object of public policy, but also draws the support of those who are indifferent to the end and those who had not hitherto envisioned it in terms of public policy.

To speak of politics as we do seems appropriate in 1968. Two great issues, each of them evoking the deepest and contrasting moral feelings, dominate our politics. They are, of course, the war in Viet Nam and race relations. We are convinced that neither issue can be comprehended, let alone resolved, if viewed solely as a moral issue. We have tried to design the readings in this book to assist in the politicization of both issues.

RACE AS A POLITICAL PROBLEM

Our political system has never managed to absorb the race problem. Its Framers tried at Philadelphia to reduce the moral tension over slavery, but even their fabled ingenuity was not adequate to the task. This is no place to retrace the history of the race question in America. It is clear that "the problem" has always stirred the deepest passions, that it still does, and that we are not yet in sight of the end of it. Jefferson, ardent opponent of slavery, democrat, and humanist, wrote chillingly in *Notes on the State of Virginia:*

> It will probably be asked, Why not retain and incorporate the blacks into the State, and thus save the expense of supplying by importation of white settlers, the vacancies they will leave? Deep-rooted prejudices entertained by the whites; ten thousand recollections, by the blacks, of the injuries they have sustained; new provocations; the real distinctions which nature has made; and many other circumstances, will divide us into parties, and produce convulsions, which will never end but in the extermination of the one or the other race.

And the ominous echo of Jefferson's despair sounds today from the throats of thousands of angry or despairing black men.

The agonies of the race problem do not, of course, arise from moral dilemmas alone. The irrational, subterranean things—mystery, dread, eroticism, and guilt, to name a few of them—continue to twist and torment the black-white relationship. But there are moral problems as well. The Negroes and millions of white people who support them raise a cry for justice and equality. But other millions of white people believe that since the legal disabilities against them have been removed, the Negroes are essentially in the same condition as everyone else, and that any further improvement of their material and psychological states is up to the Negroes themselves. To wish passionately for full equality for the Negroes is not enough in such a situation. The absolute moralist can and does denounce the moral insensitivity of the white majority. He can, also, if he is of a mind to, expatiate on the "guilt" of white society and hold himself to be alienated from so immoral a society. Political man, however, must take up the task of ending injustice in the face of the hostility or indifference of society.

Perhaps the hardest of the tasks of the man who passionately wants justice for the Negroes is to accept the fact of the injustice, to understand that history has perpetrated an atrocity against the American Negroes. If one can accept that the society has failed and also ask "Why have we failed and what can we do to remedy the failure?" he is thinking politically and stands a better chance of realizing the goal of equality for the Negroes than does the moralist who is content to point to the failure.

We offer as an example of a man who is morally committed to justice for the Negroes and who also pursues his goal politically, one of our contributors, Daniel P. Moynihan. Mr. Moynihan perceived in 1965 that the civil rights movement, or, as it might more appropriately be called, the struggle for equality for Negroes, had reached a critical point. With the passage of the federal legislation of 1964 and 1965, most of the legal disabilities against Negroes had been removed. The white majority seemed satisfied that, with the conferral of voting rights, justice had been done; and, in any case, that majority was clearly hostile to any massive legislative attack on the destructive consequences for Negroes of the long-time manifest and continuing discrimination. For Moynihan the problem was one of getting swift and significant action started in the face of the public and Congressional hostility or indifference—action on unemployment, housing, education, family life, health care. Moynihan circulated within the government a study he had supervised and written, entitled *The Negro Family: The Case for National Action*. The thesis of the study, if we may simplify, was that the centuries of discrimination which the Negroes had suffered and still suffer today had produced a radical "demoralization" of Negro family life; this demoralized family life, moreover, fed back in a "tangle of pathologies" upon the capacity now of poor Negroes to extricate themselves from the morass of underemployment, poverty, slum housing, and inferior education. The "Moynihan Report," as the document came to be known, went on to urge the development of a program of federal governmental initiatives to strike directly at the cancer of ghetto life. The tone of the report was "cool." It did not appeal directly to justice or morality. The report's primary intended audience was a governmental elite. It gave this elite a rationale for and the grounds of a program for moving beyond the tentative, traditional legislation already on the books of the Kennedy and Johnson administrations. A secondary audience was the indifferent or hostile white majority, a majority who believed that they had satisfied the requirements of justice by removing the glaring legal disabilities against the Negroes. Moynihan, in brief, was attempting to set down a basis for a national policy of preferential treatment for the hard-core Negro poor.

There is some ground for believing that Moynihan's report found favor within the administration and was, in fact, instrumental in moving the President toward a commitment to the goals Moynihan shared with the most advanced civil rights leadership. To get action started, Moynihan was willing to forsake the terms of moral exhortation. He was willing to use such terms as "demoralization" and "pathology" in characterizing family life in the black ghetto. He apparently felt that there was little potential for constructive legislation in stressing the guilt of the white community. He was willing, that is, to be "cool" or "obscure" on the moral issue for the sake of meaningful action toward achieving the moral goal. We suggest that Moynihan was, in the best sense of the word, politicizing a moral commitment.

Moynihan came under severe attack from some of the most progressive and articulate Negro and white spokesmen for the civil rights cause. Because he had not placed obvious stress on white responsibility for the plight of the Negro poor, and because he had used certain "pathologies" among the poor Negroes as the justification for launching major governmental actions to remedy the plight, Moynihan was accused of, in effect, blaming the victims for the sins of the oppressors. James Farmer, one of the ablest and most moderate of the civil rights leaders, succinctly stated the moral case against Moynihan when he noted that "Moynihan has provided a massive academic cop-out for the white conscience. . . ." Let us leave the example with Farmer's verdict. One takes the risk of appearing to his fellow moralists to have "copped-out" when he sets out to politicize a moral commitment.

THE VIET NAM WAR: POLITICS OR MORALITY?

The reader will quickly note in Chapter 10 that, although we observe the existence of a strongly moral flavor to most of the protest against the war in Viet Nam, the selections we present do not convey much of this flavor. The selection of materials is deliberately based on our belief that the national dialogue on the Viet Nam issue threatens to escape from its political context. We include no selection expressing the "There is no substitute for victory" or "Let's bomb North Viet Nam back to the stone age" mentality. Neither do we offer any representation of that species of howling jingoism which ascribes all criticism of the war to treason or cowardice. The protestor chanting "Hey, hey, LBJ; how many kids did you kill today?" will not be "turned on" by Hans Morgenthau's scholarly analysis of the uses of intervention. Chapter 10 is not for the people just described. It is for those still capable of thinking of the Viet Nam war as a political issue.

Now it bears repeating that for us a politics without passionate moral commitment is unimaginable. Such a politics would be merely squalid and not worth a man's time at all. At the same time, we argue that politics cannot be pure acting-out of one's moral commitments. What, then, do we mean when we urge politicization of moral feelings about the war?

It would be an intolerable presumption for us to survey the whole range of possible attitudes and acts concerning the war and confidently assign some to the "properly political" category, while casting out others. Some distinctions may be drawn, however, and it is worth while to try. If one believes that our participation in the war is definitive proof that our society is already so vicious and degraded that a moral man can only abandon it, or work to destroy it in the secure belief that whatever resulted would be an improvement, he has passed beyond politics; his protests against the war no longer have a political character. But this is an easy case. Despite the presence of much apocalyptic language in the protest movement, probably very few people are in so extreme a condition of alienation.

If one wishes to politicize his moral objections to the war, he must move beyond the definition of his moral position to action aimed at bringing about the end of the war. Action, in and of itself, may be undertaken solely because of a desire to bear moral witness. Voting for peace candidates, for example, or working for a "third" party or peace party, writing letters to officials, signing manifestos, marching, demonstrating, lying down before troop trains, disobeying the conscription laws, or refusing to pay one's taxes can be political acts, or they can be not political, but rather a way of bearing witness. If the actions of one opposed to the war are political actions, they are based on a kind of prediction of their consequences, a prediction that the act chosen is more likely to lead to the objective of stopping the war than some other action. Thus, bearing moral witness can be a political act if one has some sense of how his action will bring about the objective. If one is passionately concerned, it is not easy for him to choose his actions for their political effect. It is easier to choose them for their varying degrees of moral satisfaction.

It is not likely that one will be able to think and act politically in his opposition to the war if he cannot understand that millions of his fellow citizens do not think that the war is immoral. It is not likely that one will think and act politically if he begins from the belief that being in the war is itself proof of our immorality. If, on the other hand, one can believe that we are in the war because of incompetence, because of bureaucratic rigidity and stupidity, because of failure of leadership to understand the ways in which the world has changed, because of misperception of our real national interests, because of failure to realize that nationalism and communism have various meanings and various consequences for our national interests, he is more likely to be able to think and act politically. He is more likely to be able to frame his objections to the war in terms translatable to public policy. He is more likely to be able to talk with those who disagree in terms of alternative public policies. Disagreeing men who speak to one another about alternative policies are more likely to come together than are people who simply disagree about one another's moral worth. If we want an object lesson in the danger of giving too high a moral charge to the dialogue over international affairs, we need go back only a decade and a half to that time when we permitted a simplistic and highly moralized anti-communism to become a substitute for politics.

The moralistic anti-communists of the 1940s and 1950s also imagined the apocalypse. They too employed an inflated rhetoric within which there was a lurking threat of violence. They too saw public policy imposed by a conspiracy. They too imagined an Establishment in control. They too insisted upon a direct connection between appeasement abroad and socialistic policies at home. They too felt themselves distressed by the entire development of modern American life and dwelt on their alienation from it. They too hated an American President they believed was able to impose Satanic designs at will. But why go on? The point here is not to attempt the silly business of trying to confound the passionate critics of the Viet Nam war through an even sillier equation of them with the passionately moralistic anti-communists. The point is that any insistence on an unalloyed moralizing that allows no possible accommodation is not only destructive for the polity but also damaging to the prospects of achieving the moral ends.

We conclude, then, by acknowledging that politics is not easy. Loving is much nicer. In a world in which men are not always loving, however, politics is necessary. Man fulfills himself by making and acting upon moral commitment. But in a world in which men make differing and conflicting moral commitments, we must learn to express and act upon our commitments politically. In making the selections for this book we have been guided by our conviction that it is terribly important to try to present the two great, morally laden issues of 1968 in terms that are political.

2
Profile of the Electorate

The 1964 Presidential election was, in some ways, the vindication of the scholars. They knew that President Johnson could not lose unless—to paraphrase Mrs. John F. Kennedy—he ran off with Debbie Reynolds. The article that follows, by the voting-behavior specialists of the University of Michigan Survey Research Center, lays down the Republican prospects for 1968 quite clearly. The Republicans must surmount some formidable obstacles if they are to win. Approximately 50 per cent of the electorate normally votes Democratic. The Republicans, on the other hand, can count on a hard core of only about 30 per cent of the electorate. The Republicans must hold their hard core and simultaneously win over the great bulk of the independent voters as well as a sizable portion of those whom President Eisenhower used to call "discerning Democrats." Those independents and discerning Democrats, of course, are generally unmoved by a candidacy that rests on an appeal to the "principles of real Republicanism."

But the electorate is by no means frozen in its present proportions. It is no more frozen now than it was in 1952, when, despite similar gross distributions of support for the parties, General Eisenhower won a smashing victory. Clearly, a compellingly attractive personality can win for the Republicans. When the compellingly attractive personality incarnates nonpartisanship and, at the same time, the Democrats are stuck with the wrong side of an inflamed public issue, it is easy for discerning Democrats to forsake their traditional affiliation and vote Republican, at least at the presidential level. Sometimes the Republicans have a victory potential if the Democratic candidate is unattractive to some large portion of traditional Democratic voters, as happened in 1960 when Kennedy's Catholicism cost him enough normally Democratic votes to make that election the closest of modern times.

Candidates like Eisenhower, with the amazing and enduring appeal that crosses party lines, are not easy to find, though a stance of genial nonpartisanship could no doubt be created for the right man through the use of adroit salesmanship. But, for the Republicans, winning the election on the issues requires both good luck and some degree of skill. If the country is more or less content, if no really great issues are burning in people's minds, probably no amount of image manufacture and promotion can overcome the inertial power of the gross distribution of party sentiment at the present time. There are, however, two potent issues, either of which could lead to severe punishment for President Johnson and the Democrats. The two issues are the war in Viet Nam and the rising indignation and fear among white people of all strata in connection with the tumultuous, lawless, and violent behavior of Negroes in city after city the nation over.

One must be cautious in trying to predict the impact of these issues, however. It is by no means certain that they will act to dissolve entirely the huge coalition put together by the Democrats. The American people do not range themselves neatly over an ideological spectrum. Most Americans, in fact, do not have comprehensive or integral ideological perspectives on politics. So far as the masses are concerned, the Democrats are not quite the party of an integral liberalism, just as the Republicans are not the party of an integral conservatism. There is no question that the voters do perceive a difference between the parties on matters of what we might call bread-and-butter liberalism. There is no question, moreover, that most Democratic voters agree with their party leadership that national government should act decisively, without regard to the precise doctrinal requirements of free enterprise and federalism, to even out economic-life chances, to control the cycles of economic boom and bust, to succor the unfortunate, to initiate and maintain humanitarian reforms, and generally to assume a concrete responsibility for the pace and character of economic and social advance. The great social legislation of the past thirty five years is largely the achievement of the Democratic Party. It has secured for the Democrats the fairly firm loyalty of the mass of the wage earners, the young, the Negroes, the poor, the city-dwellers, the Jews, and the intellectuals. Needless to say, moreover, the party of Al Smith and John F. Kennedy has a grip on the affection of most of the nation's Roman Catholics.

While it is too much to say that this broad Democratic coalition is "jerry-built," it is clear that elements of it can be pulled. Where is the coalition the most vulnerable? That depends on the issues and the feelings the issues engender in diverse segments of the electorate. Notably, however, and despite the exception of 1964, foreign policy issues can be dangerous to the Democrats. Their coalition is based largely on a more or less accurate perception of them as the party of progress and enlightenment in domestic policy. Throughout most sections of the electorate there is far less confidence in their handling of foreign policy. Wilson, Roosevelt, Truman, Kennedy, and Johnson—the Democratic Presidents of this century—have all committed some American forces to combat overseas. If there is widespread disapproval of the war, or dissatisfaction with its progress, and at the same time no compelling domestic issue cementing the coalition, the attrition against the Democrats could be pervasive and fatal. There are puzzles, though. Catholics, who punished Wilson and Roosevelt for their English wartime alliances, tend to be "hawkish" on the current war and might well remain loyal if the Republicans field a "dovish" candidate. On the other hand, Negroes, who as a group tend to be critical of the war, are perhaps the most intensely loyal of all groups to the Democratic Party. They might, understandably, stay with the President on the grounds that he offers far more promise than the Republicans of promoting progress in civil rights and untangling the ghastly knot in the center of the cities. The academic and left intellectuals, a numerically small but qualitatively important element of the Democratic coalition, may, despite an almost hysterical hatred of the President in certain of their quarters, shrink in horror from the prospect of casting a Republican ballot and remain loyal to the party of Roosevelt, Adlai Stevenson, and Kennedy. Much, naturally, depends on the character of the Republican nominee and the stance that party adopts for the campaign. On balance, though, the war in Viet Nam offers the Republicans exactly the kind of issue that can dissolve the Democratic coalition.

The other issue, which goes by many names—"law and order," "urban crisis," "civil rights," "black power," "crime in the streets," "white backlash," etc.—could be even more fateful, for it strikes the Democrats at their very center. That center lies among the mass of low-to-modest-income folk, the blue-collar workers, hourly-wage earners, the trade-unionists, the small farmers, the Irish, Polish, and Italian city dwellers, and, to a lesser extent, the Jews. As we have noted, political attitudes in this country do not form along a neat left-right scale. Among the masses, liberalism on social welfare or class-related issues by no means indicates liberalism on foreign policy or race issues. In fact, it is in the Democratic strongholds, solidly liberal on the class issues, that the greatest resistance to the current thrust of the Negroes is felt. The President and the Democrats could not withstand a major defection in their great strongholds. But such a defection will surely threaten if the race issue burns all other issues out of the national consciousness.

Harry Truman once assured a gathering of his fellow partisans that the Republicans would always find some way "to snatch defeat out of the jaws of victory." In their analysis, Converse, Clausen, and Miller make it clear that victory cannot come easily for the Republicans, but at the same time they skillfully identify for the Republicans some of the handles of defeat.

Philip E. Converse, Aage R. Clausen, and Warren E. Miller
ELECTORAL MYTH AND REALITY: THE 1964 ELECTION

On Election Day, 1964, the aspirations of Senator Barry Goldwater and the conservative wing of the Republican Party were buried under an avalanche of votes cast for incumbent President Lyndon Johnson. The margin of victory, approaching 16 million votes, was unprecedented. Historical comparisons with other presidential landslides are left somewhat indeterminate by the intrusion of third parties. However, it is safe to observe that Johnson's 61.3 percent of the two-party popular vote put him in the same general range as the striking victories of Franklin Delano Roosevelt in 1936, Harding in 1920, and Theodore Roosevelt in 1904.

Before the fact, the election was also expected to be the most intensely ideological campaign since 1936, in no small measure because of Goldwater's reputation as a "pure" conservative. After the fact, doubts existed as to whether this expectation had been fulfilled. Goldwater supporters, in particular, expressed disappointment that President Johnson had refused to join battle on any of the fundamental ideological alternatives that were motivating the Goldwater camp. However, as we shall see, the mass public had some sense that "important differences" between the two major parties were heightened in 1964 compared with parallel data from either 1960 or, as is more impressive, the relatively

From "Electoral Myth and Reality: The 1964 Election," by Philip Converse, Aage R. Clausen, and Warren E. Miller, *The American Political Science Review*, Vol. 59, June 1965. The authors are members of the staff of the Survey Research Center, University of Michigan.

tense election of 1952.[1] And certainly no one questioned the importance of ideological differences in the factional dispute that split the Republican Party along liberal-conservative lines with an enduring bitterness unmatched in decades.

Indeed, these three prime elements of the 1964 election—faction, ideology and the contest for votes—became intertwined after the manner of a classic script. That is, the "outer" ideological wing of a party captures its nomination, leaving a vacuum toward the center of gravity of national opinion. This vacuum is gleefully filled by the opposing party without any loss of votes from its own side of the spectrum. The outcome, logically and inexorably, is a landslide at the polls.[2]

With a script so clearly written in advance, the outsider would naturally ask why any party controlled by rational strategists should choose a course likely to lead to such massive repudiation in its name. The answers to this question in the 1964 case are not particularly obscure, although they can be made at numerous levels. One answer, of course, is that Republican Party strategists were themselves in deep disagreement as to just what script was relevant: many recognized the classic script and predicted the eventual outcome, with all of its attendant losses for other Republican candidates, in deadly accuracy.

For the factional dispute within Republican ranks involved not only an ideological clash, but also major differences in the perception of that political reality which becomes important in winning votes and elections. The Goldwater faction was told by its Republican adversaries, as the conservative wing had been told for years, that a Goldwater could not conceivably defeat a Democratic President, and would instead greatly damage the party ticket at all levels. The Goldwater group countered that a victory for their man was entirely plausible despite the danger signals of the spring polls and the normal difficulties of challenging an incumbent. It is not clear how sincere or widespread this confidence was: some statements sounded as though the Goldwater candidacy had little chance of winning but would at least provide a forum for the conservative philosophy, along with control of the Republican Party. But even in their more pessimistic moments, the Goldwater people would argue that while victory might be difficult, they certainly saw no reason to believe that Goldwater would do worse than any other Republican

---

[1] The collection of data from a national sample of the electorate around the 1964 election was made possible by a grant to the Survey Research Center of the University of Michigan from the Carnegie Corporation of New York, which had also supported the 1952 election study.

[2] The most fertile elaboration of this classic script is of course contained in Anthony Downs, *An Economic Theory of Democracy* (New York, 1957).

challenger, or encounter the electoral disaster the liberals were predicting.

Similarly, at the San Francisco nominating convention, his opponents vehemently charged that Goldwater was a "minority candidate," even among Republicans in this country. In another direct clash of perceptions, Senator Goldwater is said to have remarked to a group of Midwestern delegates, "What the minority [the convention liberals] can't get through their heads is that this is a true representation of the Republican Party."[3]

In this article we wish to examine the relationship between such conflicting perceptions and what is known of the relevant reality in the context of the 1964 election. Our information comes primarily from sample survey studies of the mass public that formed the electorate in 1964, and whose reactions represent one level of political reality about which so many conflicting opinions and predictions were made. While the most important aspect of that reality was unveiled by the election outcome, there remained some of the customary latitude of interpretation as to its full significance. And with respect to the interplay between the stratagems of party elites on one hand and the grass-roots American voters on the other, the chronology of the 1964 election does indeed provide a fascinating composite of sheer myth, genuine but discrepant reality worlds, and self-fulfilling prophecies.

I. THE MYTH OF THE STAY-AT-HOME REPUBLICANS

The first theory of electoral reality on our agenda may be rapidly disposed of, for it lies more simply and unequivocally in the realm of myth than any of the others we shall treat. It should not be overlooked, however, both because of its historical persistence and because of its enshrinement in the battle cry of 1964 Goldwater supporters: "A choice, not an echo!"

In the quadrennial competition between liberal and conservative wings of the Republican Party for the presidential nomination throughout the 1940s and 1950s, the conservatives were consistently bested. One of the prime contentions of the liberals was that all of the entries of the conservative wing were so distant from the "middle-of-the-road" that they had no hope of attracting the independent votes necessary for victory over the Democrats. At an ideological level, the conservative wing coined the epithet "me-tooism" to ridicule the liberals for their refusal to reject Democratic innovations of the New and Fair Deal eras root and branch. The liberals, it was charged, were slowly selling out the

[3] *The New York Times,* July 19, 1964.

fundamental principles on which earlier days of G.O.P. ascendancy had been based.

This accusation of ideological "flabbiness" was not, however, compelling of itself without some further comment on the problem of winning votes. As a consequence, a theory became widely current among conservative Republicans that G.O.P. difficulties in maintaining much contact with the White House were in fact directly tied to the "me-tooist" flavor of its presidential candidates. Republicans running for that office tended to lose not because there was any lack of potential Republican votes (as the superficial observer might have thought), but because many of the "real" Republicans were sufficiently offended by "me-tooism" that they simply didn't bother to vote at all. Nominate a true Republican rather than a Tweedledee, the theory went, and enough of these stay-at-homes would return to the polls to put him into the White House.

As such theories go, this contention was remarkably verifiable. That is, the critic need not argue that few Republicans were disappointed by the nominees of their party, for disappointment in itself is irrelevant for argument. The question is simply whether or not Republicans, however disappointed, did continue to turn out and vote even for "me-tooist" candidates through this period—a matter much easier to ascertain. Nor is there any point in arguing that there were *never* any stray Republicans who in the last analysis vented their frustrations by refusing to go to the polls. Undoubtedly there were. But the theory hinges less on the question as to whether such people existed, than on the contention that they existed in significant numbers: not merely several hundred or several thousand or even a few hundred thousand, but in the millions needed to overcome the persistent Democratic majorities.

Such a pool of potential voters would be large enough to be discriminated reliably in most sample surveys. And we know of no reputable sample surveys at any time in this period that gave any shred of reason to believe that this significant pool of stay-at-home Republicans existed. Indeed, such findings as were relevant pointed massively in the opposite direction. From 1944 on, for example, one can contrast turnout rates between Democrats and Republicans of comparable strengths of identification. And over election after election featuring "me-tooist" Republican nominees, one finds that turnout rates are consistently higher —and often much higher—on the Republican side. Indeed, each time we isolate that polar minority who not only have an intense commitment to the Republican Party, but whose commitment is of a highly sensitive ideological sort, turnout typically reaches proportions staggering for the American system: 96 percent, 98 percent—levels almost implausible in view of registration difficulties, travel, sickness and other accidents which can keep the most devoted American from the polls upon occasion. More impressive still, we find that in 1952 those Republicans who reported during the campaign that they would have preferred the "conservative" Taft over the "liberal" Eisenhower—exactly those Republicans to whom the theory refers—actually turned out at much *higher* rates to vote for Eisenhower in the November election (94 percent) than did the set of Republicans who indicated satisfaction with Eisenhower's nomination (84 percent).[4]

These brief observations do not begin to exhaust the evidence, none of which lends any support whatever to the theory of a silent pool of frustrated conservative Republicans. Hence it is scarcely surprising that the Goldwater cause in 1964 was not buoyed up by some sudden surge of new support at the polls which other strategists had overlooked; for the hitherto silent people expected to provide such a surge existed principally in the imaginations of conservative strategists who in time of adversity needed desperately to believe that they were there. It is less of a wonder that this theory was generated, particularly before sample survey data took on much scope or stature in the 1940s, than that it persisted with greater or lesser vigor into the 1960s in the face of repetitive contradictory evidence readily available to any proponents with an edge of interest as to what the facts actually were.

II. THE MINORITY CANDIDATE OF A MINORITY PARTY

On the eve of the Republican nominating convention, an irate Goldwater supporter wrote to the Paris edition of the *Herald Tribune*, upbraiding it for the doubts it had expressed as to the extent of Goldwater sentiment beyond the convention delegates themselves, and pointing out that a massive groundswell of support had built up for Goldwater throughout the country "west of Madison Avenue."

The charge of the liberal wing of the G.O.P. that Goldwater not only was unattractive to Democrats and Independents but was not even the majority preference of Republicans was a particularly severe allegation in view of the constraints under which the Republican Party has been obliged to operate in recent years. It has been the consensus of observers for quite some time that the Republican Party is a minority

[4] This datum is not as absurd as it might appear if the reader has failed to grasp the import of the preceding text. That is, in 1952 it was the most intense and ideologically "pure" Republicans who tended to prefer Taft to Eisenhower, much as 12 years later their counterparts chose Goldwater over the other Republican alternatives. It was the less ideologically committed (either by persuasion or by lack of ideological sensitivity) who were more satisfied with the Eisenhower candidature. The erstwhile Taft supporters did not perversely turn out at higher rates because they were disappointed in the convention choice, but because their striking commitment to Republicanism compelled them to more ardent support of its candidate whatever his ideological position.

party in the affections of the American public. Our relevant data collections at frequent intervals since 1952 have left little question in our minds both as to the minority status of the Republicans, and as to the stability of that status during this epoch. For most of this time, our estimates would suggest that in terms of underlying loyalties, the Democrats could expect to receive, all other things equal, something in the neighborhood of 54 percent of the national popular vote; and if any change has been occurring in this figure in the past 15 years, it is that this Democratic majority is slowly increasing.[5] In practical terms, this means that a Democratic candidate need not have much attraction for grass-roots Republicans: he can win easily if he can but carry the votes of a reasonable share of independents, and has general appeal for Democrats. A Republican candidate, on the other hand, can only win at the national level by drawing nearly monolithic support from Republicans, attracting the votes of a lion's share of independents, and inducing unusual defection among the less committed Democratic identifiers as well. The latter was the Eisenhower formula, and one which Nixon had nearly succeeded in following in 1960. More generally, the liberal wing of the Republican Party had sought candidates with this kind of broad appeal throughout this period. In this light, the question of Goldwater's popularity was serious: for if a minority party nominates a figure enjoying only minority support within his own party, it is an obvious invitation to disaster.

In the spring and early summer of 1964, the opinion polls lent much weight to the contention that Goldwater enjoyed no broad support even among Republicans. The Goldwater supporters tended to counter this kind of evidence either (1) by ignoring the polls; or (2) by questioning the validity of the polls (some Goldwater placards were to read "Gallup didn't count us!"); or (3) by questioning the immutability of the early poll readings. Of these reactions, certainly the last-mentioned was entirely appropriate. That is, in the very early stages of a push toward the presidency, even a person who has been something of a "national" figure as Senator or major Governor for a considerable period may not be recognized by very large portions of the public. Until he has received much more intense national exposure in the limelight of presidential primaries and the nominating convention, "straw polls" as to his popularity can be highly misleading and unstable, particularly if the polling pits such a candidate against other figures with more long-standing national prominence and "household" names.[6]

---

[5] See "The Concept of a 'Normal Vote,' " ch. 1 in A. Campbell, P. Converse, W. Miller and D. Stokes, *Elections and the Political Order* (New York, 1965).

[6] In our estimation, some challengers of this description have been prematurely discouraged from competition by poll results which might well have changed radically with greater exposure.

However, survey data gathered over the course of 1964 can be put together with "hard" data from the presidential primaries to provide an illuminating picture of Goldwater's general popularity and, in particular, the reactions of grass-roots Republicans to him. In January, 1964, before the beginning of the spring primaries, we asked a national sample of the electorate:

> Many people are wondering who will run for President on the Republican side this fall. ... If you had to make a choice, which Republican leader do you think would be best for our country in 1964?
>
> Who would be your second choice?
>
> Are there any of the leading Republicans that you think would make very bad candidates?

Table 1 summarizes the responses to this sequence of questions. The open-ended nature of the questions meant that individuals only rated those Republicans whom they were aware of at the time, and

TABLE 1.   *Preferences for the Republican Presidential Nomination among Selected Segments of the Electorate, January, 1964*

		Segments of the Electorate		
	Per cent mentions[a]	Score across total electorate[b]	Score within "Minimal Majority": all Independents and Republicans[b]	Score among all Republicans[b]
	(%)			
Nixon	42	+25	+32	+37
Lodge	10	+11	+13	+13
Romney	11	+ 9	+11	+10
Rockefeller	49	+19	+10	+ 1
Scranton	11	+ 7	+ 6	+ 5
Goldwater	54	− 8	− 5	+ 9

[a] The percentage entered represents the proportion of individuals in the total sample mentioning the Republican leader indicated, either as one of two best or one of two very bad candidates.

[b] Each mention of a leader as the "best" candidate received a score of +2. Each mention as second best received a score of +1. The first-mentioned "bad" candidate received a score of −2. Any negative second mentions were scored −1. The entries in the table represent the net balance of positive or negative scores for the leader, expressed as a proportion of the maximum possible positive score an individual would have received had he been awarded all of the "best" choices given by the indicated segment of the electorate.

thought of as plausible candidates. The table excludes a thin scattering of other mentions. Since the scoring used reflects both the breadth and the intensity of support, a Republican receiving relatively few mentions could not achieve any very high score. Thus, for example, another possible scoring could have shown Henry Cabot Lodge vastly outdistancing all other aspirants, as his references were almost unanimously positive, whereas the other Republicans suffered numerous descriptions as "very bad candidates." However, at this time he was not commonly regarded as an aspirant for the nomination, and the scoring deliberately puts this warm but limited positive feeling toward him in perspective.

The table speaks for itself as to Goldwater's attractiveness as a candidate. Clearly Goldwater's problem was not that he was still too little known: he received mentions from a wider proportion of the electorate than any of his competitors. But for much of the electorate he was an object of antagonism even in January, 1964. And among grass-roots Republicans, where his strength was concentrated, he remained fourth in a field of six.

The sequence of Republican primary elections in the succeeding months tended, with some local variation, to fit the lines suggested by these January reactions. The table presages the startling Lodge write-in victory over both Goldwater and Rockefeller among New Hampshire Republicans in March, as well as his numerous subsequent strong showings. It contains ample warning as well of the amazingly poor Goldwater record in the primaries throughout the spring, including the scattered victories in such seemingly congenial states as conservative Nebraska, where by standing alone on the ticket he managed to win about half of the votes cast over a flood of Nixon and Lodge write-ins. It even renders intelligible the crucial Goldwater victory in California, where write-ins were not permitted, where the sole opponent was Rockefeller, and where Democrats had a hotly fought primary of their own. Indeed, there is room to wonder whether any presidential aspirant has ever contested so many primaries with as disastrous a showing, and still captured the nomination of his party's convention.

No evidence from polls of the period, moreover, suggests that Goldwater's popularity showed any sudden increase, even among Republicans, in the short interval between the final primary and the San Francisco convention. In interviewing our sample of the national electorate in September and October, we asked respondents to recall their reactions to the decisions of the Republican convention, including the identity of the candidates they had preferred at the time the convention began, as well as their gratification, indifference or disappointment at the outcome. While these responses suffer the inevitable frailties of any retrospective accounts that go back over an evolving situation, the social and political lines of support and antagonism for the various major contestants in July as reported during the campaign bear so close a resemblance to the lines of support visible in the January, 1964 data, as to make it unlikely that they are badly distorted by selective recollection, *post hoc* rationalization, and the like.

It is most instructive, perhaps, to set these popular reactions to the 1964 Republican convention against a fairly comparable set of data collected in 1952 after the conservative wing had lost its bid to nominate Senator Taft for the presidency against the liberal wing's offering of General Eisenhower, for the bitterness engendered in the 1952 struggle came closer to matching that of 1964 than either of the intervening conventions. Our question in 1952 asked respondents irrespective of partisan allegiance whether they would have preferred to have seen any other candidate nominated in either of the major-party conventions held in Chicago. Thus Republican identifiers could focus their remarks on the Democratic convention in a way that the 1964 question did not permit. However, partisans tended to comment primarily on the outcomes of their own party's nominating conventions.

Among Republican identifiers in the fall of 1952, about one in five recalled having felt a preference for Taft at the time of the convention. Another eight percent had preferred some third candidate. The vast majority of the remaining 72 percent indicated that they had been indifferent to the choices at either convention, or expressed gratification in the selection of Eisenhower as the Republican candidate. Some other Republicans responded that they would have preferred a candidate other than Stevenson from the Democratic convention. Presumably, however, these citizens were satisfied with the Republican convention, and it seems reasonable to conclude that a maximum of some 30 percent of all Republicans in 1952 had ground to recall any disappointment over their party's nomination.

The picture from 1964 is remarkably similar in one respect, and drastically different in another. Among Republican identifiers in this latter year, slightly less than 20 percent of all Republicans recalled having preferred Goldwater at the time of the convention. This figure is only one percent less than the proportion of Taft supporters among Republicans in 1952. What was different, of course, was that in 1952 Taft lost the nomination on the first ballot, whereas in 1964 Goldwater won it handily on the first ballot. Although in our 1964 data a large segment (30 percent) of Republican identifiers indicated that they had held no preference for a specific candidate at convention time, very nearly half of all of our Republicans did recall some preference other than Goldwater. Thus these grass-roots Republicans with non-Goldwater choices outnumbered the Goldwater supporters within Republican ranks by a margin of better than two and one-half to one. A clear majority (60 percent) of those with other preferences, when asked "Were you particularly unhappy that Goldwater got the nomination, or did you think that he was nearly as good as your man?," expressed their lingering unhappiness about the outcome.

In sum, then, it is hard to turn up any bit of evidence to challenge the conclusion that Goldwater was, in rather startling degree, a minority candidate within a minority party. If his camp actually believed that the San Francisco delegates represented a true cross-section of grass-roots Republican sentiment, then they had grossly misunderstood the situation. There was, however, at least one extenuating circumstance: the support among Republican citizens for other candidates than Goldwater was split badly among the four or five other leading candidates. Thus while any of several pairs of other candidates had grass-roots party support at convention time which would have outnumbered the Goldwater faction quite readily, the fact remains that the 20 percent Goldwater support represented a plurality for any single candidate.

However this may be, disappointment at the convention outcome in 1964 had radically different consequences in November than the comparable disappointments among Republicans in 1952. As we have seen above, the former Taft supporters in that year turned out at the polls in near-perfect proportions and cast a very faithful Republican vote for Eisenhower. In 1964, however, the widespread defections among Republicans necessary to account for the Johnson landslide tended to follow rather closely the lines of lingering discontent with the nomination.

These recollections of San Francisco varied according to the different camps in which rank-and-file Republicans had located themselves at the time. So, for example, about three Lodge supporters in four reported they were unhappy with the Goldwater nomination; for Rockefeller supporters, the figure was closer to two in three. Slightly over half of the Nixon supporters, however, indicated that they thought Goldwater was "nearly as good" as their man, Nixon. With minor departures, similar patterns marked the ultimate defections to Johnson among these varying Republicans. Since Nixon supporters were, like Goldwater's, more frequently "strong" Republicans than the adherents of some of the other camps, lower defection rates here were only to be expected. However, defections to Johnson among Republicans who had preferred Nixon at convention time remained about double what could be expected from past norms for Republicans of this particular mixture of strengths of identification. Over three times as many Republicans for Lodge and Scranton defected to Johnson as parallel "normal" expectations would suggest, and—perhaps surprisingly—defections among Republicans who expressed no pre-convention favorite at all were in this range as well. Most extreme were the Rockefeller and Romney supporters, with defection rates at the polls exceeding expectation by a factor of greater than four.

These differences across the several non-Goldwater camps are intriguing, in part because they appear related to reactions of the various G.O.P. leaders to the Goldwater candidacy. That is, of the set of major Republicans under discussion, Nixon took greatest pains to maintain relations with the Goldwater group before the convention, and undertook to help unify the party behind him after the nomination. Therefore it seems fitting that dismay at the nomination was least in his camp, and defections relatively limited. Neither Rockefeller nor Romney made any major show of reconciliation after the nomination, and subsequently went to some lengths to dissociate themselves from the Goldwater aspects of the Republican campaign.

Yet if it were true that nothing more than a "follow-the-leader" response is needed to account for these variations in defection rates among Republicans, the data would cast a somewhat different light on the question of conflicting perceptions between liberal and conservative wings of Goldwater's voting strength. For in such a case the Senator's problem would have been less one of gross overestimates of his strength, than of self-fulfilling prophecy on the part of the disgruntled liberal leaders. In other words, they first refused to support Goldwater on grounds that he could not win enough votes, and then proceeded to withhold in large quantities the votes of their "followers" to assure exactly this outcome.

No airtight way is available to determine whether or not Republican defections at the presidential level might have been reduced significantly had Rockefeller or some of the other liberals effected a more genuine reconciliation with Goldwater to unite the party for the campaign. Nevertheless, if we were to compare the issue positions and ideological persuasions of 1964 Nixon Republicans with those of Rockefeller or Romney Republicans and find no substantial differences, we might be tempted to judge that differences in leader behavior did play some independent role in minimizing or maximizing Republican defections in November. Preliminary analyses suggest rather clearly, however, that substantial ideological differences did exist across the range of Republican factions. Republicans enthusiastic about Goldwater showed a rather unique (or "extreme") pattern of ideological positions. Nixon supporters, while unmistakably different, looked more nearly like the Goldwater people than the adherents of any of the other camps. Next in order moving away from the Goldwater position were the Scranton and Lodge followers, and the Rockefeller and Romney adherents show slightly more liberal positions still. Ideological differences, therefore, plainly existed between grass-roots supporters of the various factions, and these differences were indeed correlated with defections from a Goldwater vote. This does not exclude the possibility that the defections might have been lessened by a genuine "unity" move on the part of more liberal Republican leaders. It indicates nevertheless that the desertions were rooted not only in leader-follower behavior, but in a more personal sense of ideological distance between many rank-and-file Republicans and the Goldwater faction—a distance that would have produced increased defections quite apart from examples set by the leadership.

However this may be, it was a significant feature of the election that the customary post-convention reconciliation between party factions was in the 1964 Republican case lack-lustre at best, and at many levels simply non-existent. Many of the liberals wished to avoid the Goldwater platform. At the same time, Goldwater seemed to do less than most candidates in making it easy for the dissident brethren to return to the fold. Among several possible reasons, one may have been that in the blueprint laid out by Goldwater strategists for a November victory, the support of most of these leaders did not appear to be critical.

III. CAMPAIGN STRATEGY: THE SOUTH AS REPUBLICAN TARGET

The strategy of the Goldwater camp for a November victory was both simple and relatively selective. Goldwater felt, to begin with, that he could hold on to essentially the same states that Nixon had won in 1960. This meant a clean sweep of the populous states of the Pacific Coast, most of the Mountain and Plains states, and a scattering east of the Mississippi. To reap the additional electoral votes for victory, Goldwater believed that the way lay open, under proper circumstances, for the Republican Party to make further major inroads in the once solidly Democratic South. The plan implied that Goldwater could largely afford to write off the populous industrial states of the Northeast and some, if not all, of the Midwest—a matter which greatly reduced the importance of the dissident liberal Republican bloc. And it represented a dramatic departure from any past Republican strategy in making of the South a fulcrum for victory.

Such a strategy was not only unusual but, against the long sweep of American electoral history, it might even be thought of as implausible. Yet it was no hastily devised scheme. For years Goldwater had participated in the Congressional coalition between conservative Republicans and Southern Democrats. The same drive for ideological neatness that led him to call for the reorganization of American politics into "Conservative" and "Liberal" parties impressed upon him the grotesque incongruity of a Democratic South. The South had no reason to be a Democratic bastion; by all of its affinities and traditions, it should long since have become Republican. Part of the problem lay with the national Republican Party, which, in the control of the Northeastern bloc, had failed to present national-level candidates making clear that Republicanism was the natural home of the Southern voter. This had been a frustrating fact since Goldwater's entry into national politics—a period during which political observers had frequently predicted an imminent partisan realignment of the South; but gains in the region, while very obvious, had remained rather modest. In discussions of Republican difficulty in recapturing majority status in the land, Goldwater had opined that the Party had to learn to "go hunting in the pond where the ducks are"—the South. As bitterness began to mount in that region toward the civil rights pressures of the Kennedy Administration, the time seemed more ripe than ever for the presentation of a purely conservative Republican candidate who could appeal to the Southern ethos in a most direct way, thereby breaking the Democratic hold on the region in one dramatic and decisive stroke.

This long-planned strategy had suffered two temporary but alarming setbacks. The assassination of President Kennedy suddenly placed a Southerner in the White House, and removed from power the most feared personal symbols of federal intrusion. The continuation of the Kennedy beginnings by the Johnson Administration, however—particularly in the 1964 Civil Rights bill—helped to reset the stage. So did the increased signs of Negro unrest, and the new element of "white backlash" in the North as well as the South that seemed apparent in the spring primaries. The capping touch was Goldwater's vote against the Civil Rights bill. This vote, to be sure, represented no condoning of segregationism *per se*, but rather a blow for states' rights against the encroachment of the federal government. Nevertheless, white supremacists in the South had so long paraded under the states' rights banner as to leave little room for fear lest the Goldwater gesture go unappreciated. The liberal wing of the Republican Party, having worked for years to prevent the Democrats from "gaining position" on the civil rights issue, was further horrified as it envisioned the G.O.P. suddenly transformed into "the party of the white man" at just the moment when the Negro vote was becoming effectively mobilized.

The second setback threatened when Governor Wallace of Alabama decided to enter the presidential race as a states' rights candidate. This was especially alarming, for Wallace would have competed for exactly the same votes that Goldwater had been wooing toward the Republican column. However, Wallace's subsequent withdrawal left the field open again for the original victory blueprint, and the implementa-

tion began in force. Mid-campaign accounts of the Goldwater organizational efforts spoke of a high-powered, modernistic campaign apparatus
in the South stocked with volunteer labor in numbers that would have
been unbelievable for the earlier Eisenhower and Nixon campaigns.
While this machine had been humming efficiently from the start, the
Goldwater organization in the West was described as effective but less
advanced; in the Midwest it was chaotic, and in the Northeast next to
non-existent. At few if any points in recent political history have so many
campaign resources—in both issue positions taken and organizational
efforts made—been devoted to the cultivation of a single region. The first
discordant note came when, during the campaign and apparently as the
result of new poll data, Goldwater remarked to reporters that he was not
as strong in the South as everybody seemed to think.

After the votes were counted, what was the success of this
strategy? The verdict must come in two halves. From one point of view,
the strategy was a brilliant success, and it left its imprint on the geo-
graphical voting returns with greater strength than any other of what we
have called "short-term forces" in the 1964 election. One crude way of
separating these immediate or new effects from those better attributable
to long-term standing loyalties is to create a different kind of electoral
map, entering state by state or region by region the departure of a
particular presidential vote in a more Republican or more Democratic
direction than the normal voting of the area involved. A map so constructed for 1964, with pro-Goldwater deviations regarded as "high
ground" and pro-Johnson deviations as "low," would show one primary
"tilt" or gradient across the nation. The very lowest ground would appear
in the northern reaches of New England, and the gradient would move
upward with fair regularity all the way west to the Pacific Coast. The same
gradient would appear, but much more sharply tilted still, as one moved
southward to the Gulf of Mexico. In other words, Goldwater's regional
emphases were indeed profoundly reflected in the vote.

As soon as one leaves the relative question of the regional and
the geographic, however, the strategy was a dismal failure. For while the
whole continent tilted in the expected direction, the strong Democratic
tide nationally left virtually all of the country submerged under what
from a Goldwater point of view was "sea level"—the 50–50 mark in
popular votes. In terms of electoral votes, Goldwater was stranded on a
few islands which remained above the tide on the outer Southern and
Southwestern fringe of the continent. These islands represented stunning
"firsts" or dramatic historic reversals in states like Georgia, Alabama,
Mississippi and South Carolina. But their historic interest did not bring
Goldwater any closer to the presidency.

Indeed, while Goldwater scored sharp Republican gains through the "Black Belt" of the deepest South, his assault on the South as a whole produced rather pathetic results. All observers agree, for example, that the South has been drifting away from its old status as a one-party Democratic bastion for at least two decades, if not for five or more. Hence Goldwater could have hoped to profit from four years more of this drift than Nixon, and a decade more than Eisenhower. Secondly, all observers are equally agreed that not only in the Black Belt but well north into the Border States of the South, civil rights was the prime political issue, and there is no doubt where the mass white population stood on the matter. Our data from the late 1950s and the early 1960s have consistently made clear that the potential of this issue for dramatic partisan realignment in the South had been muffled because of lack of clarity in the eyes of the mass population, prior to 1964, that either of the two major national parties offered much hope to the Southern white. It was exactly this ambiguity that Goldwater set out to remove by providing a clear party differentiation on civil rights at the national level. Putting these two ingredients together, the actual 1964 election results from the South as a whole might seem astonishing. For Goldwater actually did less well in the region than either Nixon in 1960 or Eisenhower in 1952 and 1956. One has to return at least to 1948 to find a comparably poor showing for a Republican presidential candidate; and there are reasonable treatments of the 1948 Thurmond vote which would send one back to 1944 for a parallel. Given the fact that Goldwater wooed the South so straightforwardly, and injected the new and potent ingredient of clear party differentiation on civil rights into the 1964 picture, this retrogression of Republican popular voting strength for a presidential candidate back to levels of the 1940s may seem quite incomprehensible.

A possible explanation, although one that we can summarily reject, would be that the clear party differentiation on civil (or "states'") rights which Goldwater tried to communicate failed to come across to the mass voters. Perhaps to the dismay of the liberal wing of the Republicans, however, the communication was near-perfect. In our 1960 election study, a measure of association between the two parties and the policy extremes of the civil rights controversy showed values of .02 and .05 (the Democrats only very slightly associated with a pro-civil rights position) on two different civil rights policy items. In 1964, the perceived association in the same terms on the same two items had risen to values of .54 and .50. The change in *volunteered* identifications of the two parties with the issue, among the much smaller subset of people so concerned that they brought the matter up themselves, showed even more dramatic change. In 1960 these civil-rights-concerned people had tended to associate Kennedy somewhat with a pro-civil rights position, and Nixon with more of a "go-slow" approach (an association of .30). For Johnson and Goldwater in 1964, the association had mounted to .84, approaching consensus. The same volunteered materials include images of the parties, as well as of the candidates, and it is a matter of some interest to know in what measure Goldwater's 1964 position "rubbed off" on the Republican Party as a whole. In 1960, the civil rights association appeared to lie more clearly with the Kennedy-Nixon pairing (.30) than with any differences between the two parties, for these volunteered references to the parties showed only an association of .08. The comparable figure for the two parties in 1964 was .86. In short, we cannot explain why Goldwater produced a retrogression of Republican presidential voting strength in the South by suggesting that his key civil rights position failed to get across.

The Southern vote for Goldwater becomes intelligible if we add three elements to the consideration. First, while civil rights lent an important new pro-Goldwater force to the situation, various strong short-term forces which had pushed the Southern electorate in a pro-Republican direction in 1952, 1956 and 1960 were no longer present. We have argued elsewhere that the popular vote for Eisenhower and Nixon in the South was a very misleading index of the degree of solid Republican advance there. While our data do show the Republican Party inching forward in the affections of mass Southern voters, the pace has been slow; the South remains a preponderantly Democratic region. In 1952 and 1956, the Southern presidential vote swung far to the Republican side of normal for the region, just as it did in all other parts of the United States. In 1960, with the Eisenhower appeal gone, most other regions moved back toward the Democrats as we expected. This return toward normal was almost invisible in the South, since a new and offsetting short-term force—Kennedy's Catholicism—had arisen which was peculiarly repugnant to the Southern population with its concentration (Louisiana excepted) of devout and fundamentalist Protestants. Thus if any other of the Republican aspirants had run in 1964, we might have expected a delayed return toward a much more normally Democratic vote in the South. From this point of view, the injection of a new civil rights differentiation by Goldwater did not occur in a void, but was something of a replacement for other forces which had kept the Southern vote extended in a remarkably pro-Republican direction for three consecutive presidential elections.

Once we take this into account, the Republican retrogression is less perplexing, although intuitively we would expect civil rights to have an impact on the southern voter more potent than either Eisenhower's appeal or fear of a Catholic president. It is here that the second and third considerations enter. While Goldwater's civil rights position drew Southern whites toward the Republicans, Negroes both South and North moved monolithically toward the Democrats. Although Southern Negro voting was still limited by registration difficulties, it increased over 1960 and was almost unanimously Democratic for the first time. If this sudden new increment of Negro votes could be removed from the Southern totals, the Goldwater vote proportion would undoubtedly appear to be a slight progression, rather than a retrogression, over the Eisenhower and Nixon votes.

Finally, it must be recognized that civil rights, while the primary issue in the South, was not the only one. Beyond civil rights, Southerners reacted negatively to the Goldwater positions much as their fellow citizens elsewhere. Many Southern white respondents said in effect: "Goldwater is right on the black man, and that is very important. But he is so wrong on everything else I can't bring myself to vote for him." From this point of view, the civil rights issue did indeed have a powerful impact in the South: without it, the 1964 Goldwater vote probably would not only have slipped to normal Republican levels, but would have veered as elsewhere to the pro-Democratic side. The more general ideological appeal to what Goldwater saw as Southern "conservatism" aside from the Negro question, did not have major impact.

Much the same comments hold for the failure of "white backlash" to develop in the way many expected outside the South. Our data show that civil rights feeling did not lack impact elsewhere. But for many non-Southern whites who resented the advance of the Negro cause and the summer of discontent, the election involved other important issues as well; and Goldwater's positions on them struck such voters very negatively. Thus "white backlash" feelings were translated into Goldwater votes by Democrats only where fear of the Negro was so intense as to blot out virtually all other considerations. Voters fitting this description existed in fair number and geographic concentration in the deepest latitudes of the South. Elsewhere, they were thinly scattered.

IV. THE ELECTION "POST-MORTEM"

Up to this point we have referred only vaguely to the many negative reactions Goldwater occasioned in all sectors of the country, which tended to dim out isolated attractions he did present. The Goldwater "image" was indeed phenomenally unfavorable. We have measured such images in the past, among other ways, by tallying the simple number of favorable and unfavorable references made by respondents to broad questions inviting them to say what they like and dislike about each of the candidates. Typically, American voters have tended on balance to speak favorably, even about candidates they were about to send down to defeat. The least favorable image we have seen—in Adlai Stevenson's second try in 1956—involved only about 52 percent of all responses that were favorable. Less than 35 percent of the Goldwater references were favorable.

Just after the election, Goldwater observed that "more than 25 million people" voted "not necessarily for me, but for a philosophy that I represent. . . ." At another time, in assessing the magnitude of his defeat, he chastised himself for having been a personally ineffective spokesman for that philosophy. This seemed particularly odd against the descriptions of Goldwater before his nomination, in which even opponents concurred that at long last the right wing had found an articulate spokesman with a magnetic personality.

The candidate references we collect are a mixture of observations concerning the personality and leadership qualities of the individuals themselves as well as reactions to policy positions they represent in the public eye. Ideally, we could take this image material and split it cleanly into references to personal attributes as opposed to policy positions, in order to judge the accuracy of the proposition that what the public repudiated was the spokesman, and not the philosophy. Practically speaking, such divisions present many difficult coding decisions.

Nevertheless, we have sifted Johnson and Goldwater references into categories more or less purely reflecting "policy" as opposed to "personality" significance. Among the most pure policy references, Johnson's were favorable by an 80–20 margin, visibly ahead of the 69–31 balance of his total image. Mentions of Goldwater policies ran less than 30–70 favorable, thereby trailing the rest of his image slightly. In general, the farther one moves from pure policy to pure personality, Johnson's advantage declines. His "wheeler-dealer" style and the aura of conflicts-of-interest which dogged him during the campaign came through to dilute his attractiveness. Against this backdrop, Goldwater's personal "integrity" and "sincerity" drew praise. Throughout, the data suggest that Johnson was carried along to an image nearly as positive as Eisenhower's best, less by his personal characteristics than by the policies with which he was associated (many of them identified by respondents as continuations from the Kennedy Administration). For Goldwater, if anything, the reverse was true.

Aside from civil rights and a faint flutter of approval brought by Goldwater's latter-day stand against immorality, none of his major positions was attractive to voters outside the most hard-core Republican ranks. In general, the mass of public opinion has been quite unsympathetic to traditional Republican thinking in areas of social welfare and other domestic problems for several decades. A major Goldwater theme involved attacks against the increasingly heavy hand of "big government," yet this struck little in the way of a responsive chord. Most Americans in the more numerous occupational strata do not appear to feel the governmental presence (save for local civil rights situations) in any oppressive or day-to-day manner, and as a consequence simply have no reactions to the area which have any motivational significance. Among those more aware of the practices and potentials of federal government, a slight majority feels that if anything, governmental services and protections are inadequate rather than overdone. Thus for better or for worse, such contentions on Goldwater's part had little popular resonance.

Goldwater's failure to make much capital of domestic policy was not uncharacteristic of a Republican presidential candidate. What was new for a Republican, however, was his performance in the area of foreign policy. In a degree often overlooked, the 1950s were a period during which, from the point of view of many Americans inattentive to the finer lines of politics and reacting to the parties in terms of gross associations and moods, something of an uneasy equilibrium prevailed between the two major parties. Much more often than not, for these Americans the Democratic Party was the party of prosperity and good times, but also the party more likely to blunder into war. The Republican Party, conversely, was more skilled in maintaining peace, but brought with it depression and hard times.

The foreign policies proposed by Goldwater and refracted through the press and other commentators, shifted this image more dramatically than one might have thought possible (Table 2). Setting

TABLE 2.   *Perceptions as to The Party Most Likely to Keep the United States Out of War in the Ensuing Four Years*

	1956	1960	1964
	(%)	(%)	(%)
Democrats would handle better	7	15	38
No party difference	45	46	46
Republicans would handle better	40	29	12
Don't know, not ascertained	8	10	4
	100	100	100

aside the large mass of voters who throughout the period did not see any particular differences between the parties in foreign policy capability, the balance of expectations in the area favored the Republicans by better than a 5–1 margin in 1956. This margin deteriorated somewhat in the late stages of the Eisenhower Administration, but remained at an imposing 2–1 edge. During the Goldwater campaign it reversed itself to a 3–1 margin favoring the Democrats.

Thus to the many ways of describing the public's repudiation of the Goldwater candidacy, another may be added: between a party of prosperity and peace, as against a party of depression and war, there is little room for hesitation.

V. LEVELS OF PUBLIC OPINION AND THE BASES FOR MISPERCEPTION

From at least one point of view, it is less interesting that Goldwater lost the 1964 election than that he thought he had a chance to win. What most of our descriptions of the election year have had in common is a sort of chronic miscalculation of electoral reality: miscalculations of standing strength, of new strength that might be won, and of what appeals were necessary to win that new strength. Since "electoral reality" is at many points a nest of uncertainties, and since we are told that in the face of uncertainty personal needs are likely to color perceptions the more strongly, there is little surprising in the fact that Goldwater overestimated his strength and drawing power. But as these misperceptions of Goldwater and his aides went grossly beyond what many observers felt were the margins of uncertainty, they deserve closer comment.

Rather than write off these perceptions as figments of imagination, let us suppose that to persist in the way many electoral misperceptions of the right wing have persisted, there must be some sustaining reality bases; and let us ask instead what such bases might be. For "public opinion" is a protean thing, and we shall discover that there are perfectly sound ways of measuring public opinion during the 1964 campaign which, instead of illustrating Johnson's towering lead in the opinion polls, would actually have shown Goldwater enjoying a slight margin.

As is well known, public opinion was spoken of and roughly gauged long before the operations of public opinion polling were developed. What was gauged was opinion from a variety of kinds of sources: informal reactions to events among ancillary elites around the centers of government; the writings of intellectuals and newspaper editors; representations from leaders of interest groups, and the like. While it was apparent that this conglomerate of opinion came disproportionately from relatively elite and informed sources and hence need not have coincided with what the "real public" thought, beyond mass elections themselves there were (and *are*, for those who totally distrust the polls) few further ways of understanding what the public below an elite level was thinking. One of those few ways of "digging down" into the real population was letters of opinion: letters sent from unassuming constituents to public officials, "letters to the editor" composed by non-professional writers reacting to daily events and even, in no few cases, to the opinions of the editor himself. This was one level of public opinion that seemed to be generated below the elite level and that, for the observer interested in opinion beyond the localisms of municipal government, could be monitored regularly on a wide geographic base.[7]

In our 1964 interview schedule we spent some time investigating the behavior of our respondents with respect to the writing of politically relevant letters. We ascertained first whether or not they had ever written such a letter either to any kind of public official, or to the editor of a newspaper or magazine. Then, among the minority who could recall ever writing such a letter, we went on to ask about the frequency of such activity—whether any of the letters had been written in the past four years, and if so, roughly how many such letters the respondent would estimate he had written to each of the two types of targets over that recent period.

Many aspects of these data remain intriguing despite their general predictability. Thus, for example, the materials demonstrate handsomely that the large bulk of letters to public officials or the printed media come from a tiny fraction of the population, which tends to write very repetitively. Thus, in the data summarized in Figure 1, we find that

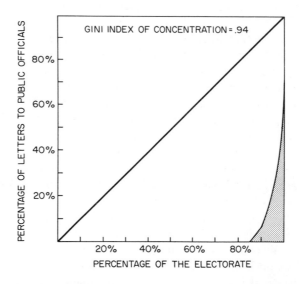

F I G. 1.   *Letters to Public Officials and Letter-Writers within the Electorate.*

---

[7] Undoubtedly, for such an observer, letters were not weighted equally in his impressions as to how opinion stood: some were more cogent than others, some were more distressed, and so on. But as a rough first approximation, one can imagine that what registered as "public opinion" on a particular issue in the mind of such an observer was closely related to the simple frequency of letters pro and con.

only about 15 percent of the adult population reports ever having written a letter to a public official, and of the total stream of such letters from the grass-roots, two-thirds are composed by about 3 percent of the population. Where letters to newspapers or magazines are concerned, the constituency is even more restrictive still: only about 3 percent of the population recalls ever having written such a letter, and two-thirds of such letters are turned out by not more than half of one percent of the population.[8] Needless to say, there is fair overlap between those who write to the printed media and those writing to public officials, so that the observer monitoring both lines of communication would tend to count the same people twice.

Furthermore, as these few people write more and more letters over time, they are counted again and again, and this of course is the phenomenon that interests us. What we have done is to reconstruct our data on various preferences relevant to the 1964 election *not* by a raw head-count, which is what a mass election measures, but rather with each individual's preference on an item weighted by the number of letters that he has reported writing to either target in the four preceding years. This provides a basis, within reasonable limits, for a fair replication of the different kind of "public opinion" as it might be assessed by a hypothetical observer.[9]

Figure 2 contrasts "public opinion" in the head-count sense, with that form of public opinion as measured by letter-writing. We suggest that this figure may usher us into the reality world on which many of Goldwater's assessments and stratagems were based. This is not to say that Goldwater had no other bases from which to calculate public opinion. He had, among other things, public opinion as measured by the polls, and he did not entirely discredit this information. Yet as we have noted there was evidence that poll data perplexed him, not simply because they customarily brought bad news, but also because they failed to square with all of his other intuitive impressions as to what the public

[8] Data on letters to the news media are not presented graphically, in part because the inequality is so complete that there is little one can discriminate in the figure. The Gini index of concentration for the newspaper and magazine letters is .99. See H. Alker and B. Russett, "On Measuring Inequality," *Behavioral Science*, Vol. 9, No. 3 (July, 1964), pp. 207–18.

[9] We wish to stress that it remains a crude approximation, in part because we do not know, letter by letter, what political opinions the respondent was expressing. Conceivably in many cases they lay outside the range of any of our items. But the exercise is worth completing in part because it is likely that our hypothetical observer generalizes beyond the specific content of letters ("if ultra-conservative opinion on issue x is running about 30 percent, then it is likely that ultra-conservative opinion on issue y would run about the same level if something made that issue salient"); and in part because the systematic lines of displacement of "letter opinion" from "public opinion" in the mass electoral sense are undoubtedly valid in their general direction, whatever the details.

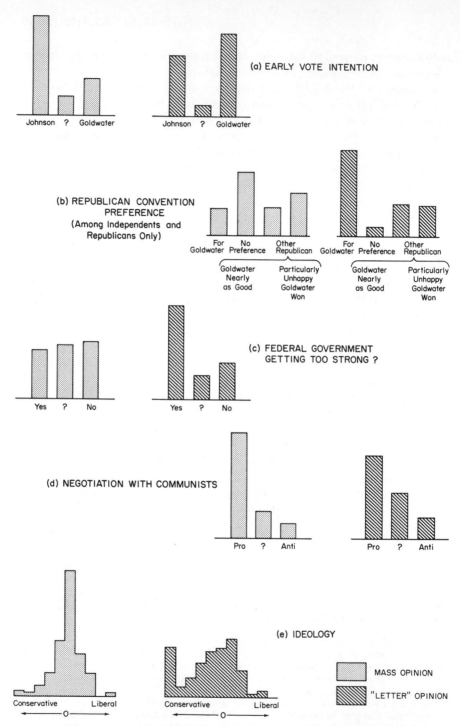

(a) EARLY VOTE INTENTION

Johnson ? Goldwater   Johnson ? Goldwater

(b) REPUBLICAN CONVENTION
PREFERENCE
(Among Independents and
Republicans Only)

For   No   Other   For   No   Other
Goldwater Preference Republican   Goldwater Preference Republican

Goldwater   Particularly   Goldwater   Particularly
Nearly   Unhappy   Nearly   Unhappy
as Good   Goldwater   as Good   Goldwater
               Won   Won

(c) FEDERAL GOVERNMENT
GETTING TOO STRONG ?

Yes   ?   No   Yes   ?   No

(d) NEGOTIATION WITH COMMUNISTS

Pro   ?   Anti   Pro   ?   Anti

(e) IDEOLOGY

Conservative   Liberal   Conservative   Liberal
         O   O

MASS OPINION

"LETTER" OPINION

FIG. 2.   *Public Opinion as Measured by People or Political Letters.*

was thinking. In the measure that these impressions came from a variety of sources not very different from the letter-writers among the public (*i.e.*, from party activists, from campaign personnel and from informal associations), it is not hard to believe that they may have been displaced from the head-count of public opinion in much the same ways.

If we accept letter-writing for the moment then as a relevant indicator of public opinion, we see a rather marvelous change in the state of political affairs. In Figure 2 (a), instead of trailing Johnson sadly in the anonymous crowd in mid-campaign, Goldwater holds a visible lead. Moving back to the time of the San Francisco convention (b), Goldwater is no longer the candidate of a small minority among Republicans and Independents, but rather is the toast of an absolute majority, even counting "no preferences" against him. In (c), we discover that not only is a vast majority of the public interested in the problem of the growing strength of the federal government,[10] but those upset by this growing strength outnumber their opponents by a ratio approaching 3 to 1! In Figure 2(d), the displacement of "letter opinion" from public opinion is much less, in part because the item wording brought a relatively consensual response. However, it is clear that Goldwater's "hard" inclinations in foreign policy are somewhat overrepresented as well in the letter-writing public.

In some ways, Figure 2(e) contains more grist than any of the others, however. First, the very form of the distributions of ideological preference differs rather dramatically. Where "public opinion" is concerned, nearly half the population falls in the "zero" category, making no affective distinction whatever between conservatives and liberals.[11] In

[10] The wordings of the issue items involved in Figure 2(c) and (d) were as follows:

(For 2c) "Some people are afraid the government in Washington is getting too powerful for the good of the country and the individual person. Others feel that the government in Washington has not gotten too strong for the good of the country. . . . What is your feeling?"

(For 2d) "Some people think our government should sit down and talk to the leaders of the Communist countries and try to settle our differences, while others think we should refuse to have anything to do with them. . . . What do you think?"

Figure 2(e) is based on a set of questions that asked people to indicate their affective reactions toward a variety of groups, including "conservatives" and "liberals." The scores for the figure are based on the difference in reaction to the two stimuli.

[11] It is likely that this contingent is roughly coterminous with that 40–50 percent of the American electorate which we have described elsewhere as having no impression as to what such terms as "conservative" and "liberal" mean. See Philip E. Converse, "The Nature of Belief Systems in Mass Publics," in David E. Apter, ed., *Ideology and Discontent* (New York, 1964), pp. 206–61. The data presented there were gathered in 1960. In the 1964 study we collected the same data on recognition of ideological terms, thinking that perhaps the nature of the Goldwater campaign might render these terms and meanings more salient to a wider public The data show that it did not.

addition, the clustering around this zero-point is very tight: over three-quarters of the population is located within one category of the zero-point. The distribution of "letter opinion," however, is quite different. The central mode of indifference or ignorance shrinks dramatically, and voices from more extreme positions on the continuum gain in strength. Other analyses show that virtually all letter-writers rank very high on measures we have used of ideological sensitivity. Hence those who remain toward the middle of the continuum in the right half of Figure 2(e) are not there through indifference or ignorance: they understand the ideological alternatives and place themselves toward the middle of the road with forethought. And, as the bimodal shape of the distribution suggests, political discourse becomes most notably a dialogue between very mild liberals and ultra-conservatives.

It is to the world of letter opinion or one like it that the Goldwater campaign, in its original design, was addressed. At least until its late stages, it assumed an electorate with near-total ideological comprehension and sensitivity. The appeal to the Southern conservative tradition in any abstract vein was indeed joyfully received in the South, and created great ferment among a part of the Southern population. Except as this theme became concretized in day-to-day problems with Negroes, however, the part of the population affected was tiny, even though in the letter-writing and related senses it was so visible as to appear to be "most of the South," politically speaking.

Similarly, the distribution of the population in this world of letter opinion helped maintain persistent overestimations of strength. Empirically speaking, the center of Goldwater support lay roughly in the third bar of the figure on the conservative side. It weakened rapidly with any further steps toward the center, and was relatively solid in the outer two bars of the graph. If one looks at "letter opinion" with this zone in mind, it would appear that the base of standing Goldwater support was very substantial. Goldwater hoped to firm up the support on his side of the center sufficiently to create a majority, and in this figure it would have taken only a modest extension of influence to achieve this. In the world of public opinion relevant for mass elections, however, the distribution of actual and potential support was radically different. Rather than starting from a solid base of support on the conservative wing, the initial springboard was scarcely populated at all. To win a majority, a much deeper penetration into the center would have been required.

In the measure that we have delineated in Figure 2(e), the kind of political environment familiar to many practicing politicians, we can also better understand the first of our puzzles, the myth of the stay-at-home Republicans. For ultra-conservatives who found a wide measure of social support and resonance for their views in the world of public opinion which they understood, it must indeed have been perplexing that uniquely at election time, and uniquely in vote totals, this vigorous support had a habit of evaporating. How could one interpret this gross discrepancy between what one heard and read about public sentiments and what happened at the polls? The easiest explanation was that strong conservatives in large numbers simply refused to go to the polls, however vigorously they would express themselves otherwise. And as soon as a useful reason was worked out as to why this willful non-voting should occur, a theory was born. It persisted in part because it was a handy tactical weapon; but it persisted in some part as well because the discrepant realities which helped to catalyze the theory also persisted. For its proponents, the election of 1964 was a sobering reality test.

VI. CONCLUSIONS

It should be apparent that the phenomena we have examined in this paper have a significance that stretches considerably beyond the 1964 election, or questions of the credibility of public opinion polls, or the playing of games with the epistemologies of practicing politicians, fascinating though each of these subjects may be.

But the more important implications flow from the reflection that while these opinion worlds may be discrepant from one another in many regards, and it behooves us not to confuse them, it is not a simple matter of fact *vs.* fantasy: both worlds are real, and have real effects on the political process. Save for the obvious fact that the reality of "one man, one vote," governs the mass election with greater or lesser modification, while other public-opinion realities like the letter-writing world tend to hold sway otherwise, we know all too little empirically about the counterpoint between the two in actual political systems, and the normative significance of motivation-weighted votes is largely unexamined.

However this may be, if the reality of one of these worlds was manifest on Election Day, 1964, then the reality of the other was equally apparent in the San Francisco convention. For it is obvious that the intense levels of political motivation which underlie the letter-writing of the ultra-conservative wing are part and parcel of the ingredients which led to a Republican convention delegation so markedly discrepant from either the rank-and-file of the Party or its customary leadership. What had been lacking around the country in bodies was made up for in dedication; but the outcome of the convention was in no sense the less real for it. And from this juxtaposition of two worlds, the oddities of the 1964 election grew.

3
Parties and Politics

For eighteen months following the death of John F. Kennedy, the national government was seized by a paroxysm of legislative energy. President Kennedy's domestic program, most of which had been on the national agenda for a decade or more, was gained by President Johnson from Congress with a mastery and ease reminiscent of Franklin D. Roosevelt in his zenith. Civil rights, the "new economics," federal aid to education, medical care for the elderly, a war on poverty, the declaration, through nearly a score of bills, of a national governmental interest and role in solving the problems of the cities burst out of a Congressional barrier first raised effectively in Franklin Roosevelt's second term. Truly, the "deadlock of democracy" seemed to have been broken. But what is the "deadlock"? Was it broken in the early years of the Johnson Presidency? Did the Presidential election of 1964 signify some fundamental change in the political order?

The phrase, "deadlock of democracy," is used by James M. Burns to summarize a two-part indictment that he, as well as numerous other critics, makes of the party system. The first part of the indictment offers a critical description of the parties as they really are. The national parties are described as little more than broad coalitions representing differing regional, social, and economic interests, which come together not out of common commitment to a set of discrete and specific principles—and much less to discrete, specific, and significant programs of national legislation—but out of a common interest in the fruits of electoral victory. The requirement of electoral victory for a broad coalition of different interests means that a party's platform—its program of legislation which it will deliver to the country if it is victorious in the election— cannot contain anything repugnant to any of the major elements of the coalition. What is worse, the critics maintain, the major national parties are not only combinations of differing interests; they often combine truly discordant or incompatible interests, as, for example, the national Democratic Party contains Negro-hating whites and militant Negroes and civil rights liberals. The Republicans, of course, have a less dramatic, less incendiary, but almost equally immobilizing division of their own between such metropolitan problem-oriented liberals as, say, John Lindsay, on the one hand, and spokesmen for a kind of rural and small-town fundamentalism such as Iowa's Representative H. R. Gross, on the other.

Such parties, the critics insist, can only be fragmented and weak in their organization and, hence, irresponsible—that is, unable to deliver even such modest legislative programs as they do manage to promise in their election campaigns. Here, then, we have the two-part indictment of the party system of modern America. The parties, by their nature, fail as vehicles of a vital electoral process in which significant solutions to major problems are thoroughly debated and judged. They are also too fragmented and weak to serve as the legislative engines of modern government. They immobilize the government in a time when, the critics say, the government must be imaginative, energetic, adaptable, and responsive.

Congress, the critics say, is the prime arena of the debacle of the parties. The long reign of the Democrats illustrates the problem. Democratic Presidents, from Roosevelt to Johnson, elected by the votes of the city masses, the poor, the Negroes, and other ethnic minorities, and primed and supported by the intellectuals, reformers, and problem-solvers of the society have repeatedly proposed programs of governmental activism to deal with most of the problems of modern social and economic life. President Truman, for example, first proposed hospital insurance under Social Security in 1949. Or, again, the "new economics," passed in the 1964 tax legislation, was already the old new economics when Congress cut its principles out of the Employment Act of 1946. Such examples could be multiplied many times. The critics of the parties do not conjure dreams when they describe a politics of liberal Presidential activism arrayed against a Congressional obstruction of thorough governmental action to solve social problems. The party critic, of course, finds the cause of this in the weakness and fragmentation of the parties and in the correspondingly fragmented organization of Congress.

But a skeptic, paraphrasing Cassius, might observe, "The fault, dear Professor, is not in our parties, but in ourselves." We have noted that

Congressional conservatism is no myth. But, on the other hand, neither is Congress simply a *melee* of rampaging particular interests. As research over the years has indicated, party lines do count very much in voting in Congress. Also, as we have seen, the electorate does make a roughly accurate discrimination between the parties, especially on the "positive government" issues. The successful Presidential activists have always had the benefit of large party majorities, usually coupled with emergency circumstances. In other words, they have had fairly clear mandates from the electorate.

Of course there is a conservative coalition in Congress. It is made up of the majority of the members from the South and the majority of the Republicans. The coalition has a distinct small-city and/or rural orientation. Due to the internal organization of Congress and also to the weak structure of the parties, its members have considerable influence over legislation. On issues involving federal governmental programs to improve the quality of life in the cities, the coalition is sometimes decisive. On President Johnson's proposal to appropriate 40 million dollars to assist local communities to exterminate rats in the slums, for example, the House voted 207 to 176 against even considering the bill. It was a classical instance of the conservative coalition in action; 59 Democrats, almost all of them from the South, joined 154 Republicans against the bill. The President had the support of the great majority of his own party and of a handful of Republicans, but that was not enough.

Still, the conservative coalition is not always decisive. Sometimes it can be, and is, cracked wide open, as it was during the outpouring of reform legislation in 1964 and 1965. Is Congressional conservatism, then, largely a function of party weakness and Congressional structure based on that weakness? Is it a conspiracy of a little band of small-town reactionaries openly flouting the expressed will of the majority? Or is there some great rough but just tidal relationship between the moods and movements within the government and those among the electorate? Is the country, for example, angered or repelled by the failure of the House to support the President's rat extermination program? What are the circumstances and requirements of successful Presidential activism? Is Congress unrepresentative when it obstructs the President?

Oscar Gass, himself a liberal activist, roams over some of these questions in a rather somberly reflective article. David Danzig makes the very important point that conservatism is neither a miniscule nor a deviant political posture in modern America. Danzig also refreshingly eschews the terms and categories of psychopathology in his discussion of the origins and future distribution of conservative strength. Senator Percy of Illinois gives us a representative portrait of the modern liberal Republican and suggests that his party, by following his road, can roll on to victory in 1968. Andrew Kopkind, in the context of a not unsympathetic examination of the "Bobby Kennedy phenomenon," speaks for a small but influential segment of left intellectuals—alienated from the conventional political scene—who are looking for a radical reconstruction of political life.

Oscar Gass
TENSIONS AND CONSERVATISM IN AMERICAN POLITICS

During this third year of Lyndon Johnson's Presidency, the United States has continued to grow richer in goods and stronger in arms. This year, however, unlike 1963–65, dissatisfaction with the course of public life has heightened. Convictions of public injustice—and of relative neglect and deprivation—have gained strength. The image of the Great Society is distinctly tarnished.

Nevertheless, in my judgment, these present discontents are more evidences of the transient distempers of the times than advance signals of profound changes. Among the issues overtly posed by public controversy in 1966, only two touch the fundamentals of American life: the role of the United States in Southeast Asia; the status of the Negro. In no other matter is there even the color of basic challenge, together with sponsorship of a magnitude to have general political import.

In Washington, both the White House and the Congress have treated 1966 as a year for consolidation, not major innovation. On September 1, not a single piece of legislation had been enacted which would deserve to be remembered five years later (though consideration was far advanced on increased minimum wages and new auto safety requirements). In 1966, as usually, American politics seeks peace through avoidance of the bone of social conflict. Congressmen and publicists, feeling their way toward an undangerous liberalism, concentrate on the aesthetic critique of *the affluent society* and strive to make an ideology of "pollution"—or anti-pollution. Even the highbrow fringe of political discourse steers away from economic and social deprivation, to find suitable objects

From "Tensions and Conservatism in American Politics," by Oscar Gass, *Commentary*, November 1966, pp. 63–68. Reprinted from *Commentary* by permission; copyright © 1966 by the American Jewish Committee. Mr. Gass is a consulting economist in Washington, D.C.

for distaste in such safe themes as "the shame of the cities." By these evidences, American society remains profoundly conservative, though not so totally immobile as it was in 1953–62.

Only at a few moments has the Johnson image of a Great Society touched the heart of America. One of these may have occurred on July 1, 1966, when Medicare went into operation. To the best of my awareness, there has been no second such moment this year.

II

In the perspective of decades, the most important development of 1965–66 may well be the new dimension of American commitment in Asia. Already sixteen years ago, in response to Communist unwillingness to accept a partitioned Korea, the United States made itself the foremost logistically-provided, deployed, and committed military power in Northeast Asia and off the coast of China. Now, in 1965–66, as the result of Communist unwillingness to rest content with a partitioned Vietnam, the United States has made itself the foremost logistically-provided, deployed, and committed power in Southeast Asia. These are events of great further consequence.

Whoever would counsel policy in these matters must make up his mind alike on some particulars of Vietnam, on the related movement of world affairs, and on the continuing role of the United States among the nations. And even an affirmatively resolved mind may not find it easy to bear the incidents of this war in which soldiers fight among civilians. Resolution does not exclude pain, nor suppress the wish for a better alternative.

Dividing and distressing as this issue is, I do not believe that current American tensions regarding public affairs are due primarily to the war in Vietnam. (Even in 1966, Americans are killing about ten times as many of their own people on U.S. highways as are being killed fighting in Asia.) The war *does* make a crisis of life or conscience for some of our best—particularly among the young. Their profound (and, as I think, mistaken) estrangement from United States' policy in Southeast Asia, and their passionate rejection of the public men who direct this policy, are important facets of American life.

Still—and bitter as the observation may be to one who weighs all that war destroys—Vietnam continues to play only a minor role in American politics and economics. No figure has emerged, either in the Congress or among publicists, to put the case for withdrawal at its maximum strength. Electorally, the war has not been made a serious issue. The Republican party has backed away from sponsoring either withdrawal or decisive escalation; Republican candidates hope to garner votes among the war-weary, while contending only that their party would do better what Lyndon Johnson is doing already. The "anti-Vietnam" nominees do poorly. The great public accepts neither involvement in Southeast Asia nor unqualified withdrawal: its program is to hit the enemy hard, to win quickly, and to come home.

In economic measure, the war is small. Its cost for 1966 may run about $12 billion. But U.S. personal consumption spending will be in the range of $465 billion and private investment (domestic and foreign) in the range of $125 billion. The American economy is not a war economy in 1966; it is a lavish consumers' and investors' economy, where the President even chose to spend nearly $6 billion, in the single fiscal year just closed, for the bauble of space exploration. Only a convergence of imbecilities brings the light-minded Left to concur with the hard-faced Right in asserting that the Vietnam war imposes neglect of the poor.

III

Fundamental political controversies within organized societies may be categorized—though with some simplification—as relating to one or more of four groups of issues: the derivation or structuring of government; the distribution or use of income and wealth; the status or consideration to be accorded various orders of persons; the support to be given to alternative styles of life, as expressed in faith, morals, or personality. A profoundly revolutionary politics, like that of contemporary China, endeavors to effect permanent and far-reaching transformations in all four of these spheres. A conservative consensus makes only accommodating adaptations in any of them.

We may dismiss out of hand the idea that any considerable force in the United States now proposes to use political instruments to make some great change in the faiths, morals, or personalities of Americans. And also with respect to the derivation and structuring of government, we should, I believe, see the United States of the 1960's as involved only in limited melioristic changes. If there does, one day, emerge a great pressure for some radical transformation of American government, that pressure will find expression in new political ideas, in a new programmatic character of parties, and probably in a new level of participation by the electorate. (Only 62 per cent voted for President in 1964.) All such new things are now absent.

Matters of the derivation of government—particularly voting rights and the apportionment of representation—have, of course, been in controversy in the 1960's. It is evidence of the mobility of the Great Society in 1964–65 that the federal government enacted two important pieces of voting legislation. These (sections of the Civil Rights Act of 1964 and the Voting Rights Act of 1965) also reflect the overcoming of old resistances: their adoption involved the two times, in all American history, that cloture of debate has been successfully invoked in the U.S. Senate on a civil-rights issue. Additionally, thirty-one states have redistricted their congressional representation since 1964, to follow more closely the present distribution of population. Moreover, the United States has now gone far—through forty-six state reapportionments—toward effectuating the principle that, in state government too, ". . . as nearly as practicable, one man's vote . . . is to be worth as much as another's." Still, it must be emphasized that, even with the accomplishment of these things, only a small minority of elected officers was made to feel the earth shift beneath them. Urbs and suburbs now have more weight. The gains are decided. Nevertheless, both the improvement of apportionment and the enlargement of voting make only for a slow cumulation of change.

In economic matters, distempers are highly visible. Though the United States still has the most stable price level of any advanced country, its prices have not been so stable in 1965–66 as they were in 1961–64; the cry of "inflation" is consequently renewed. The Democratic party, which is suspected of being more indulgent of "inflation," fears electoral consequences. Also, organized property (which has recently done very well) complains of the excessive demands of organized labor (which has done less well). Neither, however, challenges the fundamental position of the other.

During the first eight months of 1966, American unemployment has hovered above three million, and involuntary short-time work has averaged over two million—without any trend—while the top managers of the economy, public and private, have become steadily more jittery and disoriented. (In Washington, in early September, for the first time, alert and independent people were beginning to say that, particularly in its handling of economic questions, the Johnson administration was beginning to resemble the Eisenhower administration.) Few sober voices were heard to emphasize the real growth of the economy and its further large possibilities of growth—now and in the next years. On the contrary, what passes for respectable opinion largely concurred that the "overheated" economy needed to be "cooled off," by reducing demand—and consequently employment. (As always, the poor—whose role it was to be the ultimate coolants—found little voice.) On September 8, President Johnson joined the consensus of coolers, though only hesitatingly and in limited degree. Perhaps it was his intention to enter the November election period as much an anti-inflation hero as possible, without directly reducing consumers' incomes and without immediately slowing the rate of real economic growth.

"Inflation," "overheating," and "cooling" are active subjects of American economic debate in 1966. But the *distribution,* among individuals, of by far the greater part of the national income is not today an overt issue in American public life, even on the Left. (In dozens of conversations with young adherents of the "New Left," nothing has been evidenced more consistently than their total lack of interest in income distribution, unless it be their uninterestedness in all structured economic issues.) Only the *use*, in public expenditure, of a small fraction of the national income is in fact a live public issue in the United States. And here perspective turns on a grasp of the economic magnitudes; otherwise we are in danger of being bemused by the mere multiplicity of pieces of legislation. President Johnson said proudly in his message to the Congress on September 8: "If we [the federal government] had spent the same percentage [of the national product] as in 1955, our administrative budget would have been $15 billion higher last year." The current "antipoverty program" requests a 1967 budget under one-quarter of one per cent of the national product. Apart from social insurance, President Johnson's three year (1964–67) *increase* in the whole federal welfare program—including education, health, labor, housing, community development, and all aid to the poor—comes to $6.2 billion, or less than one per cent of the national product. For comparison, the fiscal year 1966 value of the *reductions* in taxes accomplished in 1962–65 was officially estimated at $20 billion.

The struggle over the status of the Negro is no transient squabble over "inflation." Its issues have such reach that, in speaking to their substance, a man may characterize his whole mind and personality. Who finds love or brotherhood the remedy generally for the problems of states and societies, he will find the remedy apt for the Negro's status too. Who puts first the recognition of equal standings for all men in law and social practice, will put first that recognition for the Negro also. Who generally prescribes socialism, will again here prescribe it.

The self-centeredness of the American Negro today is not unique, nor are his intellectuals unique when they find the Negro the key to utopia. Some Jewish spokesmen also once said, "Whoever solves my problem will have incidentally solved the problem of all mankind." And in the Jewish case, similarly, the statement was both tautologically true and operationally useless. If the Gentiles had known how to create the land of heart's desire, they would not have required any incidental benefit to the Jew as an inducement. And if Americans are capable of making a Great Society, they will make it—without requiring the additional inducement that the Negro will be more comfortable there. The world was not made for Israel, and America will not be remade for the Negro.

In 1966, the Negro in America is still a severely repressed minority, now eleven per cent of the U.S. population, but with a double share among the poor. Though he is eleven per cent in numbers, he is far less than eleven per cent in political weight. (Measured by the standard of the Jewish organized strength which in 1946–50 supported the establishment of Israel, the American Negro has no continuing organization at all.) By various measures of health, education, income, and economic insecurity, the representative Negro individual now stands where the whole United States stood less than three decades ago. But these gross measures of time lags do not begin to do justice to the Negro's sustained feeling of relative deprivation, or to the tiny place of Negroes—then and now—in U.S. leadership roles and especially among those who wield the authority of American government. There are only 6 Negroes among the 535 members of the present U.S. Congress; there are 17 Jews.

In areas of the old South and in some Northern cities, the Negro is still subjected to the traditional indignities and brutalities, designed to assure his subservience. Where these gross things are most done, they are done with the collaboration of sheriffs, police chiefs, states' attorneys, and judges. In contrast, over large parts of the nation, white people long ago discovered that Negro civil rights—and even legal desegregation—do not hurt. In these last years, "civil rights" and "desegregation" are even becoming conservative causes, in good standing. The acceptance of these limited things is the easy part of a wider process. A decade of opinion surveys demonstrates (as Paul B. Sheatsley has shown) a sustained trend of increasing favor among white Americans, North and South, not only for civil rights and legal desegregation but even for some degree of actual integration. There is a descending scale of consent: the right to vote, eligibility for jobs, access to public accommodations, sharing schools, neighborhood, personal society, and intermarriage. But for each position on the scale of intimacy, acceptance of the idea of Negro equality—at the antiseptic distance of an opinion survey—has increased steadily during the past decade.

Where then is the Negro going, in these next years? *Toward civil rights?* Yes. And new federal legislation, while desirable, is not of the essence. But further gains will be slow if dependent exclusively on sustained, local Negro pressures. A quick advance is possible only if the federal government can be brought to adopt new standards of exacting compliance with existing laws. *Toward legal desgregation?* Yes. At much the same rate and on the same conditions of civil rights. *Toward actual integration?* No, or little of it. Washington stands here as the gray image of the future—legally entirely desegregated, actually integrated only in spots. White America is not integrated; it is divided by barriers of origin, religion, status, and income. The barrier before the Negro is higher. *Toward economic equality?* I would dearly love to see it. But who can believe it? Who can believe that the size distribution of Negro incomes

will shortly coincide with the white? American society is not economi
cally equalitarian. It is certainly possible that, in these next years, the
United States will come to show more consideration generally for its
poor, but hardly for the Negro alone or preferentially. *Toward racial
assimilation?* I welcome it—for those who individually wish it. But it is
not a near-term solution. And it is never the kind of thing in which one
may require of individuals that they make themselves instruments of a
general policy. *Toward negritude?* Yes. Or rather toward several negri-
tudes, though never embracing all Negroes or perhaps even most of
them. It seems to me a blind spot in Nathan Glazer's learned, generous,
and sensitive study of the Negro that he writes:

> . . . it is not possible for Negroes to view themselves as other ethnic
> groups viewed themselves because—and this is the key to much in
> the Negro world—the Negro is only an American, and nothing else.
> He has no values and culture to guard and protect.

Alas, one must not be severe in determining what are "values and
culture." A kind of social intercourse; a distinctive humor; a music; a
rhythm of movement; an attitude toward bodily strength; a style of
religion; the sharing in a common rejection; battles won and lost together; a political program: these are enough to make values and a
culture. If some Negroes do increasingly find that these or other things
do make a negritude—and I think they will—other Negroes or white
people will hardly be in a position to say them no.

By creating great tensions in American society, by shaking the
American conservative consensus hard, and by continuing to shake,
something may be accomplished, in these years, which it will not be
entirely myopic to call "a Negro revolution"—a great change in the status
or consideration accorded to Negroes in the United States. But I see no
reason to believe that this change, if accomplished, will otherwise transform American society. Though the biblical image still makes captive our
imaginations, none of us, not even the Negro—latecomer aspirant to the
role—can be the suffering servant through whom all humanity is re-
deemed.

IV

Every alert and honest observer of a political scene must reflect
each day on how much is in the eye of the beholder. Where one observer
sees a violent struggle of interests, principles, and personalities, another
sees only a shared inertia. In the end, after seeking clarity of inquiry, and
utilizing such controls as may be contrived, one can only bear witness.

As far as my acquaintance with the U.S. government in Washington extends, in 1966 new ideas are very scarce in the executive branch.

Washington's high-level bureaucrats—those characteristic figures of a "new class" imaginatively constructed and lavishly admired by some of my contemporaries—have no idea where to go; they are waiting for their bosses to tell them. On Capitol Hill, in the Congress, there is more political mind. One studies it best where work is done, at the meetings of committees and still better of subcommittees. And, as one listens to speech, observes demeanor, and judges sentiment, the thought arises, "How little divides these people! How like they are to one another, in mind and purpose!" Here a little more pollution, there more anti-pollution. Here more shame of the cities, there less. Here more favor for school lunches, there disfavor. Of such things are current American political blocs made.

I do not deny that there is a more resistant (or, as some would say, though inaccurately, "reactionary") minority. That can be identified, in rough justice, with the affiliations of the forty-two senators (twenty-one Democrats and twenty-one Republicans) who blocked cloture on the Civil Rights Act of 1966. But it would be a great error to believe that, even on this issue—perhaps the sharpest "confrontation" of the congressional session of 1966—a moral gulf opened between the Senators who declared themselves on one side and the other. Nothing of the sort! Even Senator Mansfield, the Democratic majority leader who invoked cloture, was not regarded as an enthusiastic supporter of the bill. Senator Long, the Democratic majority whip, voted against cloture with Senator Dirksen. (Long has consistently voted against civil rights, medicare, and foreign aid. Yet he was elected majority whip with the support of Senator Paul H. Douglas, perhaps as good an example as one can find of the liberal conscience in today's Senate.) The Democratic party's Senate Steering Committee—though it includes such men as Douglas, Clark, Mansfield, and McCarthy—is probably the most conservative authority of the kind in the legislature of any Western nation; of its fifteen members who were present, eight voted with Dirksen against cloture on Civil Rights.

It will not be useful to drown these particular facts in some general cynicism over the universal proclivities of democratic legislatures. (Robert de Jouvenel accomplished all that a half-century ago.) And I am not referring to any supposed permanent characteristic of American politics. To some unhelpful guides, American history is one long consensus. They would have us forget even that Americans fought a Civil War, and inflicted on one another six-hundred thousand deaths. And they would have us make little of the differences among all Presidents and Congresses. That is not my perspective. What I see involved here is the particular fact of 1966 consensus—the particular breadth of agreement in this Congress, in 1966, regarding what the U.S. government should do and not do, just now. This consensus is, of course, in part, a phenomenon of "tired blood," and that will not last. The important question is: will this passive consensus turn out to have more durable characteristics, or will it give way, after 1966, to new and important Great Society initiatives?

Quite understandably, the congressional sessions of 1964 and 1965 have been compared with those of 1933 and 1934. President Johnson even proclaimed, in pardonable hyperbole, during a "Salute to Congress" (Oct. 7, 1965): "From your committees and both your houses has come the greatest outpouring of creative legislation in the history of this nation." Also for 1964 and 1965, however, one must shield oneself from being blinded by the deluge of trivial bills. Even a Congress which does little of substance still enacts each year about 350 public laws and 200 private laws.

In 1964 and 1965, the Congress actually did five important groups of things, relating to domestic affairs. *First:* it brought tax reductions to a cumulative total of about $20 billion a year (including earlier investment incentives and accelerated depreciation). As these reductions made the greater percentage additions to the retained incomes of prosperous people, many solid citizens found confirmation for the judgment that the Great Society was no bad thing. *Second:* the Congress enacted the most important civil-rights legislation since Reconstruction. Negroes particularly, who were estimated (by Gallup) to have voted about 94 per cent for Lyndon Johnson in November 1964, might also be confirmed in the belief that they had voted wisely. *Third:* the Congress increased social security and related benefits by amounts which, from July 1, 1966, are in the range of $6½ billion annually. Part of this (about $2¼ billion) consisted of an immediate 7 per cent increase in old-age payments, in favor of some twenty million beneficiaries. But the larger part was the new system of medical benefits, for aged persons and some others. And in an important fiscal departure, these medical benefits were to be financed, to the extent of about $1.4 billion annually, out of general tax revenues. *Fourth:* the Congress enlarged federal support for education and, to a much lesser extent, for housing and community development. Federal budget expenditure for education rose by $1½ billion in the two fiscal years 1964–66, while net spending for housing and community development rose by $358 million. *Fifth:* the Congress combined old and new measures to constitute an "anti-poverty" program, which spent just over $1 billion in the year ending June 30, 1966.

In contrast, the Congress of 1966 will have little of permanent character to its credit. In civil rights, formally a total defeat. In labor legislation, substantive failure, because of the gutting of the one important measure—enlarged and reconstructed unemployment compensation.

In federal support for education and welfare services, some small positive things. In federal support of community development—demonstration cities, water pollution control, etc.—also some small positive things. Yet, no doubt, when even this pallid session closes, the trumpeters will not hold back from trumpeting.

There is a view, which gains plausibility the further one is removed from Washington, that major domestic programs were held back in 1966 because of fear of inflation. The White House made a large contribution to public miseducation on this matter. From week to week, in one press conference after another, the President paraded his indecision on whether the economy was not just crossing some imaginary hair-breadth line where tax increases become indispensable. The President also repeatedly blew up, out of all proportion to any rational significance, the issue of whether—in a $750 billion economy, and where the President had just underestimated budget revenues by $4.6 billion—the Congress might increase, by $3 billion or $4 billion, the year's appropriations for what the executive branch *might* spend. And indeed, quite apart from the President's, voices never lacked to cry, "Beware, inflation!" Yet, again to bear witness, I am not acquainted with the name of a single senator or congressman who, in 1966, advocated reducing federal expenditure, on any program which he greatly valued, on the ground that total spending had to be specially restrained. The threatening excessive volume of total expenditure was used only as an argument against programs which one did not favor to begin with.

It would be an error to conclude that the congressional session of 1966 "just turned out thin." No, it was largely planned that way. Or, more accurately, the known and even self-conscious exhaustion of Great Society impulses, ideas, and initiatives, from the beginning, condemned this session to mediocrity. The keynote of this exhaustion was struck by Senator Mansfield as early as September 28, 1965. The Senate majority leader then said, very deliberately:

> The President has stated that "we look forward to the Congress being able to get out of here early next year." . . . I welcome . . . the President's view that he does not expect anything like the volume of substantive legislation next year. . . . The scope of achievements in the last eight or nine months makes any repetition of the volume of significant legislation which has been cleared in the present session not only unlikely but, in my judgment, undesirable. . . . [Therefore] the main concern of the Senate in the second session will be the perfection, the elaboration, and the refinement of the basic legislation which underpins major federal programs. . . . Indeed, that is likely to be the main concern not only for the next session but for some time to come.

In this view—and one cannot deny it considerable authority—at the end of September 1965, the Great Society was substantially a completed thing. Then, in 1966, there was necessarily nothing very important to do. . . .

David Danzig
CONSERVATISM AFTER GOLDWATER

Now that the Republican party has been overwhelmingly repudiated for its secession from contemporary American society, and the efforts of reconstructing it have begun, there has developed a tendency to view the Goldwater candidacy as a temporary aberration that was decisively corrected at the polls by the American consensus. Indeed, those who originally underestimated Goldwater's strength now find in President Johnson's victory a belated confirmation of their original judgment. However nervous one may have been made by those four days last July at the Cow Palace in San Francisco, the strength of hard-line nativist conservatism is now seen, in perspective, to have been more apparent than real. The Goldwater forces reduced President Eisenhower to political impotence, humiliated Governor Rockefeller, beat down one effort after another to broaden the political base of the platform, and ended on a rousing note of affirmation for extremism in the defense of freedom. But this show of power has generally come to be regarded as the result of a successful infiltration of the Republican organization by the wily and determined faction of the Right, a coup that was greatly abetted by the complacency and disunity of the moderate leaders. Similarly, the 27 million votes that Senator Goldwater received are taken to be largely an expression of last-ditch Republican party loyalty and Dixiecrat resistance to civil rights. A recent poll in the New York *Times,* according to which only 5.4 million "who voted the Republican ticket may still be devotees of Mr. Goldwater," lends support to this interpretation of the election campaign.

Yet just as it was incorrect to regard the Goldwater candidacy as merely a conspiratorial coup, so it is misleading to take the bare statistics of Goldwater support as a true index of rightist strength in the United

From "Conservatism after Goldwater," by David Danzig, *Commentary,* March 1965, pp. 31–37. David Danzig is Associate Director, American Jewish Committee. Reprinted from *Commentary* by permission; copyright © 1965 by the American Jewish Committee.

States. For the rightist cause in this country has traditionally been regional and ethnic both in character and appeal, and its failure in a *national* election involving a broad spectrum of issues and interests does not mean that it has failed altogether. Just before the election, for example, when the Johnson tide of moderate progressivism was running at its full, a national poll of voters taken by Louis Harris found that 88 per cent agreed with Senator Goldwater that prayer should be restored in the public schools; 94 per cent believed that the government had been lax in security matters; 60 per cent that the federal government should be trimmed, that some of its welfare and relief programs had a demoralizing effect on their beneficiaries, and that a federal right-to-work law should be enacted. To the extent that these findings are at all representative, the election did not test the strength of the conservative appeal; far from engaging the above issues, it failed even to sort them out.

What does this mean? It means, I would suggest, that the 1964 campaign tells us less about the potency of the political Right than it does about the character that Presidential contests have come to acquire in America. The evidence is now as overwhelming as President Johnson's majority that contemporary American politics is so much based upon the pragmatic self-interest of many different contending groups and blocs that the victory will go to the man who can achieve the broadest consensus among them. Thus, until San Francisco, the nominating convention had become the place where the deep divisions within each party were either reconciled or, more usually, papered over, and a candidate chosen who was less an initiator than a mediator, one who could impart some degree of unity and conviction to a campaign without undue doctrine or commitment. This explains in good part why a politician like Robert Taft—who most adequately embodied the core ideology of his party and remained first in the hearts of his fellow Republicans—was never chosen to lead it, and why the vague, middle-ground consensus politics of its Presidential candidates from Willkie to Eisenhower indeed gave voters an echo rather than a choice. Meanwhile, however, hard-core conservatism, whether Democratic or Republican, continued to lead a thriving existence and to exercise its power in local and state governments, as well, of course, as in the halls of Congress. A vivid example of this phenomenon was portrayed last November in these pages by Willie Morris, whose article "Legislating in Texas" shows how painfully little relation there is between the moderately progressive programs of President Johnson and the reactionary politics of his home state, where the liberals still comprise a small and virtually powerless faction.

Viewed in this perspective, Goldwater's candidacy and campaign appear as the first serious effort to translate the conservative individualism of the hinterlands into the terms of national policy and to recapture the Republican party from the lures and snares of the consensus politics of the past two decades. This is why, from his acceptance speech forward, Goldwater conducted a type of campaign which had not previously been seen in America during the 20th century—an ideological crusade that seemed designed to cast out heretics and schismatics and unite the true believers in a fundamentalist drive for "freedom." If the New Deal is to be taken as our "bloodless revolution," Goldwater is best understood as the leader of a delayed counter-revolution.

It was Goldwater's crusading zeal, rather than his ineptness, as many observers would have us believe, that was mainly responsible for his having alienated large blocs of voters. By no means an inexperienced politician, Goldwater insisted upon the unpopular and even somewhat ominous William Miller as a running mate in order to confirm that he was campaigning on ultra-conservative principles and these alone. His speeches were informed by statements that expressed the "conscience" rather than the programs of a conservative, as though the main issue were personal integrity rather than the relevance or attractiveness of a political program. "Do you think I don't know what labor wants to hear . . . what housewives and diplomats and white-collar workers want to hear?" he repeatedly asked. "Do you honestly think, after all these years in politics, that I don't know the easy way to get votes?" What Goldwater realized, however, was that the strength of his political appeal and the glue that would continue to hold the conservative movement together, even after he lost, was doctrinal purity. And it was doctrinal purity that led him into adopting certain positions—or better, impassioned attitudes—which enjoy an almost religious status in the minds of his followers: no corrupting compromises with liberals, no tolerance of "collectivism," the soft line on "extremism," the "better dead than red" approach to international affairs, the resistance to revisions of the immigration quotas, concern about the low state of public morality, and so forth. One has only to enumerate the groups that Goldwater thus went out of his way to alienate—farmers, trade unionists, Negroes, ethnic minorities, advocates of public power, the aged, the unemployed, as well as those who have lost the courage to die in a nuclear holocaust—in order to perceive the narrowness of his appeal. Conversely, the fact that so negative an approach to bi-partisan American policies could still gain more than 27 million votes must surely be attributed to more than party loyalty, for the Republicans who voted for Goldwater were either affirming or, at the very least, acquiescing in this approach. In other words, while the rejection of consensus politics brought disaster to the Republican party, it may well have accomplished precisely what the conservatives in the GOP and the Dixiecrats in the Democratic party have been seeking since the late 1940's—the marshalling of a formidable potential of popular opposition to the moderate liberalism and internationalism we inherited from the New Deal.

The political writers who have appraised this development most accurately are those with a right-wing orientation. Shortly before the election, John Dos Passos explained that "what is going on is not the death struggle of the G.O.P. but the birth of a coherent, effective, conservative opposition. . . . If it does nothing else, Barry Goldwater's capture of the . . . nomination has proved that dissent exists on a large enough scale to be politically effective." And the "victory" of a new grass-roots movement was spelled out in a post-election piece in the *National Review:*

> Is it seriously believed that the 25 million votes cast for Goldwater were cast by a sort of catatonic Republican who supported his party out of habit, and in reckless ignorance of the charges that had been made against the ticket? The opposite is more likely; that a substantial majority of those 25,000,000 Goldwater voters knew precisely for whom and for what they were voting, and would have stuck their hands into a barrel of rattlesnakes to pull the Goldwater lever.

Or again, just before the election a reporter for the *Wall Street Journal* asked a number of Goldwater voters: "Does a continuing conservative crusade carry much weight if its hero Mr. Goldwater is crushed next Tuesday?" The overwhelming majority replied that they would find another hero, preferably one who could represent their opposition to the growth of federal power more articulately and prudently.

Writing in the same publication after the election, William Henry Chamberlain raised the question of what would have been the results of the campaign if Goldwater had been denied the nomination, and went on to argue that they would not have been very different due to "a massive secession" of rightist voters. Chamberlain's conclusion was that in the forseeable future "there is no winning prospect, on a national scale, for a Republican party which alienates or proscribes either its conservative or its liberal wing." A Republican leader in California, who helped elect George Murphy, summed up the new situation in similar terms: "The Republican party just can't tell the Goldwater people to go to hell; there are too many of them. We can't let them have the leadership, but we do have to integrate them into the party."

This idea that serious account must now be taken of the extreme conservatives—that they have become for the first time an identifiable bloc with demands to make on the *national* scene and with the power and organizational skill to press those demands—constitutes a recognition of a truly important change in American politics. During the Roosevelt administrations the right-wing movement confined itself, for the most part, to scattered sniping at the New Deal, at "one world" Republicans such as Wendell Willkie, and at the personalities and hegemony of the Roosevelts. In 1948, the conservative group which tried to block the nomination of Governor Dewey was easily brushed aside, and even in 1952, when the Eisenhower-Taft contest seemed to offer an opportunity for more successful opposition, the conservatives still found that once in the arena of the national convention, they lacked sufficient strength to force the moderates to negotiate with them. By 1960, however, the remarkable demonstration for Senator Goldwater indicated that a new man-of-the-hour had emerged from the Right, and though the Senator immediately and effectively threw his support to Richard Nixon, it was with the calm confidence of a politician who felt certain that a genuine new movement had formed behind him and that its strength would soon have to be reckoned with. From having been local and sporadic, this movement was becoming organized and self-conscious; from having been composed of people who saw themselves as an intolerably encroached-upon and outmaneuvered majority, it was acquiring the character and psychology of a new minority bloc determined to win its rights by borrowing the tactics of the older minorities who had usurped the national power.

The difference between Taft and Goldwater Republicanism is not only that Goldwater is well to the right of Taft (who, after all, strongly supported federal aid to education, pushed through the public housing bill that bears his name, and was instrumental, along with Senator Vandenberg, in forging the bi-partisan foreign policy that President Eisenhower was to inherit). There is also the difference that Taft's power derived from his position on the national political scene. As "Mr. Republican" in the Senate, he articulated and effectively implemented an economic philosophy that legitimized conservatism as a reasoned and coherent, if not overly popular, alternative to the increasing centralization of power in modern society. Taft conservatism was responsible politics, capable of accommodation and adjustment, rather than a holy cause; its programs were worked out to compete with moderate progressivism as national policy rather than to whip up evangelical fervor. It is worth noting in this connection that Taft remained aloof for the most part from his party's fateful romance with Senator McCarthy, and though he died before the final rupture, the motion to censure McCarthy was carried through the Senate by exemplars of "Taft Republicanism" such as Arthur Watkins and Ralph Flanders. Goldwater, on the other hand, was one of few men in the Senate who remained with McCarthy to the bitter end and who identified his brand of conservatism with McCarthyism. Nor did his strength in the succeeding years grow, like Taft's, from his performance in the Senate, which was curiously hollow and perfunctory;

it grew, rather, from his efforts to carry the Republican message to the people during campaigns, to keep the right-wing effectively in the party, and to increase its influence at the local and state levels.

Closely related to the rise of Goldwater was the spread of discontent in many quarters over the direction that American society was taking. This reaction has been highlighted by the appearance of the far-out "radical right," but it in fact expresses a political fundamentalism whose religious and cultural roots run deep and wide. Fundamentalism itself is not a sect or a denomination or a specific church; it is a rigidly orthodox point of view which dominates some Protestant denominations and has adherents in others. However, it does provide a core ideology through which the stress upon purity and literalness of doctrine in religious matters carries over into an intransigent opposition to liberalizing the "Protestant ethic" in political, economic, social, and moral matters. Its other salient features are an anti-historical perspective which readily supports the conspiracy theory of social change, and an apocalyptic conception of the world as strictly divided into the saved and the damned. Thus the conflict with Communism is not one of power blocs but of faith, part of the unending struggle between God and the devil, and the danger of Communism comes, therefore, from within—from the corrosion of faith by insidious doctrines. It comes, that is to say, from the fostering by federal power of "collectivism"—the modern fundamentalist's secular counterpart of atheism.

Present-day fundamentalism provides a religio-ethnic matrix that naturally joins the segregationist in Mississippi to the nativist farmer and small business man in the Corn Belt, to the super-patriot in Colorado, to the leader of Spiritual Mobilizers in Los Angeles who says, "We are not going to give the city away to the Jews, Negroes, and Mexicans." Moreover, this movement serves as a rallying ground for other conservative groups, like the right-wing Catholics who supported McCarthyism a decade ago. But whereas McCarthyism lacked stable bases of local, popular support, the new reaction derives from the growing power of an important religious and nationalist group which has long felt denied its rightful share in shaping the policies of the nation and feels increasingly threatened by the modern pluralist society.

Some spokesmen of this ethos such as Bruce Alger of Texas were defeated in the Johnson landslide, but it should be noted that (like Alger himself) they usually polled many more votes in their districts than did Goldwater, which indicates that they were hurt rather than helped by the national ticket. Other local California rightists like George Murphy and James B. Utt were sent to Congress from California and a declared member of the John Birch Society became a state senator. In general, indeed, hard-core conservative candidates did not fare so badly in the election. Of the 193 Congressmen who were rated 50 to 100 per cent "Conservative" by the "Americans for Constitutional Action"—a leading radical-right group—148 were returned to Washington, and of the 32 rated "Elite" conservatives, 23 were re-elected.

The fact that the new "extremism" can continue to thrive on local issues while being roundly defeated on national ones was graphically brought home by the overwhelming vote in California—almost 2 to 1 —for repeal of the state fair housing law. According to one report, during pre-election canvassing in Long Beach and Lakewood, precincts which were 70 per cent Democratic, sentiment was 2½ to 1 against fair housing and 2½ to 1 for Johnson. Similarly, in Akron, Ohio, a fair housing ordinance was repealed that had been enacted only a few months before. Other instances suggest that the potential for a reactionary conservative bloc was not magically dissolved by Johnson's victory, that such issues as civil rights, "right to work" laws, prayers in schools, social welfare, "Communist" infiltration, and "statism" still attract powerful support when raised in the context of *local* decisions and laws. Accordingly, the organizational strength of the right-wing bloc has been concentrated in community, state, and regional networks which, if anything, were strengthened and not weakened by the opportunities provided during the campaign. For example, some 17 million copies of the Goldwater camp's rabble-rousing literature—notably *A Texan Looks at Lyndon* and *None Dare Call It Treason*—were distributed during the campaign, a feat that would hardly have been possible without an elaborate and efficient organization staffed by dedicated volunteers. Perhaps even more significant, the number of small campaign contributions was the largest ever received by the Republican party. . . .

The absence of relatively fixed classes in America has led numerous observers to believe that there is no solid social basis for right-wing conservatism in America. Hence our recurrent reactionary movements have been looked upon as essentially deviations from the basic traditions of American democracy and as better explained by social psychology than by legitimate political interests. In a recent essay in these pages, Hans J. Morgenthau exemplified this perspective in his discussion of the Goldwater candidacy. Regarding the Senator and his supporters as "romantic" and potentially fascist, Mr. Morgenthau argued that "Europe, in contrast to America, has known classes, determined by heredity or otherwise sharply and permanently defined in composition and social status which have had a legitimate stake in defending the status quo. But for the defense of what status quo could the American conservative have fought?"

Now it is true, of course, that America has not had "hereditary classes" in the European sense, but we do have hereditary *groups*—

ethnic, religious, and racial. However loose and informal in structure, these groups possess a quite concrete identity by virtue of common backgrounds and values and by their mutual interest in defending or improving, as the case may be, their status and privileges. For example, the opposition of the white supremacists to integration expresses nothing if not their "stake," whether "legitimate" or not, in "defending the status quo." Being highly pragmatic and self-serving, as political behavior generally has been in America, the segregationist's commitment to the status quo of 1954 does not give rise to a coherent ideology comparable to that of classical European conservatism. Instead it produces typically ideological slogans such as "states' rights" which permit the segregationist to fight for his privileged position and, at the same time, to regard himself as a latter-day apostle of individual freedom against the tyranny of the state. In this way, he screens his attachment to a caste system by an image carved from the grain of American resistance to tyranny. . . .

None of this is to say that direct economic class interests have not also been a major source of American conservatism. Even here, however, the conservatism that resulted was less a product of classical economic theory than of the imprint left on business values by the dominant religio-ethnic ideology. Much more so than in Europe, Puritanism and the Protestant ethic provided the economically elect with their faith in thrift, self-reliance, and independence. Thus, the reverence for the "balanced budget," which joins frugality to personal responsibility, is usually justified more in moralistic than in economic terms. In similar fashion, opposition to government welfare programs is mainly objected to on the ground that it undermines the individual's sense of personal responsibility, for in the fundamentalist business ethic, freedom of the individual to pursue his self-interest is held to be the only way to achieve the welfare of the community. Such beliefs still continue to fortify the conservatism of small business—not necessarily small in size but typified by the family-managed, entrepreneurial concern whose advertising appears in journals like the *National Review*.

The intense religio-ethnic battles of the "Tribal Twenties"—between liberal and fundamentalist Protestants, between Catholics and Protestants, as well as between the nativists and the immigrant minorities—show how deep group conflict runs in this country. That the significance of this species of conflict for American politics has not been fully recognized may be ascribed to the fact that ethnic hostilities were to some extent healed and to some extent concealed by the Depression and the pluralist coalition of the New Deal. Roosevelt's economic philosophy provided for the first time a rallying point for a labor and farm movement that cut across ethnic and racial lines and at the same time destroyed the sectional loyalties which had dominated American politics since the Civil War. But these very developments also gave rise to a new class-consciousness and political awareness among businessmen. Trading charges of Communist and Fascist leanings respectively, the labor movement and the capitalist conservatives reacted powerfully to each other as well as to the general reshuffling of opportunities which the New Deal was trying to effect. In this way, the traditional patterns of regional and ethnic political identification were broken apart by the revolution of the 1930's, and economic status and ideology became the main grounds for party attachment.

The vote in 1964, however, indicates that the economic issue on which American politics continued to turn for a generation has ceased to be the main determinant of political affiliation, just as sectionalism ceased to be the one main determinant in the 1930's. The division created by New Deal planning and the advent of the welfare state is neither as broad nor as deep as it once was. Indeed, as Samuel Lubell remarked in the course of analyzing the results of the last election, "we have developed an inflation-propped, managed economy which makes the thought of drastic change a terrifying fear to most voters." Among those converted to the managed economy are large numbers of middle-of-the-road Republicans who no longer oppose public welfare programs as a matter of course. Moreover, the Big Business executives who once believed the country to be imperiled by Marxist-inspired unions, and the labor leaders who regarded the N.A.M. as an organizing stage of fascist capitalism, no longer gaze at each other across their sword points. Both groups may continue to argue about their rightful share of the GNP, but they have found that they can live together by recognizing that their ultimate interests are equally tied to an expanding economy and to the federal policies that help to promote it.

The decline of the economic conflict suggests that the liberal-conservative split may be settling again on its traditional religio-ethnic basis and that the driving force behind the Goldwater movement was a recrudescence—in a new, updated, and more sophisticated form—of the nativist anxiety and aggression of the 1920's. It is important to realize that while the alignment under Roosevelt of labor liberalism against capitalist conservatism allayed some of the going group hostilities, it also served to foster others which have only now come to political flower. For the emergence of labor as a political force was accompanied by the growth in influence of the minority groups—the Catholics, Jews, Negroes, and nationality communities. After 1936, the Democratic party became a coalition that gave the minorities a significant role in shaping national policy, their influence having formerly been confined mainly to city politics. The bitter hostility of the ultra-conservatives to the federal government which dates from this period can, indeed, be viewed in part as stemming from the recognition that it was under the auspices of federal power that the minorities were able to achieve the political leverage which was to turn the victories of the nativists in the 1920's into a succession of defeats in the 1940's.

What makes the 1964 election a turning point, then, is not the overwhelming repudiation of the candidate of the extreme conservatives for the Presidency. This outcome had been prepared for long in advance by the population growth of the immigrant minorities whose loyalty to the Democratic party rested upon personal economic welfare and group status, by the acceptance among many Republicans of the moderate managed economy and welfare state, and by the shifts in population from the rural areas to the cities. Moreover, there was the growing acceptance of the fact, expressed most concretely by the election of John F. Kennedy, that America has become a pluralist society, however much pluralism may still be beaten down in the local and state politics of the hinterlands. And it is precisely this new pluralistic political context which gives the 1964 election its special character. In the ethnocentric 1920's, nativist conservatism represented the majority interest; in our pluralist age, it is a minority one. If Goldwater's defeat signifies the end of nativist conservatism as a majority ideology, it also signifies the transformation of such conservatism into the driving force of a definite, self-conscious, organized minority ethnic bloc. What has happened, in other words, is that the extreme conservatives, nourished by fundamentalist convictions and animated by group resentments, have reappeared on the national political scene after a period of submergence during which their influence was confined to scattered local communities. . . .

Senator Charles Percy
THE REPUBLICAN FUTURE

Not long ago a Republican friend complained to me that as far as he could see our party had nowhere to go. The Democrats, he said, had usurped all the problems that require attention in the Sixties. I was surprised by his attitude and I told him why.

From "The Republican Future," by Charles Percy, *Saturday Review*, October 29, 1966, pp. 19–21. Reprinted by permission. Charles Percy is the junior United States Senator from Illinois.

For the past several years I have been deeply involved in many of these problems, including literacy education, slum housing, and job opportunities. Consider just one of these—slum housing. More than 15,000,000 occupied dwelling units in the United States—or 27 per cent of the nation's housing—are substandard. To understand the grim reality behind these figures, one must see firsthand how such housing affects its inhabitants.

Take a seemingly insignificant thing such as paint peeling from ceilings and walls in slum buildings. Children often put the paint chips in their mouths, and the lead poisoning which results goes undetected until the damage is done. If a child survives the poisoning—and 25 per cent who are poisoned do not—it is more than likely that he will be severely and permanently retarded.

How the peeling paint and the falling plaster, the rats, the cockroaches, the tenements without heat in winter, and the buildings where five large families share a single bathroom affect the human spirit cannot be measured or charted. But the problems of the slum are very real, and they *must* be met. They are *not* being met today. Nor are many others like them. So when I am told that there are no problems left for Republicans to solve, I cannot agree. Rarely has there been such an opportunity for a major political party to come forward with progressive, imaginative, responsible solutions to a host of serious problems.

In the past, the Republican party too frequently has forgotten that urgent human needs cannot wait for ideological hair-splitting. Now we must make it clear that from the most wretched tenement on Chicago's West Side to a pocket of unemployment in Tennessee, the full range of American problems and aspirations reflects the full range of Republican concern.

In the cities alone, the Republican party has an unprecedented obligation and opportunity. By 1980, it is estimated, seventy-five of every hundred Americans will live in great unbroken crescents of city and suburb. The problems that already plague our cities are multiplying much faster than the solutions. There exists no more glaring failure of government than Democratic rule of the cities, and therein lies our most significant opportunity.

Our schools are overcrowded and understaffed.

Building code enforcement is a farce.

Traffic clogs our streets.

Smoke, soot, and carbon monoxide pollute the air we breathe.

Urban mass transit often is inadequate and inefficient.

Crime and corruption are the hallmarks of city life.

These situations *can* be remedied. They call for imagination and they call for leadership. There is no reason why the Republican party can't provide both. We have long demonstrated our concern for rural America. Let us now seize the banner of the city-dweller as well.

In New York, Mayor John V. Lindsay is showing what Republicans can do in the cities if given the chance. In less than a year, he has confronted the problems of his city with a vigor and imagination which are in sharp contrast to the stale approach of the preceding Democratic administrations. What John Lindsay is doing for the Republican party is almost as important as what he is doing for New York. He is proving in dramatic fashion that Republicans *care* about people—about people who live in cities, about poor people, about people who are not white.

Millions of Republicans, including many party leaders, share these concerns. Unfortunately, in recent years Republicans have not always been in the vanguard of social and economic development in this country. Rather, standing fast on traditional grounds—often on overly strict constitutional grounds—we frequently have said "no" to the present and "no" to the realities of American life in the mid-twentieth century. We have not been consistently progressive. We have not even been soundly conservative. All too often, we have been merely negative, both in word and deed.

We have taken the term "party of opposition" too literally; more often than not we have been content merely to oppose Democratic programs when we could have been suggesting constructive—and superior—alternatives. When we have proposed such alternatives, as when Senator Everett M. Dirksen shaped the 1964 Civil Rights Bill, our party has made its most significant contributions, not only to good government but to its own vitality.

In part, what has kept us from contributing enough are our differences. Like the Democrats, we are still ideologically divided. It is difficult, if not impossible, to speak of *a* Republican philosophy. Our party is in the midst of a re-examination of its policies and its politics. The best one can do, then, is to speak of those beliefs which all Republicans still share, and then to define what one individual Republican believes the Republican party must do and what it must be.

I suspect that the tie that binds all Republicans is a sincere and stubborn belief in the individual—in his capacity to grow as an individual, in his right to function as an individual, in his desire to *be* an individual rather than an anonymous appendage to the faceless crowd. Too many Democrats tend to consider collections of individuals; Republicans think each individual makes a difference. Democrats see government as the most fruitful source of initiative; Republicans believe that too much government will stifle initiative.

For many years, another bond between most Republicans was their alarm at the diminishing role of state and local government. Too often, however, state and local government failed to respond adequately to the needs of the people. We listened to ourselves deplore the shift of power to Washington, when really the people had nowhere else to turn. The states were not doing their jobs; the blame was bipartisan.

Today, however, some of the states *are* doing their jobs, and most of these states are governed by Republicans. These states are moving ahead in education, civil rights, medical care, mental health, conservation, and highways. In some cases, they are taking the lead away from the federal government; if every state did the same things, the necessity for a continuing transfer of responsibility to Washington might be sharply relieved.

Republican governors are demonstrating that the GOP is capable of serving compassionately and efficiently in administrative posts. But what should the Republican party work for in the halls of Congress and in the state legislatures? What should it stand for? What are our choices in the years just ahead?

Domestically, the most sensitive issue will continue to be civil rights. The Republican party cannot approach this issue timidly. Morally, we have an obligation to continue the work which we originally started in behalf of equal opportunities; politically, we have an opportunity to prove that we are worthy of minority trust. We must do what is necessary to guarantee the legitimate rights of every citizen, whatever his color, his creed, his cause. Every American must have equal opportunity in voting, housing, health care, education, and employment.

In addition to supporting legislation which is still needed, Republicans can take the lead in demanding enforcement of legislation already on the books. The Civil Rights Act of 1964, supported by 80 per cent of Republicans in Congress, has not been adequately enforced. This is a Democratic failure and a Republican opportunity.

What of our opportunities in other areas of social and economic legislation—in housing, education, poverty, labor relations, crime, conservation, employment? Was my friend right? Has the opposition in fact usurped our opportunities for creative government in these fields?

Hardly. In our Illinois campaign for the Senate this year we have advanced a number of positive proposals. They are not perfect, and they are not perfectly refined. But they *are* constructive attempts to get at some of the needs confronting the nation. I think they represent the search for solutions which Republicans should be conducting every waking hour of the day.

In education and housing, for example, we have proposed positive, practical programs.

We have suggested the establishment of universal pre-school education as a matter of high priority. It has long been recognized that the period of greatest development in children is the pre-school period when the child learns quickly and the patterns of a lifetime are set. Today, pre-school education is available only to the rich, who can afford to send their children to private nursery schools, and to the poor, a few of whom can send their children to Project Head Start classes in summer. I would like to see pre-school instruction made available to all children, regardless of their parents' income.

Similarly in the housing field we have proposed a broad program to make home ownership available to low-income families in our cities. Drawing on the successful experience of local groups in Tulsa, St. Louis, and Philadelphia, we have developed a national program in which government and the private sector can cooperate to help people move out of slum housing and into their own homes. This program would make a major contribution to the redevelopment and restoration of presently declining and blighted urban areas. At the same time, it would have the effect of creating a new spirit of independence and self-reliance in the low-income families involved.

I would hope that the Republican search for solutions to domestic problems will be in this mold in the years ahead. I would hope, too, that we will try to be equally constructive in foreign affairs.

Since the implementation of the nuclear test ban treaty, American foreign policy has shown little sensitivity to the subtleties of a changing world. President Johnson, less sophisticated in foreign affairs than was President Kennedy, has been obsessed with the war in Vietnam at the expense of American relationships in the rest of the world. As a result, we are shocked at the disruption of NATO when instead we should have prepared for its evolution in the world of the 1960s. We are frustrated at the recalcitrance of our allies even though we have made little effort to involve them in our goals or to be sensitive to theirs. In Western Europe, where there had been accord with friends, there is now disarray among dissidents. With the Soviet Union, where there had been détente, today there is only impasse.

I see an opening here for Republican leadership, if only we will grasp it. Let Republicans pursue a policy directed toward the reduction of tensions among nations. In the nuclear age this must be our goal. As much as some Americans might like to pursue a holy war against Communism, the stakes in human life are too high. The only rational policy is to pursue peace with at least as much vigor and invention as we now pursue war.

Early last July I proposed that the nations of Asia convene a conference to work toward a peaceful settlement of the war in Vietnam. The enemy had clearly indicated that he was not prepared to negotiate directly with the United States. Therefore, new approaches toward ending the war were in order. It was unrealistic to expect Hanoi and Peking to submit the problem to a reconvened Geneva Conference chaired by the Soviet Union and the United Kingdom. A different environment for negotiation was required, and perhaps the only forum in which North Vietnam and China might participate would be a forum of Asian nations. In such an environment, Hanoi and Peking would not be subject directly to the demands of either the U.S.S.R. or the Western powers.

No one could guarantee the success of such a peacemaking conference, but I am convinced that we cannot achieve peace by military means alone. Moreover, it is a simplistic view of world affairs which fears negotiation with the Communists and which never really trusts our allies to support Free World interests.

I felt—and continue to feel—that the continued escalation of the war makes it imperative that we quicken and intensify efforts to seek a just peace. By bombing within 900 yards of large civilian centers, we have multiplied the risks of this war—the risk of Chinese intervention, the risk of enemy escalation, the risk of still more casualties among innocent people. If we must accelerate the war—as the Administration believes we must—then let us also accelerate the pursuit of peace.

The Republican party should continue to seek new approaches to peace in the world. We clearly need more imagination and more flexibility in our foreign policy. The Administration is not providing it. Therefore, in a two-party system, the responsibility falls to the opposition.

There are many possibilities. We can encourage greater U.S. cooperation with the U.N. in seeking settlements of international conflicts. We can exert greater efforts for cooperative exploration of space and for a treaty to keep outer space free of military activity. We can extend the nuclear test ban treaty to include underground testing as soon as adequate detection devices are available—and we can press for the prompt development of such devices. We can negotiate a nuclear nonproliferation treaty now. We can seek agreement on nuclear-free zones in Africa, the Middle East, and Latin America.

Let us begin to develop a multinational agency through which prosperous countries of the East and West can more effectively channel assistance to the less developed nations. Perhaps there would also be value in periodic regional forums where both Communist and Free World nations could meet to deal with regional problems. This would stimulate regional initiative and tend to reduce regional tensions. Such policies should be shaped and sponsored by the Republican party. Still a minority out of power, our party has the time, the talent, and the resources to pursue new approaches.

Both in foreign and domestic policy, the opportunities for creative government are countless. The challenge for the Republican party is to seize these opportunities. If we can be responsive to the individual's needs without destroying the individual; if our responses are sensible *and* sensitive; if we will forget our liberal-conservative obsessions and devise solutions that are responsible and realistic—if we do these things, we can regain the confidence of the American people. If we do not, we are doomed to minority status, and we would deserve nothing more.

Andrew Kopkind
WAITING FOR LEFTY

In America, the cult of personality is the faith of the outcast, the politics of salvation. To be revered beyond reason, the cult-hero need not be particularly talented (Barry Goldwater, for example) nor especially commanding (Adlai Stevenson). But he must express, however ambiguously, the unrealized hopes of the disaffected of his age for a new order of life. The only mandatory article of faith is the belief that the qualities of his personality can somehow become the values of their society. The unhappy few who were madly for Adlai saw in their hero all the elements of compassion, intelligence, and wit which a generation of official liberalism had failed to secure. Twenty-six million Americans knew in their hearts that Goldwater would infuse his own virtues of individualism, morality, and simplicity into the social fabric. Disconfirmation of the prophetic vision by electoral defeat served only to strengthen the faith and spur the efforts of the believers. Stevensonism's wildest expression was in the galleries of the 1960 Democratic convention. The biggest batch of bumper-stickers for Barry was affixed after the rout of November, 1964. Stevenson Democrats swarmed into Washington with John Kennedy (himself the object of only a posthumous cult) and made much of the New Frontier in the image of their old guru. The Goldwaterites did the same for the Reagan campaign in California.

Now Stevenson is gone and Goldwater forgotten, and the hero who has succeeded them is Senator Robert Francis Kennedy. By luck and pluck he has become the last, best hope of the Sixties and the first of

"Waiting for Lefty," by Andrew Kopkind. A review of *R.F.K.: The Man Who Would Be President*, by Ralph de Toledano. Reprinted from *The New York Review of Books*, June 1967. Copyright © 1967, The New York Review.

the Seventies. The luck is his family, his fortune, and the assassin (or assassins) of Dallas. The pluck involves the development of a style and a rhetoric compounding some of the more attractive aspects of Bob Dylan and Fidel Castro: tousled hair, plaintive croon, under-doggedness, undefined revolutionism. His special charm is for those temporarily or permanently out of power; they sense that he is, either directly or metaphorically, their ticket to the top. They are more than willing to overlook his shortcomings; they invent virtues and powers for him quite beyond the possibilities of natural endowment. His past is rationalized into a prologue for greatness, and his future is divined as its realization. . . .

Anyone who has spent even a few minutes with Kennedy knows how he can get under the skin—by a word or the omission of it, by a glance or the diversion of it. Those who must deal critically with Kennedy *should* stay as far from him as possible or, alternatively, tie themselves like Odysseus to a mast of opposing politics and sympathies if they must listen to his songs. For he gives an impression utterly at odds with the one taken from the clippings. He is charming and tender, not brutal and rough; he is spontaneous, not scheming; witty, not humorless; self-critical, not cocky. More than the other ninety-nine senators and as much as any public official, he abjures the easy political response, the hypocritical canned answer to serious questions. He is the only non-Rotarian in the club, the one who tells it like it is: as they all say, he is "one of us." . . .

Whatever his hang-ups and his moods, Kennedy's politics are determined by the same perceptions which have produced Lyndon Johnson and George Romney, and in the long run his Administration would have much the same effect as theirs. There is no way of knowing whether Kennedy will continue to be a cult-hero, much less whether he will become a candidate for the Presidency. There are too many variables, which are best left to the newspaper columnists to pick over in the next five years. But, at this point, there is an assumption of popularity and eventual candidacy on the part of the political commentators, Kennedy and his staff, and a large population of demoralized and frustrated voters waiting for the coming of the once and future Kennedy.

So, as the future Kennedy moves to a position of political power and responsibility, the latitude he allows himself decreases. He may or may not predicate his actions on a cold assessment of political reward; but that is not the point. He has to deliver, he has to show his effect, and he has to keep winning. Because he cannot think of doing that outside political convention, he must become increasingly conventional.

At first, Kennedy appeared to be on the outer margins of the "system," poised for a swing beyond, into a position of attack. He exhibited a certain identification with the insurgents of this world: the grape-pickers in California, the Negro political movement in Mississippi, the rebels in Santo Domingo, the blacks in South Africa—even the Viet Cong, whom he thought entitled to the blood of his countrymen. It was not entirely clear how far that identification went; Kennedy always had an inexplicit appreciation for the poignant, the powerful, and the talented. But his support remained primarily moral. He was no insurgent himself.

But whatever swing has come has been inward, toward traditional methods of dealing with social problems. Kennedy supported the grape-pickers' merger into the AFL-CIO, which may have been helpful to their strike, but which surely limited their capacity to attack political and economic institutions beyond immediate objectives. He made television commercials for Rep. Jeffery Cohelan to use in his Democratic primary fight against the peace-and-civil-rights campaign of Robert Scheer in California. He helped raise funds for the Young Democrats in Mississippi, an elitist, "moderate" grouping allied with the national Democratic Administration and opposed to the politics of the Freedom Democrats. He chided critics of CIA's activities by reminding them of the complexities of international affairs.

Kennedy's interest in foreign policy waxes and wanes with the phases of some private moon which he alone observes. Perhaps his cult, and not his own behavior, is responsible for the incredible fuss when he goes abroad—to Latin America and Africa last year, to Europe recently. But in spite of the returns in newspaper column inches, they seem to be more trouble than they are worth. Back home, he delivers occasional speeches on Latin America which describe in fine detail the malignancy of the established order, the misery of the poor, and the failure of US policy. But he makes no assault on the root causes of that failure—the manipulation of US corporate interests and the habit of military support. He saves his complaints for the examples of obvious breakdown. One can look in vain in his speeches for a convincing critique of the sources of imperialism, although it is clear that he would like to clean it up a bit. The same is true for his treatment of South Africa. Kennedy's visit there last year gave heart to both internal and external opponents of *apartheid*, and he seemed to understand the depressing realities of resistance. But there his understanding stopped; never a mention of Charles Engelhard nor of the Chase Manhattan Bank, nor a recommendation that the US withdraw support from the South African regime.

Most perplexing, because most tantalizing, has been his position on the war in Vietnam. In February, 1966, he proposed acceptance of the National Liberation Front's role in any Vietnamese settlement, then backed away when questioned sharply, and remained silent (or contrite?) for a year. His second annual Vietnam address, presented to an expectant Senate this year on March 2, criticized the President for a reluctance to negotiate with Hanoi, and included a moving account of the horrors of war. It was a fine attempt to legitimize the moral issues, which hard-nosed politicians like to ignore. Kennedy's staff claims the second speech went further against official policy than did the first, but to many listeners it seemed somewhat less of a break. In any case, it came at least two weeks too late to have any specific effect on negotiations for de-escalation. Kennedy knows now that he waited too long; he confided recently that the Administration fooled him into thinking that real progress toward peace talks were being made, and that a critical speech might ruin their chances of success.

What is maddening is that Kennedy *always* appears to know better. Staughton Lynd and Tom Hayden emerged from a lengthy interview (which Kennedy requested) believing that he understood the basic error of the Administration's policy: that the refusal to entertain the possibility of a unified, Communist-controlled Vietnam only prolonged the war. "We're in the same ballpark," Kennedy told the two visitors as they left his East River apartment. But that was not the way it came out on the floor of the Senate. Some weeks later, after General Westmoreland's bullying visit to the mainland, Kennedy indicated to friends that he thought the war would soon get much worse, that there would be new escalation, and that the dangers were enormous. He thereupon made a few mildly critical comments about Administration policy in the course of an exchange among "doves" after the wide-ranging assault by Senator George McGovern. But even then Kennedy could not see himself risking his place inside the system to lead the attack—the only attack which might mobilize effective opposition to the war in the foreseeable present.

It should hardly be surprising that Kennedy acts like a normal politician. There is nothing in his background, his performance, or his prospects which suggests that he behave otherwise. He may be impulsive and keen on the issues, but he sees them with the eyes of a traditional political operator. It is not necessary to suppose that he feeds every alternative into some Lou Harris poll or a computer to see which one will get him the most number of votes for some office in some future election. He goes out of his way to talk with poor sharecroppers in the Mississippi Delta, or attacks Sam Yorty in a Senate hearing, or supports legislative reapportionment, because he is genuinely concerned. Most of his advisers (outside his dovish office staff) warned him of the negative political consequences of this year's Vietnam speech; Ted Sorensen, for one, was adamantly opposed. But Kennedy went ahead, because he did not like the war nor the way the President was conducting it. To Kennedy cultists, those qualities of spontaneity and honesty are absolute virtues, and even to critical observers there is something rare and refreshing in the way he swings around the issues. But it is all perfectly safe. His impulses never take him beyond the limits of accepted behavior. He would not join a peace march in Central Park nor withdraw his account from a bank supporting the South African economy nor make a TV spot for a peacenik candidate against a good Democrat. Nor will he fail to support the Johnson-Humphrey ticket for re-election in 1968. He can conceive of doing no less.

All that may be obvious to the politically sophisticated, but the Kennedy cult is based on the hope, if not the tenet, that the man can operate without as well as within the boundaries of the system, that he can lead a revolution of attrition against the dominant institutions of the society. The myth will die hard. It is based on the shaky assumptions of pluralism: that the structure of American life is open enough and democratic enough to allow for whatever reforms are necessary, if only a formula for gathering political power can be found.

Arthur Schlesinger, Jr., a peripatetic theoretician in Kennedy's Lyceum, appears to have arrived at such a formula. In an article in the April *Progressive*, he restates his argument that Americans have most of the things they need for the good life. What they want now is quality control. The new "qualitative" issues replace the old "quantitative" ones. Instead of "a job, a suit of clothing, three meals a day, a roof over one's head, and a measure of security for old age," people now are concerned with "civil rights, civil liberties, education, urban planning, the state of the arts and the beauty of the environment ... and, in addition, foreign policy." These issues, he concludes,

> are no longer social and economic so much as they are cultural and moral. It is no longer the common man against the economic royalist or the worker against the boss so much as it is the rational against the indignant, the tolerant against the bigoted, the planner against the spoiler, the humanist against the materialist, the educated against the uneducated, the young against the old.

To deal with them, Schlesinger would weld a new coalition of urban innovators (Cavanaghs instead of Daleys), the unorganized (or Reuther-organized) poor, the newly diplomated middle class, the remaining progressive ethnic groups, the churches—"and the most vital group of all, the youth." Discarded are the repressive elements of the old New Deal coalition—the satisfied labor unions, the grasping lower-middle class, and the backlashing minorities. To lead the new forces must be a leader "sufficiently free, cool, and brave, to relate to the young and recover their allegiance for American society." Schlesinger need be no more specific.

Despite the echos of Dylan and Marcuse, Fannie Lou Hamer and Erik Erikson in Kennedy's speeches, Schlesinger's formulation indicates the basis and the limits of the new Kennedy politics. It can all be seen in Kennedy's project in the Bedford-Stuyvesant section of Brooklyn. In January, 1966, Kennedy presented a series of speeches on urban problems which included several policy suggestions for community development, but no specific plans for action. A few weeks later, he began to hear complaints from Negroes in Bedford-Stuyvesant about the lack of follow-up. Kennedy's New York staffmen went to work seeing what might be done, and by the end of the year they had developed a "total program" for employment, education, community organization, social services, and economic growth such as Kennedy outlined in the second of his addresses.

A committee of influential businessmen—Thomas Watson of IBM, William Paley of CBS, financiers Douglas Dillon and André Meyer —was established as a development corporation. A local organization of the poor was set up to "govern" the project. City and state officials were asked to help, and proposals for federal aid (including financing from a Labor Department program which Kennedy pushed through Congress last year) were drawn. Before long, however, the poor people's organization developed a malfunction. It was being controlled by the traditional manipulators in the community. The Kennedy men in New York had not known how to reach the underclass, but when they saw that the council was making no impact in the area, they abandoned it and established a new, *poorer* people's organization as a rival. The Citizens' Crusade against Poverty, a liberal coalition of community action organizations set up by Walter Reuther, was called in to get the poor moving. The Astor fortune was requisitioned to build "superblocks" in the slum.

The Bedford-Stuyvesant project is almost too good a test of Kennedy's ideas and the direction he intends to go. It is relatively small and self-contained. There is no strong existing governmental organization, nor local leadership with deep roots. The typical problems of urban slums are acute. Kennedy can marshal considerable political power in New York to effect change, and his staff is rather immodestly eager to assume executive functions to relieve the boredom of legislative life. Kennedy, too, is restless under the restrictions of the senatorial role. The operation in Brooklyn amounts to a kind of mini-Administration, until the real thing comes along.

But it is far too early to tell whether Kennedy's plan for Bedford-Stuyvesant will develop the new forms of community government, and achieve the physical and social rehabilitation its backers envisage. The basic scheme suggests that something less than radical reconstruction will result. The Kennedy assumption is the Schlesinger thesis: that the highly motivated poor can work with the corporate elite and the planners with the politicians to produce a "qualitatively" Greater Society. It does not, however, seem likely. The cultural and moral issues are still inextricably bound up with the social and economic ones. Air pollution may be an aspect of the quality of life, but all the technological adjustment in the world will not reduce the smog one particle if economic pressure cannot be applied against the polluting industries. Urban planning is still a political problem; there is no end to the plans, and no end to the political obstacles in the way of their execution either. Banks and factories for the slums might be nice, but something much more profound—"more social and economic" in the sense that Schlesinger's formula rejects—has to be done to bring the poor out of the culture of poverty. Kennedy's men in Brooklyn will find that the poor and the middle class do not share a universe of interests. In trying to improve education, for example, they will see that new buildings and bright teachers and modern curricula make little difference in learning among the poor. As the parents of East Harlem's p.s. 201 have been trying to say for a year now, changes in educational quality will not come until the community gains new measures of power—money, and status, and social effect. That process comes through political struggle; it will not be freely given by businessmen or social workers, much less by senators or mayors or directors of human resources. For the act of *taking* power is the condition of *being* powerful.

At best, the Bedford-Stuyvesant plan seems to be an attempt to apply the principles of American development aid overseas to an "underdeveloped" community at home. The idea of local counter-insurgency obviously appeals to Kennedy. Riot control is the first responsibility of the modern Prince. But there is no assurance that the local effort will have any more success than the foreign one has had. Aid programs have largely failed because of an inability to arrange a redistribution of power in the "target" countries. US money and technical assistance is monopolized by the elites, who use it to tighten their grip on the underclasses. The same has been true of the antipoverty program in this country; city machines and welfare bureaucracies have been the major beneficiaries of the money and the effort expended so far.

Still it is very difficult to criticize the Kennedy project in Brooklyn, as it is to bad-mouth his efforts and exercises in other fields. There is precious little in the country that is any better. Only a handful of senators criticize the war, few even *talk* about Latin America, and in any event Kennedy is so much brighter and more appealing personally than any of them. But it may be a serious mistake to consider what Kennedy is doing—in Bedford-Stuyvesant as elsewhere—a healthy "first step" toward significant change. For Kennedy would impose his own kind of elitist reform before any independent forms of social reconstruction could begin.

To realign US foreign policy, there must be basic changes in the operation of the corporatist system, so that its decision-makers no longer perceive their interests to lie in destroying the independence of other countries. Along with those changes, there would have to be drastic revisions in military strategy and a dismantling of the defense establishment. No president elected within the normal political procedures by the constituencies that now exist could achieve that. But Kennedy would tend to strengthen, not weaken, the structure of imperialism: by encouraging American overseas corporations to behave liberally, to allow foreign governments to exert superficial control over corporate operations, and to keep cool when political currents seem to threaten their interests. At the same time, Kennedy would encourage the development of a large counter-insurgency capability (as begun by his brother) to put down the really serious threats.

At home, Kennedy would be drawn to analogous illusions of reform. Larger governmental units might be decentralized to bring policy-making "closer to the people," while the old power relationships are maintained. It would always be necessary to control independent political constituencies, whether they are Freedom Democrats in the South or Liberation Parties in the ghettoes or unaffiliated labor insurgencies on the farms. The job of political leaders is to force such groups into coalitions which they already manipulate: the national Democratic Party, the city machines, the big labor unions.

A Kennedy Administration would try to implement the Schlesinger formula on a grand scale. There is a strong suggestion in that thesis that there is a "crisis" in the order akin to the failure of American institutions in the years before the New Deal, which Schlesinger has chronicled so brilliantly. The New Deal saved the order then by appearing to reform it. If things are really falling apart now, if the war and the Negro revolt and the alienation of the suburban middle class and the loss of "allegiance" of the young is as serious as Schlesinger suspects, Kennedy may indeed be the only leader able to maintain the order, however readjusted it may have to be internally. Certainly the Bedford-Stuyvesant coalition—corporation heads, liberal intellectuals, welfare politicians, progressive unionists, militant Negroes, and eager young volunteers— offers the best hope to keep the center holding. But it is absurd to suppose that the social finagling will produce essential change. The Schlesinger doctrine invests the "free, cool, and brave" leader with powers he cannot logically have. The kind of top-down reforms he is capable of will result *only* in the superficial readjustments that can buy off the cutting edge of resistance. To do more requires the kind of dislocation and reconstruction of underlying relationships which can only come from a new politics, based on movement and conflict, not coalition and consensus. It is not Kennedy's fault that he can do no other; it is his situation.

For those who cannot believe in the essential efficacy of "cultural and moral" (or technical and legislative) solutions to basic social and economic problems, the next few years will present a series of painful choices. The Kennedy camp will gather much of the brightest, most energetic, most effective talent in the country. Some may join up in full agreement with the prospects as they now appear; others may try, as Robert Scheer recommended in a recent *Ramparts* profile of Kennedy, to "up the ante," to make Kennedy's reforms a little more broad than they might otherwise be. Only a few will remain outside. Only a handful will continue to build independent constituencies—of intellectuals, of the poor, of the Negro underclass. It is far from clear what the outsiders will accomplish. But in the end Kennedy will not remake the society, either by his personality or with his programs, and we will have need again of a saving remnant.

4
The Presidency: Nature of the Office

After Lord Bryce returned to England from his visit to the United States in 1883, he observed in *The American Commonwealth* that Americans only infrequently select great men as Presidents. He pondered about the reasons for this and concluded that "after all, a President need not be a man of brilliant intellectual gifts." He noted that while profundity of thought, a wide range of knowledge, and imagination might be assets to the President, these qualities really were not necessary. This, he maintained, was true because "four-fifths of his work is the same in kind as that which devolves on the chairman of a commercial company or the manager of a railway, the work of choosing good subordinates, seeing that they attend to their business, and taking a sound practical view of such administrative questions as require his decision."

Lord Bryce can be excused for this observation. When he viewed the Presidency in 1883, Chester Arthur was sitting in the White House and President Arthur could not be called an energetic President. In the busiest time of the year, when Congress was in session, President Arthur did not arise until nine. He would then eat a "continental breakfast" while dressing, and his official day would be under way. But the day would usually end at four in the afternoon, at which time he went out for a drive or a horseback ride.

In the 1880s, the President exercised certain narrowly defined constitutional, ceremonial, and political duties. He was chief of state, commander in chief of the small military and naval forces, chief of

America's diplomatic corps—a diplomatic corps that did not even contain one diplomat with the rank of ambassador—and he was also chief clerk of the federal administration and titular head of his political party.

By the end of the first decade of this century, it was still appropriate to discuss the relative merits of William Howard Taft's "constitutional" or literal view of presidential powers versus Theodore Roosevelt's "stewardship" theory of the Presidency. Today, such theories are of historical interest only. In the 1960s, a President has no choice between being a weak or strong chief executive. As the late Henry Jones Ford noted some fifty years ago, the Presidency has evolved from a semipopular institution into a broadly representative office. This evolution, or aggrandizement as the late Edward Corwin characterized it, has added not only popular support to the office but also national and international responsibilities. All of the President's traditional duties have mushroomed, and many new responsibilities have been added. Wars, cold wars, depressions, and the welfare state have thrust upon the Presidency continuing responsibilities of such magnitude that no President can safely ignore them. Today, the President must execute his traditional duties and also be the leader of the Congress, the overseer of the national economy, the tribune of the people, and the leader of the free-world alliance.

In order to discharge effectively the constantly increasing burdens of the Presidency, it has been necessary to equip the office with such staff agencies as the National Security Council, the Council of Economic Advisers, and the Bureau of the Budget. There is no longer just a President, but a President and a Presidency—a man and an institution. The President's personal responsibility to take a policy lead for the nation—to seize the initiative—has become institutionalized in such agencies as the Bureau of the Budget and the Council of Economic Advisers.

Few would seriously contend that Presidents have not needed policy-planning agencies. The President must be free from petty details before he can assume the responsibility for decisions. Woodrow Wilson states: "Men of ordinary physique and discretion cannot be Presidents and live, if the strain be not somehow relieved. We shall be obliged to be picking our chief magistrates from among wise and prudent athletes—a small class."

It may well be that scholars have paid too much attention to the "institutionalized" Presidency. There is still an office which is quite personal to the incumbent and does not lend itself to easy generalizations. Despite the institutionalization that has occurred since the beginning of the FDR era, a considerable portion of presidential power still remains personal to the man in the office. The organization of the

Presidency has not undergone any major changes in the past decade, yet the Presidency of Lyndon Johnson is quite different from the Presidency of John Kennedy, and both differ from the Eisenhower Presidency.

These differences raise a problem. If certain events in American history have transformed the Presidency into the focal point of American government, should the discharge of these important responsibilities be dependent upon the accident of an incumbent's personality and style and his personal attitude toward presidential power? In other words, should the institutionalization of the Presidency be carried to the point that executive responsibilities and power would attach less to the man and more to organizational units within the executive branch?

The issue raised by these questions is only one aspect of the still broader question of the power of the modern Presidency. From almost the beginning of the Republic, American presidents have made commitments outside of the system of checks and balances. Jefferson did so in the case of the Barbary pirates, McKinley in the Boxer Rebellion, and Wilson in Mexico. Yet none of these compares to the commitments made by Truman in Korea, Eisenhower in the Formosan Straits, and Johnson in Viet Nam. Has this popular office, so closely involved in the evolution of democracy in the United States, reached the point that it can operate outside the political process and thus constitute a standing menace to democracy? Or is the modern Presidency a refutation of those critics who hold that democracies must fail because they can neither decide quickly nor act forcefully?

James MacGregor Burns
THE PRESIDENCY: POWER AND PARADOX

A few years ago some grade-school children in the Chicago area were polled on their attitudes toward political authority. Two figures, it developed, first appeared on their political horizon—the local policeman and the President of the United States. The children saw their President as something of a superman. To almost all the children he appeared as

From "The Presidency: Power and Paradox," by James MacGregor Burns, *Saturday Review*, February 5, 1966, pp. 30–31. This article is based on the author's book *Presidential Government*. Boston: Houghton Mifflin Company, 1966. Reprinted by permission. Mr. Burns is Professor of Government, Williams College.

either a good person or the "best in the world." Even the youngest seemed to know a good deal about him.

That was in Eisenhower's time. We have just concluded a year in which the obsession with the President's personality, health, and state of mind has reached new heights. We used to think that the obsessive interest in John Kennedy, his family, and his friends was due to Kennedy's youthfulness, glamour, wife, and other special attributes. But the absorption with Lyndon Johnson is just as great. The press has followed his every movement, mood, and motive in endless detail.

So we know a great deal about Presidents. But how much do we know about the Presidency? Most studies of the office are really accounts of Presidents in office, the men around them, their decisions and crises. While we have been focusing on personality, the office itself has been changing drastically. Today it may have a far greater effect on its incumbents than we have recognized.

One by one the Presidency has absorbed the men and institutions that once were centers of separate and countervailing power. There was a time when Presidents had to cope with opposition—or at least foot-dragging—in their Cabinets, Vice Presidents, and party leaders. Today Cabinet members, Vice Presidents, and national party chairmen are essentially assistants to the President. The process of "Presidential aggrandizement" has been accelerating. Not more than once or twice since the mid-1930s has the Supreme Court been a major deterrent to Presidential action. The Chief Executive has become virtually "President of the Cities" through his control of urban funds and policy, and hence has pulverized some of the barriers of federalism established by the Founding Fathers to limit national power. Thanks to Barry Goldwater's dragging scores of Republican Congressmen down to defeat in 1964, Congress has overcome its old deadlocks and has occasionally even moved ahead of the President on items of the Great Society. And a close study of two social power centers, the press and the intelligentsia, would reveal, I think, that they have been drawn—far more than they would admit—into the orbit of Presidential influence.

I am not, of course, predicting eternal joyous harmony between President and Congress. Doubtless Mr. Johnson will lose some of his strongest congressional boosters in this year's elections, and the Democrats cannot hope for another Barry Goldwater to overwhelm in 1968. But in the long run Congress will be drawn increasingly into the orbit of executive power as a result of reapportionment, the erosion of one-party districts, party realignment, and the widening consensus over quantitative liberalism—over social welfare, federal regulation, and even Negro rights.

For years American conservatives have been jumping up and

down and pointing to Presidential aggrandizement. In this the conservatives have been profoundly right. But where they have been profoundly wrong is in seeing Presidential power as a direct threat to individual liberty. Quite the opposite has happened. In the protection of civil liberties, in the broadening of civil rights, in the pressure for social welfare legislation such as aid to education and to the poor that has done so much to expand individual liberty, the President has been the leader, the innovator, the cutting edge in the immense widening of social, economic, and individual liberty that has occurred in this nation during the last three decades. In this sense the power of the Presidency has been paradoxical.

That power may become more paradoxical, but for a different reason. As we increasingly achieve freedom and equality for the great number of Americans, Presidential government may exhaust the purpose for which it has been such an eminently suited means. The great machinery of government that has been shaped to distribute welfare and overcome poverty and broaden opportunity and protect liberty will become devoted to increasingly automatic tasks of dividing up shares in the welfare state. The old passions, the old compulsion of purpose, will be dissipated. Purpose will no longer be toughened in conflict; creativity will no longer rise from challenge and crisis. As the consensus widens— that is, as the ends of government become increasingly agreed upon between President and Congress, between the parties, between national and state and local governments—issues will revolve mainly around questions of technique. And the more humdrum these matters become, the more Presidents will turn to their ceremonial and symbolic roles to provide circuses for the people—the bread already being in abundance.

Many would reject any call today for high purposes and fighting issues. They prefer a polity that is not rent by great issues, scarred by savage conflict, absorbed in passionate controversy, or even distracted by political problems. The very realization of the historic goals of freedom and equality would, they believe, create a basis on which people could turn to the enduring problems of the richness and quality of life, and could forsake some of the old ideological quarrels.

Those who spurn ideology will contend, moreover, that progress flows not from the pursuit of central, synoptic visions or plans or purposes, but from the pursuit of a wide range of alternative policies, from flexible methods, from refusal to make ultimate commitments to any means or any end, from incremental and adjustive tactics that permit day-to-day reconciliations of differences. Such an approach, they hold, produces innovation, creativity, and excitement. It rejects the grand formulations of interrelated ends and means in favor of special angles of vision, the social dynamics of a loosely articulated, highly accessible, and open-ended polity. The incrementalists would proceed step by step, renouncing passion and commitment in favor of prudence and calculation.

Yet many who have lived through decades of traumatic and even bloody political conflict at home and abroad will wonder about a nation in which the great issues have dwindled to matters of technique. They will worry first about a people so bored by the relatively trivial political issues of the day that they have become largely absorbed in the minutiae of their private lives. They will worry that people may fall into adjustment, conformity, undiscriminating tolerance, and aimless, time-filling activities, and that this will lead to the acceptance of mediocrity and a compulsive togetherness rather than the pursuit of excellence and individuality.

They will be concerned about the governors as well as the governed. For a government agreed on the larger issues and proceeding by calculation and adjustment is likely to attract to its service the little foxes who in Archilochus's phrase know many little things—the operators, the careerists, the opportunists, the technicians, the fixers, the managers. Some of these men may be resourceful, flexible, and prudent. But they will be so absorbed in adjusting things and mediating among people that it will be difficult for them to separate issues of policy from questions of their own immediate self-enhancement. Certainly there would be little room for the Churchills who give up office in pursuit of broader principles, or even for the innovators who wish to create something more exalted than a better administrative mousetrap. Thus the governors, too, would lose their way, become lost in technique, become absorbed in private motives, and substitute the means for the ends.

For this is the corruption of consensus—the attempt to find universal agreement on so many issues that great public purposes are eroded by a torrent of tiny problems solved by adjustment and adaptation. Ways and means are more and more rationally elaborated by mounting numbers of technicians for a society having less and less human purpose.

In the Presidency this trend would mean the submergence of the nation's supreme political decision maker in an ever-widening tide of incremental adjustments. The President might still be a hero to most of his people, but his policy and program would not be heroic, only his image. He would still seem a potent figure to children—and grown-ups—but his actual influence over events would be dwindling. He would still be visible as he mediated among the technicians and occasionally coped with crises; but it would be the visibility of the tightrope walker whom the great public watches, entranced but uninvolved. The defeat of Presidential government would be inherent in its very success. Having taken over the Cabinet and the rest of the government, Presidential government would finally have taken over the President.

Can we exploit the immense potential of Presidential government for power and creativity and still escape creeping consensus and enervation? Not, I think, by reimposing the old constitutional barriers against the President. The main hope of keeping the Presidency as an alert and daring agency of popular government lies in a vigorous and vibrant opposition. Such an opposition cannot be built on Capitol Hill, for Congress fragmentizes minority-party power just as it does the majority. It must be built anew. The Republicans have a fine opportunity to fashion party machinery—an annual conference or convention, for example, to keep its platform and leadership up to date—that could empower a clear, unified, and loyal "Shadow Presidency."

Presidential government is a superb instrument for realizing our national purpose as we redefine it over the years. But purpose in turn is steeled not amid agreement, adjustment, conformity, but in crisis and conflict; it was out of crisis and conflict that Roosevelt, Nehru, Lenin, Churchill, and the other great leaders of the century emerged. A great society needs not consensus but creative leadership and creative opposition—hence it needs the sting of challenge in a society rich in diversity, in a politics rich with dissent.

Henry Jones Ford
THE PRESIDENCY AS A POPULAR INSTITUTION

The new character impressed upon the presidential office by the democratic movement at once made it the basis of political control. Every national party which has come into existence since Jackson's time, no matter how purely legislative its programme, has felt impelled to nominate a presidential ticket. Unless it is able to control the presidential office, no party can accomplish its purposes. The Whig party, which was animated by the old spirit of parliamentary control, was the first party to find this out by experience. In electing Harrison in 1840, it secured a President who fully assented to the parliamentary principle of government. In his inaugural address he contended that by no fair construction

From *The Rise and Growth of American Politics*, by Henry Jones Ford, Chapter 15. New York: The Macmillan Company, 1911, pp. 188–193.

could anything "be found to constitute the President a part of the legislative power." His duty to recommend legislation was simply "a privilege which he holds in common with every other citizen." He regarded it as "preposterous to suppose that a thought could for a moment have been entertained that the President, placed at the capital, in the centre of the country, could better understand the wants and wishes of the people than their own immediate representatives"; so, therefore, "to assist or control Congress in its ordinary legislation could not have been the motive for conferring the veto power on the President." In particular he held that the President "should never be looked to for schemes of finance."

This was very satisfactory doctrine to the Whig party leaders in Congress, but there was no way by which it could be made obligatory. When Harrison died, his doctrine died with him. Tyler, although elected on the same ticket with Harrison, did not scruple to use the veto power to defeat the Whig schemes of finance adopted by Congress. Polk, the next President, had occasion to review the whole subject of the relations between the President and the Congress, and in his message of December 5, 1848, he laid down the constitutional principles governing the case as follows:

> The people, by the constitution, have commanded the President, as much as they have commanded the legislative branch of the government, to execute their will. They have said to him in the constitution, which they require he shall take a solemn oath to support, that if Congress pass any bill which he cannot approve, "he shall return it to the House in which it originated, with his objections." If it be said that the representatives in the popular branch of Congress are chosen directly by the people, it is answered, the people elect the President. If both Houses represent the states and the people, so does the President. The President represents in the executive department the whole people of the United States, as each member of the legislative department represents portions of them.

The course of our political history since Jackson's time has conformed to the constitutional principle that the President is the direct representative of the people as a whole. The establishment of this principle was accompanied by a marked change of popular habit in the exercise of the suffrage. Originally, the House of Representatives was not only the designated medium for the expression of public sentiment, but in most of the states there was no means of popular participation in the government of the United States, save in the election of members of the House. And even in states where presidential electors were chosen by the vote of the people, the interest in such elections was small as compared with that taken in congressional elections. *Nile's Register* of November

18, 1820, reports that very few votes had been polled for presidential electors in Maryland and Virginia. In the whole city of Richmond only seventeen votes were cast. Yet this was the period when the country was convulsed over the admission of Missouri with a slavery constitution, and congressional elections were attended by great excitement. Even during the presidential election of 1824, with four candidates in the field, each with enthusiastic partisans, the total vote cast in Virginia was less than 15,000; and Massachusetts, which had cast more than 66,000 votes for governor in 1823, cast only 37,000 votes at the presidential election. Ohio polled 50,024 votes; but the election for governor two years before had drawn out 10,000 more votes, and in the same year as the presidential election the vote for governor aggregated 76,634. The Jacksonian era marks the beginning of a concentration of popular interest on the presidential election. After 1824, the popular vote shows a rapid increase. The aggregate in 1824 was 356,038. The aggregate vote cast by the same states in 1828 was 817,409. The increase in some of the states was amazing. In New Hampshire, the vote rose from 4750 to 45,056; in Connecticut, from 9565 to 18,286; in Pennsylvania, from 47,255 to 152,500; in Ohio, from 50,024 to 130,993. The popular tendency thus suddenly developed has been constant. It is now a commonplace of politics that the presidential vote is the largest cast at any election. In the presidential election of 1896 there were cast for President 218,658 votes more than were cast for Congressmen. When it is considered that the practice of putting presidential and congressional candidates on the same ballot is almost general, this popular disposition is certainly very remarkable.

This change in the attitude of the people towards the President took away much of the importance of Congress, and had effects upon its character which soon became very manifest. The framers of the constitution anticipated for the House of Representatives a brilliant career, something like that of the House of Commons. The natural ascendency which the House would possess as the immediate representative of the people, is the stock argument of "The Federalist" in justification of the exclusive privileges conferred upon the President and the Senate. It was held that no danger to the constitution could result from an excess of power in them, since "the House of Representatives with the people on their side will at all times be able to bring back the constitution to its primitive form and principles"; while, on the other hand, the coördinate branches of the government could not withstand the encroachments of the House without special safeguards. The result, on the whole, during the early period of the republic, verified this calculation. Although never developing such an authority as that of the House of Commons, the House of Representatives was the most important branch of the government. The Senate was composed of provincial notables who sat as a privy council, transacting business behind closed doors. The floor of the House was the field where political talent might obtain distinction. The Senate became tired of its dull seclusion from popular interest, and in 1799 admitted the public to its debates; but the superior prestige of the House was maintained until the Jacksonian era. Calhoun remarks that the House was originally "a much more influential body than the Senate." Benton says, "For the first thirty years it was the controlling branch of the government, and the one on whose action the public eye was fixed." The democratic revolution overthrew the pillars of its greatness. It ceased to make presidents; it ceased to control them. Instead of being the seat of party authority,—the motive force of the administration,—it became in this respect merely a party agency. National party purposes, having to seek their fulfilment through the presidential office, had nothing to ask of the House but obedience to party demands, and at once began the task of devising machinery to enforce submission.

Richard Neustadt
KENNEDY IN THE PRESIDENCY: A PREMATURE APPRAISAL

There are many ways to look at the performance of a President of the United States. One way—not the only one—is to assess his operational effectiveness as man in office, a single individual amidst a vast machine. This has been my own approach in previous writings on past Presidents. Regarding our most recent President, John F. Kennedy, it is foolhardy to attempt appraisal in these terms. He died too soon and it is too soon after his death. Still, the *Political Science Quarterly* has asked me to attempt it. And assuming that my readers will indulge the folly, I shall try.

I

In appraising the personal performance of a President it is useful to ask four questions. First, what were his purposes and did these run

From "Kennedy in the Presidency: A Premature Appraisal," by Richard E. Neustadt, *Political Science Quarterly*, Vol. 79, September 1964. Reprinted by permission. Mr. Neustadt is Professor of Government at Harvard University.

with or against the grain of history; how relevant were they to what would happen in his time? Second, what was his "feel," his human understanding, for the nature of his power in the circumstances of his time, and how close did he come in this respect to the realities around him (a matter again of relevance)? Third, what was his stance under pressure in office, what sustained him as a person against the frustrations native to the place, and how did his peace-making with himself affect the style and content of his own decision-making? This becomes especially important now that nuclear technology has equipped both Americans and Russians with an intercontinental capability; stresses on the Presidency grow apace. Fourth, what was his legacy? What imprint did he leave upon the office, its character and public standing; where did he leave his party and the other party nationally; what remained by way of public policies adopted or in controversy; what remained as issues in American society, insofar as his own stance may have affected them; and what was the American position in the world insofar as his diplomacy may have affected it?

With respect to each of these four questions, the outside observer looks for certain clues in seeking answers.

First, regarding purpose, clues are found in irreversible commitments to defined courses of action. By "purpose" I mean nothing so particular as an endorsement for, say, "Medicare," or anything so general as a pledge to "peace." (All Presidents desire peace.) By "course of action" I mean something broader than the one but more definable than the other: Harry S. Truman's commitment to "containment," so called, or Dwight D. Eisenhower's to what he called "fiscal responsibility." By "commitment" I mean personal involvement, in terms of what the man himself is seen to say and do, so plain and so direct that politics—and history—will not let him turn back: Truman on civil rights, or Eisenhower on the Army budget.

Second, regarding feel for office, sensitivity to power, clues are drawn from signs of pattern in the man's own operating style as he encounters concrete cases, cases of decision and of follow-through in every sphere of action, legislative and executive, public and partisan, foreign and domestic—Truman seeking above all to be decisive; Eisenhower reaching for a place above the struggle.

Third, regarding pressure and its consequences, clues are to be drawn again from cases; here one examines crisis situations, seeking signs of pattern in the man's response—Truman at the time of the Korean outbreak, or of Chinese intervention; Eisenhower at the time of Hungary and Suez, or of Little Rock—times like these compared with others just as tough in terms of stress.

And fourth, regarding the man's legacy, one seeks clues in the conduct of the *next* administration. Roosevelt's first New Deal in 1933 tells us a lot about the Hoover Presidency. Truman's troubled turnabout in postwar foreign policy casts shadows on the later Roosevelt Presidency. And Kennedy's complaint at Yale two years ago about the "myths" retarding economic management is testimony to one part of Eisenhower's legacy, that part identified with the redoubtable George Humphrey.

To list these sources of the wherewithal for answers is to indicate the folly of pursuing my four questions when the object of the exercise is Kennedy-in-office. He was President for two years and ten months. Were one to assess Franklin Roosevelt on the basis of performance before January 1936, or Harry Truman on his accomplishments before enactment of the Marshall Plan, or Eisenhower had he not survived his heart attack—or Lincoln, for that matter, had he been assassinated six months after Gettysburg—one would be most unlikely to reach judgments about any of these men resembling current judgments drawn from the full record of their terms. We cannot know what Kennedy's full record would have been had he escaped assassination. Still more important, we can never know precisely how to weigh events in his truncated term.

Truman's seven years and Eisenhower's eight suggest a certain rhythm in the modern Presidency. The first twelve to eighteen months become a learning time for the new President who has to learn—or unlearn—many things about his job. No matter what his prior training, nothing he has done will have prepared him for all facets of that job. Some aspects of the learning process will persist beyond the first year-and-a-half. Most Presidents will go on making new discoveries as long as they hold office (until at last they learn the bitterness of leaving office). But the intensive learning time comes at the start and dominates the first two years. A President's behavior in those years is an uncertain source of clues to what will follow after, unreliable in indicating what will be the patterns of performance "on the job" once learning has been done. Yet the fourth year is also unreliable; traditionally it brings a period of pause, dominated by a special test requiring special effort—the test of reelection. The way that test is taken tells us much about a President, but less about his conduct on the job in other years. The seventh year is the beginning of the end—now guaranteed by constitutional amendment—as all eyes turn toward the coming nominations and the *next* administration.

So in the search for signs of pattern, clues to conduct, the key years are the third, the fifth, the sixth. Kennedy had only one of these.

Moreover, in this Presidential cycle, retrospect is an essential aid for sorting evidence. What a man does in his later years sheds light on the significance of what he did in early years, distinguishing the actions which conform to lasting patterns from the aspects of behavior which were transient. The man's early performance will include a host of clues to what is typical throughout his term of office. But it also will include assorted actions which turn out to be unrepresentative. Looking back from later years these become easy to distinguish. But in the second or the third year it is hard indeed to say, "This action, this behavior will be dominant throughout." That is the sort of statement best reserved for retrospect. Kennedy's case leaves no room for retrospect; he was cut off too early in the cycle. (And when it comes to sorting out the legacy he left, Lyndon Johnson has not yet been long enough in office.)

No scholar, therefore, should have the temerity to undertake what follows.

II

Turning to appraise this President in office, I come to my first question, the question of purpose. This is not a matter of initial "ideology," fixed intent; far from it. Franklin Roosevelt did not enter office bent upon becoming "traitor to his class." Truman did not swear the oath with any notion that he was to take this country into the cold war. Lincoln certainly did not assume the Presidency to gain the title of "Great Emancipator." The purposes of Presidents are not to be confused with their intentions at the start; they are a matter, rather, of responses to events. Nor should they be confused with signs of temperament, with "passion." Whether Kennedy was "passionate" or not is scarcely relevant. Truman certainly deserves to have the cause of civil rights cited among his purposes, but were he to be judged in temperamental terms according to the standards of, say, Eastern liberals, he scarcely could be called a man of passion on the point. And F.D.R. goes down historically as "Labor's friend," although his coolness toward the greatest show of that friendship in his time, the Wagner Act, remained until he sensed that it was sure to be enacted. What counts here is not "passion," but the words and acts that lead to irreversible *commitment*.

In his three years of office, what were Kennedy's commitments? Never mind his private thoughts at twenty, or at forty; never mind his preferences for one thing or another; never mind his distaste for a passionate display—taking the real world as he found it, what attracted his commitment in the sense that he identified himself beyond recall?

The record will, I think, disclose at least three purposes so understood: First, above all others, most compelling, most intense, was a commitment to reduce the risk of holocaust by *mutual* miscalculation, to "get the nuclear genie back in the bottle," to render statecraft manageable by statesmen, tolerable for the rest of us. He did not aim at anything so trite (or unachievable) as "victory" in the cold war. His aim, apparently, was to outlast it with American society intact and nuclear risks in check. Nothing, I think, mattered more to Kennedy than bottling that genie. This, I know, was deeply in his mind. It also was made manifest in words, among them his address at American University on June 10, 1963. That speech is seal and symbol of this purpose. But other signs are found in acts, as well, and in more private words accompanying action: from his Vienna interview with Khrushchev, through the Berlin crisis during 1961, to the Cuban missile crisis and thereafter—this commitment evidently deepened with experience as Kennedy responded to events.

Another speech in June of 1963 stands for a second purpose: the speech on civil rights, June 11, and the message to Congress eight days later launched Kennedy's campaign for what became the Civil Rights Act of 1964. Thereby he undertook an irreversible commitment to Negro integration in American society, aiming once again to get us through the effort with society intact. He evidently came to see the risks of social alienation as plainly as he saw the risks of nuclear escalation, and he sought to steer a course toward integration which could hold inside our social order both impatient Negroes and reactive whites—as tough a task of politics as any we have known, and one he faced no sooner than he had to. But he faced it. What Vienna, Berlin, Cuba were to his first purpose, Oxford and then Birmingham were to this second purpose: events which shaped his personal commitment.

A third speech is indicative of still another purpose, a speech less known and a commitment less apparent, though as definite, I think, as both of the others: Kennedy's commencement speech at Yale on June 11, 1962, soon after his short war with Roger Blough. He spoke of making our complex economy, our somewhat *sui generis* economy, function effectively for meaningful growth, and as the means he urged an end-of-ideology in problem-solving. His speech affirmed the notion that the key problems of economic growth are technical, not ideological, to be met not by passion but by intellect, and that the greatest barriers to growth are the ideas in people's heads—"myths" as he called them—standing in the way of reasoned diagnosis and response. Kennedy, I think, was well aware (indeed he was made painfully aware) that only on our one-time Left is ideology defunct. Elsewhere it flourishes, clamping a lid upon applied intelligence, withholding brainpower from rational engagement in the novel problems of our economic management. He evidently wanted most of all to lift that lid.

Failing a response to his Yale lecture, Kennedy retreated to the easier task of teaching one simple economic lesson, the lesson of the recent tax reduction: well-timed budget deficits can lead to balanced budgets. This, evidently, was the most that he thought he could manage in contesting "myths," at least before election. But his ambition, I believe, was to assault a lot more myths than this, when and as he could. That ambition measures his commitment to effective growth in the economy.

Stemming from this third commitment (and the second) one discerns a corollary which perhaps would have become a fourth: what Kennedy's successor now has named "the war against poverty." During the course of 1963, Kennedy became active in promoting plans for an attack on chronic poverty. His prospective timing no doubt had political utility, but it also had social utility which evidently mattered quite as much. Historically, the "war" is Lyndon Johnson's. All we know of Kennedy is that he meant to make one. Still, for either of these men the effort, if sustained, would lead to irreversible commitment.

Each purpose I have outlined meant commitment to a course of action which engaged the man—his reputation, *amour propre*, and sense of self in history—beyond recall. The question then becomes: how relevant were these, historically? How relevant to Kennedy's own years of actual (and of prospective) office? Here I can only make a judgment, tentative of course, devoid of long perspective. These purposes seem to me entirely relevant. In short perspective, they seem precisely right as the pre-eminent concerns for the first half of this decade.

III

So much for Kennedy as man-of-purpose. What about the man-of-power?

He strikes me as a senator who learned very fast from his confrontation with the executive establishment, particularly after the abortive Cuban invasion which taught him a great deal. On action-issues of particular concern to him he rapidly evolved an operating style which he maintained consistently (and sharpened at the edges) through his years of office. If one looks at Berlin, or Oxford, Mississippi, or the Cuban missile crisis, or at half a dozen other issues of the sort, one finds a pattern: the personal command post, deliberate reaching down for the details, hard questioning of the alternatives, a drive to protect options from foreclosure by sheer urgency or by *ex parte* advocacy, finally a close watch on follow-through. Even on the issues which were secondary to the President and left, perforce, primarily to others, Kennedy was constantly in search of means and men to duplicate at one remove this personalized pattern with its stress on open options and on close control. Numbers of outsiders—Hans Morgenthau and Joseph Alsop for two— sometimes viewed the pattern with alarm and saw this man as "indecisive." But that was to consult *their* preferences, not his performance. Kennedy seemed always keen to single out the necessary from the merely possible. He then decided with alacrity.

Not everything was always done effectively, of course, and even the successes produced side effects of bureaucratic bafflement, frustration, irritation which were not without their costs. Even so, the pattern testifies to an extraordinary feel for the distinction between President and Presidency, an extraordinary urge to master the machine. This took him quite a way toward mastery in two years and ten months. We shall not know how far he might have got.

Kennedy's feel for his own executive position carried over into that of fellow rulers everywhere. He evidently had great curiosity and real concern about the politics of rulership wherever he encountered it. His feel for fine distinctions among fellow "kings" was rare, comparable to the feel of Senate Leader Johnson for the fine distinctions among fellow senators. And with this Kennedy apparently absorbed in his short time a lesson Franklin Roosevelt never learned about the Russians (or de Gaulle): that in another country an *effective* politician can have motives very *different* from his own. What an advantageous lesson to have learned in two years' time! It would have served him well. Indeed, while he still lived I think it did.

The cardinal test of Kennedy as an executive in his own right and also as a student of executives abroad was certainly the confrontation of October 1962, the Cuban missile crisis with Khrushchev. For almost the first time in our foreign relations, the President displayed on that occasion both concern for the psychology of his opponent and insistence on a limited objective. Contrast the Korean War, where we positively courted Chinese intervention by relying on Douglas MacArthur as psychologist and by enlarging our objective after each success. "There is no substitute for victory," MacArthur wrote, but at that time we virtually had a nuclear monopoly and even then our government hastened to find a substitute. Now, with mutual capability, the whole traditional meaning has been taken out of "victory." In nuclear confrontations there is room for no such thing. Kennedy quite evidently knew it. He also knew, as his performance demonstrates, that risks of escalation lurk in high-level misjudgments *and* in low-level momentum. Washington assuredly was capable of both; so, probably, was Moscow. Accordingly, the President outstripped all previous efforts to guard options and assure control. His operating style was tested then as not before or after. It got him what he wanted.

In confrontations with Congress, quite another world than the executive, the key to Kennedy's congressional relations lay outside his feel for power, beyond reach of technique; he won the Presidency by a hair, while in the House of Representatives his party lost some twenty of the seats gained two years earlier. The Democrats *retained* a sizeable majority as they had done in earlier years, no thanks to him. With this beginning, Kennedy's own record of accomplishment in Congress looks enormous, indeterminate, or small, depending on one's willingness to give him credit for enactment of the most divisive, innovative bills he espoused: the tax and civil rights bills passed in Johnson's Presidency. Certainly it can be said that Kennedy prepared the way, negotiating a bipartisan approach, and also that he took the heat, stalling his whole program in the process. Equally, it can be said that with his death—or by it—the White House gained advantages which he could not have mustered. Johnson made the most of these. How well would Kennedy have done without them? My own guess is that in the end, with rancor and delay, both bills would have been passed. But it is a moot point. Accordingly, so is the Kennedy record.

Whatever his accomplishment, does it appear the most he could have managed in his years? Granting the limits set by his election, granting the divisiveness injected after Birmingham with his decisive move on civil rights, did he use to the fullest his advantages of office? The answer may well be "not quite." Perhaps a better answer is, "This man could do no more." For Kennedy, it seems, was not a man enamored of the legislative way of life and legislators knew it. He was wry about it. He had spent fourteen years in Congress and he understood its business, but he never was a "member of the family" on the Hill. "Downtown" had always seemed his native habitat; he was a natural executive. They knew that, too. Besides, he was a young man, very young by Senate standards, and his presence in the White House with still younger men around him was a constant irritant to seniors. Moreover, he was not a "mixer" socially, not, anyway, with most members of Congress and their wives. His manners were impeccable, his charm impelling, but he kept his social life distinct from his official life and congressmen were rarely in his social circle. To know how Congress works but to disdain its joys is an acquired taste for most ex-congressmen downtown, produced by hard experience. Kennedy, however, brought it with him. Many of the difficulties he was to encounter in his day-by-day congressional relations stemmed from that.

But even had he been a man who dearly loved the Congress, even had that feeling been reciprocated, nothing could have rendered their relationship sweetness-and-light in his last year, so long as he persisted with his legislative program. As an innovative President confronting a reluctant Congress, he was heir to Truman, and to Roosevelt after 1936. Kennedy's own manner may have hurt him on the Hill, but these were scratches. Deeper scars had more substantial sources and he knew it.

In confrontations with the larger public outside Washington (again a different world), Kennedy made a brilliant beginning, matched only by the start in different circumstances of his own successor. The "public relations" of transition into office were superb. In three months after his election, Kennedy transformed himself from "pushy," "young," "Catholic," into President-of-all-the-people, widening and deepening acceptance of his Presidency out of all proportion to the election returns. The Bay of Pigs was a severe check, but his handling of the aftermath displayed again superb feel for the imagery befitting an incumbent of the White House, heir to F.D.R. *and* Eisenhower. That feel he always had. I think it never failed him.

What he also had was a distaste for preaching, really for the preachiness of politics, backed by genuine mistrust of mass emotion as a tool in politics. These attitudes are rare among American politicians; with Kennedy their roots ran deep into recesses of experience and character where I, as an outsider, cannot follow. But they assuredly were rooted in this man and they had visible effects upon his public style. He delighted in the play of minds, not of emotions. He doted on press conferences, not set performances. He feared "overexposure"; he dreaded overreaction. Obviously he enjoyed responsive crowds, and was himself responsive to a sea of cheering faces, but I think he rarely looked at their reaction—or his own—without a twinge of apprehension. He never seems to have displayed much fondness for the "fireside chat," a form of crowd appeal without the crowd; television talks in evening hours evidently struck him more as duty than as opportunity, and dangerous at that; some words on air-raid shelters in a talk about Berlin could set off mass hysteria—and did. At the moment when he had his largest, most attentive audience, on the climactic Sunday of the Cuban missile crisis, he turned it away (and turned attention off) with a two-minute announcement, spare and dry.

Yet we know now, after his death, what none of us knew before: that with a minimum of preaching, of emotional appeal, or of self-justification, even explanation, he had managed to touch millions in their private lives, not only at home but emphatically abroad. Perhaps his very coolness helped him do it. Perhaps his very vigor, family, fortune, sense of fun, his manners, taste, and sportsmanship, his evident enjoyment of his life and of the job made him the heart's desire of all sorts of people everywhere, not least among the young. At any rate, we know now that he managed in his years to make enormous impact on a world-wide audience, building an extraordinary base of public interest and affection (interspersed, of course, with doubters and detractors). What he might have made of this or done with it in later years, nobody knows.

IV

So much for power; what of pressure? What sustained this man in his decisions, his frustrations, and with what effect on his approach to being President? For an answer one turns to the evidence of crises, those already mentioned among others, and the *surface* signs are clear. In all such situations it appears that Kennedy was cool, collected, courteous, and terse. This does not mean that he was unemotional. By temperament I think he was a man of mood and passion. But he had schooled his temperament. He kept his own emotions under tight control. He did not lose his temper inadvertently, and never lost it long. He was observer and participant combined; he saw himself as coolly as all others—and with humor. He always was a witty man, dry with a bit of bite and a touch of self-deprecation. He could laugh at himself, and did. Often he used humor to break tension. And in tight places he displayed a keen awareness of the human situation, human limits, his included, but it did not slow his work.

Readers over forty may recognize this portrait as "the stance of junior officers in the Second World War"; Elspeth Rostow coined that phrase and, superficially at least, she is quite right. This was the Kennedy stance and his self-confidence, his shield against frustration, must have owed a lot to his young manhood in that war.

This tells us a good deal but not nearly enough. At his very first encounter with a crisis in the Presidency, Kennedy's self-confidence seems to have been severely strained. The Bay of Pigs fiasco shook him deeply, shook his confidence in methods and associates. Yet he went on governing without a break, no change in manner, or in temper, or in humor. What sustained him? Surely much that went beyond experience of war.

What else? I cannot answer. I can only conjecture. His family life and rearing have some part to play, no doubt. His political successes also: in 1952 he bucked the Eisenhower tide to reach the Senate; in 1960 he broke barriers of youth and of religion which had always held before; on each occasion the Conventional Wisdom was against him: "can't be done." Beyond these things, this man had been exceptionally close to death, not only in the war but ten years after. And in his Presidential years his back was almost constantly a source of pain; he never talked about it but he lived with it. All this is of a piece with his behavior in a crisis. His control, his objectivity, his humor, and his sense of human limits, these were but expressions of his confidence; its sources must lie somewhere in this ground.

Whatever the sources, the results were rewarding for this President's performance on the job. In the most critical, nerve-straining aspects of the office, coping with its terrible responsibility for use of force, Kennedy's own image of himself impelled him neither to lash out nor run for cover. Rather, it released him for engagement and decision as a reasonable man. In some of the less awesome aspects of the Presidency, his own values restrained him, kept him off the pulpit, trimmed his guest list, made him shy away from the hyperbole of politics. But as a chief *executive*, confronting action-issues for decision and control, his duty and his confidence in doing it were nicely matched. So the world discovered in October 1962.

V

Now for my last question. What did John Kennedy leave behind him? What was the legacy of his short years? At the very least he left a myth: the vibrant, youthful leader cut down senselessly before his time. What this may come to signify as the years pass, I cannot tell. He left a glamorous moment, an engaging, youthful time, but how we shall re-member it depends on what becomes of Lyndon Johnson. He left a broken promise, that "the torch has been passed to a new generation," and the youngsters who identified with him felt cheated as the promise, like the glamor, disappeared. What do their feelings matter? We shall have to wait and see.

May this be all that history is likely to record? Perhaps, but I doubt it. My guess is that when the observers can appraise the work of Kennedy's successors, they will find some things of substance in his legacy. Rashly, let me record what I think these are.

To begin with, our first Catholic President chose and paved the way for our first Southern President since the Civil War. (Woodrow Wilson was no Southerner *politically;* he came to the White House from the State House of New Jersey.) While Texas may be suspect now in Southern eyes, it certainly is of the South in Northern eyes, as Johnson found so painfully in 1960. Kennedy made him President. How free the choice of Johnson as Vice-Presidential candidate is subject to some argument. But what appears beyond dispute is that once chosen, Johnson was so treated by his rival for the White House as to ease his way enormously when he took over there. Johnson may have suffered great frustration as Vice-President, but his public standing and his knowledge of affairs were nurtured in those years. From this he gained a running start. The credit goes in no small part to Kennedy.

Moreover, Kennedy bequeathed to Johnson widened options in the sphere of foreign relations: a military posture far more flexible and usable than he himself inherited; a diplomatic posture more sophisticated in its whole approach to neutralists and leftists, markedly more mindful of distinctions in the world, even among allies.

On the domestic side, Kennedy left a large inheritance of contro-versies, opened by a youthful, Catholic urbanite from the Northeast, which his Southwestern, Protestant successor might have had more trou-ble stirring at the start, but now can ride and maybe even "heal." This may turn out to have been a productive division of labor. However it turns out, Kennedy lived long enough to keep at least one promise. He got the country "moving again." For in our politics, the *sine qua non* of innovative policy is controversy. By 1963 we were engaged in controversy with an openness which would have been unthinkable, or at least "un-American," during the later Eisenhower years.

Events, of course, have more to do with stirring controversy than a President. No man can make an issue on his own. But Presidents will help to shape the meaning of events, the terms of discourse, the attention paid, the noise-level. Eisenhower's years were marked by a pervasive fog of self-congratulation, muffling noise. The fog-machine was centered in the White House. Perhaps there had been need for this after the divisive Truman years. By the late nineteen-fifties, though, it fuzzed our chance to innovate in time. Kennedy broke out of it.

Finally, this President set a new standard of performance on the job, suitable to a new state of Presidential being, a state he was the first to face throughout his term of office: the state of substantial, deliverable, nuclear capability in other hands than ours. Whatever else historians may make of Kennedy, I think them likely to begin with this. There can be little doubt that his successors have a lighter task because *he* pioneered in handling nuclear confrontations. During the Cuban missile crisis and thereafter, he did something which had not been done before, did it well, and got it publicly accepted. His innovation happened to be timely, since the need for innovation was upon us; technology had put it there. But also, in his reach for information and control, his balancing of firmness with caution, his sense of limits, he displayed and dramatized what Presidents must do to minimize the risk of war through mutual miscalculation. This may well be the cardinal risk confronting his successors. If so, he made a major contribution to the Presidency.

Joseph Kraft
PRESIDENTIAL POLITICS IN LBJ STYLE

Style is not the man, much less a government or a party. But paperback books and TV have made psychological awareness rampant. Ideology is dying, and legislative programs are necessarily complex, and

From *Profiles in Power* by Joseph Kraft. Copyright © 1966 by Joseph Kraft. Reprinted by arrangement with The New American Library, Inc., New York.

hence too boring for wide comprehension. Personality, accordingly, has become the touchstone of politics—the measuring rod by which programs, policies, and parties are assessed and compared. The fashion is to deduce matter from manner. And in that respect, at least, President Lyndon B. Johnson is preeminently in fashion. To see him in the White House—or even more at home on his ranch in Texas—is to experience as pronounced a style as any public man can boast.

Cyclonic activity is the hallmark of the Johnson style. The President approaches his job like a spirited football team breaking out of the huddle. For more than eighteen hours every day—from six-thirty in the morning to past one at night—he is on the go. It is typical that Mrs. Johnson, in order to caution him to take it easy, had to pin a warning note to his pillow, and not only hand-wringers must be concerned about his health. It is said that he takes more than a hundred phone calls per day. He must be the only man in the world who has had a phone installed beside a hammock. Visitors not only stream in and out of his office, but join him at meals or in swims before lunch and dinner.

At almost all his meetings, the President forces the pace, walking up and down, sawing the air, raising and lowering his voice, jabbing with his index finger. After one session, the venerable dean of the Senate, eighty-eight-year-old Carl Hayden of Arizona, was heard protesting: "You know, Mr. President, I'm older than you are." To which the President replied: "I don't care how old you are. Do it. Do it now."

If anything, the pace the President sets while ostensibly on holiday at the ranch is even more formidable. During a recent Christmas vacation, every day on the ranch was a permanent floating press conference, with the President first addressing reporters, then allowing them to trail behind as he loped over his acres. Relatives, friends, politicos and publishers, most of the Cabinet, the Joint Chiefs, a goodly share of the White House staff, and a full delegation from West Germany headed by Chancellor Ludwig Erhard came and went. The President did everything. He chaired negotiations; he shot deer; he guided visitors; he drove friends in his car; he made appointments and signed bills; he acted as MC at a barbecue, attended the opening of a synagogue, the funeral of a local mayor, and a New Year's Eve party thrown by the press. One official, working on an exceedingly complicated program, discussed the matter with the President in at least ten different forums—including a dinner for fifteen people, riding in a helicopter, driving around the ranch, and at the mayor's funeral.

The mode and manner of Presidential discussion is perhaps the most distinctive feature of the Johnson style. The President's idiom is earthy to the point of vulgarity. It is true that he has spoken of "piss-ant correspondents" asking "piss-ant questions" and that he once said (of a prominent official), "He can't reach his ass with his right hand." Mr. Johnson is also prone to ramble on for what seem like hours at a time, almost pointlessly. I once heard him give, certainly not on purpose, the impression that he had canceled the visits of two leading Asian statesmen because it would look bad, at a time of civil-rights tension in this country, to have black men staying with the white women of his family in the Presidential mansion. My own feeling is that these verbal tours de force are intrinsically innocuous. Rather than any particular meaning, they express in the President the weakness for hyperbole which once caused one of his aides to liken him to Baron Munchausen. But if the words don't say anything, the music again announces a strong, individualistic style.

✤ ✤ ✤

Like all public styles, the Johnson style mixes nature with art. Nothing shows the mixture more plainly than the LBJ ranch. The basic elements are the authentic stuff of Western life: hard-scrabble soil and a scraggly river; sunsets and sage; boots, saddles, and guns; horses and cattle; foreman and hands; Howdies and Hi Podners; towns marked only by a widening of the road and a post office. But the President wears his Western shirts monogrammed. He tours the ranch in a whitish Lincoln Continental. The barbecues are catered by a firm from Fort Worth. Muzak pipes "The Yellow Rose of Texas" into his living room.

The combination suggests an instinctive understanding of the role of image in politics. For in image politics, aspiration replaces identity as the bond between voter and candidate. The cement is not so much self-interest as dreams. There lies the strange connection between the angry racists of the extreme Right and the part-Jewish merchant, personally the least angry man in the world, who is named Barry Goldwater. Between them one would have expected deep antipathy. But in fact Goldwater is the perfect symbol of the world as his followers would like it to be: simple and easygoing, and the place where the veriest *arriviste* finds himself snugly at home. John F. Kennedy, for the same reason, appealed to the Irish: far from being like them, he was what they wanted their children to be like. Similarly with Adam Clayton Powell and his Harlem constituency. In the case of Lyndon Johnson, he has played to a small-town clientele with dreams of the big time. The LBJ ranch is a faithful reflection of local aspiration—a brilliant example of image politics in action.

It is one of the features of image politics that where style doesn't work, issues must be brought into play. There is what Sidney Hyman calls a "policy of reverse images." In line with that theory, President Johnson, being relatively secure in the rural South for personal reasons, has developed a program that caters almost exclusively to the urban North. In 1964, he went down the line for the most important innovations of the Kennedy Administration: the tax cut designed, not in respect to federal revenues, but, for the first time, in order to foster continued prosperity; a civil-rights program outlawing discrimination in public places and authorizing the federal government to enforce its provisions by withholding payments to states; and the poverty program. The following year, the President pushed several more items dear to the urban population, all of which went beyond what President Kennedy seemed able to accomplish: an equal voting rights law; the Medicare bill, providing health insurance to the aged on the social-security program; the establishment of a Department of Housing and Urban Development (HUD); a housing program that included, for the first time, a rent supplement permitting low-income families to live outside the limited and unsatisfactory public housing facilities; a program for ending air and river pollution; an immigration bill that did away with the odious national quota system in effect for more than forty years; a farm program that, by stressing direct welfare payments to farmers, brought closer the possibility of easing the great majority of inefficient farmers off the land as jobs in the urban society opened up; and, perhaps most important of all, a program for federal aid to elementary and secondary schools. By 1966, he had fulfilled the Kennedy legacy beyond question and was off on his own. Off and running. He refused to let the claim of the Vietnam war pose a test between guns and butter. His record budget of 1966 provided for expansion in all his domestic welfare, or Great Society, programs, and added such favorite Northern liberal features as proposals to bar racial discrimination in housing and a plan to rebuild, as a whole, the decayed downtown centers of major cities. Measuring that record against the interest of the Northern urban middle and lower classes, it is probably already fair to say that Lyndon Johnson is the most liberal President in American history.

But if the Johnson program is in the liberal tradition, there is a pronounced discontinuity in the mode of operations in the White House and the rest of government. Nowhere else, indeed, do the President and his predecessor contrast more sharply. John F. Kennedy liked to act the part of the desk officer. He would get into his mind the elements of a problem, and reach decisions by sifting, sorting out, arranging, and rearranging the elements until the pattern that seemed right emerged. Principal advisers in the Cabinet and the White House staff were frequently brought into the analytic process. As in the Cuban missile crisis, they would thrash out issues and explore alternatives in a way that became known as a "dialogue." The intrusion of personalities into the "dialogue" was abhorrent to Kennedy; when it seemed to be developing in the Cuban missile crisis, he deliberately absented himself from the meetings of the executive committee of the National Security Council. The White House staff he chiefly used to bring before him and his advisers the raw material for decision. Staff members would watch over the work of the Departments and agencies, and pull issues into the White House before they had worked their way up the bureaucratic ladder. In that sense, the staff served as a kind of super-Cabinet.

For President Johnson the source of light seems to be much less analysis than experience. The poverty program, with its heavy New Deal overtones, was congenial to him from the beginning; in talking privately of the program, he repeatedly cited the work of Roosevelt's Secretary of Interior, Harold Ickes. He was particularly adept at cutting the space and defense programs, because he had known them (and their weaknesses) from the beginning. Indeed after his thirty years in the thick of things, there is almost no issue that the President does not approach with strong convictions. His characteristic gambit in dealing with aides is: "I want to do this—you tell me why I shouldn't." Perhaps more than any President since Theodore Roosevelt, he has a strong inner sense of what he wants. He has an even stronger sense of what he doesn't want. "To convince Lyndon Johnson of anything," one of his aides once said, "you have to convince him six times."

In translating impulses into action he is extraordinarily sensitive to personality. If Kennedy's instinct on confronting a problem was to analyze it, Johnson's is to manipulate the men who hold the levers of power toward the answer that most people want—the consensus. Nothing is more revealing in this respect than the President's major appointments: Hubert Humphrey as Vice President; Arthur Goldberg as Ambassador to the United Nations; Nicholas Katzenbach as Attorney General; John Connor as Secretary of Commerce; Lawrence O'Brien as Postmaster General; John Gardner as Secretary of Health, Education and Welfare; Robert Weaver as Secretary of Housing and Urban Development; Henry Fowler as Secretary of the Treasury; Abe Fortas as his first justice of the Supreme Court. All of them, to be sure, fit a familiar mold. Humphrey and Fortas were old-time New and Fair Dealers. Goldberg, Katzenbach, O'Brien, and Fowler had been first appointed by Kennedy. Gardner and Connor were the kind of sophisticated Republicans Kennedy could easily have appointed. But if the appointments themselves were not remarkable, the process of selection was. President Johnson seemed to set as much store by surprising people as by satisfying them. It is widely believed—though I myself doubt it—that he has canceled major appointments when advance word leaked in the press. He certainly takes visible pleasure when a nomination takes people off guard. Twenty-four hours before announcing the appointment of Justice Fortas, the White House indicated that he was not being considered, and the President himself said he had given the matter no thought. No one can forget the months-long agony of mysterious hints and misleading winks that preceded the final, last-minute selection of Hubert Humphrey as running mate in 1964. And what is the purpose of these "acts"—for they are really nothing more than that? It is to underline in the most visible public and dramatic way that there is really only one man running the show in Washington—Lyndon Johnson. Even the Cabinet officers, those masters of great Departments, are his men—his to mold and manipulate, to call up at all hours, and to move from place to place at his merest whim. They are the visible instruments of his power.

As to finding which way the winds are blowing, determining consensus, President Johnson, besides using polls and his own antennae, is always checking his impulses with other men, men whom he has long known and trusted. That is why he is on the phone so much, and there lies the real function of the so-called kitchen cabinet of informal advisers: the Washington lawyers and ex-New Dealers—Abe Fortas, Ben Cohen, James Rowe, and Thomas Corcoran; the Texas banker and former Secretary of the Treasury in the Eisenhower Administration—Robert Anderson; Harry Truman's Secretary of State—Dean Acheson; and White House counsel, Clark Clifford. Some of them may undertake special jobs for the President: Fortas, before moving to the Supreme Court, put together the Warren Commission to investigate the assassination of President Kennedy. But mainly the kitchen cabinet serves as a sounding board for the President. Its members comprise a miniature spectrum of opinion. And by testing their reactions to his impulse, the President gets a fast reading of more general public reaction.

The White House staff, in these circumstances, has far less scope for substantive work. The President's personal entourage are men of undoubted ability. But their talent runs to expediting—arranging appointments, getting meetings together, turning out the immense volume of paperwork connected with high office. "We fit pipes together," one of them said.

The changed status of the White House staff opens a place that can be filled by other institutions of the government. Foremost of these, of course, is the Congress. As he reminded the nation in his first formal statement as President, Mr. Johnson had spent thirty years of his life on the Hill before entering the White House. As President he has played elaborate court to the Congress and its peccadillos. He has repeatedly invited the legislators to all sorts of White House functions. No action is ever taken without advance Congressional briefing. Senator Harry Byrd was humored by being allowed to see the 1965 budget before its presentation to the nation. Congressman Richard Bolling was also humored with White House backing for a discharge petition to move the 1964 civil-rights bill out of the Rules Committee—a wholly unnecessary procedure. But most of all, Lyndon Johnson showed that he was a man of the Congress in his foreign policy.

This is not to say, as some foreigners apparently believe, that the President is a mere pork-barrel politician concerned only with domestic affairs. "The ripe melon of foreign affairs," as Ambassador David Bruce once put it, is by so much the most tempting morsel of business in the White House that even a President who had never done anything but run mail on a rural delivery route before reaching the White House would soon find himself trammeled in international matters. While President Johnson spent his first year cementing the transition—and building a domestic record to reassure his election—he was inevitably drawn more and more into international matters. By the end of 1964 he was thoroughly initiated into European policy, and, thanks to the issue of the Multilateral Force (MLF), especially into the mysteries of dealing with Germans, British, French, and other Europeans on nuclear sharing. The Panama and then the Dominican crises brought him to concentrate on Latin-American matters. Vietnam became a never-ceasing headache beginning in February 1965. By that time, Lyndon Johnson was probably spending as much of his efforts and time on foreign policy as any previous President.

What set him apart, and marked him as a man of the Congress, was that he moved to integrate foreign policy into the framework of domestic politics. Four previous Presidents had seen foreign-policy issues shake, if not shatter, their majorities. Aid to the Allies cost Roosevelt the support of the progressive Western wing of the New Deal coalition. Resistance to Soviet designs in Europe cost Truman some of his left-wing urban support, while resistance in Korea cost him the farm vote that had put him over the top in 1948. As for Eisenhower, the truce in Korea and the huge military expenses required to stay abreast of the Soviet Union forced a break with the conservative wing of his own party, and drove him into the hands of the Congressional Democrats under the Senate Majority Leader Lyndon Johnson. That John Kennedy's relations with the conservative wing of his own party were not more strained by his refusal to go all the way in Cuba and by the test-ban agreement was only because they had already been ruptured when he took office. Since they could not count on purely partisan political support, each one of the four Presidents turned, in putting across foreign-policy measures, to a grouping of prestigious figures from the worlds of law (John McCloy, Dean Acheson, and Foster Dulles), finance (Averell Harriman, Eugene Black, and Robert Lovett), the press (Henry Luce, Arthur Hays Sulzberger, and Barry Bingham), and the military (Generals George Marshall, Bedell Smith, and Lucius Clay). Time after time, when Administration foreign policy objectives were in hazard before the Congress, members of this group were wheeled up to cow, cajole, or charm the legislators into submission. Because they were all internationalist in outlook, generally connected with the East and its bigger schools and foundations, and usually members of the Council on Foreign Relations in New York, as the years wore on, the group acquired, from an English counterpart, the name of the Establishment. And to a large extent, it can be said that from 1940 through 1965, the United States followed the Establishment foreign policy.

Lyndon Johnson has moved to change that. Instead of following a foreign policy that forced him to depend on outsiders for support in the Congress, he followed a policy that built Congressional support. Thus, when troubles broke out in Panama and the Dominican Republic, the President moved ahead of the Congressional jingoes to occupy the high ground of defense of the flag and to utter the cry "no second Cuba." In Vietnam, he tried to talk peace with the Congressional doves and make war with the Congressional hawks. His foreign-aid policy, grounded in the general interest in selling agricultural products and machinery abroad, catered to the liberal Senate interest in long-term development and to the more conservative House interest in short-term agreements, which made it not only possible but easy to punish recipient countries which took the American name in vain. Perhaps best of all, the President expressed himself when, in the winter of 1964, explaining why he was against the united recommendations of his advisers to honor a commitment to push the MLF in Europe, he seems to have declared: "Nobody in the Congress is for it. I asked Bill Fulbright; and he's not for it. I asked Dick Russell, and he's not for it. I asked Paul Douglas, and he's not for it. I asked Jim Eastland, and even he's not for it."

Potentially, at least, the tipping of influence away from the White House and toward the Congress and the Departments has its dangers. If he can only choose between rival views, if he has to be broker among competing interests, if he must play Solomon to two mothers each wanting the baby, the President is in trouble. To make good decisions, he needs to have the raw materials of decision in his hands before possibilities are narrowed by bureaucratic interests and Congressional committees. Still, to write off the President as the captive of the bureaucracy and the Congress is to make an evident error. It may be true that no normal man has the working capacity to run that vast machine the United States government and the flexibility and adroitness to steer around the pitfalls of the bureaucracy and to backtrack from the blind alleys of public opinion. But Lyndon Johnson does these things, and to say that is to say perhaps the ultimate truth about Lyndon Johnson. He is not only big physically. He hates more, loves more, worries more, boasts more, talks more, cries more, laughs more, eats more, conceals more, exposes more, works more, plays more than normal men. He is a giant in all things, something larger than life and out of size. But a touch of the common man—deriving perhaps from roots in Texas, in the Democratic party, and in the Congress—saves him from being a grotesque figure. His genius is to be the average writ large.

Robert and Leona Rienow
CHECKS ON PRESIDENTIAL POWER

The Founding Fathers were fanatic in their insistence on "checks and balances" against the excessive accumulation of power by any arm of the federal government. Influenced by Montesquieu and William Blackstone, they were convinced that excesses in government could be avoided only by compartmentalizing it and then setting off one branch against the other. John Adams, with great satisfaction, listed no less than eight such checks:

> States and territories against the central government
> The House of Representatives against the Senate
> The President against the Congress
> The Judiciary against Congress
> The Senate against the President in matters of appointments and
>   treaties
> The people against their Representatives
> The state legislature against the Senate
> The Electoral College against the people

Adams' list actually contains but two checks on the President: those of states' rights and of the Congress. To these might be added (for what it may be worth) the ex post facto check of the Supreme Court, or Judiciary, on the President.

Corwin and Koenig assume that adequate safeguards automati-

From *The Lonely Quest: The Evolution of Presidential Leadership,* by Robert and Leona Train Rienow, pages 253–265. Copyright © 1966 by Robert Rienow and Leona Train Rienow. Reprinted by permission of Follett Publishing Company.

cally come into play to counteract a too ambitious Chief Executive. They list these additional checks on the President: the undeniable pressure of public opinion, biennial elections, an alert press, freedom of legislators to criticize, and the vast number of vocal, private interest groups, all of whom avidly watch the President for any misstep. But in any consideration of countervailing powers there must loom, overshadowing all else, the great lethargic bulk of the Congress of the United States.

Between Andrew Johnson and Lyndon Johnson a century-long river of history flows. When Thaddeus Stevens pointed his scrawny finger in the direction of the White House and announced a hundred years ago, "He [the President] is the servant of the people *as they shall speak through Congress*," Andrew Johnson bristled. The subordination of the Presidency to the Congress, he decided, was insupportable; it was the most flagrant sort of distortion of constitutional doctrine. Recalling Alexander Hamilton's declaration that "Congress forgets itself when it tries to play the executive," Johnson truly strove to be a "strong Chief," but he was a hundred years in advance of his times. Alone in his constitutional trenches, unable to summon any logistic aid from the grass roots, bereft of public backing, he was forced to surrender to the Congress, more ignominiously than anyone before or after.

Yet today the party leaders gather amiably in the White House every Tuesday morning for bacon and eggs. Three times a week the Senate majority leader and the Senate whip (being of the President's party) pay their political Chief a special visit. How different this camaraderie from the day not only of Andrew Johnson, but of most of our Presidents. Are there underlying causes (more basic and of longer duration than the new presidential powers) which have brought all this about?

The history of our government has been one of constant strife between the Congress and the Chief. When the Senate cabal conspired to meddle with Lincoln's cabinet, he rose in angry defiance, declaring unequivocally, "I AM MASTER, and *they shall not do that.*" Only the powers conferred by the emergency supported him. Andrew Johnson called the Senate "the damned scoundrels," and cared not who heard him. And President Cleveland in 1895 complained bitterly: "Think of it! Not a man in the Senate with whom I can be on terms of absolute confidence. . . . Not one of them comes to me on public business unless sent for, and then full of reservations and doubt. We are very far apart in feeling and, it seems to me, in purpose."

But the lordly and pre-eminent Senate is not alone in badgering the Chief; the attitude of the House may be discerned in the words of eighty-year-old, tobacco-chewing "Uncle Carl" Vinson when a member of the press accosted him as he was impatiently awaiting the eight o'clock opening of the House cafeteria. Bill Surface asked the old Georgian, who had an unequaled record of service in the House (since 1914), if it was true that he had served under nine Presidents? "I didn't serve *under* nine.... I served *with* nine. I don't serve *under* anybody," returned the venerable gentleman, with some acerbity. Presidents all down the corridors of time have learned this disillusioning fact about the Congress of the United States.

The cordial relations that exist today between the Chief and congressional leaders have developed not because the President has at last adopted more tact, but because during all the long years of conflict, when the Congress was energetically trying to crush the President's independence, it was failing, increasingly, to meet the nation's legislative needs. The Congress failed to offer integrated leadership, satisfactory response to the exigencies of time, to sift out the important measures sorely demanded. It spent most of its time in agitating, in Finer's words, "for those hundreds of small (often private) bills which confer benefits on individuals and pork-barrel tidbits on cities, counties and states, and bills which cater to pressure groups, of which no congressman need be proud."

Thus the President, on Congress's default, has moved in to become the chief legislator. He must work through Congress, but he does so with ever more assurance, using his new pressures and public backing to make whatever deals he must perforce make to put his program into effect.

We have already noted that it was F.D.R. who fashioned his intimacy with the electorate into the telling weapon which today's Presidents use to challenge the Congress. That new leadership persisted even through Eisenhower, although the General had no great personal taste for the role. Under Lyndon Johnson, it is at its peak. We hear no denials of legislative authority from the Chief today! Instead, it is his set of proposals that gives unity to the actions of Congress. More and more we tend to grade the Congress by the President's assignments. If the lawmakers measure up to what he expected of them, we applaud them as diligent; if they fall short, we stamp the Congress as "do-nothing."

President Johnson was refreshingly frank about his relationship to the lawmakers. Just before a big lawn party for the Eighty-eighth Congress and their families, even as he bemoaned what the preparations were doing to the White House lawn, he said: "You don't think I'd be having 1,000 of them down here if their record had not been very good. This is one of the best Congresses in history. Out of 50 bills I submitted, they passed most of them." And following on Johnson's landslide election in 1964, the heavily Democratic Eighty-ninth Congress passed such a series of landmark laws as to alarm some observers by the lawmakers' docility.

In view of this co-operation it is hard to believe that only a few years ago the traditional interpretation of separation of powers still persisted. Mr. Justice Douglas, in his concurring opinion in *Youngstown Sheet & Tube Co.* v. *Sawyer* (1952), while acknowledging the President's unique power to "formulate policies and mould opinions," adds that, nonetheless, "the impact of the man and the philosophy he represents may at times be thwarted by the Congress. Stalemates may occur. . . ." Then the famed Justice, weighing a proposal to allow some legislative authority to the President, concludes that to do so would distort the constitutional pattern. Today it is not likely that the *fait accompli* could longer be ignored. The President is openly exercising the proscribed authority. One cannot depend on the phrase "separation of powers," hallowed though it may be, to serve as countervailing power when in reality it has come to lack both force and full meaning.

We have considered at some length the Chief's newly acquired ability to sway the people to exert pressure upon the Congress. But for a considerable period the President has been developing many other, though lesser, weapons of congressional control. For example, there is tremendous significance in the way in which the President today shares his popular standing with those legislators who commit themselves to his legislative program. It is they who are privileged to have their campaign photos taken in the company of the Chief. When a new project is undertaken by any federal agency in such a Congressman's district, the announcement is made through the lawmaker's office, thus implying that he may share the credit.

A cold shoulder by executive agencies to the importunities of a Congressman for local recognition could, if prolonged, be a devastating blow to his standing in his home district. There are many occasions when community leaders *must* be ushered into the presence of the Chief Executive, when a study group *must* hear the head of the Peace Corps, when the Queen of the Great Lakes or "Miss Distilled Turpentine of 1966" *must* be greeted with full White House ceremony by the President's lady herself. A Congressman who is locked out will cut a sorry figure with his constituents.

What a President gives, he demands payment for. The Chief is a horse trader. The interminable conferences, phone calls, breakfasts, messages, the sending of trusted Cabinet members to the congressional lobbies, the caucuses, information leaks, the providing of friends with the drafts of favorite bills, the explanatory briefings, the jockeying, the secret "understandings," the "reasoning together," the backslapping and coddling of visiting constituents, the quietly applied thumbscrews—all these are old and tried techniques of the protector of all the people. Patronage, too, is never dead or out of style. The President, although losing much to civil service, has thousands of favors to grant, funds to dispense, jobs to give or to take, contracts to allocate.

Moreover, the very reasons why Congress has lost, or is losing, its pre-eminence in legislating—its recalcitrance, provincial orientation, absorption with minor matters, and blocking tactics carried too far—confound it once more when it would present a rival national leadership to that of the President. The opposition of the House often deteriorates into a sniping action in which the shots are fired from committees by chairmen who, although they ignore the party label, are chosen because they have been returned to Congress many times by a "safe" constituency. Because, therefore, they tend to be ultraconservative, their opposition is often described as mere obstructionism.

By an incredible stroke of luck, both Johnson and Humphrey are born conciliators, artists unexcelled at compromise and persuasion. By exercising their amazing talents to soften harsh opposition, they not only strengthen the Chief's leadership, but actually tend to preserve congressional authority from the imposition of too angry and drastic reform.

However, because of this congressional irresponsibility, the House in particular continually discredits itself as a center of sensible countervailing power to a possibly overbearing Chief Executive. The Congress *should* be such a countervail. Such was the intention of the Constitution. But provincial attitudes and often senseless opposition have in recent times prevented its playing such a role.

That the Founding Fathers did not foresee the corrosions of history is unfortunate. Or perhaps some of them did foresee the provincialism but, fatigued with arguments and compromise, surrendered to Hamilton's contention that our government was "as good as could be devised," and that if its vices were corrected it would no doubt be rendered impractical.

Those who propose the "streamlining" of the Congress might resolve certain questions before outlining their plans. Can a government be made to function "too smoothly for wisdom"? Is, as former Governor Edmund S. Muskie of Maine contends, the stability of our government (which astonishes Europeans and Asians alike) dependent in great part on our very deliberation, our "counterbalanced and constitutionally inhibited" institutions? How much do we want to restrain the opposition in order to get quick action? How may we strike a good balance between too cumbersome a democracy and too autocratic a one? Past dalliance must be corrected; but can powers once wrested from the Congress ever be restored to it? When we decide we are getting too much "instant democracy" from the President, will the restoration of former checks be possible?

But what of the other checks against the President mentioned earlier? Much has been made of our "pluralistic society." The question now arises, How long can we preserve a pluralistic society, with its great variety of opinions, when the centers of mass communications blanket the entire nation with conformist "news"—news that very often follows the "line" of a federal bureau or agency? The news on insecticides has long been doctored by the Department of Agriculture. The news on the effects of atomic fallout was long belittled by the Atomic Energy Commission as it sought to reduce the public's opposition to its atomic testing program. (Today the government's position is reversed, since it wants public support for the test-ban treaty, and the executive gives us the facts about the amounts of strontium 90 in the bones of babies.) It so happens that heretofore the A.E.C. was engaging in deception and that now the President is giving the nation the truth.

But the duplicity of federal agencies is not at issue here. The question is, How much of a countervail is the much-touted "pressure of public opinion" going to be against a magnetic, persuasive President who has greater television "projection" than scruples? It would seem that such a President's appeal would be able to overwhelm, for example, a states' rights issue, whatever the principle involved. What will "public opinion" of the future be if not the opinion of the authoritative, ever-present leader? The President will make public opinion.

There are those, then, who put much store in corporations and private interest groups as counterforces to the Chief. The great American corporation emerged from World War II as the characteristic institution of American society; Professor Andrew Hacker of Cornell University, quoted in *Current* in December 1963, declared that "all signs are that the future lies with the great corporate institution" with its ever agglomerating masses of wealth and power. As far as a counterforce is concerned, it is unlikely that ever again will we be blessed with a poor man in the White House; to reach the pinnacle the Chief is becoming daily more dependent on millions of dollars in campaign contributions or from his own fortune. Whatever quietus he has made with big business and its cause, the President of the future is not exactly its "man on the spot." Too many of these corporations have their destinies influenced by a regulatory commission he controls or by government contracts he approves or by the government investment and tax policy he directs.

One must recognize that in itself the great bulk of America is a protection against excessive domination. The dissident press can still be influential, but the journalistic forces of opposition to presidential policies tend to have no place to focus their efforts. The President, on the other hand, personalizes *his* policy.

There is still the Supreme Court as a restraint on an overambitious President. The Supreme Court has been making its power felt so much in the last decade that it is being accused of usurping the constitutional roles of both the Congress and the Chief Executive by continually amending the Constitution. Arthur Krock of the New York *Times* notes that the Justices have attained so much supremacy that "the President automatically enforces the decrees of the Supreme Court, and . . . appeals to Congress to use its limited power to vacate them get nowhere." It proclaims "revolutions in the American political process," and the "revolutions are immediately accomplished."

Friction between the Chief Executive and the Supreme Court, like friction between the Chief Executive and the Congress, is in good American tradition. As early as 1832 Andrew Jackson, enraged at a Court pronouncement, said angrily of Chief Justice Marshall: "He has made his decision: *now let him enforce it!*" With that one sentence, he cleaved to the heart of the Supreme Court's weakness. While the lovely black robes and dignified surroundings bemuse the populace, and reverence clings to its dictums like lint on velvet, the Supreme Court is hopelessly handicapped against any President of the future who may not display the conscientious, Constitution-respecting attitudes to which it is accustomed. The Supreme Court may pontificate and hand down its honored decisions. But what does it mean? Federal troops must be called out to enforce the really important ones. The Supreme Court cannot execute its decisions. And who must call forth the federal agencies of enforcement? None other than the President of the United States—*if, and when, he so chooses.*

An entirely different counterforce to the Chief's dominance has not yet been mentioned. Like the corporation, it is neither crumbling nor desirable as an offset. This institution is quite modern, is endowed with massive power, has large sums of independent funds, and has no responsibility to speak of to the people. It is beyond their control. It is also, for the most part, beyond the control of Presidents, who come and go while it remains. It is the federal bureaucracy.

Because the bureaucracy is a mammoth, headless "thing," because it is becoming daily a greater political force, which must be reckoned with, it cannot be ignored in any discussion of presidential stumbling blocks. Bureaucracies that go on and on with the same personnel decade after decade, becoming ever more hidebound and inflexible, can seriously impede even the most persuasive executive. Marriner S. Eccles, in *Beckoning Frontiers*, offers us a picture of what was encountered by one of our most ingratiating Presidents, Franklin D. Roosevelt. He quotes the President:

"The Treasury is so large and far-flung and ingrained in its practices that I find it almost impossible to get the action and results I want—even with Henry [Morgenthau] there. But the Treasury is not to be compared with the State Department. You should go through the experience of trying to get any changes in the thinking, policy, and action of the career diplomats and then you'd know what a real problem was. But the Treasury and the State Department put together are nothing compared with the Na-a-vy. The admirals are really something. . . . To change anything in the Na-a-vy is like punching a feather bed. You punch it with your right and you punch it with your left until you are finally exhausted, and then you find the damn bed just as it was before you started punching."

It is true that bureaucrats bow more to congressional sentiment and cater more to it than to either public opinion or the President. It is to the Congress that they must look for their appropriations, for their daily bread. Bureaucrats, like many a Congressman, were there before the incumbent Chief, and they expect to be there long after he is gone.

But even the bureaucrats may be brought into line by the Chief Executive. Equal representation, which is surely coming to the House, will tend more and more to align House members with the President as their constituencies become one and the same. Bureaucratic snubbing of the Chief will disappear. Exactly how? We have already noted that the electoral college is gerrymandered to give dominance to the urban vote and urban viewpoint, thus imposing an urban outlook upon the President himself. Reapportionment and redistricting of the House will, of course, alter that body drastically, imposing on it, also, an urban outlook. When the interests of both President and House are joined, foolhardy indeed will be the bureaucrat who fails to bow deeply to both.

What is true of the executive departments is true also of the many independent commissions that depend so heavily on congressional appropriations. But even if certain of these independent, irresponsible nuclei of concentrated power were to continue for some time in their errant, irritating ways, they would not be counterforces, but mere stumbling blocks. One-purposed, narrow-horizoned entities, each pursuing its small and special goal, they could oppose little of reference or relevance to the national welfare as a whole. The heads of departments and commissions are often large-souled and earnest men, even self-sacrificing men. But they are caught in a bureaucratic net toughened by the decades. It is the bureaucracy that rules itself. As for the nation, the leadership of the most daring and whimsical President would be infinitely preferable to the leadership of one of these "things."

The old order, the ancient pattern of checks and balances, is crumbling. Restraints upon the President by the great new forces rising in our society—the bureaucracies, the departments, and the massive new corporate entities which Professor Hacker so greatly fears—are unthinkable and must be circumvented. Yet ought we not give some thought to reconstructing and modernizing the political devices of restraint that are at hand?

5
The Presidency: Emergence of the Candidates

The American Presidency makes incredibly imposing demands on the man in the White House. The office calls for a man who has the dignity of a monarch, the sagacity of an elder statesman, the adroitness of a professional politician, and the physical stamina of a track star. The question discussed in this chapter is: How do we find the man to meet the demands of the office? The answer is that "we" do not find the man, but rather that a political party at its national convention "finds" a man who claims to be able to meet the challenges of the office. The central problem, then, is to examine this method of selecting presidential candidates, viewing it against the nature of the presidential office.

The national conventions date back to the early 1830s as a product of Jacksonian democracy. Prior to this time, a small group of party and congressional leaders, "King Caucus," determined who would be the presidential candidate. Along with the increase in suffrage that accompanied Jacksonian democracy came demands for a nominating method that would allow a far greater number of people to participate directly in the selection of the nominees. Thus the convention system was born.

However, the convention system has long been under attack. Many have asked just who the delegates represent. Others have questioned the appropriateness of its circus atmosphere. In the words of one critic, it is a "colossal travesty of popular institutions." Dissatisfaction with the system grew to such proportions that toward the end of the last century many states adopted the presidential-preference primary. By this method, the voters of a state select the delegates to the national convention. These delegates are pledged to support a specified candidate—at least on the first ballot. Today, twenty states have some form of preference primary; but the majority of the delegates continue to be selected by state or district conventions or by the state party committees. Even in the states that use the primary, some people criticize the primaries as hardly more than popularity polls. Yet, popularity is not necessarily a meaningless term in a democratic society.

Despite this doubt, the presidential primary has taken on added dimensions that probably have been strengthened by the coming of television. For Senator John F. Kennedy in 1960, the hard primary route was his only means of competing for the nomination. He entered a series of contests culminating in a "showdown" primary in West Virginia against Hubert Humphrey. The California primary played an important part in Barry Goldwater's bid for the GOP nomination in 1964. Goldwater's California victory demonstrated popular support for his nomination and, perhaps more significantly, it ended the candidacy of his principal opponent, Nelson Rockefeller.

In any given presidential-election year only a limited number of potential candidates appear. In a broad sense, there is a natural political aristocracy; membership in this group of white males is equivalent to "availability" for the nomination. These political aristocrats have certain features in common: a middle-to upper-class social and economic status; residency in a large urban state; an unblemished family life; and some political experience. Formerly, the unwritten rules of availability excluded non-Protestants. Kennedy's election broke that tradition, as well as the tradition favoring candidates of English, Scotch, or German background. How soon a Jew, an Italian, or a Negro will break the rule against his candidacy is unknown.

The most "available" candidate for any party's nomination is a White House incumbent. Thus the 1968 Democratic nomination is probably a foregone conclusion. The 1968 Republican nominee will be selected from fewer than a dozen available candidates. All are politicians, all are members of the upper socioeconomic group, and all are Protestants. They vary in family life, in political philosophy, and in their urban identification. While Robert Novack contends that the pragmatism of "availability" tests failed at the Republican convention in 1964, it seems likely that in 1968 the Republican delegates will examine Rockefeller, Nixon, Goldwater, Romney, Reagan, and Percy in the more traditional context of "who can win?"

The Presidency has an urban bias, for the reason that under the "winner-take-all" electoral system, the large urban centers in any given state have a major voice on election day. In 1964 the Republican convention ignored this bias and gambled on a Southern strategy. But Goldwater's candidacy alienated substantial numbers of urban voters, and the GOP carried only one state outside of the Deep South, Arizona. Rarely can a convention ignore the "swing states." New York, Michigan, Illinois, Texas, California, Pennsylvania, and Ohio have a combined vote of 210 in the electoral college, and only 268 votes are needed for victory. It should also be noted that, with the exception of Texas and Illinois, each of these states has a Republican governor. Indeed, in 1968 the Republican party controls 25 governorships.

In 1960, it was obvious that the primary campaigns largely predetermined the nomination of Kennedy. In 1964, with the important exception of the California Republican primary, primaries did not play a significant role. Whether the 1968 GOP nomination will be predetermined is largely dependent on whether the major contestants engage in a series of tough primary battles. In the absence of primary battles, the nominating convention will again loom large. It might be possible for the "smoke-filled room" of Harding's era again to take over the nominating process, and to dictate the Republican standard-bearer for 1968. Although the national nominating convention developed as a democratic response to "King Caucus," the convention has been the subject of a long series of attacks. One of the earliest, and one of the most acid, was by a European observer, M. Ostrogorski. Yet for all of the seemingly antidemocratic qualities of the convention system, Professor Wildavsky finds that the system is superior to its alternatives.

Preconvention primary battles can mean that the national conventions serve only as rubber-stamps—to ratify the previously fought popularity contests. On the other hand, a convention where smoke-filled rooms dominate the scene could imply that conventions are controlled by the party elite, the bigwigs. The question is whether either alternative is consistent with the nature of the Presidency or responsible government.

V. O. Key, Jr.
THE PRESIDENTIAL PRIMARY

The primary has introduced a considerably higher degree of popular participation in the choice of presidential nominees. That partic-

From *Politics, Parties & Pressure Groups*, Fifth Edition. Copyright © 1964 by Thomas Y. Crowell Company. Reprinted by permission. The late V. O. Key was Trumbull Professor of American History and Government, Harvard University.

ipation may not be determinative of the candidates, but those who would be nominees must ordinarily conduct campaigns directed to the voters to a greater degree than when the nominations were more exclusively in the hands of the party professionals. The primary probably makes some men presidential hopefuls who would not have been in an earlier day. Thus, Estes Kefauver, with a reputation developed through the televising of his crime investigations, became a far more serious contender for the nomination in 1952 and in 1956 than he would have been in the days before the presidential primary.

On occasion it seems as though the effect of the primaries is to kill off candidates rather than to determine which of the two or three aspirants who reach the convention with considerable blocs of delegates will be nominated. In 1944 Wendell Willkie withdrew from the race for the Republican nomination after an early defeat in the Wisconsin primary. He lost to a slate of delegates pledged to Dewey, who had disavowed the slate and not even bothered to campaign. Or in 1956, Stevenson's victory in the California primary was regarded as the death blow to the Kefauver candidacy. On the other hand, a spectacular performance in a primary may give a candidate a powerful boost and bring leaders to his bandwagon. In the 1952 "Minnesota miracle," when over 100,000 persons took the trouble to write in the name of Eisenhower in the primary, Republican leaders all over the land could see that a vote-getter had arrived on the scene. Similarly, in 1960, Kennedy, the front runner, strengthened his cause by his demonstration of vote-pulling power among Protestants in his West Virginia victory over Humphrey.

While the primary has modified nominating practices, it has not produced conventions of automata that mechanically record the preferences expressed by the voters at home. Party organizations in many states retain a fairly high degree of autonomy despite the primaries. Candidates for the presidency choose not to enter many primaries. State delegations often retain their freedom of choice by commitment to favorite sons through the primary as before; the voters may even vote for uncommitted delegations. Indeed, for the convention to be capable of achieving its broad objective of developing party consensus on a candidate, delegations must possess a range of discretion.

When the memory of the Republican convention of 1912 was fresh, numerous proposals were made for the establishment of a nationwide preference primary, which perhaps would have required a constitutional amendment. President Wilson, in his first message to Congress, urged a national system in these words: "I turn now to a subject which I hope can be handled promptly and without serious controversy of any kind. I mean the method of selecting nominees for the Presidency of the United States. I feel confident that I do not misinterpret the wishes or the expectations of the country when I urge prompt enactment of legislation which will provide for primary elections throughout the country at which the voters of the several parties may choose the nominees for the Presidency without the intervention of nominating conventions." Congress did not act on the recommendation. From time to time renewed flurries of interest in the matter develop. In 1952 a Senate committee even reported a bill to encourage the states, by financial assistance, to hold presidential preference primaries; the proposal died at that stage.

The invention of the straw poll has introduced a sort of nationwide preference primary. In recent conventions the nominations and the rankings of candidates for the nomination have followed fairly closely the sentiments of party members as revealed by the polls. It is doubtful that the polls control convention actions, though they may establish that convention actions do not deviate nearly so far from popular sentiment as some advocates of the presidential primary would have us believe. It has been contended that during the past half-century the convention has become, in fact, the captive of the forces of mass democracy. It is limited in its deliberations to consideration of those who have achieved, by one means or another, the status of a celebrity. When one person is clearly the national favorite the convention has, or so it is argued, no choice but to nominate him.

M. Ostrogorski
THE AMERICAN CONVENTION SYSTEM

At last, after a session of several days, the end is reached; the convention adjourns *sine die*. All is over. As you step out of the building you inhale with relief the gentle breeze which tempers the scorching heat of July; you come to yourself; you recover your sensibility, which has been blunted by the incessant uproar, and your faculty of judgment, which has been held in abeyance amid the pandemonium in which day after day has been passed. You collect your impressions, and you realize what a colossal travesty of popular institutions you have just been witnessing. A greedy crowd of office-holders, or of office-seekers, disguised as delegates of the people, on the pretence of holding the grand council

From *Democracy and the Organization of Political Parties*, by M. Ostrogorski, pp. 278–279. New York: The Macmillan Company, 1902.

of the party, indulged in, or were the victims of, intrigues and ma-
nœuvres, the object of which was the chief magistracy of the greatest
Republic of the two hemispheres,—the succession to the Washingtons
and the Jeffersons. With an elaborate respect for forms extending to the
smallest details of procedure, they pretended to deliberate, and then
passed resolutions settled by a handful of wire-pullers in the obscurity of
committees and private caucuses; they proclaimed as the creed of the
party appealing to its piety, a collection of hollow, vague phrases, strung
together by a few experts in the art of using meaningless language, and
adopted still more precipitately without examination and without conviction; with their hand upon their heart, they adjured the assembly to
support aspirants in whose success they had not the faintest belief; they
voted in public for candidates whom they were scheming to defeat. Cut
off from their conscience by selfish calculations and from their judgment
by the tumultuous crowd of spectators, which alone made all attempt at
deliberation an impossibility, they submitted without resistance to the
pressure of the galleries masquerading as popular opinion, and made up
of a *claque* and of a raving mob which, under ordinary circumstances,
could only be formed by the inmates of all the lunatic asylums of the
country who had made their escape at the same time. Here this mob
discharges a great political function; it supplies the "enthusiasm" which
is the primary element of the convention, which does duty for discussion
and controls all its movements. Produced to order of the astute managers,
"enthusiasm" is served out to the delegates as a strong drink, to gain
completer mastery over their will. But in the fit of intoxication they yield
to the most sudden impulses, dart in the most unexpected directions, and
it is blind chance which has the last word. The name of the candidate for
the Presidency of the Republic issues from the votes of the convention
like a number from a lottery. And all the followers of the party, from the
Atlantic to the Pacific, are bound, on pain of apostasy, to vote for the
product of that lottery. Yet, when you carry your thoughts back from the
scene which you have just witnessed and review the line of Presidents,
you find that if they have not all been great men—far from it—they were
all honourable men; and you cannot help repeating the American saying:
"God takes care of drunkards, of little children, and of the United
States!"

Dwight D. Eisenhower

OUR NATIONAL NOMINATING CONVENTIONS ARE A DISGRACE

In my opinion—and I think most Americans will agree—our Presidential nominating conventions have become a thoroughly disgraceful spectacle which can scarcely fail to appall our own voters and create a shockingly bad image of our country abroad. Now that we are midway between the conventions of 1964 and 1968, it seems time to discuss this matter frankly. We can view the events of two years ago with some perspective, and there is still time to adopt reforms before the summer of 1968 is upon us.

First, I want to make it clear that I am not among those who wish to abolish the nominating conventions in favor of a national primary. Over the years, the conventions have done a reasonably good job of choosing men of ability and honor. There are, moreover, compelling arguments against a national primary. In most Presidential years at least two primary elections would be necessary. With perhaps four or five men seeking the nomination in each party, it is unlikely that any one of them—except an incumbent President—could win a majority vote on the first round. Unless we nominated by plurality, which certainly is not desirable, a runoff would be necessary. All this would prolong the selection of candidates almost unbearably and wear down the interest of voters long before the main event.

Furthermore, if we nominated by primary, only wealthy men could normally run for the Presidency. Any campaign which attempts to cover this big country is enormously expensive. Once a candidate is nominated, of course, he is backed by the resources of his party. But in a primary campaign the aspirant must find a way to pay his own expenses—and I certainly do not think we should close the door of the Presidency to any man of integrity and ability simply because he cannot afford to run. Therefore I feel that the nominating conventions must be retained.

POINT OF DISORDER.   There is, however, no reason under heaven why these conventions must be exercises in chaos and tumult—

unmannerly, undignified, ridiculous. Here we have men and women meeting to perform a vital task. The same atmosphere of dignity should prevail that we find in Congress or in any other major deliberative body. Yet our conventions now resemble a rioting mob of juvenile delinquents.

The floor often becomes a scene of milling humanity, and the din is such that delegates frequently cannot hear what is said on the podium. The thumping of the chairman's gavel, as he futilely tries to restore order, is an endless refrain to television viewers, many of whom turn off their sets in frustration.

Press, radio and television reporters roam the aisles at will, and often work their way into the center of a delegation for an interview. Reporters and delegates alike chatter into walkie-talkies, thereby increasing the hubbub. The confusion becomes so frustrating that it is almost impossible for a delegation to hold a caucus on the floor.

The ultimate in mob scenes occurs, of course, after each candidate is placed in nomination. The band plays the candidate's theme song *ad infinitum,* and the parade of demonstrators begins. The doors at the rear of the hall are opened, and imported shouters—who have no official status whatsoever—swarm in with their banners and placards and noise-making devices. The moment the uproar begins to diminish a bit, the candidate's managers whip up the frenzy of the faithful and prod the mercenaries into new feats of raucous clamor. The theory seems to be that the man who gets a 20-minute ovation would make twice as good a candidate as the 10-minute man.

BESMIRCHED BY TRAVESTY. Sometimes the artificiality of these demonstrations is so ludicrous as to be acutely embarrassing. I recall one such instance some years ago. The hour was late, and most of the delegates had left the hall. But one more name remained to be placed in nomination—the name of a distinguished American who had served his country long and well. Finally, the speeches were ended, and the time had come for the joyous ovation. With few delegates left to participate, a motley assortment of characters from the city streets—obviously hired for the occasion—came in. Their performance, in a hall littered with waste-paper and debris, was lifeless and pathetic. Yet all this went out on television. As an American, I was embarrassed for my country. As a human being, I was outraged that the name of a prominent citizen should have been besmirched by such a travesty.

In times past, bad manners at our conventions—such as talking and visiting during a speech—have been largely due to thoughtlessness and the delegates' preoccupation with their own affairs. At the 1964 Republican convention in San Francisco, however, a new note of deliberate rudeness was injected. Booing and hissing were common, and insulting remarks were exchanged. The low point of the convention—perhaps of all conventions—came when New York's Gov. Nelson Rockefeller found it virtually impossible to deliver his speech. Chairman Thruston Morton furiously tried to quell the shocking display of bad manners, but without much success.

I suppose that this rudeness at San Francisco was the outgrowth of the sharp conflict between opposing camps. Whatever the reason, it was unpardonable—and a complete negation of the spirit of democracy. I was bitterly ashamed. I wish to add most emphatically that none of this was caused or condoned by the principal figures of the convention. It resulted from the lack of machinery for firm control of the unruly.

THE ROAD TO REFORM. Until recent times, the spectacle of our nominating conventions was strictly for domestic consumption, and even in our own country few people ever *saw* a convention. Now, with television coverage, these riotous proceedings go into virtually every home. Worse, millions of TV viewers in foreign countries see the conventions, either live by satellite communication or from tapes flown across the oceans.

Now, I am all for television, radio and press coverage of the conventions. It is one way to bring home to our own people the issues and problems of government and to make them conscious of their duties as citizens. It is a way to show the workings of our brand of democracy —which is still the best form of government on earth—to our friends overseas. But certainly we should show all these people, at home and abroad, a dignified deliberative body at work, not "Operation Chaos."

I am happy to say that my own party is now making a determined start toward reform. Our national chairman, Ray Bliss, has appointed a committee of distinguished Republicans to study convention procedures and make recommendations. Somewhere along the way, I am told, the committee may ask for my suggestions, and I shall be most happy to coöperate.

My recommendations will be about as follows:

1. The permanent chairman should have better means for controlling convention procedure. If a violation of the rules occurs—a disturbance, an exhibition of rudeness—he should have the power to eject the disorderly or even to clear the hall and reconvene the convention at a later hour. If this were done even once, I think that people would soon get the idea that dignified and courteous deportment is obligatory.

2. No one except delegates and those with official convention business should be permitted on the floor. Even the alternate delegates should be seated in the gallery; when needed, they could descend to the floor.

3. The above rule should apply to all reporters—television, press and radio. They could be provided with ample facilities *off the floor*. This recommendation may bring loud protest from some of our public media, but I think it is highly necessary. Congress wouldn't think of letting reporters come onto the floor of the House or Senate to interview members. The business of a convention is just as important as that of Congress, and the convention should have the same right to reach its decisions undisturbed. I have discussed this problem with one top network official, and I gather that at least some of the broadcasting people would be happy and relieved to operate under more orderly rules.

4. Walkie-talkies should be banned from the floor. Closed telephone circuits should be set up in the hall *for the delegates,* so that they could reach anyone in the hall quickly and easily, but these phones should not be connected with outside circuits. If a delegate wished to talk with someone outside the hall, he could go to a telephone elsewhere in the building.

5. All noisemaking devices should be banned from the hall, and any delegate or spectator using one of these abominations should be ejected. Moreover, there should be only one band inside the building—the official one. It could play some rousing music at the beginning and end of sessions, and play the theme song of each candidate during his demonstration—but at no other time.

6. Demonstrations should be restricted to ten minutes—ample time for a display of genuine enthusiasm. Participation in demonstrations should be limited to delegates and alternates—no hired hands from the streets, no pretty high-school girls in cheerleader costumes.

7. Any booing or hissing or other disorderly conduct from spectators in the galleries should be quelled instantly and firmly, and the culprits should be evicted from the hall.

8. Although the convention should in no way interfere with protest demonstrations by legitimate groups *outside the hall,* it should have the right to expect that its business will not be impeded by them. Demonstrators who try to prevent the entry or departure of delegates by lying down in streets or doorways should be removed by the police. Any city unwilling to give a firm guarantee of such protection should be avoided as a convention site.

These are my recommendations. If they were adopted and enforced, I am sure that they would make our conventions respectable exhibits of democracy at work. It may be objected that such rules would be so inhibiting as to take all the steam and enthusiasm out of party procedure. I believe that the opposite is true. I am aware that genuine emotion—loyalty to a candidate, deep conviction on issues, patriotism—is an essential ingredient of political gatherings. But I believe that, within the framework of these rules, there would still be full scope for honest emotion and the kind of enthusiasm that makes party wheels turn.

THE URGENT NEED.   There is one other suggestion which I think merits careful consideration by both parties. Each of the two conventions now lasts four days. That is much too long. If the recommendations I have offered were adopted, and if speeches were reduced in number and duration, the entire business of a convention could easily be accomplished in two days. This would be highly desirable for virtually everyone concerned, including the long-suffering public.

In any case, the urgent job before us now is to reform convention procedures—so that the summer of 1968 will not find us once more presenting to the world an inept, inane interpretation of the democratic process. As a Republican, I am delighted that my party is diligently studying the problem. As an American, I ardently hope that *both* parties will take the proper steps as soon as humanly possible.

Aaron B. Wildavsky
ON THE SUPERIORITY OF NATIONAL CONVENTIONS

The appraisal of national conventions as mechanisms for nominating presidents involves many problems of political theory. Who should be entrusted with the task of nomination? Can we reconcile the desirability of popular participation with the need for maintaining a strong party leadership? To what extent does the nominating convention contribute to the maintenance of the political system in which it is imbedded? Does the apparent lack of decorum in this high political body adversely affect the kinds of decisions it makes? What are the implications of increasing the visibility of convention nominations? Any attempt to deal with these and similar questions necessarily involves an admixture of normative and descriptive theory. Postulation of what ought to be can hardly be separated from consideration of the actual or likely consequences of alternative courses of action. The merits of existing party

From "On the Superiority of National Conventions," by Aaron B. Wildavsky. *The Review of Politics*, Vol. 24, July 1962. Reprinted by permission. Dr. Wildavsky is Professor of Political Science, University of California, Berkeley.

platforms, for example, cannot be fruitfully discussed apart from knowledge of the relevance of issues to voters. In this context, I propose to evaluate national conventions and the various proposals for altering or abolishing them in the light of the degree to which they meet widely shared goals for the American political system.

No one will deny that presidential nominating conventions are peculiar. After all, they perform a peculiar function. The task of the convention is to unite a party which is not inherently united, behind a popular candidate who is unpopular with many delegates, in order to speak for all the people after battling half of them in an election. It would be surprising if a political institution which must accomplish these goals did not reflect some of the contradictions it is designed to embody.

The critics of national conventions find them gay when they should be solemn, vulgar when they should be genteel. In a word, they find the conventions somehow too American. The reforms proposed by these critics suggest that grave decisions should be made at a solemn convention or that the convention system should be abolished entirely. Yet we shall see that every major change suggested has the unfortunate result of leading to consequences much worse than the evils they are supposed to remedy.

In order to evaluate national conventions, and the alternatives to them, we need a set of goals which most Americans would accept as desirable and important. The following six standards appear to meet this test: any method for nominating presidents should: 1. aid in preserving the two-party system; 2. help secure vigorous competition between the parties; 3. maintain some degree of cohesion and agreement within the parties; 4. produce candidates who have some likelihood of winning voter support; 5. lead to the choice of good men; 6. result in the acceptance of candidates as legitimate.

Let us first evaluate the alternatives to national conventions to see if they are superior to the existing system.

A national primary has often been suggested. This, however, would have serious disadvantages. It is quite probable that as many as ten candidates might obtain enough signatures on nominating petitions to get on the ballot. Nor would it be surprising if they divided the vote equally. The victor would then have to be chosen in a special run-off primary. By following this procedure, the United States might have to restrict its presidential candidates to wealthy athletes: no poor man could ever raise the millions required for the nominating petition, the first primary, the run-off primary, and the national election; and no one who was not superbly conditioned could survive the pace of all these campaigns.

National primaries might also lead to the collapse of the party system as we know it. It is not unusual for a party to remain in office for a long period of time. If state experience with primaries is any guide, this would result in a movement of interested voters into the primary of the winning party where their votes would count more. As voters deserted the losing party, it would be largely the die-hards who were left. They would nominate candidates who pleased them but who could not win the election because they were unrepresentative of a majority of the nation. Eventually, the losing party would atrophy, thus seriously weakening the two-party system and the prospects of competition among the parties. The winning party would soon show signs of internal weakness as a consequence of the lack of opposition necessary to keep it unified.

A national primary is also likely to lead to the appearance of extremist candidates and demagogues who, unrestrained by allegiance to any permanent party organization, have little to lose by stirring up mass hatreds or making absurd promises. A Huey Long or a Joe McCarthy would have found a fertile field in a national primary, an opportunity sufficient to raise the temperature of American politics to explosive levels even if he did not win. The convention system rules out these extremists by placing responsibility in the hands of party leaders who have a permanent stake in maintaining the good name and integrity of their organization. Some insight into this problem may be had by looking at the situation in several southern states where most voters have moved to the democratic primary and where victory in that primary is tantamount to election. The result is a chaotic factional politics in which there are few or no permanent party leaders, the distinction between the "ins" and "outs" becomes blurred, it is difficult to hold anyone responsible, and demagogues arise who make use of this situation by strident appeals, usually of a racist variety. This functional theory of demagoguery (in which extreme personality takes the place of party in giving even a minimal structure to state politics) should give pause to the advocates of a national primary.

The remaining radical alternative is nomination by one of the branches of Congress. This, though, would be out of the question. The caucus system of nomination was rejected in Andrew Jackson's time because it did not give sufficient representation to the large population groups whose votes were decisive in the election. Furthermore, the large fluctuations of party membership in Congress lead to serious difficulties. If a party happened to do very poorly for a few years in several sections of the country, the representation in Congress from those areas would be small and they would, in effect, be deprived of a voice in nominating a president. Thus, if northern Democrats suffered a serious reverse one year, the southern members of that party would be in complete control.

This nominating procedure would advertise itself as being national in scope, but it would be far more likely than the present system to produce candidates with a limited, sectional appeal. The attempts of leaders in areas where the party is weak to strengthen themselves by nominating a candidate who might help increase their vote would be stymied.

Perhaps, it may be argued, what is required is not some radically new method of nominating candidates, but reform of some of the more obnoxious practices of the present system. High on the list of objectionable practices would be the secret gathering of party leaders in the smoke-filled room. Some liken this to a political opium den where a few irresponsible men, hidden from public view, stealthily determine the destiny of the nation. Yet it is difficult to see who, other than the party's influential leaders, should be entrusted with the delicate task of finding a candidate to meet the majority preference. Since the head-on clash of strength on the convention floor has not resolved the question, the only alternatives would be continued deadlock, anarchy among scores of leaderless delegates, splitting the party into rival factions, or some process of accommodation.

Let us suppose that the smoke-filled room were abolished and with it all behind-the-scenes negotiations. All parleys would then be held in public, before the delegates and millions of television viewers. As a result, the participants would spend their time scoring points against each other in order to impress the folks back home. The claim that bargaining was going on would be a sham, since the participants would not really be communicating with each other. No compromises would be possible, lest the leaders be accused by their followers of selling out to the other side. Once a stalemate existed, it would be practically impossible to break and the party would probably disintegrate into warring factions.

An extensive system of state primaries in which delegates were legally compelled to vote for the victorious candidate would lead to the disappearance of the smoke-filled room without any formal action. As the delegates could not change their positions, there would be little point in bringing their leaders together for private consultations. Sharply increasing the number of pledged delegates would introduce such rigidity into the convention that it would perpetually be faced with stalemates which could not be overcome because no one would be in a position to switch his support.

While candidates are being nominated and during the balloting at national conventions, demonstrations, partly spontaneous, largely prearranged, take place on the floor. Much criticism has been leveled at this raucous display. But criticisms of demonstrations as unseemly and vulgar seem to me to be trivial.

There is no evidence which would substantiate a claim that the final decision is in some way worse than if demonstrations were banned. Lincoln, Bryan, and Willkie are the prime examples of men aided in their nomination by the exuberance of their supporters.

The criticism neglects the important communicating function of demonstrations. Imagine the scene if a candidate were nominated or scored an advance in the balloting and this was accompanied by a brief, polite moment of applause. Surely, no one would believe that a candidate who worked up so little response could stir any enthusiasm among the people. It is possible that this criticism of demonstrations comes from the individuals who prefer rule by the genteel. A sedate convention might be more appropriate for a sedate country.

In still another way the demonstrations help meet the need of many delegates for an active function which they can perform and tell about when they get home. As in almost any large political gathering (the number of delegates and alternates is in the thousands) only a small number actively participate in planning strategy or in trying to influence other people. The rest often find that they have no well-defined political role other than casting one vote out of many and may feel at a loss to explain their lack of activity to themselves as well as to the people back home. The demonstrations provide an opportunity for the delegate to enhance his feelings of importance by active participation in a colorful event which he can recount when he returns. Since one of the advantages of the convention is to gather the party faithful and imbue them with a sense of belonging to a national party, a mechanism which increases the delegate's sense of satisfaction is by no means unimportant.

Undoubtedly, demonstrations have been overdone and might be cut short. This task can safely be left to the requirements of television. As the 1960 conventions showed, televising dictates briefer demonstrations to retain the attention of the vast audience which the party would like very much to influence in its favor.

The members of each party may love it on a sentimental basis; they certainly love the idea of getting into office; but do they love each other? The convention provides the acid test of party unity by determining whether the disparate elements which make up each party can agree on one man to represent them—a man who cannot possibly be equally attractive to all of them. The much maligned party platform is exceedingly important in this regard not so much for what it says but for the fact that it is written at all. The platform tests the ability of the many party factions to agree on something even if, on crucial points, the differences have to be papered over.

The problem of the platform does not lie in evil, scheming politicians who want to confuse the public, but rather in the nature of the American people and their extraordinary diversity. In order to gain a majority of electoral votes, a party must appeal to all major population groups. Since all these interests do not want the same thing in all cases, it is necessary to compromise and, sometimes, to evade issues which would split the party and lead to drastic loss of support. A perfectly clear, unequivocal, consistent platform on all major issues presupposes an electorate which divides along such lines, and that is not the case in this country.

The concern of reformers with party platforms stems primarily from two assumptions: first, that there is a significant demand in the electorate for more clear-cut differences on policy; second, that such elections are likely to be a significant source of guidance on individual issues to policy makers. Yet both these assumptions are either false or highly dubious. Herbert McCloskey and his associates have shown that on a wide range of issues leaders in both parties are much further apart than are ordinary members who, in fact, are separated by rather small differences. To the degree that party platforms do spell out clear and important differences on policy—and these were considerable in 1960— this probably results far more from a desire of party leaders to please themselves or from misinformation about what the voters desire than from any supposed demand from the electorate. Moreover, as Robert A. Dahl has demonstrated so well, it is exceedingly difficult (if not sometimes impossible) to discover just what an election means in terms of the policy preferences of a majority. Given a reasonable difference in the salience of issues for voters, it is quite possible for a candidate to win 75 per cent of the vote although 75 per cent of the voters opposed each of his policies. Finally, the Michigan Survey Research Center points out that the number of people who (a) know about most issues, (b) differentiate between the positions of the candidates, (c) care about the issues, is very small. And these are likely to be the most interested and involved section of the population whose allegiance to party is strongest and who are least likely to change their votes on the basis of one or a few issues. About all that one can expect from an election is an indication of the general direction in which a candidate and the dominant factions in his party intend to go, and the party platforms do reasonably well in this respect.

Some critics object to the convention's stress on picking a winner rather than "the best man" regardless of his popularity. Now this is a rather strange doctrine in a democracy where it is presumed that it is the people who should decide who is best for them and communicate this decision in an election. Only in dictatorial countries do a set of leaders arrogate unto themselves the right to determine who is best, independently of the popular preference. An unpopular man can hardly win a free election. An unpopular President can hardly secure the support he needs to accomplish his goals. We deceive ourselves when we treat popularity as an evil condition instead of a necessary element for obtaining consent in democratic politics.

Although popularity is obviously a necessary condition for nomination, it should not be the only condition. The guideline for purposes of nomination should be to nominate the best of the popular candidates. But "best" is a slippery word. A great deal of what we mean by best in politics is "best for us" or "best represents our policy preferences." And this can hardly be held up as an objective criterion. What is meant by "best" in this context are certain personal qualities such as experience, intelligence, and decisiveness. Nevertheless, it is doubtful whether an extreme conservative would prefer a highly intelligent radical to a moderately intelligent candidate who shared the conservative's policy preferences. Personal qualities are clearly subject to discount based on the compatibility of interests between the voter and the candidate.

Insofar as the "best man" criterion has a residue of meaning, I believe that it has been followed in recent times. Looking at the candidates of both parties since 1940—Roosevelt, Truman, Stevenson, Kennedy for the Democrats, and Willkie, Dewey, Eisenhower, Nixon for the Republicans—there is not one man among them who could not be said to have had some outstanding qualities or experience for the White House. Without bothering to make a formal declaration of the fact, American political leaders and their followers have apparently agreed to alter the requirements of availability. They have restricted their choice to those popular candidates who give promise of measuring up to the formidable task of the President as preserver of the nation and maintainer of prosperity. The nominee whose sole virtue is his innocuousness or pleasant smile seems to have disappeared.

It has been alleged, however, that this criterion has been violated because nominations have come to be determined by popularity, that is, by expressions of mass preferences as reported in polls and state primaries. Merely defining the candidate who won the nomination as most popular is not sufficient to prove the thesis; it must be shown that the voters agreed who was the most popular candidate, that this was communicated to the delegates, and that they nominated him. It would be hard to say that William Howard Taft, Warren Harding, Alfred Landon, Wendell Willkie and Thomas Dewey, to name a few, were indisputably the most popular Republican candidates. Dwight Eisenhower might fit in this category (though he had to fight for the nomination) but he represents just one case and is counterbalanced by Theodore Roosevelt's failure to obtain the nomination in 1912. There is no evidence to suggest that, among Democratic candidates, Woodrow Wilson was more popular than Champ Clark in 1912, that James M. Cox and John Davis fit the most popular category, or that Franklin Roosevelt could have been placed there with certainty before his first nomination. If anyone was most popular in 1952 it was Estes Kefauver and not Adlai Stevenson.

A surface view of the situation in 1960 might suggest that John F. Kennedy's nomination was due to an irresistible current of public opinion. Obviously, Kennedy's excellent organization and the difficulty of refusing the nomination to a Catholic who had won important primaries must be taken into account. Furthermore, the Republican experience suggests another important factor. We never discovered whether or not Nelson Rockefeller was more popular with the voting public than Richard Nixon because the latter had such strong support among party professionals that the former decided it was not worth running. A crucial difference between the two conventions was that there was no Democrat to oppose Kennedy who could claim a widespread preference among party leaders as was the case with Nixon in the Republican Party.

To be sure, popularity as evidenced through victory in primaries is important. But the unpledged delegates, comprising some two-thirds of the total, may use their judgment to disregard this factor as they did in nominating Willkie and Stevenson who entered no primaries. The significance of primaries derives not nearly so much from the delegates they bring to an aspirant's side as from the indication they give that he is likely to win the election. The candidate who feels that he already has considerable delegate strength would be foolish to enter a primary unless he was quite certain he could win. All he can gain is a few additional votes but he can lose his existing support by a bad showing that would be interpreted to mean he could not win the election. Naturally, primaries are the vehicles of candidates who must make positive demonstrations of support in order to be considered and are hardly worse off by losing than if they had not entered at all. Candidates who are strong at the outset can pick and choose the one or two primaries they wish to enter and can use the most favorable circumstances to defeat their opponents. It does not seem too great an emphasis on popularity to ask that an aspirant be able to win at least one or two primaries. Alternately, it does not seem too shocking that the candidate who wins all the contested primaries, as Kennedy did, should be given prime consideration.

No doubt the primaries, though held in different sections of the country and in different kinds of states (Wisconsin, California, West Virginia) are by no means a perfect representation of the electorate. Yet this is a rather peculiar argument coming from those who wish to downgrade the importance of primaries; for if primaries were truly representative of the nation their importance would be enormously enhanced. How could the nomination be denied to a candidate who had apparently proved that he had the support of a majority of a very large and accurate sample of the voting population?

The conclusion I would draw is that the primaries, together with other methods of delegate selection which give predominance to party activists, provide a desirable balance between popularity and other considerations which party leaders deem important. Without denying an element of popular participation, the decision is ultimately thrown into the hands of the men who ought to make it if we want a strong party system—the party leaders.

For some critics the defects of conventions lie not only in their poor performance in nominating candidates but also in their failure to become a sort of superlegislature enforcing the policy views in the platform upon party members in the Executive Branch and Congress. This is not the place to become embroiled in the seemingly endless debate over "party government." But it is in order to suggest that such a role for the conventions implies a radical change in our entire political system and might well result in a breakdown of the existing nominating structure by saddling it with unbearable burdens. To make the convention's policy decisions truly effective—that is, binding on the President and Congress—would mean a radical shift in power from the constitutionally delegated authorities, and from the people who elect them, to the delegates and those who elect and control them. There is no evidence that anyone will either try to do this or, indeed, has any chance whatsoever of proving successful at it. There is certainly no reason to believe that such a change would meet with the preferences of more than an insignificant minority of citizens.

Let us suppose, nevertheless, for the purposes of argument, that the conventions would somehow become much more influential on matters of national policy. How could either party retain a semblance of unity if the stakes of convention deliberations were vastly increased by converting the platform into national policy? If one believes that heated discussion necessarily increases agreement, then the problem solves itself. Experience warns us, however, that the airing of sharp differences, particularly when the stakes are high, is likely to decrease agreement. Today, the choice of nominees at the convention is accepted as legitimate by all but a few delegates. The fact that platforms are not binding permits the degree of unity necessary for the delegates to stay long enough to agree on a nominee. By vastly increasing the number of delegates who would bitterly oppose platform decisions, and who would probably leave the convention, the proposed change would jeopardize the legitimacy of its nominating function. Paradoxically, the temptation to make the platform utterly innocuous so as to give offense to no one would be difficult to resist.

There are also good reasons for opposing the desires of those who love the conventions so well that they would like to see them convene once every year or two years. If the purpose of these meetings is to give free advice there would seem to be little point to them. Congressmen are likely to pay as little attention to convention talk as they did to the pronouncements of the Democratic Advisory Committee. After all, Congressmen are subject to different risks and sanctions than are most delegates, get no great help from the national party in securing nomination and election, and have no reason to be beholden to it for suggesting policies which may get them into trouble. As they have uniformly decided in the past, Congressional leaders will likely refuse to participate in organizations in which they cannot control the result but are committed to support the proposals. The differences between the convention and Congressional constituencies are such that in a convention the legislative leaders are bound to suffer many defeats which could well render them ineffective. The notion of getting delegates together under circumstances where their disagreements are certain to come out into the open, merely for the purpose of making recommendations, does not seem promising. It is doubtful whether most delegates, who could not be expected to take an active part in formulating proposals, would feel it worthwhile to participate in a convention which lacked its major rationale and interest—the choice of a presidential nominee.

Although I hope to have avoided the error of assuming that whatever is is right, the superiority of national conventions to the available alternatives is clearly demonstrable. Only the convention permits us to realize in large measure all the six goals—the two-party system, party competition, some degree of internal cohesion, candidates attractive to voters, good men, and acceptance of nominees as legitimate—which we postulated earlier would commonly be accepted as desirable. We get good candidates but not extremists who would threaten our liberties or convert our parties into exclusive clubs for party ideologists. Leaders are motivated to choose popular candidates who will help maintain vigorous competition between the parties but who are unlikely to split them into warring factions. The element of popular participation is strong enough to impress itself upon party leaders but not sufficiently powerful to take the choice out of their hands. The convention is sufficiently open to excite great national interest but it is not led into perpetual stalemate by pseudo-bargaining in public. Voters have a choice between conservative and liberal tendencies—a choice which is not absolute because a two-party system can be maintained only if both parties moderate their views in order to appeal to the large population groups in the country. In all these ways, national conventions make an essential contribution to the maintenance of the peculiarly American political system, a contribution which could not be made by any competitive mechanism now on the horizon. It would be interesting to speculate on the reasons why a political institution, which no one consciously set out to create in its present form, should have evolved in such a way that the delicate balance between its parts serves us so well.

Robert D. Novack
WHERE PRAGMATISM ENDS

How did it happen?

This was the question asked incessantly after Barry Goldwater had astounded so many to become his party's nominee. It was asked by laymen, by disconsolate Republican liberals, by conservatives who could not quite believe that they had finally succeeded after so long in the wilderness.

The answer usually given was a wrong answer, which in turn led rapidly to the propagation of a Goldwater myth. The trouble is that the answer was usually given by people who had seen what happened in San Francisco and nothing before. It was akin to analyzing a winning football team based on watching it in the last quarter of a game, after its opponent has been ground down to impotence. Watching the Goldwater juggernaut crush the feeble opposition in San Francisco and forgetting all that came before led to this answer:

"Goldwater was nominated because behind him was a smooth-working, well-disciplined, well-led political organization that had so dominated state conventions that Goldwater had enough delegates at San Francisco to win no matter what happened in the primaries. Therefore, for the future, primaries are obsolete and Goldwater-style organizations are absolutely essential." This is the Goldwater myth.

In the first place, this book has tried to show that all the confusion, the indecision, and the blunders that are inherent in political-

Reprinted with permission of The Macmillan Company from *The Agony of the G.O.P.*, by Robert D. Novack. Copyright © Robert D. Novack, 1965. Mr. Novack is a nationally syndicated correspondent.

campaign organizations were to be found in abundance within the Goldwater organization. These were scarcely robot-like supermen running Barry Goldwater's campaign.

In the second place, it is almost certain that Goldwater could not have been nominated if he had lost to Rockefeller in the California primary on June 2. And if Goldwater had won his earlier primary tests in New Hampshire, Oregon, and elsewhere, he would have been the certain nominee, without much opposition—quite probably by acclamation. So primaries *do* count. Despite their limitations, they are the only way (other than the much abused polls), that a candidate's popular appeal can be tested prior to the convention.

The truth is that the Goldwater organization really picked up no more than four hundred absolutely hard-core delegates (not counting California's eighty-six). The remaining delegates had to come from delegations whose support for Goldwater was something less inviolate than a sacred vow. If Goldwater had lost to Rockefeller in California, he would have lost more than eighty-six delegates. He would have lost much of Ohio, Colorado, Florida, Wisconsin, and parts of Illinois, Georgia, and Washington. In other words, Goldwater would have had an extremely difficult time being nominated—*if* thirty thousand voters in California had voted for Rockefeller instead of Goldwater. This is just the first of many such *ifs*. They are worth recording only to show that the Goldwater nomination was something a good deal less than inevitable:

If Nelson Rockefeller had not remarried in May, 1963, he would have been difficult to beat, if not unbeatable, for the nomination—particularly if Goldwater campaigned no better than he actually did in 1964.

If Rockefeller had been realistic enough to withdraw from the Presidential race after his remarriage, the gap probably would have been quickly filled (particularly after the Kennedy assassination). That would have meant Lodge, Nixon, or Scranton as Goldwater's principal contender. It is questionable whether Goldwater could have won in California against any of these three.

If Lodge or Nixon or Scranton had actively entered the race even though Rockefeller stayed in it, it is likely that one of these three would have won in Oregon and California.

If Nixon had either been elected Governor of California in 1962 or had not entered that race at all, he would have been difficult to stop for the 1964 Presidential nomination after the assassination—whether an active candidate or not.

The point here is that the Goldwater organization and the Goldwater campaign were not invincible. But it was different. From a strictly organizational standpoint, its distinctiveness was a matter of its insinuating itself so early in the delegate-selection process—right down to the precinct mass meetings. It meant that hundreds of delegates went to San Francisco who were Goldwater men from the beginning, their progress from precinct to county to district to state conventions carefully followed by national tacticians in the Goldwater campaign.

This was the great contribution of F. Clifton White, Goldwater's chief delegate hunter. From the time that White put together the Draft Goldwater nucleus, not long after the 1960 election, he exercised a degree of personal control and personal observation of the delegation-selection process not seen before in American politics.

But the organization that Clif White built was not the invincible machine that some of the postnomination newspaper accounts portrayed it to be. Not long after the nomination, the Goldwater organization was put in proper perspective by one of the originals in the Draft Goldwater group—Representative John Ashbrook, thirty-five, a militant and attractive conservative Congressman from Ohio. "I get a kick out of all this praise heaped on us," said Ashbrook. "We booted a lot of them. We almost lost Florida by backing the wrong people down there. We could have lost Ohio. We *did* lose Minnesota by not coming to an agreement with Walter Judd. We made a lot more bobbles. The only reason we came out all right is the people at the grass roots."

Ashbrook's "people at the grass roots" are the warriors of the Goldwater Movement—the real heroes and the real winners of the Republican fight of 1964. These were the foot troops who swarmed into precinct meetings from Seattle to Atlanta to take over the Republican Party. Often, their sleeping foes didn't oppose them. But even when opposed, the Goldwaterites proved hard to outnumber. The Minnesota Republican Party fought a year-long war to prevent the Goldwater onslaught in the precincts, but only partially succeeded and then only through the gimmick of using Walter Judd as a Presidential candidate to oppose Goldwater.

The real question of the 1964 Republican fight should be not "How did it happen?" but "How does the Goldwater Movement manage to flood the precinct meetings in every part of the country?" The Movement cannot outpull a Lodge in New Hampshire or a Rockefeller in Oregon, but it can find more people who care enough to sit through a precinct meeting.

Why?

The answer to this is the real answer to the nomination of Barry Goldwater in 1964 and the sudden dominance in the Republican Party of the new conservatives. For without the Movement, Goldwater would have been finished after New Hampshire.

It is not enough to dismiss the Goldwaterites as kooks. A more

penetrating answer is suggested by a senior staff member in the organization of one of the unsuccessful contenders for the 1964 nomination. In a
brief unsigned monograph on the 1964 campaign called "Where Pragmatism Ends," this staff member blames the hold of pragmatism—the test of
"Does it work?"—on what used to be called the progressive wing of the
Republican Party. The paper depicts Rockefeller as the archetype of the
political pragmatic:

> ... he tends to shy publicly from discussions of political doctrine,
> arguing the pragmatic line that government is a matter of "problem
> solving" rather than of adherence to abstract political philosophies.
> He gave currency to the rather mealy-mouthed label "moderate" to
> describe his own position.

After quickly tracing the dismal course of the party's non-
Goldwater wing in 1964, the monograph comes to this conclusion:

> Pragmatism failed the moderates and the progressives in the Re-
> publican Party in 1964, not only because it prevented them from
> developing a positive alternative to ... "Goldwaterism," but also be-
> cause it prevented their leaders from giving free rein in crucial
> moments to those moral checks or moral impulses which might have
> enabled them to maintain their supremacy within the party. The argu-
> ment against Goldwater was based too much on his "electability," too
> much on the damage that his presence might do to other candidates
> running on state or local tickets. . . .

For all the *ifs* that show how many different ways Goldwater
could have been stopped, this monograph points to the true weakness of
his opposition. It is true that the anti-Goldwater forces were victims of an
unlucky chain of events, beginning with the Rockefeller remarriage. But
if they had had some nonpragmatic moral philosophy to oppose Goldwater and his conservatism, they might have survived the bad breaks.

In the final analysis, then, Rockefeller and Scranton lost because
they had nothing to offer the people but themselves. Goldwater had a
moral philosophy that stirred enough people to the heights of enthusiasm
so that the nomination was his. Indeed, this attraction was so strong that
the Goldwaterites could not see disaster looming ahead in November.

6
The Process of Persuasion

Is a presidential campaign really a national soap opera, or is it a national effort to educate and inform the public about the political issues confronting the nation? Has Madison Avenue invaded political parties to the degree that the process of persuasion is simply the systematic manipulation of the mass mind? Has television basically altered the nature of campaigns, or are they today essentially the same as in 1860?

If we could turn the clock back to Lincoln's first presidential campaign, the four-party race of 1860, we would watch a number of campaign tactics that are still in use today. The nation was bitterly divided over the slavery issue, the aftermath of which is still an issue in 1968. The recently born Republican Party smelled victory in the winds. Out of caution, their nominee assumed a lofty, noncommittal pose. An "old campaigner," William Cullen Bryant, advised Lincoln to make no speeches, write no letters as a candidate, and enter into no pledges. Why alienate large groups of voters already committed to Lincoln, for the sake of a few uncommitted voters? Lincoln stayed in Springfield during the entire campaign and never made a single campaign speech.

Thus, Lincoln's strategy in 1860 was what has been described as the "front-porch" campaign: he waited in Springfield for the press and the party workers to visit him—and they did. The campaign had wide press coverage, and Lincoln's party had most of the Northern press "sewed up"—a press which at least on the editorial page is still largely committed to the same party one hundred years later.

But Lincoln's principal opponent, Senator Stephen A. Douglas, could not afford to conduct a "front-porch" campaign. The "Little Giant" had to carry his cause to the people. Undaunted by imminent defeat, Douglas conducted a "whistle-stop" campaign. Harry Truman, laboring under similar odds, achieved different results when, in 1948, he decided to "give 'em hell" via a whistle-stop campaign.

Although the 1860 campaign was sobered somewhat by the threat of secession, still it had its ballyhoo and color. Republican speakers made an estimated 50,000 speeches, and the people flocked to political rallies all over the nation. There are few torchlight parades today, yet a lot of martial music, political rallies, and stomping of feet still exist. Another Senator from Illinois, Paul Douglas, one hundred years later, said that there is nothing to replace this old strategy of meeting the voters face to face.

What has changed since 1860? It does not seem likely that a "front-porch" campaign is still possible. Modern political campaigns are placing incredibly heavy demands on the candidate, and some feel that showmanship is replacing ideas. In other words, there is some concern that a premium is being placed on huckstering rather than political statesmanship.

The discussion of campaign issues has been filled with ambiguities and distortions. The Chairman of the National Republican Committee for the 1964 campaign, Dean Burch, contends that the campaign never really presented the substance of the issues to the voters. Mr. Burch calls for a campaign of full debate, particularly television debate. Such a proposal should be judged, at least in part, with William Glaser's study, "Television and Voter Turnout," in mind. Glaser's study indicates that television has not had the impact on voting that many anticipated it would, and Glaser concludes that television has not been exploited as an instructive political media. His conclusions tend to refute the earlier fears of many scholars that politicians would be able to exploit this media and easily manipulate the voters.

While Dean Burch felt that the 1964 presidential campaign was a sham, the late V. O. Key suggests in his thoughtful book, *The Responsible Electorate*, that even if presidential campaigns are phony, voters are not fools. While recognizing that there is a great deal of sound and fury in a presidential campaign, Key concluded that, by and large, the electorate behaves about as rationally and responsibly as can be expected, given the clarity of the information presented to it. Key's study is not a full answer to recent critics who contend that American political campaigns are antithetical to the rationalism assumed in democratic theory. His study, however, does suggest that these fears are not entirely well-founded. Relying upon extensive voting-behavior data, Key discovered that a rather large percentage of voters switch parties and that these "switchers" do so on the basis of their policy attitudes. Key concludes from his data that the American voter and American electoral institutions, particularly the presidential election, are rational. In effect, he rejects the fear of some scholars that presidential elections are characterized more by the cult of personality than by rational principles. Presidential campaigns may indeed be short on rational dialogue, but voters do not judge candidates exclusively by what is presented in a campaign. Rather, they judge by campaigns as well as by past events and previous personal experiences.

Stanley Kelley's analysis of the 1964 campaign is particularly interesting in view of Key's analysis of the electorate and Dean Burch's comments on the 1964 campaign. Professor Kelley concludes that, given the situation which any Republican candidate would have faced in 1964, the Goldwater strategy was not unreasonable. In any event, he suggests, no campaign strategy can reasonably be predicated on the assumption that the opposition will enter into a full dialogue of the "issues" as presented by one party.

V. O. Key, Jr.
THE RESPONSIBLE ELECTORATE

In his reflective moments even the most experienced politician senses a nagging curiosity about why people vote as they do. His power and his position depend upon the outcome of the mysterious rites we perform as opposing candidates harangue the multitudes who finally march to the polls to prolong the rule of their champion, to thrust him, ungratefully, back into the void of private life, or to raise to eminence a new tribune of the people. What kinds of appeals enable a candidate to win the favor of the great god, The People? What circumstances move voters to shift their preferences in this direction or that? What clever propaganda tactic or slogan led to this result? What mannerism of oratory or style of rhetoric produced another outcome? What band of electors rallied to this candidate to save the day for him? What policy of

Reprinted by permission of the publishers from V. O. Key, Jr., *The Responsible Electorate*. Cambridge, Mass.: The Belknap Press of Harvard University Press, Copyright, 1966, by the President and Fellows of Harvard College.

state attracted the devotion of another bloc of voters? What action repelled a third sector of the electorate?

The victorious candidate may claim with assurance that he has the answers to all such questions. He may regard his success as vindication of his beliefs about why voters vote as they do. And he may regard the swing of the vote to him as indubitably a response to the campaign positions he took, as an indication of the acuteness of his intuitive estimates of the mood of the people, and as a ringing manifestation of the esteem in which he is held by a discriminating public. This narcissism assumes its most repulsive form among election winners who have championed intolerance, who have stirred the passions and hatreds of people, or who have advocated causes known by decent men to be outrageous or dangerous in their long-run consequences. No functionary is more repugnant or more arrogant than the unjust man who asserts, with a color of truth, that he speaks from a pedestal of popular approbation.

It thus can be a mischievous error to assume, because a candidate wins, that a majority of the electorate shares his views on public questions, approves his past actions, or has specific expectations about his future conduct. Nor does victory establish that the candidate's campaign strategy, his image, his television style, or his fearless stand against cancer and polio turned the trick. The election returns establish only that the winner attracted a majority of the votes—assuming the existence of a modicum of rectitude in election administration. They tell us precious little about why the plurality was his.

For a glaringly obvious reason, electoral victory cannot be regarded as necessarily a popular ratification of a candidate's outlook. The voice of the people is but an echo. The output of an echo chamber bears an inevitable and invariable relation to the input. As candidates and parties clamor for attention and vie for popular support, the people's verdict can be no more than a selective reflection from among the alternatives and outlooks presented to them. Even the most discriminating popular judgment can reflect only ambiguity, uncertainty, or even foolishness if those are the qualities of the input into the echo chamber. A candidate may win despite his tactics and appeals rather than because of them. If the people can choose only from among rascals, they are certain to choose a rascal.

Scholars, though they have less at stake than do politicians, also have an abiding curiosity about why voters act as they do. In the past quarter of a century they have vastly enlarged their capacity to check the hunches born of their curiosities. The invention of the sample survey—the most widely known example of which is the Gallup poll— enabled them to make fairly trustworthy estimates of the characteristics and behaviors of large human populations. This method of mass observation revolutionized the study of politics—as well as the management of political campaigns. The new technique permitted large-scale tests to check the validity of old psychological and sociological theories of human behavior. These tests led to new hunches and new theories about voting behavior, which could, in turn, be checked and which thereby contributed to the extraordinary ferment in the social sciences during recent decades.

The studies of electoral behavior by survey methods cumulate into an imposing body of knowledge which conveys a vivid impression of the variety and subtlety of factors that enter into individual voting decisions. In their first stages in the 1930's the new electoral studies chiefly lent precision and verification to the working maxims of practicing politicians and to some of the crude theories of political speculators. Thus, sample surveys established that people did, indeed, appear to vote their pocketbooks. Yet the demonstration created its embarrassments because it also established that exceptions to the rule were numerous. Not all factory workers, for example, voted alike. How was the behavior of the deviants from "group interest" to be explained? Refinement after refinement of theory and analysis added complexity to the original simple explanation. By introducing a bit of psychological theory it could be demonstrated that factory workers with optimistic expectations tended less to be governed by pocketbook considerations than did those whose outlook was gloomy. When a little social psychology was stirred into the analysis, it could be established that identifications formed early in life, such as attachments to political parties, also reinforced or resisted the pull of the interest of the moment. A sociologist, bringing to play the conceptual tools of his trade, then could show that those factory workers who associate intimately with like-minded persons on the average vote with greater solidarity than do social isolates. Inquiries conducted with great ingenuity along many such lines have enormously broadened our knowledge of the factors associated with the responses of people to the stimuli presented to them by political campaigns.

Yet, by and large, the picture of the voter that emerges from a combination of the folklore of practical politics and the findings of the new electoral studies is not a pretty one. It is not a portrait of citizens moving to considered decision as they play their solemn role of making and unmaking governments. The older tradition from practical politics may regard the voter as an erratic and irrational fellow susceptible to manipulation by skilled humbugs. One need not live through many campaigns to observe politicians, even successful politicians, who act as though they regarded the people as manageable fools. Nor does a heroic conception of the voter emerge from the new analyses of electoral behavior. They can be added up to a conception of voting not as a civic decision but as an almost purely deterministic act. Given knowledge of certain characteristics of a voter—his occupation, his residence, his religion, his national origin, and perhaps certain of his attitudes—one can predict with a high probability the direction of his vote. The actions of persons are made to appear to be only predictable and automatic responses to campaign stimuli.

Most findings of the analysts of voting never travel beyond the circle of the technicians; the popularizers, though, give wide currency to the most bizarre—and most dubious—theories of electoral behavior. Public-relations experts share in the process of dissemination as they sell their services to politicians (and succeed in establishing that politicians are sometimes as gullible as businessmen). Reporters pick up the latest psychological secret from campaign managers and spread it through a larger public. Thus, at one time a goodly proportion of the literate population must have placed some store in the theory that the electorate was a pushover for a candidate who projected an appropriate "father image." At another stage, the "sincere" candidate supposedly had an overwhelming advantage. And even so kindly a gentleman as General Eisenhower was said to have an especial attractiveness to those of authoritarian personality within the electorate.

Conceptions and theories of the way voters behave do not raise solely arcane problems to be disputed among the democratic and antidemocratic theorists or questions to be settled by the elegant techniques of the analysts of electoral behavior. Rather, they touch upon profound issues at the heart of the problem of the nature and workability of systems of popular government. Obviously the perceptions of the behavior of the electorate held by political leaders, agitators, and activists condition, if they do not fix, the types of appeals politicians employ as they seek popular support. These perceptions—or theories—affect the nature of the input to the echo chamber, if we may revert to our earlier figure, and thereby control its output. They may govern, too, the kinds of actions that governments take as they look forward to the next election. If politicians perceive the electorate as responsive to father images, they will give it father images. If they see voters as most certainly responsive to nonsense, they will give them nonsense. If they see voters as susceptible to delusion, they will delude them. If they see an electorate receptive to the cold, hard realities, they will give it the cold, hard realities.

In short, theories of how voters behave acquire importance not because of their effects on voters, who may proceed blithely unaware of them. They gain significance because of their effects, both potentially and in reality, on candidates and other political leaders. If leaders believe the route to victory is by projection of images and cultivation of styles rather than by advocacy of policies to cope with the problems of the country, they will project images and cultivate styles to the neglect of the substance of politics. They will abdicate their prime function in a democratic system, which amounts, in essence, to the assumption of the risk of trying to persuade us to lift ourselves by our bootstraps.

Among the literary experts on politics there are those who contend that, because of the development of tricks for the manipulation of the masses, practices of political leadership in the management of voters have moved far toward the conversion of election campaigns into obscene parodies of the models set up by democratic idealists. They point to the good old days when politicians were deep thinkers, eloquent orators, and farsighted statesmen. Such estimates of the course of change in social institutions must be regarded with reserve. They may be only manifestations of the inverted optimism of aged and melancholy men who, estopped from hope for the future, see in the past a satisfaction of their yearning for greatness in our political life.

Whatever the trends may have been, the perceptions that leadership elements of democracies hold of the modes of response of the electorate must always be a matter of fundamental significance. Those perceptions determine the nature of the voice of the people, for they determine the character of the input into the echo chamber. While the output may be governed by the nature of the input, over the longer run the properties of the echo chamber may themselves be altered. Fed a steady diet of buncombe, the people may come to expect and to respond with highest predictability to buncombe. And those leaders most skilled in the propagation of buncombe may gain lasting advantage in the recurring struggles for popular favor.

The perverse and unorthodox argument of this little book is that voters are not fools. To be sure, many individual voters act in odd ways indeed; yet in the large the electorate behaves about as rationally and responsibly as we should expect, given the clarity of the alternatives presented to it and the character of the information available to it. In American presidential campaigns of recent decades the portrait of the American electorate that develops from the data is not one of an electorate straitjacketed by social determinants or moved by subconscious urges triggered by devilishly skillful propagandists. It is rather one of an electorate moved by concern about central and relevant questions of public policy, of governmental performance, and of executive personality. Propositions so uncompromisingly stated inevitably represent overstatements. Yet to the extent that they can be shown to resemble the reality, they are propositions of basic importance for both the theory and the practice of democracy.

To check the validity of this broad interpretation of the behavior of voters, attention will center on the movements of voters across party lines as they reacted to the issues, events, and candidates of presidential campaigns between 1936 and 1960. Some Democratic voters of one election turned Republican at the next; others stood pat. Some Republicans of one presidential season voted Democratic four years later; others remained loyal Republicans. What motivated these shifts, sometimes large and sometimes small, in voter affection? How did the standpatters differ from the switchers? What led them to stand firmly by their party preference of four years earlier? Were these actions governed by images, moods, and other irrelevancies; or were they expressions of judgments about the sorts of questions that, hopefully, voters will weigh as they responsibly cast their ballots? On these matters evidence is available that is impressive in volume, if not always so complete or so precisely relevant as hindsight would wish. If one perseveres through the analysis of this extensive body of information, the proposition that the voter is not so irrational a fellow after all may become credible.

Dean Burch
PRESIDENTIAL CAMPAIGNS ARE A SHAM

The presidential campaign of 1964 was a mockery of the democratic process. At best, it was a waste of time, money, and energy. At worst, it was an absolute sham.

The blame for this must be shared by the two great political parties, the candidates and the managers for both sides—though I am convinced that none of us on either side wanted it that way. All of us were only doing what comes naturally—following outmoded, ineffective, irrational but traditional patterns. These made of the presidential contest a nine-week marathon bicycle derby, driving the candidates to the point of physical exhaustion while they whizzed past the real issues. Thus were the American people cheated of the thorough, rational discussion that the times and the problems demand.

As Republican national chairman, I was keenly disappointed by the results of the balloting in November, but that is not the point at issue here. My present concern is not so much with the outcome as the way it

From "Presidential Campaigns Are a Sham," by Dean Burch, *Saturday Evening Post*, March 25, 1965. Reprinted by permission. Mr. Burch is former chairman of the Republican National Committee.

was reached. In retrospect, it is clear that despite all the frantic efforts, the campaign was a bore. The substance of the issues never really got through to the voters.

When the campaign began on Labor Day, our private polls showed us that almost 90 percent of the electorate had already made a choice. This was in keeping with political surveys over the last 20 years, which have consistently indicated that the voting pattern is set before the campaign paper even starts.

During the weeks of intense activity which followed, Senator Goldwater was able to win over more of the previously undecided voters than President Johnson was able to attract. The senator was also able to win over almost three voters who had favored the Democrats before the campaign for every voter the President was able to win from him. However, all these shifts were far from enough to change the outcome. Our polls show that 79.2 percent of the voters stuck by the decisions they had made before the campaign began. Incredibly, shortly after election day fully one-third of those interviewed still knew little or nothing about the Republican candidate.

It may be said that this was our own failure—but if so, it was not for lack of effort. Senator Goldwater traveled about 75,000 miles. He averaged five speeches a day, shook hands with thousands, kissed his quota of babies and conferred with hundreds of politicians, each one eager to tell him how to win.

The pace was almost inhuman. Goldwater's own overwhelming memory of the campaign is of Charlie Justice, his personal aide, standing over him with a pocket watch in a crowded hotel room saying, "It's time to go . . . it's time to go." The Republican vice-presidential candidate, Congressman Miller, was rarely able even to take a shower without some aide standing just outside the curtain shouting instructions about the next appearance. In early October we managed to reschedule an entire Monday of the Miller itinerary so that he could calmly tape some important television shows—but he was so exhausted he couldn't get out of bed. For myself, holed up in Washington headquarters with a supporting cast of 695 full-time employees, I was often so tired at the end of the day that I could not bring myself to lift a telephone.

In the calm light of today it is reasonable to wonder what difference all this made. Some of the exertions, in fact, seemed ridiculous even at the time. Nevertheless, they went forward partly for lack of a clear alternative and partly because of the seemingly unbreakable pattern set in 1960 when two keenly ambitious young politicians engaged in a jet-powered test of stamina. At one point both Goldwater and Miller reached the conclusion, independently, that the campaign grind was senseless and ineffective. At a strategy meeting their protests were hooted down by those who cried that this was "the way it has always been done."

Much of a presidential campaign elevates the demands that the politicians make on the candidates over the needs of the voters. One such facet is the "prop-stop," the aviation-age variant of the old whistle-stop. It is idiotic to think that any but the fondest supporters would drive miles to a remote, noisy airport to hear a few fragments of a speech. Nonetheless, political managers the nation over expected and demanded such appearances "if we are going to carry the state for you."

The value of the personal appearance is greatly overrated. On a trip through the South in September, Goldwater spoke for six days to the largest crowds that had ever been assembled there to hear a presidential candidate. We were greatly encouraged. Later on, however, our surveys disclosed that barely two percent of the eligible voters of the South had seen him.

Thus, in a modern campaign, we elevate sheer motion over everything else. We ask the candidates to travel constantly, sleep when they can find time, live out of suitcases, endure unbelievable fatigue—and then we expect these worn and harried men to communicate to us their deepest thoughts on issues of great complexity.

In practical fact they end up largely talking to their friends in a race against exhaustion, mouthing dreary ghost written speeches which often miss the true issues and influence virtually no one—all at monumental expense. When by heroic efforts they manage to surmount the obstacles to serious discussion, their words are filtered and condensed by the rewrite men—or snipped to a 60-second film clip on TV news, again screened to fit the demands of "equal time, equal coverage."

Under the circumstances, is it any wonder that politicians tend to sell personality rather than serious argument? Is it any wonder that a President can clamber over cars and shout at crowds through a bullhorn, and be hailed as a model campaigner in the Grand Style? Is it any wonder that the electorate can be swayed by outrageous slogans and distortions, despite every effort to set the record straight?

Less than five months after election day we are deeply enmeshed in some of the same problems that the campaign so neatly skirted. One is the continual drain on our national reserve of gold. Already the President has had to recommend to Congress emergency legislation to meet the crisis. Even more urgent is the war in Vietnam. From the campaign you may recall an occasional cry of "trigger happy." But does anybody remember any discussion in depth or substance of this explosive situation?

I'm not suggesting that such discussions were not offered—on our side, at least. But the fact is that nobody seemed to be listening.

Could it be that the professional politicians are right when they say that anything more complex than wide roads and free beer cannot possibly register on the consciousness of the American electorate?

I think the professionals are wrong. Moreover, there is one obvious way to reach the people directly: television—or, if you prefer, the "boob tube." In this case the tube can become the indispensable ally of our democratic Republic, for it is the greatest medium ever devised for transmitting the essence and the substance of politics.

To realize this full potential, however, is almost impossible in today's circumstances. To begin with, the costs are enormous. A 30-minute telecast on a network costs in the neighborhood of $125,000, cash in advance, exclusive of production charges of reimbursements to the program which has been bumped. A one-minute spot advertisement can cost $36,000. Even with cash in hand, obtaining desirable time is difficult, for the TV executives are usually anxious to protect their most popular shows from the incursions of a mere candidate for the presidency of the United States.

The greatest problem, however, is simply attracting the attention of the public to a political broadcast at any hour. The rating services reported that on the evening of October 29, for example, some 14 million Americans watched *Peyton Place* while on a rival network, Goldwater drew his peak audience of the campaign—7.3 million. Most of the senator's viewers were already his faithful supporters (though some who were not wrote angry letters because *Baileys of Balboa* was cancelled to make way for the candidate). None of President Johnson's sponsored TV appearances did even this well.

What was missing, of course, was the drama of 1960 when 65 million to 70 million viewers watched each of four debates by the presidential candidates. It can be argued convincingly that the format of those debates—the disjointed questions and the brief chances for explanation—put a premium on glibness over force of argument. But it is clear that, whatever the faults, those broadcasts caused more Americans to look and to listen for themselves than ever before or since in a presidential race. It is hardly an accident that the 1960 race drew the greatest proportion of eligible voters ever to go to the polls.

Something of that interest and excitement must be recaptured, for it is the only way to get the candidates and the issues to the great mass of voters so they can make an intelligent choice. I am not talking about the synthetic interest and the contrived excitement of the traditional political rally, which was exemplified by Senator Goldwater's tumultuous appearance at Madison Square Garden in New York City on October 21. Some 18,000 screaming partisans crammed every corner of the vast arena to urge their tiger to "give 'em hell." He proceeded to oblige. The speech that resulted could hardly have convinced any wavering voter—if one could be found in this improbable place. When we broadcast this event on television the following day, we were appalled by the excessive belligerence and harshness that came through. It was obvious that what is appropriate for the bull ring is out of place in the drawing room.

There is one way to circumvent outlandish costs, the senseless hurly-burly and the torrent of trivia that marked the 1964 campaign. As a basis for discussion I propose that in 1968 the major presidential candidates share eight one-hour television shows—one a week, on all networks—for the eight weeks prior to Election Day. In at least four of the shows the two candidates would divide the program into equal segments, with both men discussing a predetermined topic. They need not be in the same studio or even the same city. The format of the other four programs would be as flexible as candidate preference and circumstance might dictate.

If the two parties paid for this television effort, it would not even be necessary to amend the unwieldy "equal time provision" of the Communications Act. The cost would be about $750,000 per viewing hour, or a total of six million dollars for the eight weeks, to be shared equally by the two parties. This is less than half of the sum spent on television by the two parties in the recent campaign, with negligible results in terms of public enlightenment.

I believe that as a condition of accepting the nomination of a political party, a candidate should agree—not by force of law but by force of reason and public opinion—to participate in these TV presentations. There seem to me only three objections to such a procedure, none of which has real merit.

First, there are many people who object to having their entertainment interrupted by anything so mundane as a discussion by presidential candidates of national issues. To state this objection is to answer it.

Second, there are fears in some quarters that an incumbent President who is a candidate might inadvertently make some security slip. To meet this objection, the programs could be taped and screened by security experts.

Third, there is the doctrine "Never Give a Sucker an Even Break"—the idea that an incumbent should refuse to help his opponent become well known to the public. President Johnson apparently used this reasoning in refusing Senator Goldwater's invitation to appear with him on a paid telecast, at Goldwater's expense or with expenses shared by the two parties. This reasoning may make sense from an incumbent's point of view, but not in the perspective of the public interest.

The American people have both a right and an overriding need to make their decision on a better basis than the frantic and yet somehow dull and dreary campaign of 1964. This sorry situation will continue to exist so long as the public allows politicians to worship the past and ignore the real problems of the modern campaign. A better way is readily available. Motion and emotion are no substitute for the good sense and full debate that the election of a President demands.

William Glaser
TELEVISION AND VOTING TURNOUT

Whenever an innovation enters politics or any other area of social life, people speculate about its effects. The search for effects has been a central theme of mass media research for decades. And since television from the start seemed such a gripping instrument and so widely distributed, it was assumed that television "must" affect the political behavior of its audience. This paper will examine whether television use is associated with voting turnout, whether television's association with voting turnout differs from the effects of other mass media, and whether television affects some people more than others. The article is a secondary analysis of data from several nationwide sample surveys.

Some observers have guessed that television has important effects on voting turnout. They believe that television has direct effects by continually reminding people to vote through exhortations in spot announcements and in speeches. They believe that television raises the level of political interest by graphic presentation of the news and by creating a closer contact between a candidate and viewer than can be provided by other media. Like commercial advertisers seeking higher sales, civic organizations attempt to stimulate turnout by heavy investments of their budgets and efforts in television. These hypotheses appear plausible: research before the age of television suggested that communications media are increasingly persuasive over attitudes and actions as they come closer to personal influence; and since television presents the viewer face-to-face with messengers and persuaders, one might think it

From "Television and Voting Turnout," by William A. Glaser. *Public Opinion Quarterly*, Vol. 24, Spring 1965. Reprinted by permission. Dr. Glaser is a Research Associate, Bureau of Applied Social Research, Columbia University.

peculiarly effective. Some early research provided apparent corroboration: as television watching rates increased among individuals, so did turnout.

But one might approach the subject more hesitantly. Research about the other mass media has failed to reveal the clear-cut effects once predicted for them, and one might expect that television, too, would have only limited effects upon certain types of people under special circumstances. Some research seems to corroborate this skeptical view. Herbert Simon's ecological data from Iowa showed that counties with widespread ownership of television sets had turnouts no higher than counties with low television density. Comparing national turnout rates over the period since women's suffrage, Angus Campbell finds that they have risen because of other social factors—including the advent of radio several decades ago—but do not appear to have increased because of the introduction of television. Comparing successive interview surveys, Campbell finds that levels of interest and information—both correlates of political participation—have not risen since the advent of television. Doubt about the special efficacy of television alone is consistent with several studies suggesting that the effects of television on candidate choice depend on many other personal predispositions, social stimuli, and media effects.

RECALL OF REMINDERS TO VOTE

Television acquaints many people with political information that they might have missed or underemphasized in the newspapers and over radio. Several studies have documented the immense public exposure to politics that has resulted from television, an exposure far greater than that achieved by previous media, particularly during presidential elections.

The widespread public use of television has led to heavy reliance upon it during the get-out-the vote campaigns sponsored by civic organizations, although the other media are not neglected. Conducted by the American Heritage Foundation, the Advertising Council, and other public service associations, these promotional campaigns consist of one-minute, thirty-second, and twenty-second films that remind people to register and vote. Kits including both films and literature are furnished without charge to all American television stations and networks. Similar recorded statements and literature are given to all radio stations, while mats for ads are sent without charge to newspapers and magazines. The television and radio stations are expected to donate time for such public service announcements as a condition for keeping their licenses from the Federal Communications Commission, but no statutory obligations control the newspapers.

At first sight, the data seem to document the superiority of television. According to Table 1, people recall reminders through television more than through the other media, and they can describe the television reminders far more readily. The salience of television is even more evident from Table 2. Television ranks at or near the top among all types of media user. Only the radio listeners and newspaper readers recall reminders more frequently from any other channels, and even they are able to *describe* the television reminders more easily or almost as easily. Among those who rely on both television and another medium for

TABLE 1. *Percentages Recalling Reminders to Vote (N ≡ 1,645)*

Media	Reminded	Could Describe
Television	69	22
Newspapers	57	8
Radio	40	3
By mail	28	2
Posters	22	2
Outdoor billboards	20	2
Magazines	17	1
Movies	6	*
None of these	17	64

* Less than 1 per cent.

QUESTIONS: "Through which of these ways, if any, do you remember having been reminded to register or to vote?" Respondents were shown a card listing the various media in the table, in an order different from the one given here.

"Which of these appeals can you recall well enough to describe?"

SOURCE: Gallup Survey 638 K, November 1960. Data in Tables 1 through 5 are previously unpublished and are released with the permission of the American Heritage Foundation and the American Institute of Public Opinion.

information, television is consistently listed as reminding more people. Among the apathetic, too, television is cited more often.

In part, the more frequent recall of reminders over television may be due to the greater impact of the medium itself. Some experimental studies have found that people remember information best—in the order of successful recall—over television, radio, and print. On the other hand, television reminders may be recalled more often because they are encountered more often. Nielsen Ratings and other estimates suggest that the Register-and-Vote campaign conducted during 1960 by the Advertising Council and the American Heritage Foundation had the following results: 2.5 billion home impressions from commercial televi-

TABLE 2. *Recalling Reminders to Vote, by Type of Media User*

Principal Source of Information	Per Cent Reminded by			Per Cent Who Could Describe Reminders from			Number of Cases
	Tele-vision	Radio	News-papers	Tele-vision	Radio	News-papers	
Television	72	26	40	24	1	5	385
Print (magazines and newspapers)	68	43	68	20	4	12	588
Radio	38	47	36	9	10	6	87
Television and print	78	37	67	27	2	6	287
Television and radio	73	50	37	24	7	0	41
Print and radio	57	63	65	17	8	6	63
Television, print, and radio	75	52	65	22	3	7	143
None	42	29	39	13	3	6	31

QUESTION for classifying type of media user: "Where do you get most of your information about what's going on in the world—from magazines, TV, radio or newspapers?"
Source: Gallup Survey 638 K, November 1960.

sion networks and stations, where a "home impression" is one message heard once in one home; over 200 million home impressions from commercial radio networks and stations; 3,340 million lines of advertising in newspapers throughout the country; advertisements in magazines with circulation of over 25 million.

EFFECTIVENESS OF REMINDERS

If televised reminders are more salient and more frequently encountered, are they more effective in getting out the vote? Table 3 presents the voting rates among people who could recall and describe the messages from the various channels. Being reminded by any of the media—including television—may lead to higher voting rates than not receiving (or not remembering) such messages. But the special superiority of television now disappears. Reminders may be far more effective by mail and slightly more effective in the press. As other students of the mass media have pointed out, the recall of messages is not the same thing as the stimulation to action.

Of course, Table 3 must be interpreted with the usual cautions about inferring effects from respondents' reports about experience and behavior. Nonvoters may not recall reminders from certain media, thus inflating the apparent statistical effectiveness of those media. Certain media may appear to rank high because they solicit persons with con-

TABLE 3.   *Turnout and the Recall of Reminders to Vote*

| | Percentages Who Voted | | Number of Cases | |
Media	Among Those Reminded by Each of the Media	Among Those Who Could Describe Reminders	Reminded	Could Describe
Television	81	81	1,112	348
Newspapers	83	88	930	125
Radio	81	72	642	54
By mail	91	91	453	33
Posters	83	86	358	37
Outdoor billboards	84	68	324	37
Magazines	83	(10 cases)	268	15
Movies	85	(3 cases)	88	4
None of these	65	76	273	1,036

SOURCE: Gallup Survey 638 K, November 1960.

scientious voting habits: for example, reminders may be sent by mail disproportionately to those affiliated with political and civic organizations, while newspapers are read and recalled disproportionately by the better educated and by those more interested in politics.

Recalling messages declines by social class, as does turnout itself. Are there any social groups for whom television reminders make a special difference? Table 4 compares turnout rates for persons of various educational backgrounds who did and did not recall reminders to vote. Re-

TABLE 4.   *Education and Response to Reminders*

| | Per Cent Who Voted | | | | Number of Cases | | | |
Recall of Messages from Each Medium	Grammar School and Less	Did Not Complete High School	High School Graduate	College	Grammar School and Less	Did Not Complete High School	High School Graduate	College
Television:								
Reminded	71	81	83	88	263	216	347	283
Not re-minded	59	70	90	86	225	115	71	85
Newspapers:								
Reminded	80	79	83	87	192	183	282	270
Not re-minded	56	74	88	89	296	148	136	98
Radio:								
Reminded	72	79	84	86	148	115	189	187
Not re-minded	63	76	85	90	340	216	229	181

SOURCE: Gallup Survey 638 K, November 1960.

minders in general seem to make a difference for the grammar school group and for the dropouts from high school, but less so for those with more education. Television does not have special effects: hearing reminders from all three channels is associated with turnout differences; although television appears "stronger" than radio, it may be "weaker" than newspapers. When other socio-economic variables are run according to the format of Table 4, the same results occur: the lowest social class appears sensitive to reminders while higher classes are not; reminders seem to have so little effect on the higher classes that often recall is inversely related to turnout; television appears "stronger" than radio and "weaker" than newspapers, a theme that will recur throughout this paper.

The usual *caveat* must govern the interpretation of data like those in Table 4. Statistical differences may reflect an increment in turnout due to additional stimuli. Or perhaps lower-class persons who

TABLE 5.   *Knowledge and Response to Reminders*

Recall of Messages from Each Medium	Per Cent Who Voted among Those Who Gave		Number of Cases	
	Correct Answer	Incorrect or No Answer	Correct Answer	Incorrect or No Answer
Television:				
Reminded	88	73	615	497
Not reminded	87	62	179	322
Newspapers:				
Reminded	88	75	537	393
Not reminded	86	62	257	426
Radio:				
Reminded	87	71	376	266
Not reminded	88	67	418	553

Question for ascertaining knowledge: "Do you happen to know what is meant by the term 'balancing the federal budget'?" (If yes): "What?"
SOURCE: Gallup Survey 638 K, November 1960.

report recalling messages over the mass media are simply more alert and articulate generally, and higher turnout habits are part of their more active way of life. But the special sensitivity to stimuli by the less politically involved has been documented by me elsewhere, and it would be consistent to discover that otherwise comparable lower-class people are more likely than upper-class people to show large turnout differences when some are stimulated.

A more direct test of the special susceptibility to reminders among the less involved politically appears in Table 5. The questionnaire surveys available to me contained various tests of political understanding. Table 5 classifies respondents by whether they understood the meaning of "balancing the budget." As the table shows, reminders make little difference to those with greater knowledge but are associated with turnout differences among those with less. As in the other findings of this paper, television appears "weaker" than newspapers but "stronger" than radio.

ASSOCIATION BETWEEN MEDIA USE AND TURNOUT

If the transmission of turnout reminders over television has uncertain effects upon turnout, what are the results of television use generally? Tables 6 through 9 tell how watching television, reading newspapers, and listening to radio are associated with turnout. The same results appear whether the variables are mere ownership of television and radio sets, length of time using the media, or getting political information from the media.

Whether it is television watching or newspaper reading, the break comes between those who do and those who don't. Television owners (and watchers) vote at higher rates than non-owners (and non-watchers). Newspaper readers vote at higher rates than those who do not read. But length of time watching and reading does not add successively higher increments in turnout. Voting is relatively easy and socially expected—particularly in presidential years—and only low threshholds of motivation and social stimulation need be crossed. Only for more difficult acts are successive stimuli likely to affect a steadily increasing number of people. The relative ease of voting limits the sizes of the associations between media use and turnout: most of the nonusers vote anyway, because voting is socially expected, because personal contact influences them, or because of other reasons.

Perhaps uniquely powerful influences are expected from television's personal images, thorough absorption of viewers' attention, and long hours of viewing. . . . The association between television use and turnout is *lower* than the association between newspaper reading and turnout. . . . Either newspapers are more "stimulating" than television programs, or newspaper reading and television tend to be parts of slightly different styles of life, with newspaper readers being more conscientious, informed, and interested in politics.

A remarkable and consistent pattern . . . is the present weakness of radio listening, once a significant correlate of turnout. Whether the variable is set ownership or listening in general, radio use is independent of turnout. One might think that listening to campaign speeches and special events would strengthen the association, but the result according to the data . . . is a weakening. Most people do not listen to speeches and special events on radio. . . . Past predictions about the decline of radio as a political vehicle in the television age have been borne out.

Approximately the same relationship between media use and turnout holds true when the full sample is partitioned by background variables. . . . The well-known turnout differences between social categories are evident: at each level of media use men vote more than women, the upper classes more than the lower, and, in general, the better educated more than the less educated. Within each social group, turnout jumps between those who do not and do watch television and read newspapers. Classifying people by background variables does not reduce these percentage differences, and therefore something else is at work besides the well-known relationships between media use, and—on the other hand—sex, education, and social class. And something else is at work in highly publicized presidential elections besides the stimulating effects of the media alone: the basic answer seems to lie in general patterns of political involvement and political apathy, of which media use is a part.

SELECTIVE EFFECTIVENESS OF THE MEDIA

Let us assume that the turnout differences . . . reflect the effects of the mass media. (The assumption, as I have said earlier, is debatable.) Are the media in general and is television in particular more stimulating for some population groups than for others? Are certain categories of the electorate likely to drop out if they are not presented with televised stimuli? Measuring effectiveness by percentage differences between users and non-users can be done in two ways: (1) by comparing rises in the aggregate turnout rates for each population group, as in the "per cent who voted" rows of the table; (2) by comparing the success of the media in bringing out those who might not have voted in the absence of the media, as in the "Relative increment in turnout" rows of the table.

By the first criterion, television and newspapers may succeed in raising the turnout rates of the less involved groups more than the rates of the more involved. Media use brings turnout differences slightly closer together between men and women, between the rich and poor, and between the better educated and the less educated. Thus, media stimuli might bring into the electorate a larger *number* of the politically less involved than of the population groups more interested in politics. There are hints that television may be slightly less effective in narrowing the gaps than newspaper reading. . . .

If we define effectiveness as the capacity to bring to the polls people who otherwise might have stayed home . . . the case for selective effectiveness weakens. If the media are effective in bringing out the apathetic, the relative increments . . . should be consistently higher for women than for men, for the poor than for the rich, and for the less educated than for the better. But no such consistent pattern can be found for the media generally or for television alone. The less involved groups have more nonvoters in the absence of media use; therefore, even though the media may help bring more of them to the polls, many are left unaffected.

MEDIA EFFECTS ON THE EXECUTION OF INTENTIONS

A better way to infer effects is to study processes over time. Table 6 shows how pre-election turnout intentions are carried out, when persons are classified by their exposure to speeches and news during the intervening campaign.

Two common facts are evident in Table 6. As in much media research, media stimuli in real-life situations do not strike people randomly: those who intend to vote early in the campaign have the higher frequencies of subsequent media exposure. People are more likely to defect from an intention to vote than to reverse an intention not to vote; consequently, effectiveness increases as the negative trend approaches zero and as turnout rates increase among those intending to vote (i.e. the sorts of data appearing in columns 2 and 4 of Table 6).

The trends in the second column of Table 6 suggest that newspaper reading is more effective than television watching in regulating the carrying out of intentions. Readers' over-all voting behavior declines during the campaign less than nonreaders' rates; television viewers' rates do not decline consistently less than nonviewers' rates. The same difference appears in column 4 of Table 6: among those who intend to vote, newspaper reading produces a turnout increase over the absence of reading, while television viewing produces only ambiguous results. As in previously mentioned relationships between radio and turnout, listening appears to lack any effects on the fulfillment of intentions. Last-minute exposure by television and radio thus does not seem to bring out the vote.

CONCLUSION

Television leaves a more lasting impression than newspapers and radio when conveying reminders to vote. But recollection of televised messages does not appear to have a potency lacking in any other mass medium: recollection of a reminder in any mass medium is associated with higher turnout than the absence of any recollection. Newspaper reading may be more effective than television watching in affecting turnout and in affecting the fulfillment of intentions to vote. Or, perhaps a more accurate statement is that newspaper reading and television watching are associated with partly different modes of life with different political patterns. When practiced jointly, newspaper reading and televi-

TABLE 6. Media Use, Intention, and Turnout

Questions and Responses	Per Cent Who Expressed Intention to Vote in September and October (1)	Relative Trend between September–October and November* (2)	Per Cent Who Voted in November			Number of Cases		
			Total Per Cent Who Voted in November (3)	Among Those Who Intended to Vote (4)	Among Those Who Did Not Intend to Vote (5)	Total (6)	Intended to Vote (7)	Did Not Intend to Vote (8)
"Did you watch any programs about the campaign on television?"								
No	63	−8	58	90	3	233	146	87
Yes, just one or two	86	−13	75	86	4	181	155	26
Yes, several	86	−3	83	95	18	509	436	73
Yes, good many	90	−6	85	93	12	832	752	80
"Did you read about the campaign in any newspaper?" (If yes): "How much did you read newspaper articles about the election?"								
No	64	−13	56	84	16	344	220	124
Yes, from time to time; once in a great while	81	−6	76	94	6	402	326	76
Yes, often	90	−2	89	93	7	210	190	20
Yes, regularly	95	−4	91	95	5	763	722	41
"Did you listen to any speeches or discussions about the campaign on the radio?"								
No	83	−4	79	94	10	1,014	837	177
Yes, just one or two	87	−12	76	88	4	178	154	24
Yes, several	85	−4	82	94	11	303	259	44
Yes, good many	91	−9	83	89	18	255	233	22

* "Relative trend" shows the amount of change undergone by an aggregate group relative to the number of members who intended to vote at the time of the pre-election interview. It is computed by the following formula: (number who voted in November − number who intended to vote in September) / number who intended to vote in September.

SOURCE: University of Michigan, Survey Research Center, Project 440, Pre- and Post-election Panel Interviews, 1960.

sion watching are associated with very high rates of turnout, but television may "add" less to the combination than newspapers. The association between media use and turnout distinguishes only between users and non-users: extra hours do not steadily increase voting probabilities. Radio listening has become independent of turnout. Perhaps television is more effective in stimulating increases in the voting of less politically involved people, but the data are uneven and the same differential effect (if any) may be true of newspaper reading. All these generalizations are gross statistical associations based on national sample surveys; adequate verification and more specific conclusions would require more precisely designed samples and variables.

These statements are based on surveys in presidential elections, when there are abundant communications through many channels, and high turnouts; possibly, media effects differ in other situations. Possibly, television would have more specific influence in elections about which the public was more apathetic. Or, possibly, the advent of television has placed a higher floor under the public's interest in presidential elections, thus preventing repetitions of the low turnouts sometimes encountered in the past.

Although television reminders to vote appear to have only limited effects, perhaps they could be more influential if they were better adapted to the situation of the nonvoter. At present, the messages reach and are recalled disproportionately by the upper classes and better educated, who are likely to vote without reminders. Also, these messages are phrased for all audiences together. Reminders might stimulate more voting if they were aimed more frequently at the lower classes and at other groups with lower turnouts, and if they were phrased specifically to appeal to these audiences. Also, turnout reminders should not merely exhort people to vote but should explain how to overcome barriers. Although most people find voting easy, many nonvoters are confused by legal prerequisites, by registration and absentee ballot procedures, by ignorance of the electoral system, etc. Thus, turnout reminders over television must increase knowledge and skill as well as increase motivation. This implies varying turnout reminders in each community according to the situations confronted by the mobile, the sick, and the apathetic.

A common generalization in media research today is that the effect of any medium depends on how the subject responds to all other media. Therefore, the effects of television on turnout (or on anything else) can best be identified by focused interviewing involving each subject's total communications experience. Television watching is closely connected with some newspaper reading and with some personal conversations within the family, and both these other variables—particularly family behavior—have higher correlations with turnout than has television alone. Thus, one future problem is to identify how television adds to or subtracts from the influence of the press and family; another problem is to identify how television affects the collective political behavior of the family.

Finally, another common generalization in contemporary media research is that users approach the media with a variety of needs and predispositions, and thus they acquire diverse satisfactions. Thus, any precise identification of the effects of television watching on voting must identify the uses sought and made of television by the various types of viewer: the effects of television upon the viewer's political behavior will doubtless prove to be a subtle product of the total interaction between him and his set.

Stanley Kelley, Jr.
THE PRESIDENTIAL CAMPAIGN

The initial strategy of a political campaign may be usefully regarded as an investment plan in which the level of investment in the several undertakings is set in accordance with estimates of the likely return in votes from each. Strategists may revise these estimates in the course of a campaign, as reports come in from pollsters and as events work for or against the success of particular ventures. The strategists of the side that is losing are particularly likely to take a second look at their initial decisions and to alter them; thus, a campaign may change its character considerably even while it is in progress. The 1964 Republican presidential campaign is a case in point.

In July and August conditions became—or at least seemed to become—increasingly favorable to the success of the southern-backlash strategy. On July 19 Governor George Wallace of Alabama, apparently under strong pressure from his backers, abandoned his candidacy for the Presidency. By doing so he greatly increased Senator Goldwater's chance to become the political beneficiary of the feeling that the Negro revolution was proceeding too fast and going too far. That feeling was given

From *The National Election of 1964*, Edited by Milton C. Cummings, Jr., The Brookings Institution, Washington, D.C., 1966. Reprinted by permission. Dr. Kelley is Professor of Politics, Princeton University.

added force by riots in the Negro ghettos of Harlem, the Bedford-Stuyvesant section of Brooklyn, and Rochester in late July, and in Jersey City, Elizabeth, Paterson, the Chicago suburb of Dixmoor, and North Philadelphia in the month of August. When the Democratic convention opened on August 24, Democratic uneasiness about the possibility of extensive white backlash was probably at its height. In an article entitled "White 'Backlash' Scares Democrats," Robert C. Albright reported on August 30 that one Democratic tactician had said, "Some days I am convinced we are going to win big—I mean by a historic landslide. Then something goes wrong and I cross my fingers. We could be so wrong."

Both the administration and the leaders of the civil rights movement took steps to minimize backlash, and what they did removed some of the tension and attention from relations between Negroes and whites in later stages of the campaign. On July 21, three days after the rioting in Harlem began, President Johnson dispatched two hundred FBI agents to New York City with orders to investigate the causes of the riots there; he took the occasion to state his belief that "American citizens have a right to protection of life and limb—whether driving along a highway in Georgia, a road in Mississippi or a street in New York City." And the President's efforts to tame the civil rights movement for campaign purposes did not stop there. According to Theodore White, "Every form of pressure—political, financial, investigative, and persuasive—was quietly applied to the problem [minimizing white backlash] in maneuvers directed from the White House." The object of these maneuvers was to get civil rights groups to abandon "hell-raising" in favor of registration drives. On July 29 four prominent leaders of the civil rights movement did ask for a "broad curtailment, if not total moratorium" of demonstrations until after election day, and a substantial decline in the numbers of organized demonstrations followed in apparent response to their plea. There were also substantial increases in Negro registrations.

The failure of southern Democratic leaders to defect from the Johnson cause in large numbers was a further blow to the southern-backlash strategy. A few maintained silence, a few declared themselves neutral, and others did little to help the national ticket, but there were few outright bolters. On August 16 the *New York Times* had reported that Governors Orville Faubus of Arkansas, George Wallace of Alabama, and Paul Johnson of Mississippi would support Senator Goldwater. Wallace and Johnson did so, but Faubus finally came out for the President, as did six other southern governors. The only bolters in the entire southern congressional delegation were Senator Strom Thurmond of South Carolina, Representative Albert Watson of the same state, and Representative John Bell Williams of Mississippi.

As the President's relations with dissident southerners improved,

Senator Goldwater's relations with moderate Republican leaders went from bad to worse. On July 17, two days after the Goldwater nomination, former President Eisenhower declared himself unable to give active support to his party's nominee until Goldwater had explained his (Goldwater's) views on extremism, and the former President was joined in his decision to "wait and see" by many other prominent Republicans. The Senator and his aides then moved to conciliate the Republican moderates. On July 23 National Chairman Dean Burch sent a letter to Republican state chairmen, soliciting their advice on the conduct of the campaign, and assuring them that they would be consulted on appointments of the state chairmen of the Citizens for Goldwater-Miller organizations. In early August Senator Goldwater, in a letter to Richard Nixon, paraphrased the statement regarding extremism in his acceptance speech, and Nixon expressed satisfaction with the thought in its new form. At a conference of party leaders in Hershey, Pennsylvania, on August 12, which had been arranged at Goldwater's request, the Senator declared the Eisenhower-Dulles foreign policy to be his own, promised to support the United Nations and North Atlantic Treaty Organization, pledged conscientious administration of the Civil Rights Act of 1964, said that he favored strengthening the Social Security system, repudiated the support of extremists, and denied any desire to read anyone out of the Republican party. This speech persuaded General Eisenhower to endorse Goldwater but little seemed to come of it otherwise.

In September and October, more and more Republican leaders took steps to disassociate themselves from the Goldwater candidacy. Those who at first refused to give their endorsement remained adamant, and those who declared their support made it increasingly clear that such support was nominal. Governor Rockefeller was seen pocketing Goldwater buttons offered him, and Governor Scranton, who earlier had made several speeches on Goldwater's behalf, in late October introduced the Senator at a rally not, as tradition would have it, as "the next President of the United States," but as "the Republican candidate for President." Near the end of the campaign even many conservative Republican candidates for office went it alone.

Republican hopes were buoyed up very briefly by the disclosure on October 14 that Walter Jenkins, President Johnson's chief assistant and an associate of the President's for many years, had been arrested for indecent acts. The incident both drew attention to and seemed to confirm Senator Goldwater's charges that the administration was infected by corruption in the highest circles. Chairman Dean Burch said that the incident raised grave questions of national security, while bumper stickers issued by the Republican National Committee declared, "No Wonder They Turned the Lights Off at the White House." Chalmers Roberts, writing in the *Washington Post* on October 16, described the Johnson staff as "deeply worried" about the political consequences of the Jenkins case.

The sudden fall from power of the Soviet Union's Premier Nikita Khrushchev on October 15 and the detonation of a nuclear device by the Red Chinese one day later, however, relegated the Jenkins story to the inside pages of newspapers and turned the attention of voters to foreign policy. President Johnson spoke to the nation on the meaning of these developments and restated, in a nonpartisan context, one of the basic themes of his campaign: "We must be ready to defend the national interest and to negotiate the common interest.... Those who test our courage will find it strong, and those who seek our friendship will find it honorable." A survey taken by the Louis Harris organization after the Jenkins incident, Krushchev's removal, and the Red Chinese nuclear test, showed 60 percent of the voters favoring President Johnson, 34 percent Senator Goldwater, and 6 percent undecided. Only 5 percent of those who told Harris' interviewers that they intended to vote for Johnson said that the revelations about Walter Jenkins had made them think less well of the President.

The Republicans seem to have chosen mid-October, or shortly before, to reassess their strategy. That the possibility of a Goldwater victory had by this time almost evaporated must have been clear from polls commissioned by the Republican National Committee. These showed defeatism to be widespread among Goldwater supporters—only 37 percent of those stating an intention to vote for the Republican candidate thought he would win. In a list of eighteen issues there was but one that voters thought would be better handled by Senator Goldwater than by President Johnson—the Bobby Baker case—and even so, relatively few believed the case incriminated the President in any way. A significant number of voters saw Goldwater as a radical; few saw Johnson as such. Over one-third of the public believed the Senator to be opposed to Social Security, despite his many protestations to the contrary. Voters thought a nuclear war more likely under Goldwater than under Johnson, and by a margin of about 5 to 1. Extensive white backlash had failed to materialize. Opposition to the civil rights movement had increased after the riots of July and August, but most voters did not blame the administration for the unrest, nor did they see Goldwater and the Republicans as better equipped to resolve racial tensions. And as demonstrations became fewer and rioting ceased, concern with the civil rights issue also declined. By October the international situation—not civil rights—was the problem most frequently cited as the nation's most serious one.

Whether or not the Republicans consciously made minimizing

defeat the goal of their campaigning in late October, they acted as if they had. In the campaign's final three weeks Senator Goldwater for the first time visited Nebraska, South Dakota, Nevada, Wyoming, Colorado, and Washington—all states which had originally been counted on by the Republicans for hard-core support. He also gave substantial amounts of time to Arizona, Wisconsin, and Iowa in this period, while downgrading (relative to the proportion of his time given them in the campaign as a whole) New York, Illinois, New Jersey, and Michigan. In his speeches after October 15, Goldwater devoted himself to a narrower range of issues than he had earlier. He spent very little time outlining the choice he offered voters in welfare and economic policy. Instead, he denounced "forced integration," attacked the Kennedy-Johnson administration for its alleged foreign policy blunders, hit hard at corruption in government, and pronounced Lyndon Johnson incapable of providing the kind of moral leadership the nation required.

The Democrats, as the campaign came to an end, seem to have decided that they could enlarge upon a victory already within their grasp. In the last three weeks before election day, President Johnson spent a considerable amount of time in states that, for the most part, would have to be considered quite marginal to any winning strategy. It was then that he visited Delaware, Kansas, and South Carolina for the first time. He gave an inordinate amount—about one-third—of his time to New York in this period. He also devoted sizable amounts of time to Florida, South Carolina, Georgia, and Missouri. Toward the end of the campaign, reporters noted a slight change in the President's speaking style—as Richard Rovere put it, "He moved from a defense of past Democratic administrations to evangelistic and almost utopian views of the future. . . ." Illustrative of this change of tone were speeches in Pittsburgh and New York. In the former city the President heralded the advent of the Great Society. In New York he made a prediction:

> . . . this Administration has passed more legislation, made more progress and fulfilled more promises than any Administration since the New Deal of Franklin Roosevelt.
> And we've just begun.

CONCLUDING OBSERVATIONS

At this point it will be useful to compare the strategy adopted by Senator Goldwater and his staff with those which have shaped other recent Republican presidential campaigns. The comparison makes more evident both the degree to which, and the ways in which, the 1964 Republican campaign broke with the past.

The strategy of the Goldwater campaign was not distinctive in the value it assigned to get-out-the-vote efforts. The strategists of the Nixon and Eisenhower campaigns had also regarded such efforts as of great importance.

The personal attack on President Johnson in 1964 had no coun terpart in the Republican campaigns of 1960 or 1956, but this did not make it unusual either. In the 1952 campaign against Adlai Stevenson, moderate Republicans had charged President Truman with the same kind of misconduct that was attributed to Johnson. In 1964 Goldwater's leading rival for the nomination, Governor William Scranton of Pennsylvania, was ready to make the campaign against Johnson "a very personal one."

The attitude taken by Senator Goldwater toward parties and partisanship in 1964 differed only marginally from that adopted by Eisenhower in 1956 and Nixon in 1960. The speeches of the three Republican leaders contained few positive references to the Republican party and were almost entirely devoid of negative references to the Democratic party. Goldwater began his campaign by opposing *administration* policies and the record of the *administration* to *Republican* policies, and to the *Republican* record in the White House and in Congress, but he did not persist in doing so. He identified himself with his party more frequently than Nixon did in 1960, but no more often than had Eisenhower in 1956.

The strategies of the Republican presidential campaigns of 1964 and 1960 also differed only marginally in the states selected as the foci of the most intensive campaigning. Nixon and Goldwater did allocate their scheduled time among regions in a somewhat different way.... Goldwater gave less time to the Northeast and more to the South than Nixon had. The list of the ten states where Nixon was scheduled to campaign longest, however (and to which as a group he devoted about 63 percent of his time), includes seven of the ten states that appear in a similar Goldwater list. (Since a willingness to engage the Democrats in a battle for the industrial states has been regarded by some as a hallmark of the moderate Republican way, it is noteworthy that Kennedy and Goldwater lists of this sort include eight of the same states.)

Senator Goldwater's foreign policy position—in substance—was very like that of the two men who had preceded him at the head of the Republican ticket, although it differed considerably in tone. Like Eisenhower in 1952, he criticized the administration's policy toward the "captive nations" of eastern Europe and the foreign policy "blunders" of the Democrats. Like Nixon, the Senator was for peace through preparedness, and firmness in dealing with Communist nations. He put much less emphasis than either Eisenhower or Nixon, however, on negotiation as an instrument for attaining his foreign policy objectives; and he did not, as

Nixon had, ascribe virtue to refusing to "trade insults" with the Russians.

It was Senator Goldwater's stand on domestic issues that made his campaign differ in a fundamental way from the Eisenhower and Nixon campaigns. The difference was not primarily ideological. Goldwater's attack on "the regimented society," "handouts," "unwarranted intervention in our private economic lives," and on "centralized power" paralleled attacks by President Eisenhower on "big government," "paternalistic direction by Washington bureaucrats," and "socialized medicine." Goldwater's expressions of faith in "private property, free competition, hard work" echoed Eisenhower's. But General Eisenhower took pains in 1952 to assure voters that a vote for him was *not* a vote to repeal the New Deal. In 1964 Senator Goldwater gave no such assurances. Eisenhower in 1956 and Nixon in 1960 favored measures that implied an important role for the federal government in the solution of domestic problems, while Senator Goldwater had hardly any suggestions for action on the home front.

Insofar as its basic strategy was concerned, then, the case for considering the 1964 Republican presidential campaign as precedent-breaking rests on fairly narrow grounds. Senator Goldwater chose to appeal for the votes of southern whites on a basis almost certain to alienate northern Negroes. He failed to couple attacks on big government, bureaucracy, and spending with assurances that, were he elected, something very like the status quo would obtain with respect to federal welfare programs and economic and foreign policy. For the rest, his campaign, particularly in its final weeks, was not very different from the kind of campaign one would have expected on behalf of a moderate Republican leader.

What lessons can be learned from what happened?

Many observers have been quick to link as cause and effect the conservatism of Senator Goldwater's positions on issues of public policy and the one-sidedness of the outcome of the election; Goldwater's conservatism, in this view, alienated many voters who otherwise would have voted Republican, while it failed to win him the support of any sizable group of previous nonvoters. Walter Lippmann, for instance, wrote soon after the election that "the returns prove the falsity of the claim ... that there is a great, silent latent majority of 'conservative' Republicans who will emerge as soon as the Republican Party turns its back on 'metooism' and offers them a 'choice.' The Johnson majority is indisputable proof that the voters are in the center." Tom Wicker of the *New York Times* agreed, and went on to argue that Republicans in the present era can win only as a "me-too" party.

This popular view of the meaning of the presidential election of 1964 has won an easier acceptance than it deserves on the basis of the evidence thus far advanced in support of it. The election returns, in and of themselves, proved very little—certainly not that conservatism or any other particular feature of the Goldwater campaign was the cause of the Republicans' overwhelming defeat. The prospects were poor for a close race by any Republican candidate in 1964 because any Republican candidate was fated to run against a popular incumbent President of the majority party in a time of relative peace and prosperity. Moreover, Senator Goldwater was a far from ideal standard-bearer for the conservative Republican cause. Before he ever began to campaign against President Johnson, Goldwater had put himself on record as holding opinions far more extreme than any he expressed in the campaign itself; that he had done so helped the Democrats in their efforts to get voters to see him as an extremist and a radical. The Senator's campaign, finally, was marked by several blunders. To the extent that these facts had anything to do with the one-sidedness of the election's outcome, the severity of Senator Goldwater's defeat cannot be properly attributed solely to the character of the program he offered the electorate.

The strategy adopted by the Senator and his advisers may have contributed to the Republican defeat, but it may also have saved the Republicans from a defeat more disastrous than that which they actually sustained. Angus Campbell, reporting the preliminary findings of the Survey Research Center's study of the 1964 election, suggests that probably Goldwater's stand on civil rights lost votes for him in the North but won votes for him in the South. A moderate Republican candidate might have minimized these northern losses but there is little reason to think he could have matched Goldwater's gains in the southern states, since there is no reason to believe that Governor Wallace would have abandoned his presidential candidacy if the Republicans had nominated a moderate. Campbell suggests also that the broad issue of governmental responsibility raised by Senator Goldwater was "not a major contributor to movements of the vote from normal party positions." It is possible that this issue had an indirect impact on the vote not detected by the Survey Research Center's study that was disadvantageous to Goldwater; this could be the case, for example, if voters who did not react negatively to the Senator's position on domestic policy nevertheless took their cues for voting from those who did. It is also possible, however, that Goldwater's conservatism won him votes indirectly, because it stimulated a great deal of grass-roots activity in his behalf. Whatever the effect of the Republican drive to get out the vote, the Senator's candidacy apparently did inspire considerably more activity by Republicans at the grass-roots level than was in evidence in 1960 and before; and it is reasonable to relate this fact to the strength of his ideological appeal. One can justifiably conclude that the Republican strategy in the 1964 campaign was a losing one and perhaps that it was a desperate one; but, even given what we know now, it can hardly be considered an irrational response to the situation in which the Republicans found themselves.

The campaign and its outcome did show the difficulties of the Goldwater strategy, however, if not its folly. Both Goldwater's stand on civil rights and his statements regarding domestic policies were intended to bring a realignment of forces in party politics. To a certain extent they succeeded in doing so, at least temporarily. One of the more impressive facts about the campaign of 1964, however, was the scarcity of bolters in the top leadership ranks of the southern Democrats. This fact is not so difficult to understand. President Johnson was an odds-on favorite to be reelected. Southern Democratic leaders had a great deal to lose in defecting from his cause—certainly the favor of the President and possibly their congressional seniority rights. Under the circumstances, Senator Goldwater and his staff found that the leaders of the moderate Republicans could be alienated from his candidacy much more easily than southern Democratic leaders could be won to it. Rats desert a sinking ship, one anonymous observer of the 1964 campaign has observed, but they rarely jump off a floating one.

In another respect, Senator Goldwater's campaign efforts must have been even more disappointing to him. He failed to stimulate that debate of "fundamentals" he seems to have expected. Neither the President nor his running mate seriously discussed any of Goldwater's favorite themes. The Senator contended that private enterprise, and not governmental action, could most effectively insure full employment; that states and localities should have a larger share of responsibility for providing public services; that public action against de facto segregation violated the right to free association; and that the Supreme Court's reapportionment decision constituted "judicial legislation." Johnson and Humphrey never attempted to refute any of these contentions. Argument about the points Goldwater raised would have both advertised and lent respectability to them, and the President had little reason to give this kind of aid and comfort to his Republican opponent. As a result, there was certainly no greater, and probably a smaller, element of debate in the 1964 campaign than there had been in earlier ones.

Part Two
The Issues

7
The Urban Crisis

We in the United States have long had a love-hate relationship with the city. Jefferson, and, for that matter, most men of the generation of the Founders, envisioned a Republic of farmers. Sober, industrious, self-reliant cultivators, Jefferson thought, are the source and safety of Republican virtue. "Corruption of morals in the mass of cultivators," he argued, "is a phenomenon of which no age nor nation has furnished an example." But for the denizens of the cities, especially for the property-less workers, he felt horror and contempt. "I view great cities as pestilential to the morals, the health, and the liberties of man," he wrote, and his echo reverberates yet in the United States.

But neither in Jefferson's time nor in our own have men flocked to the cities to find virtue. Men thronged to the city in the eighteenth century and thither they still throng, to find—what? Glory, riches, fulfillment, excitement, sensual delight, warmth, light, and, ironically, safety against the perils of the countryside. More crucially, perhaps, the city is where the action is. The American success story is an urban story. If an American is going to "make it," he will most likely do it in the city.

Perhaps, then, Americans live in the cities only because they have to. Perhaps our cities are gigantic concrete traps in which desperate millions are harassed and threatened by inconvenience and danger, poisoned by deadly effluent both organic and inorganic, oppressed by ubiquitous ugliness, and psychically crushed by loneliness and anxiety. Perhaps, also, city governments are too constitutionally enfeebled, too impoverished, and too unresponsive to the plight of their masses to cope with the *malaise*. The metaphors of pathology characterize most of the contemporary writing about the American city. Universities and private foundations sponsor symposia about our "sick cities." President Johnson and the northern Democrats in Congress have been moved to define the urban problem as a federal problem, and many moderate Republicans, too, have indicated a willingness to attempt to make new definitions of governmental relationships to meet the problem.

Morton and Lucia White, in *The Intellectuals versus the City*, argue persuasively that American intellectuals have, by and large, always detested the city and have written voluminously of their estrangement from it and of their pity for its masses. Today's intellectuals, city men themselves, continue to act out their hostility to the city as they find it. The terms of their criticism, however, are terms of identification and renewal, rather than rejection.

If we turn away from the intellectuals, if we look at the responses of popular culture to the cities, we do not find unqualified antagonism. The movies, the comic strips, popular songs—"Chicago, Chicago's a wonderful town," or "Tell me, what street compares with Mott street in July?"—and jazz find much to celebrate in city life. Mass-produced furniture, ticky-tacky suburbs, land-gulping freeways, cavernous sports stadia, neon-lighted pizza-parlors, motels, and other familiar features of the notorious urban "sprawl" do not seem to upset the city masses so much as they upset intellectuals and city planners.

Thus, we introduce this chapter with questions. Is there really an urban crisis? Are our cities really sick? Professor James Q. Wilson, a Fellow of the Joint Center of Urban Studies, finds that big cities do have a number of serious problems—housing, "blight," crime, race relations, finance, and appropriate governmental arrangements—but he wonders whether it is "urban-ness," as such, that really troubles us and calls forth a literature of crisis.

Probably the most emotion-laden of the contemporary urban problems, the one most likely to catch fire as an issue in political campaigns, is what has come to be called "crime in the streets." The problem is complex. The absolute number of crimes committed (and reported) indubitably is, and has been, on the increase. But then our population, especially in the 15–30 age bracket, is also increasing. More people, more crimes. The more young people increase as a proportion of the population, the more does it appear that the *rate* of crime is increasing. There are more people, and more young people, in cities. There are more victims in cities, more markets, department stores, automobiles, gas stations, liquor stores, and coin boxes. Here it is worth noting that theft, the typical crime committed by young people, is the commonest crime in the cities. Murder, rape, and aggravated assault are *not* increasing any faster than the population, and the *rates* of these headline crimes may actually be decreasing slightly.

The crime that "crime in the streets" refers to is more likely to be felonious assault and/or robbery—for example, purse-snatching or mugging. These take place in the streets. The victims are women, older people, and people who look as though they might be well-heeled.

The term "crime in the streets," like complaints about "welfare loafers," and a "breakdown of law and order," is a familiar shorthand method of complaining about Negroes. Negroes do commit, proportionately, more crimes than white people do. Poor people commit more crimes than rich people. Well-to-do Negroes commit no more crimes than do their white peers. Most of the victims of crimes committed by poor Negroes are other poor Negroes, but there is enough spillover from the ghettos to raise a serious question about the safety of city streets. Because poverty, the ethnic ghetto, and crime are so intricately linked in our time, we present here, in the testimony of Claude Brown, author of *Manchild in the Promised Land,* and Arthur Dunmeyer, a statement about a number of relationships between ghetto life and crime.

Messrs. Brown and Dunmeyer are interested primarily in the cause-effect relationship between ghetto life and crime. William F. Buckley, Jr., though he explicitly recognizes that much urban crime is rooted in the deprivation and despair of poverty, believes that the immediate and crucial problem facing New York City is to find ways to increase the capacity of the police to apprehend criminals and to permit the courts to deal more severely with those apprehended. Deterrence, then, has a high priority in Mr. Buckley's program for dealing with the problem of crime in the streets. Messrs. Brown and Dunmeyer, on the other hand, are not optimistic about the chances for success of a "get tough" policy; they offer themselves as evidence that dealing severely with ghetto juveniles is not a promising approach.

While the crime issue has a high emotional content and offers neat handles for the campaigner, discussions of fiscal and tax policy tend to be muted and, for the average voter, obscure. Yet conservatives and liberals alike, do-gooders and get-toughers together, agree that the localities must very soon find vastly greater revenues if the pressing problems of city life are to be dealt with. Simultaneously, it is clear that the local property tax, the base of most municipal revenue systems, has risen about as far as it can go. Perhaps the most imaginative, but controversial, proposal for putting money into the municipalities is the so called "Heller Plan," or per capita revenue-sharing proposal. Under the proposal, funds from the rich federal income tax base would be returned without strings to the states and localities. The proposal is not without its critics. We present here a brief history of the proposal and the summary of the arguments for and against it.

James Q. Wilson
THE WAR ON CITIES

What, indeed, is the "urban problem"? The language of crisis with which this subject is normally discussed—"sick cities," "the urban crisis," "spreading blight"—is singularly unilluminating. I doubt that most residents of most American cities would recognize in such terms a fair description of the conditions in their communities. Since such words are usually uttered or printed in Washington, D.C., or New York City, perhaps the most we can infer is that life is tough in these two places—though the staggering expense the authors of such words are willing to incur in order to live in the very center of these cities suggests that the "crisis" is at least bearable.

Viewed in historical perspective, and taking American cities as a whole, the conditions of urban life have, by most measures, been getting steadily better, not worse. Nationally, the proportion of families under the poverty line—for purposes of argument, let us take that as a family income of $3,000 a year in constant dollars—declined from 31 percent to 19 percent between 1950 and 1963, and the decline was the greatest in the cities (in the rural areas of our country, by contrast, about *half* the families still live at or near the poverty line). Since the Second World War, there has been a more or less steady decline in the proportion of housing units that are substandard; this improvement has been greatest in the cities, least in the rural areas. (In 1960, less than 3 percent of the dwelling units in cities of 50,000 population and over were dilapidated by Census Bureau standards.) The "flight to the suburbs" has made most people better off—the middle-income family finds the peace and privacy of a suburban home, the lower-income family takes over the larger, sounder structures vacated in the central city. The proportion of young people who drop out of school before getting a high school diploma has been declining steadily, both absolutely and relatively, for about the last

From "The War on Cities," by James Q. Wilson, *The Public Interest*, Number 3, Spring 1966. Reprinted by permission. Mr. Wilson is Associate Professor of Government at Harvard University.

twenty years. Certain forms of violent crime—murder and forcible rape—have declined in rate for the last several decades, though other forms of crime (assault, theft) may have increased (no one knows for certain, because crime statistics are neither completely reliable nor standardized for the changing age composition of the population).

American cities have fully participated in the prosperity of the country—indeed, they have participated more than the rural areas; and this no doubt accounts for the fact that, whatever problems the cities have, people are moving to the cities in very large numbers. But it would be a mistake to try to be unreservedly optimistic about these aggregate trends. Certain classes of people within cities continue to confront problems, and these problems vary with the size and kind of the city in question. Three of these problems are especially noteworthy.

HIGH EXPECTATIONS

First, there is what might be called the "psychological urban problem"—i.e., our expectations are increasing faster than our achievements. As more affluent suburbs spring up, with neat lawns and good schools, the apparent gap between the quality of life in the central city and at the periphery increases. The suburbanites, adjusting rapidly to residential comfort, become more discontented with the conditions that surround the places where they work in the central city, even though these conditions are also (on the average) improving. Those city dwellers who cannot, for reasons of income or race, move to the suburbs, grow increasingly envious of those who can; the prizes of worldly success are held up before their eyes but out of their reach.

Because whites are gaining, in income and housing, faster than Negroes (though they are gaining also), the gap between the two groups is widening. (The full-employment economy of World War II narrowed the gap because of the need to fill manpower shortages; the underemployment prosperity of the 'fifties widened the gap; a continued Vietnamese war and the re-emergence of labor shortages may once again reduce the gap.) Moreover, within the Negro community itself, greater progress is being made in schooling than in income. The fact of Negro life is that a high school diploma is worth less to a Negro than to a white person, and the disparity is most obvious precisely where educational progress has been the greatest—in the cities.

In addition, the central city has remained the place where important members of the commercial and intellectual elite live. This is the group which, more than any other, sets the tone and provides the rhetoric of public discussion on "urban problems." By habit and tradition, it prizes the cultural amenities of the large central city and it tends to resent the spread of lower-class people into areas where these cultural and commercial institutions are established—even though that spread has been caused by the very increases in freedom and prosperity which the elite itself values. In the resulting distress, we see the conflict between the two major functions of the central city—on the one hand, the maintenance of a highly urbane style of life and of a concentrated and diverse market for the exchange of wealth and ideas; on the other hand, the provision of a place in which the lower classes, especially the immigrant lower classes, are housed, employed, educated, and by slow degrees assimilated to the standards of civility of American society. It is no longer possible to keep these two functions geographically separate within the central city, because it is no longer possible to confine the lower classes to high-density ghettoes—they have moved out into low-density ghettoes, thereby consuming much more land area than before, including land around or near the city's universities, hospitals, museums, and theaters.

The psychological urban problem cannot be solved, it can only be coped with. Indeed, it has been caused precisely because so many other problems *have* been coped with, if not solved. Efforts to lessen the gap between expectations and achievements will, in the short run, only make the discontent produced by that gap more acute. That is one of the inevitable tensions in a society committed to self-improvement.

TECHNICAL PROBLEMS, POLITICAL SOLUTIONS

The second kind of urban problem might be called the "technical" problem. By this I mean both that the problems are created because people are living in highly interdependent, dense settlements in an industrial society and that the solutions to these problems are technically feasible. If the problems are not solved, it is not for lack of knowledge. It might be more meaningful, indeed, to call them "political" problems, inasmuch as the obstacles to their solution are largely political.

These problems result partly from the fact that we are constantly getting in each other's way or otherwise committing various nuisances. We pollute the air with soft coal soot and with hydrocarbons from automobile exhausts; we pollute rivers and lakes with industrial and residential sewage; we congest city streets with cars, and sidewalks with pedestrians. The problems are also in part the result of consuming natural resources—e.g., open space and park land—and of making future generations bear the cost of this consumption. (Or to say the same thing in other words: we spend less on urban—and suburban—beauty than would be spent if everyone who will at some time enjoy that beauty were here now to vote on the matter.) Finally, the "technical" problem is also the result of an imbalance between the costs and benefits of various essential local services—education, police protection, welfare, and the like. Everyone would agree that supplying such services is a common responsibility which one should not be able to escape simply by moving away from the place where such facilities are maintained. Yet this is exactly what many of us do when we leave the central city for the suburbs. If the central city is to continue to perform its traditional function of housing, employing, educating, policing, and supporting the poor and the disadvantaged (and the only alternative is to spread the poor and the disadvantaged throughout the suburbs), then it must be able to tap the taxable wealth of all of us.

What all these problems—nuisances, scarce collective resources, fiscal imbalance—have in common is that they result from a situation in which the costs and benefits of urban life are imperfectly related. People who get the benefits of consuming attractive land, driving cars on city streets, or cheaply disposing of waste products and junked cars, do not pay their fair share of the costs of vital central city services. Similarly, people who inhale the foul air, gaze at the ruined landscape or the junked cars, or put up with the traffic congestion, have no way of being reimbursed for having these annoyances inflicted on them.

There is no reason in principle why these problems cannot be solved or significantly alleviated. We know, or can discover, techniques for stopping pollution; the crucial task is devising an appropriate combination of legal sanctions, tax policies, and incentives that will make these techniques effective. Open space and other unique natural resources can be conserved by public purchase, by easements, and by tax policies. Those persons who are determined to produce ugliness in parts of the city where ugliness is out of place (and this is not everywhere; every city, like every home, ought to have some place—the equivalent of Fibber McGee's closet—where we can store necessary ugliness) can be restrained by fines, taxes, and laws from carrying on those activities, or can be induced by subsidies to hide the ugliness by appropriate devices. There is nothing very difficult about hiding or getting rid of junked automobiles—provided that the people who are pleased by the absence of junk are willing to share the necessary cost of achieving the result. Even the design of private buildings can be improved by rewarding builders who leave open spaces around their buildings and who hire good architects and artists. The fiscal imbalance between public needs and public resources in the central city can be corrected by using a combination of transfer payments and user charges to insure that the suburbanite who uses the central city pays his fair share of the cost of that use and that everyone, regardless of whether he uses the facilities, pays his fair share of the cost of supplying essential common services such as education, police protection, and the like.

Traffic congestion is a somewhat more complicated matter, for it is not obvious in what precise sense it constitutes a problem. Congestion arises because many people want to use limited space; in a sense, as Martin Meyerson and Edward Banfield point out *(Boston: The Job Ahead)*, congestion is a means by which we ration access to a scarce resource (i.e., a desirable central city location) just as the price system is a way we ration the enjoyment of most other commodities (e.g., Cadillacs). The only way congestion could be eliminated entirely is to reduce the attractiveness of a given location to the point that no one will want to go to any one place any more than he will want to go to any other. Clearly this is both impossible and undesirable—central locations are central precisely because there are certain things people want to do in the company of large numbers of other people, or because large numbers of customers or workers are necessary to carry on various activities.

But congestion can be reduced if we provide other ways of rationing access besides traffic jams. One way—politically risky, but nonetheless likely to grow in favor—is to assess a charge on automobiles driven into central city locations, the amount of such a charge either to be based on the full cost of accommodating the car (parking space, police and fire protection, road use), in which case it is simply a user charge, or to reflect some penalty cost selected to deter the use of cars rather than merely to finance their accommodation.

The other strategy to deal with congestion is, of course, to subsidize mass transit facilities. The enthusiasm with which this proposal has been embraced by most public spokesmen suggests that their advocacy is based as much on an emotional dislike for automobiles (especially those parts made of chromium) as it is on a sober assessment of the comparative costs and benefits of various transportation programs. There are no doubt communities where the development of this kind of mass transit makes sense, either because of the population densities involved, or the investment already sunk in train tracks and equipment, or both. It is also perfectly clear, as John Meyer, John Kain, and Martin Wohl point out in their comprehensive study, *The Urban Transportation Problem,* that the vast majority of American cities could not possibly support a rail-based system without staggering subsidies. In fact, most communities would be better served by a mixed transportation plan that relied on a combination of user charges on automobiles entering the central city, high-speed bus service in reserved lanes on existing roadways, and various mechanical devices to regulate the flow of cars on and off expressways. The prosperity that produced the massive shift away from the train and bus and to the private car cannot be reversed by public policy; its effects, however, can be regulated.

THE NEGROES IN THE CITY

The third sense in which there is an urban problem is the most important. It results from the fact that the large central cities are where the immigrant lower classes congregate.

Today, with Negroes constituting the most important part of the urban lower class, the challenge to the central city is greater than ever before, because the Negroes create a unique set of problems. Unlike most previous migrants, they are marked by color. Furthermore, the Negro came originally from a slave culture in which he had no opportunity to acquire a complete range of political, economic, and social skills, and in which his family was subjected to systematic disruption and abuse. Unlike other immigrants—even other colored immigrants, such as the Chinese and Japanese—the Negro began his migration to the central city lacking the relevant skills and experience, and with a weakened family structure. Urbanization, of course, places further strains on community and family ties. The result is a central-city population with little money, few skills, a weakened capacity to cope with large bureaucratic institutions, and high rates of social disorder—crime, broken homes, alcoholism, narcotics addiction, illegitimacy, delinquency, and unemployment.

The argument over the details of the Moynihan Report on the Negro family has to some extent obscured its most important implication, which I cannot believe anyone will reject: if all Negroes were turned white tomorrow, they would still have serious problems. Whether these problems are more the result of a weak family structure, or of the impact of urbanization, or of the past history of discrimination, or of a depressed economic position, is very hard to say. But I suspect that whatever the cause, there are few aspects of this problem which will not be cured—or will not cure themselves—in time.

In time. In how much time? And what does one do in the meantime? I incline to the view that in the long run the acculturational problem of the Negro—i.e., the problem of being unable, as an individual or as a family, and as compared with previous migrants to the cities, to cope with the fact of poverty—will be reduced by improvements in income and education; habits will change as class changes, though more slowly. Perhaps I say this because it is easier to think of changing class position than cultural values, though altering the former is hard enough. Perhaps I say it because of the great and obvious differences between middle-class and lower-class Negroes, differences much greater than those between middle-class and lower-class whites. And perhaps I am wrong.

But whatever the strategic factor is, we cannot as yet say we have discovered it. The best that can be said in our favor is that we are perhaps the only free society which has ever tried to change a large racial minority by massively upgrading its condition. The debate about what the goal of "equality" means—whether a random distribution of Negroes throughout the city and the social structure, or a distinctive Negro enclave with guaranteed rights of entry and departure, or some combination of the two—is less interesting to me than the fact that, wherever we want to go, we don't know how to get there. And for the present, the urban Negro is, in a fundamental sense, *the* "urban problem."

If there were no Negroes in our large cities, or if the only difference between Negroes and whites were the accident of skin color, the rate of serious crimes in our cities would immediately be cut by about a third. The welfare rolls would be cut by a like amount. The population of our state prisons would be cut by more than one-fourth. No one can be sure how many fewer narcotics addicts or alcoholics there would be, but no one could argue the reduction would be negligible. The number of "dilapidated" homes would be further reduced by about 30 percent.

WHAT WE DON'T KNOW

If solutions to the technical problems facing our cities are impeded because our motivation does not yet equal our knowledge, then solutions to our fundamental problems are impeded because our understanding does not yet match our motivation. A dramatic crisis—an epidemic of deaths resulting from smog, for example—will quickly produce the motivation necessary to move swiftly on many of the technical problems. But we have already had our crises with respect to the fundamental problems—Watts, for example—and the result has only been a frantic and futile search for "answers." There is no ready-made knowledge stored up in our universities or foundations on how to prevent a Watts, or even on what causes a Watts. The malaise of lower-class life in the central cities has been a matter of scholarly concern for several decades, but there is not much scholarly wisdom to show for it, except a general—and probably sound—belief that higher incomes, more education, and less discrimination are desirable things. For thirty years, various experiments have been conducted in an effort to reduce juvenile delinquency; although we have occasionally been successful in eliminating gang warfare (primarily by disarming and policing the gangs), no one has been able to reduce the apparent rates of the most common form of delinquency, theft. We know that the rates of certain "private" crimes—murder, for example—cannot be changed no matter what tactics the police may use. We suspect that certain "street" crimes (auto theft, or purse snatching) can be reduced by "Saturation" police patrol, but no one knows whether what occurs is actually a reduction or simply a displacement of the crime to other parts of the city—or, if a reduction, whether it can be made permanent. No one is yet precisely certain what effect segregated schools have on Negro children, or how much of the slower rates of learning of these children is the result of family background (which is very hard to change) or of the school experience (which is somewhat easier to change). We do not even know how much narcotics addiction there is, much less what to do about it on any large scale. Above all, we do not know how much urban pathology is in some sense inevitable and how much space, therefore, our central cities must expect to reserve for the derelicts, the alienated, and the unaspiring poor.

One would suppose that we know most about one prerequisite for progress among the lower classes—employment opportunities. Yet, although the debate between the proponents of achieving full employment by stimulating aggregate demand and those who insist that we need structural change (job retraining, family allowances, vocational education, public works) has been raging for a decade or more, neither side has convinced the other. More importantly, *neither* strategy has been seriously tried. Until the war in Vietnam required a greater use of our industrial capacity, the federal government did not attempt as vigorously as it might, through tax and fiscal policies, to create a full employment economy—in part from fear of inflation, in part from a concern over the international balance of payments. Nor have the structuralists tried a program of public works, guaranteed incomes, worker resettlement, and vocational education on a scale sufficient to test the feasibility of eliminating the so-called "pockets of poverty." The war on poverty contains some of the elements of a "structuralist" strategy—for example, the Job Corps as a way of developing skills and motivation, and Project Head Start as a long-term attack on rates of learning—but it will be some time before we know how successful they are and to what extent such methods can be generalized. . . .

It is possible to conceive of a rational policy for dealing with so-called "urban" problems, once one begins to realize that the word "urban" is less relevant than the word "human." And perhaps this is implied in the Demonstration Cities Program proposed by the President this year, though the details are still sufficiently vague to make its real significance unclear. Leaving aside the obvious contradictions in the "guidelines" for determining whether a city is qualified to participate (for example, the incompatibility between maximum "co-ordination" achieved by a "single authority with adequate powers" and "widespread citizen participation" in the demonstration area or the conflict between maximum employment of indigenous workers and the development of labor-saving technologies), one may take the optimistic view that the Demonstration Cities Program is simply a fancy way of describing a new federal effort to impose federal standards on the local use of renewal money, so that renewal projects are more likely to serve legitimate national objectives rather than what ever purposes, good or bad, local leaders cook up. The demand for more local "co-ordination" and "planning" may be a tactic for creating an organized local constituency for HUD. A good case can be made for such intentions, but it is doubtful that a Congress sensitive to local interests and pressures is going to let HUD or anyone else get away with it entirely. And this, of course, should provide a good political reason for shifting federal efforts more in the direction of universalistic programs (maintaining the incomes of all poor, and subsidizing services—like education—that provide general benefits) and away from particularistic programs (tear down some buildings and subsidize others). So long as programs are designed to achieve particular effects in particular places, they will frequently be used by local groups to the disadvantage of the poor and powerless, or to produce effects that the federal taxpayer ought not have to pay for. And so long as HUD has no consistent federal policy, Congress will be able to insist that policies be set at the local level.

There is a bureaucratic as well as political reason for favoring universalistic programs—large bureaucracies are not very good at performing complex tasks requiring the exercise of a great deal of co-ordination over disparate activities, the accomplishments of which cannot be easily measured or evaluated. Direct income transfers, block grants to local governments, and increased reliance on individual choice are ways of reducing the impossible burdens on government agencies, most of which are (necessarily) staffed by men of average attainments. Making full allowance for the good intentions behind the Demonstration Cities Program, its central problem—apart from (though related to) the obscurity as to its goals and the mystery as to its means—is that it is an effort to improve on old programs, not by changing them or by substituting a wholly new strategy, but by creating a new apparatus to show how, by "co-ordination" (i.e., more administration), the job can be done better. But the failures of the past sixteen years have been precisely the failures of administration—of seeking inappropriate or incompatible goals, or of being unable to attain given goals, or of failing to take into account the consequences of working toward these goals. Overcoming the weaknesses of administration by providing more administration is likely to succeed only if extraordinary men do the administering. There are such men, but not many; simply hoping that enough of them wind up in HUD strikes me as, to say the least, imprudent.

For almost two decades we have been "attacking" the problems of the city—almost literally—by mounting successive assaults against various real and imagined difficulties. Each assault force has had its own leadership and ideology and the weaknesses of each have been the signal for a new assault, under different leadership and with a new ideology. First came public housing, then urban redevelopment, then urban renewal, and now the demonstration program. The old assaults of course never vanished, they just moved over a bit (not without complaints) to let the newcomers in. The common objective is to capture and hold central-city real estate; the differences in tactics concern the number of fronts on which the fighting is to proceed. In general, each successive assault has had broader objectives—the current President's message calls for a change in the "total environment." The motto is, "more is better." Perhaps it will all work out, if humane weapons are used and we evacuate the wounded. But I suspect that in the confusion the real enemies—poverty, ignorance, despair—may slip away, to live and strike again in another place.

William F. Buckley, Jr.
IN NEW YORK IT PAYS

The first mark of the civilized community is the ability to control its criminal element. By this standard New York City has lapsed into barbarism. Last year, 1761 major crimes were committed for every 100,000 of the city's population. During the first three months of this year the rate of crime increased 6.6 per cent over the same period of 1964. Such conditions, to be sure, constitute a "scandal"; but simply to repeat that cliché is scandalously to understate and depersonalize a very real

From *The Unmaking of a Mayor*, by William F. Buckley, Jr. Copyright © 1966 by William F. Buckley, Jr. All Rights Reserved. Reprinted by permission of The Viking Press, Inc. Mr. Buckley is Editor of *The National Review* and was a candidate for mayor of New York City in 1965.

outrage daily perpetrated on the peace of mind and body of every law-abiding New Yorker.

The basic cause of increased crime is, of course, the increasing moral and social disorder that mark contemporary society, and is thus less a problem for civil magistrates than for our churchmen and educators. (It is ironic, under the circumstances, that it has been judged by our highest civil magistrates a crime against the Court of the United States to mention the name of God in the public classrooms.) But the problem has been greatly aggravated by factors over which the city government does have control, or influence:

The city's law-enforcement facilities are inadequate. The police force is too small to cope with burgeoning crime. Current proposals (Lindsay's) to abolish two-men patrol cars, moreover, would make matters worse by diluting the effectiveness of the present force, and by jeopardizing police security. More policemen are needed.

The present Administration is doing nothing to resist the derogation of the law enforcement agencies. The disparagements of the police have created a crisis in morale and a swaggering disrespect for the policeman as the symbol of the public order. Yet far from resisting such assaults, the Wagner Administration has taken the course of appeasement: the proposed Civilian Review Board is nothing less than an agreement to elevate the campaign to discredit the police to official city policy.

Current welfare and housing policies have resulted in an undue concentration in New York City of idle and demoralized persons in an environment which breeds crime and criminals. No program to restore law and order to the city can be effective without coming to grips with New York's grave social problems.

Above all, crime has been encouraged in the city, as elsewhere, by the policies and practices of the courts. Too many judges appear to have forgotten that the primary purpose of courts of justice is to assert the demands of the public order—by meting out convincing punishment to those who transgress against it. This purpose is consistently frustrated in New York by fastidious procedural requirements that impede convictions of the guilty, and by lax sentencing policies that fail to provide an effective deterrent to crime.

To be sure, much of the trouble in bringing criminals to justice can be traced to decisions of the United States Supreme Court—for instance, the *Mallory, Mapp,* and *Escobedo* cases—which, if they indeed extend the implicit rights of the accused as guaranteed by the Constitution, raise the question, to which our judges have not addressed themselves, whether the Bill of Rights, as presently interpreted, sufficiently provides for the effective maintenance of law and order. Former Police Commissioner Michael J. Murphy has put it this way: "We are forced to fight by Marquess of Queensberry rules, while the *criminals* are permitted to gouge and bite."

But some of the courts of New York City have gone far beyond the specifications of the Supreme Court. They have institutionalized what commentators have taken to designating as "turnstyle justice." They have applied the rules of search and seizure, and other evidentiary and procedural requirements, with an extravagant, often ludicrous technicality. As one newspaper has observed, "the law itself has created so many escape hatches for criminals that nine postponements and a half-dozen separate hearings to suppress evidence or controvert a search warrant are not unusual before a case is ready for trial." The result is that our judicial system blinds its eyes on countless occasions to demonstrable guilt, and turns loose upon our streets the drug pusher, the sex offender, the mugger, the thief. The fact is that crime in New York City, both juvenile and adult, does pay. It pays, in large part, because the city's judicial system had defaulted on its primary duty to protect the public, in favor of an obsessive solicitude for those individuals who are responsible for breaking the peace of the city.

Proposals:

1. Additional policemen should be hired. Many of them could be hired from among retired policemen, to relieve younger men currently deskbound. To assure the police force a maximum efficiency, it should be provided with the most advanced technological tools now available, so that its equipment is at least as sophisticated as that now routinely employed by the criminal.

2. The new Administration should oppose the establishment of a Civilian Review Board, and should encourage the police to do their duty, and back them up when they do it.

3. The new Mayor and other city officials should bring vigorous pressure to bear on local judges to abandon criminal-coddling policies, and resume the administration of justice. The Bar Associations and other civic groups should be urged, with the support of the communications media, to mobilize an irresistible public demand that the courts of law join New York City's fight against crime.

4. Parole and probation procedures should be tightened to assure the confinement or surveillance of convicted criminals for long enough periods to guard the public safety. Studies should be conducted to determine whether enough parole officers are employed by the city to do an effective job and whether civil service regulations should be revised so as to ensure that officers not qualified or not disposed to administer the law strictly can be replaced.

5. The special treatment now accorded to juvenile criminals

should be re-examined in all its ramifications. Specifically, existing legislation should be revised to permit severer punishment of juveniles who commit serious crimes. Youth must cease to be an excuse for vicious attacks on fellow citizens.

6. As a further deterrent to juvenile delinquency, legislation should be enacted requiring the publication of the names and addresses of juvenile offenders guilty of serious offenses, and of their parents. This practice was recently adopted by Judge Lester H. Lobel in Helena, Montana. Subsequently, juvenile crime decreased by fifty per cent. While a community like New York can hardly expect such startling results, improvement would almost surely result. "The parents," Judge Lobel observed, "can't stand the heat. I have today about a thousand parents who are about the best probation officers any court can have."

7. As the protection of the individual from acts of lawlessness is a first responsibility of government, to the extent that the law-abiding citizen is victimized by the criminal, the government has failed in its duty to him. Legislation should, therefore, be enacted providing for the indemnification of victims of personal assaults and other crimes of violence.

8. Legislation should be enacted to provide (a) enticing bounties for informers who furnish information leading to criminal convictions, and (b) financial compensation for witnesses in criminal trials.

These measures are necessary inducements for wider citizen participation in the defense of the city.

Of all the crises now gripping New York, the emergence of Crime Triumphant is the gravest. The challenge to a new Administration could not be plainer: it is to make New York habitable.

There were a few scattered comments to the effect that I desired to modify the Bill of Rights—which, as a matter of fact, are half correct—and I herewith decline to terminate this sentence where logically it should be terminated, in order to make it just a little harder for the above few words to be excerpted out of the context—the current movement to fanaticize certain provisions of the Bill of Rights has of course the effect of diminishing certain other provisions of the Bill of Rights. This law of the projection of rights to the point of irreconcilability, an ancient intuition, has been brilliantly demonstrated by Professor Sidney Hook in his little book on *The Paradoxes of Freedom*. You cannot, Professor Hook maintains, extend any two freedoms indefinitely because there is a point at which they are likely to collide with each other. He gives many examples, among them: (a) the freedom of the press on one hand, and on the other, (b) the right to a fair trial; the conflict of interest between the two, at a certain point, being manifest. Another obvious example is the right to practice religion and the right to protection from religious indoctrination.

The position paper on crime sought to identify a crystallizing dilemma. The series of recent decisions by the Supreme Court reifying derivative rights of defendants that trace to the Bill of Rights are highly defensible extrapolations. For instance, if one has the "right" to counsel as of the moment one becomes *de facto* the accused, then it would appear that that right exists irrespective of whether the suspect knows of its existence; hence the Supreme Court—in its *Escobedo* decision, for example—and the Third District Court in its *Russo* decision correctly develop the Sixth Amendment. The question, however, should collaterally arise: what corresponding rights exists for the public prosecutor whose duty it is to affirm the rights of the aggrieved? The rights of the party of the first part are increasingly developed, while those of the party of the second part are relatively neglected. In England, Sir Hartley Shawcross has been waging a passionate campaign attempting to rectify the imbalance, his startling contention being that the day is past when the court is most usefully engaged as mere umpire between defendant and prosecutor, that radical revisions of the old rules are in order, revisions that aim at conscripting all parties concerned to the ascertainment of the truth. The truth is, after all, what is desired—*did* John in fact kill Jane?—and he boldly asks whether the adversary system is the most productive form of jurisprudential epistemology. For the hell of it, I spun out these considerations to a fidgety deputation from the Citizens Union of New York, a nonpartisan gathering of right-, or better, good-minded persons whose function was to ascertain, and then to report to the people, whom, in the higher interests of New York, they should vote for. The four lawyer-interrogators who—frankness requires me to confess—were clearly there to interview me only so that they could report that they had been there to interview me, and thus document their formal open-mindedness, nodded in more or less excited confusion—agreed, yes, that radical analysis was probably in order, yes—but quickly and with evident relief guided the discussion back to the fashionable sociological platitudes of the day and never again lost their hold of the conversational leash. So that the discussion, which had begun on the theme of law enforcement, turned to crime and the bearing on it of (a) unemployment, (b) insufficient housing, (c) race relations, etc.—all of which have much to do with the causes of criminals and nothing whatever to do with their apprehension or conviction.

It is conceivable that dilemmas of the kind I felt like talking about tend to occur last to lawyers, whose training commits them to the old precepts; and that may be a reason why the legal profession, of which John Lindsay is a member, has done so little reformist thinking on the subject. It is rather the philosopher Sidney Hook who comes through with the definitive destruction of the same Hugo Black whom Lindsay venerates. On the other hand, Shawcross (who was Attorney General of England in the postwar Labor government) and Mr. C. Dickerman Williams, who almost singlehandedly stopped the establishment of the emerging doctrine that no adverse inferences of any sort are to be drawn from the use of the Fifth Amendment, are lawyers; but an organization like the Citizens Union depends, for its prestige, on its respectability; and respectability in New York, as in most other parts of the country, tends to be confined within the limits of tolerability set by, e.g., *The New York Times.*

In the days ahead the dilemma is bound to harden. Either the Supreme Court will, as unfortunately has been its recent wont, more or less laze up to different specific cases in different ways, leaving the question of what are and what aren't the rights of parties in dispute, in boundless incertitude; or else basic laws will have to be rewritten, perhaps even a Constitutional Amendment or two, aimed at clarifying the rights of the public against those of the defendant. A lot can be done about law enforcement in New York City—as I indicated in the Position Paper—under existing arrangements; but, I fear, there is a lot that can't be done.

Senate Committee on Government Operations
MR. ARTHUR DUNMEYER TELLS IT LIKE IT IS

MR. BROWN. Thank you, Senator. First of all, I would like to give a somewhat broader description of Arthur Dunmeyer. We met 18 years ago—even though we were both from Harlem—for the first time at Wiltwyck School for Boys. We were at Wiltwyck School for 2 years together. We were also at the New York State Training School for Boys in Warwick, N.Y., together. There I stopped. Arthur Dunmeyer and I met for the first time 18 years ago and I was at the age of 11, he was 13—at

Condensed from "Federal Role in Urban Affair," Part 5, from *Hearings,* United States Senate Committee on Government Operations. Government Printing Office, 1966.

Wiltwyck School for Boys where I stayed for 2 years, and we became very close friends there. We were at the New York State Training School for Boys together 2 years later, at Warwick, N.Y., and at the age 16 I saw the handwriting on the wall, and knew if I was ever to accomplish anything positive in this life, that I could no longer continue my criminal activities, because at the age of 16, if you are arrested for a felony in New York State you became—well, you obtain a felony sheet, which is a criminal record, which is an obstacle in the way of any kind of economic progress for the rest of your life. It is a sad situation, but it still exists.

BACKGROUND OF ARTHUR DUNMEYER

Well, unfortunately, Arthur Dunmeyer was not of the mind that I was. He went on. He went on to Coxsackie, he went on to Elmira. He went on to Auburn; he went to Sing Sing; he went on to Dannemora; he went on to Attica, which is the top security prison in New York State. Everybody knows. So he was to run the whole roster of penal institutions in New York State, and this is why I said that he is more of a typical "manchild" than I am. Claude Brown was fortunate enough to stop at the age of 16, and to develop academic aspirations which enabled him to one day come up with "Manchild in the Promised Land." Arthur Dunmeyer was not quite as fortunate. But he has been out of Attica now for about 2 years, "isn't it, Arthur," and he has become determined.

He is 30 years old. He spent about half of his life in and out of jails. He has been determined to break a habit for the last 2 years regardless of all the social, economic, and political obstacles and abuses which he has to suffer in order to accomplish anything positive in this society, and he has done a great job of it, in my opinion. And now I would like for Arthur to tell you something about himself, which might be of interest to those listening.

SENATOR RIBICOFF. Go ahead. Tell us how old you are and what you do and what you have by way of family and some of your experiences.

MR. DUNMEYER. I am married; I am 30 years old. I have eight kids by various different women. The same problems that existed when I was a kid are existing now. It is just that I know how to handle them a little better now.

As far as making my mind up about the law, I have the same ideas I had when I was a kid. It is just that I feel now that I know how to get around those laws or I know more about the laws.

I would like to clarify something, Senator. I might go back to jail again because this is a way of life. A lot of people don't realize this. We have those who do go and we have those who don't go. I have never been ashamed of it. But as it is now right today, this moment, I have no intentions of breaking the law. But to exist where I live and how I live, you might break the law at any time without intention, and this is, I think, part of the idea, the logical questions that I feel like straightening out about, a man being criminally minded. I don't go to sleep with a crime on my mind.

CRIMINAL RECORD BEFORE 10 YEARS OLD

SENATOR RIBICOFF.   How old were you when you first came in contact with the law and received a sentence or were placed in some State institution?

MR. DUNMEYER.   I was between 8 and 10. Being a kid, I got in trouble and I had to go to juvenile courts. This was the record, the first record. They said that it wouldn't hurt me in later life, but every time I was later arrested this is what did hurt me. This is what pushed me aside without any questions or answers. I had a record.

To bring out a point, say I reached the age where I had the opportunity, where somebody was interested—

MR. BROWN.   I would like to clarify something ahead, when he refers to "Sonny." When we grew up together, that was a childhood nickname, and Sonny is Claude Brown.

PROBLEMS OF THOSE IN GHETTO NEED MORE THAN 8 HOURS' ATTENTION EACH DAY

MR. DUNMEYER.   I feel we both had the same opportunities. It is just that my interests weren't the same as his. They are not the same now. We are both the same people we were when we were kids, and I don't feel his success is the same as what I would call success. My success is just being able to live and have my family live decent, and this is not what I feel I am getting, and I resent sometimes the fact that he has it and I don't have it, because if I had someone to take an interest in me, I don't mean this 8-hour interest—we were speaking before about social workers, who come down to offices in the morning and go at 5 in the evening.

I feel that my problem, the problem of my family, of those who I was raised with is not an 8-hour problem. It is a problem that has to be tackled 24 hours a day. It consists of my mother, my father, my guardian, my friends, my neighbors, and these things were never taken into consideration.

DUNMEYER GRANDFATHER AT 30

MR. BROWN.   I wonder if you would let me interrupt you, if you don't mine. You have heard Arthur Dunmeyer say that he is 30 years old. He is 30 years old and he is also a grandfather, which makes him more of a typical "manchild" than Claude Brown.

This is one of the reasons I said he is more typical, not just having gone through the whole roster of penal institutions of New York State. Claude Brown is not yet a grandfather, fortunately, but the more typical "manchild," the more the average Negro who comes up in a ghetto whether it be Harlem, New York; Harlem, Los Angeles; Harlem, Cleveland; Harlem, Chicago; Harlem, New Haven, any of the large urban Negro ghettos throughout the country, by the age of 30 is likely to be a grandfather.

SENATOR RIBICOFF.   How old were you when you had your first child?

MR. DUNMEYER.   Fifteen.

SENATOR RIBICOFF.   You were 15. And how old was your daughter when she had her first child?

MR. DUNMEYER.   Twelve.

SENATOR RIBICOFF.   Your daughter at 12 had her child. So basically, your first child was born at 15 and your daughter's child was born when she was 12.

MR. DUNMEYER.   That is right.

SENATOR RIBICOFF.   And this is a common situation in your neighborhood and where you live?

MR. DUNMEYER.   Very much so. As I said before, it is our way of life. We have but so many ways to express ourselves, and when you are a kid you have the expressions that want to come out, and this is the closest thing that you can get as a solvent. You know, you have a girl, you have a mother, you have a friend, or you have somebody away from the crowd, and you can express yourself sexually because you do know all of the facts about sex long before society thinks you know or says, you know.

MR. BROWN.   Suspects that you might know.

HOW CITY AFFECTS RURAL NEGRO

SENATOR RIBICOFF.   What is the impact on the Negro from the rural South who comes up to the slums of New York? What happens to them physically, emotionally, mentally, morally? What do you find happens when they have to make their change? Your parents came and you were born here, or you were just a child in arms, and now you are older and you observe this. What happens to them then?

MR. BROWN.   Once they get there and become disillusioned, they can see the streets aren't paved with gold, and there exist no great economic opportunities for them, they become pressured. Many of the fathers who brought the families can't take the pressure any more, the economic pressure. How can you support a family of five kids on $65 a week? So he just leaves. He just ups one day and leaves; maybe becoming an alcoholic. Maybe he just goes out one night and he is so depressed because he missed a day's pay. During the week—he was sick. He couldn't help it. And he wasn't in the union, and this depression leads to a sort of touchiness, I will say—to become more mundane, where in a bar a person can step on his foot and he or the person gets his throat cut.

Somebody is dead. The other is in jail. He is going to the electric chair. It won't happen in New York today since they have abolished capital punishment. But this was one of the reactions.

Many of the physical reactions—they took out their frustrations on their kids—they beat the hell out of them. My father used to beat me nearly to death every day. Still they take it out on their wives. They beat their wives. It is just frustration that they feel.

The wives lose respect for their husbands. They can't really support their families. There are many affairs, you know, like when I use the term "Mama," I am using the term generally. Like, Mama is screwing the butcher for an extra piece of meat. Pardon the term. Mama is having sexual relations with the butcher for an extra piece of pork chop for the kids. She wants to see them well fed—this sort of thing.

Or maybe the number runner on the corner digs Mama or something. She has got a couple of kids. He can give her $25 a week. All her husband can make is, say, $60 at most a week, and it isn't enough, and the $25 helps because she wants her kids to have the things that TV says that they should have.

CITY DEBASES NEGRO MALE

You know, these are many of the reactions. And, then, there is the shooting. The guy comes home. He is trying. He comes home. He hears about his wife and he goes out one day, picks up a gun, he says "Oh, Lord, I have tried so hard. It is just not for me. It is my lot to always be a day late and a dollar short. But, this guy has been making it with my woman and he has got to die. This is an affront to my masculinity."

So he kills him. Then he is in jail. His family is on welfare or he is in the electric chair. These are emotional and physical reactions.

I will turn it over to you, Arthur.

NEGROES TURN TO CRIME FOR STATUS

MR. DUNMEYER.   I would like to bring this up also. In some cases this is the way you get your drug dealers and prostitutes and your number runners. You get people that come here and it is not that they are disillusioned. They see that these things are the only way that they can compete in the society, to get some sort of status. They realize that there aren't any real doors open to them, and so, to commit crime was the only thing to do, they can't go back. There is nothing to go back to. This is understood. This is why they came.

The only thing to do is to get something going to benefit yourself. It is a way to live, a way to have enough to keep your wife from going to bed with the butcher. It is a way to keep from killing the butcher. You kill him in small ways, by taking him off, by holding him up, by seeing that he don't hang out in the neighborhood after the store is closed. It is cheating. It is stealing. These things are just a way of life that come from this one particular thing.

GHETTO NOT PROMISED LAND

This Negro comes to the promised land, as he says, and he finds that it isn't a promised land and he finds that there is nowhere else to go. There is nothing else to do. And he has the physical and the mental ability to do this particular thing. So he does it as a way of life.

ATTITUDE TOWARD SOCIETY AND ITS LAWS

Society has made this law to protect itself, not to protect this man in any way, just to protect itself so there is a law that he can't do this, and he doesn't recognize this law. Really, he doesn't recognize anything in society, because of this one particular thing. He sees there are no doors really open to him; and until these doors can be open to this man and this woman, there is going to be the same thing over and over again.

It is a matter of getting caught. Not a matter of taking or doing anything. It is a matter of getting caught and this is where it comes from.

BROWN'S FAMILY LIFE

MR. BROWN.   I would like to add something more to this. In the Harlems throughout the Nation, it is like the crimes which society considers crimes, that the Negro who has migrated to the North has to resort to. My father he started—as it is related in the book—one of my most pronounced recollections is seeing my father cut a man's throat when I was at the age of 5. My father and I never got too close because there never was time. He beat the hell out of me quite often, and that was it. We couldn't talk. He had too many problems, too many frustrations. And there were times when I would be bothering my sisters. I would hit them or something. They'd say, "I'm going to tell Daddy on you and he's going to cut your throat," and I say, "No, he ain't." But I never believed that he wasn't because I had seen him do it.

Anyway, my father started when he came, the only thing he knew was what his father had taught him as a trade, considered illegitimate by Internal Revenue Service, of course, but it was making corn liquor in the bathtub—White Light, King Corn, perhaps you heard of it in those terms. And so he did this and ran his parlor parties and his crap games.

When I was coming up I wanted things, too, as a child, that my parents couldn't give me because my father he wanted to be with his family, he wasn't going to jail and had to give up his way of life, and at this time he was making a little more money. Of course, by the age of 40 or 42 he was making, say, $75 a week, because he had been working on the job for about 15 years at that time and this was a big deal to him. But still, he couldn't afford to give me the things, buy the sport jackets and things that the kids were wearing at the time to go along with the fad of the community. Anyway, I took to selling drugs.

SENATOR RIBICOFF.   How old were you when you started selling drugs?

MR. BROWN.   I was selling drugs at 13.

SENATOR RIBICOFF.   Thirteen?

GHETTO NEGROES RESPECT SUCCESSFUL CRIMINALS

MR. BROWN. Yes; heroin. Anyway, it is like, in the community, in the Negro ghettos throughout the country, these things that are considered criminal by society, the solid citizen, aren't considered criminal. It is like a war between them and us, the society which oppresses us, and us, the oppressed. When a guy goes to jail, it is OK. You are looked up to, if you are a successful hustler, you have a big Cadillac and you have always got $300 in your pocket, you are taking numbers, you are selling drugs, you are a stickup artist, you are anything, you are a prostitute, anything you may be doing, you are a con man, a hustler. Anybody you heard of, Jim Smith, the mayor, or somebody from Arkansas, this is the way you come up in Harlem. You learn these games at certain ages.

At 13 I learned how to cut drugs, how much quinine to put in cocaine. At the age of 15 I learned how to "Murphy" somebody. The "Murphy" is the flimflam. Anyway, had I been in the South, had I been in a better society, I would have been learning. I would have been in school and learning how to make it legitimately, but I wasn't. I was learning how to make it illegitimately, but these were the best possible ways to make it financially, to establish a decent place for yourself in America's greatest metropolis.

The TV's were saying, yes, get this, you know, have a car. Everybody should have a car. Even color TV, how are you going to get it? You can get it selling drugs. You can get it taking numbers. You know, you can get it playing the Murphy. You can get it if you ran around taking off people, sticking up people, this sort of thing. As long as you were making it, as long as you were a success, that is why in Harlem people respect the guy who is always clean.

A CRIMINAL WHO GOES TO JAIL IS CONSIDERED
A PRISONER OF WAR

You know, he has on a $200 silk suit every day, $55 alligator shoes and this sort of thing. He drives a big Cadillac, and, they know he is winning the war. He is a soldier, he is a real soldier. He is a general in the community. If he gets busted, well, he is just a prisoner of war. That is the way it is looked upon.

MR. DUNMEYER. Or you have a situation where you have got a white fellow from downtown. He is a gangster, and high in society. He can bring the dope in town. He imports it. He brings it uptown. He makes me feel important. I have the money that he has. I can dress the way he dresses. I can drive a car like he drives. I can take care of my family the way he takes care of his. And he is white. So if it is recognition by the white standards, then, I am getting recognition by the white. And this is very important, you are being looked up to in your community. It is just a way of life. So when you get struck, you take it until you get struck again. That is the way it is.

It is not a matter of a guy saying, "I want to go to jail. I am afraid of jail." Jail is on the street just like it is on the inside. The same as, like when you are in jail, they tell you, "Look, if you do something wrong you are going to be put in the hole." You are still in jail, in the hole or out of the hole. You are in jail in the street or behind bars. It is the same thing, a matter of existing, and this thing of feeling like a person regardless if it is illegal or not.

This is what happens to people like my mother. My mother came here under certain pressures from her family, because I was born, and in any family this is wrong when you don't have marriage. My father wasn't married to my mother. As a matter of fact, I just found out that my name isn't what I thought it to be because my mother knew no difference, knew no better, knew nothing about hospitals, and what she put on the record I never knew until recently.

DUNMEYER'S MOTHER'S LIFE

It is this type of thing. When she came here she had to scratch. She had to hold on. She had to feed herself, first, in order to feed me. She had pressures from her family. She had pressures from people that she met, whites in the neighborhood, the business people. To them she was a prostitute. To her she was just a woman that had to learn how to live by her wits and to this day I respect her for this more than I respect her for bowing to anyone or working for anybody.

I have an uncle that I respected to a certain extent, but I felt he never understood me, because he never knew what hardships were from my point of view. He worked every day and came home and mumbled about discrimination on the job and what he had to go through and how these white fellows would steal his sandwich everyday and what he had to do to stop it. He had to defecate and put it in the sandwich [mixing it with fish to take the smell away so they would eat the sandwich] and this would make him feel like a man.

But this didn't make my mother feel like a woman. She felt that just existing was her main interest. And she went out and did it, how she felt she should do it, not because she felt it was right or wrong. My mother was arrested two or three times. As far as the courts are concerned she has a record as a prostitute, an undesirable. She has been stigmatized. She has this particular brand on her.

NEGRO VIEW OF GHETTO STRUGGLE

Why? To me I can't understand because I feel she was just living and I feel it is because of conditions that we are still going through. It is just that now, as I said before, we have a way of getting around it, and it is not to me a race thing. To me it is a thing between those who have and those who haven't. If I had found a million dollars and I felt I could keep society or those who should know about it from knowing about it, I would make it just as well as the next man, because I don't get along with some of my own people, and my money would buy what I needed, and my friends, the friends I would need, whatever it is that we consider status, the money would do this.

OPPORTUNITY TO FAIL SOUGHT

The only way for us to get money at that time—my people, my mother, my father too, I guess—was to get it by our wits. If you couldn't get downtown to take the big stack, you took the little stack uptown from the little guy who lived right around you. This is just living, and I have never felt that it was wrong. I have never felt ashamed of it, as I said before, and it is going to happen over and over again until the policy-makers make it so that we, who they recognize as the minority, can get the same opportunity to reach out, to strike out, to make our errors too, to fail, just like they are entitled to fail. I feel we are entitled to fail.

Every form of success that I have ever heard about, if I listened long enough I found out that it came by flimflamming somebody.

These hearings, I always had an idea about them. I have seen fellows sitting down here sweating and going through changes and I always said to myself they know that they must go through these changes. They knew this from the beginning because they are human, and every human being has this quality, this so-called wrong in him, every human being. There is no perfect one. If there was, then he wouldn't be the same as us. He wouldn't even be a human being. He would be something else. And I also said to myself, "Well, if you take this fellow that is questioning him and sit him at this table and let me question him, I'd make him sweat too." If only about his toilet habits, you know, about things people don't want to recognize. It is there.

HOW CAN CONDITIONS BE IMPROVED?

SENATOR RIBICOFF.   I am just wondering, here you are, Mr. Dunmeyer. You come here and—let me first say this. We are very, very grateful to you. You are not only educating us. I believe you are educating all America by your appearance here today. I am grateful to both of you for coming. You did this of your free will and at my request. You were willing to come, and I am grateful to you as I am sure Senator Kennedy is.

Mr. Dunmeyer, you say that you were an illegitimate child. You have an illegitimate child. Your daughter then bears an illegitimate child. You are 30 years of age. Half of it you spent in jail or prison, reform school.

Mr. Brown, by reading your book I understand your background. You were able to make it. You now go to law school. Where do you think the cycle can be broken? Where do you believe, from your own personal experience, your knowledge, where you live, what you do? Is it possible for the fourth generation to live a normal life? Mr. Dunmeyer, you have got a job now. You have been out of prison for 2 years. Mr. Brown, you wrote this book indicating a sensitive understanding of the depth of the problems and now you are going to law school. How do we break this cycle of poverty, illiteracy, the slums, crime? How do we bring the people of the slums of the Nation, not just Harlem or Bedford Stuyvesant, but all over, how do we make them part of what we say is a normal society? How do we turn this around, in your opinion?

EMPHASIZE WHAT A PERSON CAN DO

MR. DUNMEYER.   Senator, it is not a junction, it is not a junction where you meet and you can go this way or you can go that way. It is not like that. I am not illiterate. I didn't go to Howard. What I learned I learned on my own, I got from jails. I know quite a bit about law. I got it from reading books. And this, the bum on the street can do, read. So it is not a matter of where you turn off.

It is a matter of accepting a person for what he is, regardless of what field he is in. In other words, you have some number writers who are brilliant mathematicians, see, but they are not recognized as brilliant mathematicians. They are recognized as number writers, and the guys that are getting away from the law. If he went to the police station and said "Listen, I'd like to get a job to learn how to run this IBM machine," the first thing they would say is "Have you got a record?"

They wouldn't ask "What do you know about mathematics?" Mathematics wouldn't be important to him at the time. His record would be important to him.

And for instance, at a certain time in my life I realized that anything I did wouldn't only hurt me. It would hurt my family also, and especially this one particular woman. This was a love thing. I guess we all go through regardless of what position we are in, we all go through this particular thing. And I felt afraid of hurting her, not myself, because I might have done more things than I did now.

In other words, I never went to the Army. You will find some guy will go to the Army, and he parades in the neighborhood as being a soldier, you know, this the ideal thing for a young man to do. I never had any desire to go. I said if I had to go I wouldn't go. But I have no desire. I wasn't raised up saluting and playing soldier, you know, toy soldiers and whatnot. This didn't interest me.

DOUBLE STANDARD OF MORALITY

What interests me was how this guy could have a uniform on, a policeman's uniform and still be like me, yet have this much power to hit me in the head when he felt like it or run me off the street when he felt like it, or to allow me to go my way until he felt like it. This is what always puzzled me, and I always considered him a person like me and I said I am just as smart as this guy.

I eat apples. I can take an apple off the fruit stand and wave to Mr. John or Mr. Peter or whoever it is. I can do these things too. But society wouldn't recognize me because I don't have the uniform. If I took an apple off Pete's fruit stand, he would get a stick and chase me or get this policeman who takes an apple every day. Every day he is on duty he comes by and gets a cup of coffee free or whatever it is. This is normal to him because this is accepted, this is the right person doing it. This is the person who has passed their examinations. But I haven't done this.

DUNMEYER ATTITUDE TOWARD HIS LIFE

Now if I went to school perhaps I might have been exposed to more things than I have been exposed to, but I feel that I was exposed to the criminal side of it, and I got what I could out of it. It didn't hurt me. I gained more from it. In other words, if I had to do it again, I wouldn't change it. This has allowed me to see things that I could never see unless I had the opportunity to go say to Howard or to law school and wherever this leads to.

This is not my idea. My idea is to be able to sit in my living room and listen to you and these hearings and understand both sides of these hearings, not just the fellow that is over here, because I happen to be in his world, but your side of it also, because I happen to know your history from what is written about you, or the history of these hearings.

I would like to know both sides of it. But because I don't have the formal education, no background, I am not considered an ideal person for my own kids to emulate. And anything they do wrong I am blamed for it in the sense that, they are "copying off you" meaning myself.

ILLEGITIMACY IN GHETTO

In other words, you did it a second ago, Senator. You said—you didn't carry it all the way through—you said I was illegitimate. My daughter was illegitimate and my granddaughter was illegitimate. I may have four or five more generations, Senator, of illegitimacy in my direct line from my posterity. But I don't think it is wrong. I think that until those who never think of illegitimacy can understand that this is just a way of life, until this happens, there is going to always be a question of what can I do to help you, and until you experience this, and the closest way you experience this is to try to understand to the point of forgetting any standards, any rules, and look at the person as a person. You know, what I mean, the biological thing that makes men and women go for each other, love each other and have children, regardless of what the social—

MR. BROWN.   I think he means see people simply as people and nothing else.

MR. DUNMEYER.   Right, and, as I said, this is not a race thing.

MR. BROWN.   The real cosmopolitan attitude that very few Americans have.

MR. DUNMEYER.   Our people happen to be the minority, and are in the ghettos, and so this is where all the limelight is focused, and because of this, we are considered people with problems, people with something that has something wrong with them. But, believe it or not, I would never think of going on the roof and jumping off. I would never think of going on the roof and taking a rifle and shooting five or six people for no reason at all.

But I might think of having some children, not thinking of the woman being married to me or not, because I want to have children, not thinking if it's right or wrong. This is because I want to have children, you see. But I would never do some of the things I see that the accepted standards allow and make excuses for it.

UNIMPORTANCE OF RACE

These things never come across my mind. I wouldn't steal just to be stealing. I steal for a purpose, if I steal. It means to me, but perhaps not to you or the other person who is always asking why do we steal. They are not even thinking of what I stole. They are not thinking that I stole an orange because I was hungry, whereas another person may steal $10,000 and not be hungry. I might steal just an orange, but I am considered a criminal because of two reasons. I was caught, and because society says to steal is wrong, you see.

And as I said before, it is not a matter of race. It is a matter of the upper class and the lower class, those who have and those who haven't got.

MR. BROWN.   Arthur, I would like a minute, baby, right here, if you don't mind. Excuse me, Senator, I am going to elaborate on your question, or on the answer to your question. But first of all, I would like to point out a few other things, while we are on the subject.

LIFE OF JOHNNY D

You know there are many guys who come up in the Harlems throughout the Nation. They recognize the system of oppression and become hopeless at a very early age. You have read "Man-Child." You have read, perhaps you remember a character by the name of Johnny D. You know I was shot at 13. Well, I also shot Johnny D at 13 and he respected me so much for it that he taught me how to pull my first stickup. Well anyway, Johnny D is now in the death house. He just got out of Attica Penitentiary last spring, and I got a letter from him in September. At the age of 16 Johnny D was saying: "Baby, like we ain't going to make it. Like I'm never going to have any job. The only thing that is going to happen to me is that I am going to be dead or I may have a whole pot full of money."

And I would see him from time to time—even though then we started going in different directions—and he would be out of jail in between terms, and I would say, "Damn, if I only had two bills, Johnny, it would straighten me out. I've got a problem."

He would say "Sonny, baby, don't worry about it. If you see me Friday, I will give you five bills."

MR. DUNMEYER.   Five bills is $500.

MR. BROWN.   It is $500. We didn't talk any more once I started going to school, I knew what he meant. He is a stickup artist and he was going to pull a stickup. He had gotten away from the pimp thing. Once he started taking drugs he could no longer be a pimp.

You understand the biochemistry of this. Anyway, he had become a stickup artist at this time, and since I was in a different life he never told me what he was going to take off and this sort of thing. He knew I wasn't going to stick up anybody. He had some money. I would be 17 or 18 at the time.

He would say "Sonny, baby, if you see me Friday I will give you five bills, but don't worry about it."

I knew he had a job, like something, 10 grand, maybe 25 he was going to try and take off.

He would say, "If you don't see me after Friday, or if you read about me in the papers, like send me some cigarettes, baby, or send me some flowers and come to the funeral if you can make it."

Well, he was thinking this way since 16. He was not going to work because he knew society. He was so perceptive that he saw where society offered no opportunities for him. He was illegitimate also. At 16 he knew, and he just never changed. This was it. It was them against us, and he was little meaner than many of us, you know.

He had just gotten out of Attica around April, and he came around to my house. At the time I was living in Washington. I had finished school but I was still living here for awhile, and my mother wrote me a letter and told me, you know, "Your friend, Johnny D has been around and he wants to see you."

I said "Yeah, it would be great to see him." I hadn't seen him in 5 years. He had been in jail, 5 years in Attica.

I said, "I will be up in June and I want to see him." So, when I got up to New York in June, I asked my mother, "Where is Johnny shacking now?"

She said, "Man, you didn't read the papers?"

I said, "No; what happened?"

"You didn't hear about that stickup in Jersey, bus company, 25 grand, and somebody took one guy's head off who was going to be bold enough to turn around with a sawed off shotgun?"

I said, "I heard about it; why?"

She said, "That was Johnny, baby. They popped him off for it."

They had just abolished capital punishment and he had to go to Jersey where they still have capital punishment, and, you know, a felony murder is automatically No. 1, I mean first degree murder. Anyway, he is now in the death house, and he wrote me a letter from the death house. He says:

> Well, Baby, they got me for the big one this time, and they mean to get all of me, but I don't care. All I want to do before they turn on the frying pan is read that tough book I heard you wrote. Like well I guess you were better off than I was to cope with it. I wish I could have made it your way, but I had to do it my way and here I

am. I've got no regrets and have got no sweats. Just send me a copy of the book when you get a chance and go on, baby, you are ready for it—kill them.

Not in the sense of actually killing anybody, but just making it—go all the way. And there were many guys like this in the Harlem community and in the Harlem area.

At the age of 16—remember Rocky in the book. When I was 8 years old, he was 14 at the time; I saw him throw a guy off the roof just like that, and everybody, you know, scattered. It was a gang fight. I was 8. And, you know, you are so shook up. It is like everybody is wondering what is he going to look like. How does he feel about it afterward?

Rocky was always a mean guy. He would kill a guy in a minute. He was one of the nicest guys I have ever met, you know, but if he was wronged he wouldn't hesitate to kill somebody. Of course, he was a little psychopathic.

Library of Congress
THE HELLER PLAN

One proposal which may receive serious consideration by the 89th Congress and which may stir up considerable controversy is the recommendation that the Federal Government channel excess Federal revenues to State and local governments.

This proposal is not new. More recently it has been espoused by Dr. Walter W. Heller, who recently resigned his official position as chairman of the President's Council of Economic Advisers. As far back as in June of 1960, while still chairman of the Economics Department of the University of Minnesota, he proposed that rising Federal revenues be distributed to State and local governments with little or no Federal strings attached. . . .

Two basic considerations have prompted the administration to consider the possibility of sharing additional Federal revenues with State and local governments.

First of all, the steady and the more recent rapid growth of our

From "Library of Congress Analyzes Tax Sharing," prepared by the Library Reference Service, *Congressional Record*, Aug. 25, 1965.

gross national product and the leveling off of defense expenditures due to the closing-down of certain military installations is expected to produce a budgetary surplus by the end of fiscal year 1966. It is feared by administration economists that the realization of these surpluses before full employment of manpower and resources is achieved will cause a fiscal drag on our economy and will retard the business expansion we are currently enjoying.

The second underlying factor is that State and local governments are badly in need of new revenue sources to meet the ever-growing needs of their citizens for additional schools, hospitals, health and welfare services. State and local expenditures are continuing to climb at a rapid rate. During the 10-year period from 1954 through 1963 the expenditures of these governments more than doubled, having increased from $36.6 billion to $74.9 billion. State and local indebtedness increased even more rapidly during this same period—from $38.9 billion to $86.4 billion. With archaic tax systems which place heavy reliance on sales taxes, fees and property taxes rather than taxes on incomes, it is becoming increasingly difficult with each passing year for State and local governments to support the rising costs of those programs so vital to the well-being of their citizens.

The full details of the task force report on this proposal are not known. However, it is understood that a formula has been recommended which will provide that 1 or 2 percent of the Federal personal income tax base (which is taxable income after exemptions and deductions) will be set aside annually in a trust fund for distribution to State and local governments. With a tax base of $250 billion anticipated for fiscal year 1965, State and local governments would receive anywhere from $2.5 billion to $5 billion annually should such a formula be formally approved. As the economy expands and Federal revenues rise, more would automatically become available for distribution to State and local governments under this plan.

It has been proposed that this money be given to the States unconditionally. This means that State and local governments would be free to make their own determinations on just how the money will be spent. Also, there would be no Federal supervision or administration of the expenditure of these funds once they are disbursed.

These amounts would be in addition to payments which are already made under various programs of Federal aid, some of which have been in operation for years. In the current fiscal year 1965 such payments to State and local governments are expected to amount to $10.6 billion. They are disbursed for specific purposes such as for highway construction, airport construction, school construction and maintenance, public assistance, etc. They are allocated under varying formulas prescribed by law. These formulas frequently require State matching and have generally been devised so that the poorer States receive more aid than the richer States. Each program is subject to close supervision and control by the administering Federal agency.

It is not known just how these additional funds will be allocated among the States. They may be disbursed according to a formula based upon population or average income or both. It has been reported that the task force studying this proposal has recommended that perhaps a relatively small proportion of the payments be distributed on the basis of average income and the remainder on a population basis.

These block grants represent a departure from the conventional method of disbursing Federal aid. The disbursement of $28 million to the States under terms of the Surplus Distribution Act of 1836 represents the only instance in U.S. history when Federal funds have been granted to the States without conditions governing use of the funds. However, the money was originally deposited with the States; but its return never was requested.

Canada and Australia have both made unconditional payments to local governing bodies.

Assuming that legislation embodying this general proposal is introduced during the next Congress, the earliest date that it would become effective would probably be at the end of fiscal year 1966, or possibly 1967, contingent, of course, upon a continued expansion of economic activity.

Since the precise details of the administration proposal have not yet been worked out, it is not possible to give a specific evaluation of it. However, some of the basic arguments for and against a general proposal that the Federal Government redistribute to State and local governments certain tax revenues are briefly given below.

ARGUMENTS IN FAVOR OF THIS PROPOSAL

In an expanding economy and under present tax rates Federal revenues increase on the average by about $6 billion per year. Administration economists fear that these additional taxes will siphon off too much money from the private sector of the economy. A Federal surplus will thus result before full employment of manpower and resources is achieved. Such a surplus has the effect of retarding economic growth, and in time, the forces of recession set in. It is believed that enactment of this proposal will avert this fiscal drag which such budget surpluses may exert upon our national economy.

It is true that appropriate tax reduction measures will also counteract the restrictive effects on the economy that a budget surplus produces. However, tax reduction bills take too long to enact, and a recession may be well on its way before such legislation can take effect. By making excess revenues available to State and local governments automatically, action gets underway immediately to offset the contractive effect of such surpluses.

Once it is agreed that it is the wisest economic policy to spend these excess Federal revenues, it can be demonstrated that the largest area of unmet national needs lies in the services provided by State and local governments. Additional Federal grants to these needy governments will provide them with additional revenues upon which they can depend and will relieve in some measure the critical shortage of funds which constantly harasses them. Such grants will enable them to better meet the growing requirements of their people for more schools, hospitals, health and welfare services.

State and local governments have been increasing their outlays much more rapidly than the Federal Government during the past few years in an attempt to meet their mounting obligations. State and local governments are currently spending about $75 billion per year; by 1972 their expenditures are expected to reach $120 billion. On the other hand, Federal spending has remained relatively stable and may rise from the current level of $98 billion predicted for fiscal year 1965 to only $110 or $115 billion by that time.

Because of the severe shortage of funds which has faced State and local governments in the past, the Federal Government has found it necessary to intervene by means of special aid programs to help to bring about some solution to this difficult problem. Without additional Federal aid these governments are not going to be able to fully meet the burgeoning demand of their citizens for necessary services.

It may be argued that State and local governments will not use these Federal funds wisely if they are granted or will reduce their own taxes and expenditures for necessary programs. Experience of the past, however, indicates that such fears are groundless, and that this will not be the case. A large proportion of total State and local outlays over the past years have been used for educational, health, and welfare purposes—an indication that they are cognizant of the needs of their people in these areas and are attempting to meet them.

Grants made to State and local governments without the usual strict supervision will enable these bodies to operate more independently—free from Federal control. Local officials will be free from Federal domination, and the spread of a growing Federal bureaucracy will be halted. State and local governments will thus be in a stronger financial position, and a better fiscal balance will be achieved between Federal, State, and local governments.

Unconditional grants will free the Federal Government from much red tape and overhead currently necessitated in the administration of Federal aid programs. Present aid programs are becoming so numerous and diverse that they are becoming unmanageable. During the fiscal year 1963 the Treasury Department itemized some 66 programs of direct aid to State and local governments. These do not include numerous other programs of assistance disbursed directly to individuals and institutions within the States. During the past 10 years direct payments to State and local governments have almost tripled—increasing from $3.8 billion in fiscal year 1956 to an estimated $10.6 billion in the current fiscal year 1965. During the last Congress some 10 to 30 additional aid programs were authorized, depending upon how one considers a separate program. Making additional revenues available to State and local authorities without the usual strict controls would enable Federal officials to devote more of their time and energy to more pressing problems of national defense, international relations, etc. They would also be freed from constant pressuring from lobbying groups seeking special projects or benefits for their particular districts.

Unconditional grants will be a boon to low-income cities and States. Stringent matching requirements currently imposed by the Federal Government on numerous programs make it difficult for some of these governments to take full advantage of the proffered assistance, or, if they do take advantage of this aid, frequently it must be at the expense of other vital services. If the funds are allocated primarily on the basis of population (as has been proposed by the task force report), the poorer and more needy areas will stand to benefit more than the richer districts.

Since States and localities may well spend these excess funds for educational purposes, it can be argued that this would relieve the Federal Government from making a decision on the controversial question of granting Federal aid to religious institutions.

Federal grants made with few or no strings attached will foster healthy competition among the State, county, and city governments for this aid.

ARGUMENTS AGAINST THIS PROPOSAL

First of all, such a plan presupposes continued prosperity and the realization of Federal budget surpluses. While it is true that since 1961 we have been enjoying an expansion of economic activity, full employment of our labor force and full utilization of our industrial capacity have yet to be attained. During the past 30 years budget surpluses have been the exception rather than the general rule. A Federal surplus has been realized in only 6 years out of the 30-year period from

1935 through 1964. Still another deficit is anticipated for the current fiscal year 1965, and in the years following there is no guarantee that a surplus will automatically be produced. If such Federal assistance were made available only in those years when a surplus is expected, State and local governments would find it difficult to plan their spending programs with such an indefinite and uncertain arrangement. Once they received Federal funds under this program, they would automatically count on receiving them year after year. It would not be fair to make such a distribution contingent on the state of our national economy from year to year, the condition of which may abruptly change overnight.

Some fear that without strict Federal supervision and control, State and local governments will not use the funds in the right way. Knowing that additional funds are forthcoming from the Federal Government, they may be tempted to reduce their own taxes and curtail vital programs. There is apprehension that rural-dominated State legislatures will make allocations of the funds which will not be in the best interest of the majority of citizens. County leaders are fearful that the money may never trickle down below the State level. Similarly, civil rights advocates fear that in the South the funds will be spent to support segregated schools, housing, and other facilities. Failure of the Federal Government to control the actual distribution of funds below the State level will undoubtedly cause bitter controversy among State, county and city leaders as to just how these funds will be spent.

It is argued that additional funds forthcoming from Washington will only cause State and local governments to become more and more dependent on our National Government rather than stronger and more self-reliant as advocates of this proposal assert. It is also feared that Federal power will be enlarged rather than diminished by giving further aid to these governing bodies.

Rather than doling out excess funds to State and local governments, some feel that any surplus funds should be used to reduce our large national debt. This fall, the public debt reached its highest point in history, and latest Treasury Department releases report that it now amounts to $315.5 billion (as of November 13, 1964). There is also strong sentiment by Cabinet and other Federal officials that the funds can better be spent to support needed Federal programs such as mass transit, cancer research, welfare programs, etc., and that these programs should not be sacrificed for the sake of aiding State and local governments.

8
Poverty

By the middle of the twentieth century most Americans believed that mass poverty had been eliminated in the United States. In 1958 John K. Galbraith wrote in his famous *The Affluent Society* that poverty was "no longer a massive affliction [but] more nearly an afterthought." In a nation where the average family income was approximately $7,000, how could poverty be a problem? However, in 1962 Michael Harrington wrote *The Other America,* in which he described our "invisible poor." Harrington developed the thesis that the economic advances and guaranteed forms of security, such as social security, have by-passed a large percentage of Americans. He contends that millions of Americans are ill-housed and ill-nourished, but not so ill-clad that we could readily recognize them. He maintains that the poor in America are invisible— that poverty lies off the beaten track of middle-class America. The general economic prosperity of the past quarter of a century has not trickled down to all and, in consequence, we have a hard-core class of poor—those who because of age, race, or physical or mental defects cannot be lifted out of their poverty by economic booms. A detailed account of one class of poor, the rural poor, is contained in Robert Sherrill's article, "It Isn't True That Nobody Starves in America."

The Harrington thesis gained widespread acceptance in the early 1960s and led to demands that the federal government undertake new measures to eliminate poverty in America. In 1961 Congress passed the Area Redevelopment Act and in 1962 the Food and Agriculture Act.

Then came the Manpower Development and Retraining Act of 1963. Finally, in 1964 President Johnson, in his first State of the Union address, requested the Congress to enact an omnibus bill as a part of his "war on poverty." Congress responded with the Economic Opportunity Act of 1964 and 750 million dollars in funds. The legislation provided for a Jobs Corps, for Vista, the "domestic peace corps," and for a variety of measures allowing for urban and rural community action programs. By the fiscal year 1967 the program had been expanded and the funds enlarged to over one and one-half billion dollars. However, Congress does not always react favorably to proposals designed to eliminate the conditions of poverty in America. The debate in the House of Representatives on the proposed Rat Extermination Act of 1967 is illustrative of a certain level of Congressional response to poverty proposals. The act was subsequently passed by the House in September of 1967, but only after considerable public outcry against the earlier vote. The public response to the House's July vote may have been influenced by the Detroit ghetto riots of late July.

The new awareness of poverty has resulted in a widening discussion about the role of government in the elimination of poverty. Within the past two years there has been growing criticism of the traditional welfare and relief programs sponsored by the government. The criticism is by no means limited to conservatives. Increasing numbers of liberals are saying that these welfare and relief programs not only are degrading but also are designed to perpetuate poverty rather than eliminate it. Out of this discussion one major proposal has emerged, the proposal that the federal government undertake some form of guaranteed income program. It is unlikely that the guaranteed, or negative, income tax proposals will enter in any major way in the 1968 presidential campaign. It does seem likely, however, that these proposals will receive increasing attention by both major parties over the next few years.

There have been a number of different proposals for guaranteed income. One of the first major proponents was Professor Milton Friedman, economic adviser to Barry Goldwater during his presidential campaign. All of the proposals have one thing in common—the federal government would make payments to families and individuals whose incomes fall below a stated amount. Professor Rolph's article presents one such proposal. Professor Hildebrand's article expresses one of many possible criticisms that could be raised against the negative income tax. Henry Hazlitt, writing in an April 1967 issue of *The National Review*, found the proposals to be economically and morally indefensible. If the guaranteed income is to assure everyone a life of dignity, then Mr. Hazlitt questions whether the government could simply give the money to individuals without determining whether they used the money in dignity, or, instead, used it as a means to guarantee a life of dissipation, drunkenness, dope addiction, or crime. Mr. Hazlitt points out that a guaranteed right to an income is simply another way of saying that somebody else must earn more than he needs, or wants, to live on so that the surplus can be taken by the government and turned over to those who can't or won't earn an income sufficient to live in dignity.

If the existing federal programs fail to solve the problems of poverty in America, then stronger measures, such as the negative income tax or family allowances, will receive increasing political attention. It is unlikely that the discussion will remain free of charges and counter-charges. What the perplexed voter must look for, then, are politicians who discuss poverty without resorting to shibboleths or slogans.

Robert Sherrill
IT ISN'T TRUE THAT NOBODY STARVES IN AMERICA

Heywood Broun, watching a breadline in 1932, is said to have remarked with cynical sympathy, "Poor people wouldn't be such a bother if they didn't starve so publicly." Since the end of the Depression, and especially in recent years with the development of more sophisticated welfare programs, poor people have been much more discreet about their starving.

Occasionally, the public peace of mind is elbowed by a news story indicating that something may not be quite right—a Mississippi family is reported to have eaten a cat; some Kentucky coal miners are seen eating only potato peelings for lunch; in Washington, D.C., pensioners scramble for discarded lettuce and cabbage leaves behind one of the largest markets. But most poor people are not observed in their ingenuities, and, in any event, the Government lists only 1,279 deaths from "malnutrition" and 197 deaths from "hunger, thirst, and exposure" in 1965, the last year for which there are statistics.

This, coupled with the natural optimism of Americans, has pushed into public faith an almost religious tenet—a second miracle of the loaves and fishes—called Nobody Starves in America, with the alternate title, No Adult Is Completely Broke for Long.

As with most economic dogmas, both are false, yet the founda-

From "It Isn't True That Nobody Starves in America," by Robert Sherrill. © 1967 by the New York Times Company. Reprinted by permission. *New York Times Magazine*, June 4, 1967. Mr. Sherrill is Washington Correspondent for *The Nation*.

tion heaves a bit when either is challenged. And this may account for the present unease and unhappiness among some high Washington officials as they observe the Senate Anti-Poverty Subcommittee going around the country holding meetings and reviving the political topic of hunger as it has not been revived since the nineteen-thirties. (When, on Senator George Murphy's motion, the subcommittee unanimously asked President Johnson to send emergency food to Mississippi to stop wide starvation, even the Office of Economic Opportunity jumped in to belittle the subcommittee's findings.) With all the powerful antagonisms the tour is arousing, its revival mood would probably not achieve much, except that one of the evangelists on the subcommittee happens to be Senator Robert F. Kennedy, whose disciples fill many a grotto and thrive on opposition.

The problem that a majority on this subcommittee—Joseph Clark of Pennsylvania, both Kennedy brothers, Jacob Javits of New York, *et al.*—is attempting to attack is illustrated perfectly in the two charity food programs administered by the U.S. Department of Agriculture.

The older program deals in surplus commodities. The men who put it through Congress never posed as humanitarians—the basic purpose of the commodities program is to support and stabilize farm prices, not support and stabilize needy people. It distributes free food from a larder stocked with whatever the Government's price support program has piled up, and the major items include flour, cornmeal, rice, grits and dry beans.

None of this is expected to supply more than three-fourths of minimum diet requirements. The only meat, when there is any, is a canned variety which the department states in its literature is not expected to provide a family with more than one-seventh of its needs. Each member of the family gets about $5.50 worth of food a month, but the food never includes eggs, citrus fruits, green or yellow vegetables, potatoes, sugars or sweets.

A diet of nothing but "commodities" is guaranteed to produce physical lethargy, mental depression and frequent onslaughts of disease. But, after all, this is called a supplemental program, and the optimistic Agriculture Department assumes that there is other food in the house to be supplemented. As for the quality of the commodities, that is debated. I attended a welfare rights conference at which the delegate from New York City said the commodities are "not fit for pigs." This came as something of a surprise to the delegate from Mississippi, who pointed out that in those relatively few parts of the South which have permitted this Federal program to operate, thousands of Negroes live on nothing else.

The other Federal anti-hunger program run by the Agriculture Department is food stamps.

Enaction of this program was the first thing President Kennedy did in the White House. Today 41 states participate to varying degrees; all major cities are in it except New York and Boston, and New York may join if pending Congressional legislation increases its funds.

Theoretically, it is a gorgeous program, constructed around the notion that everybody spends something for food each month, but poor people just don't spend enough. Solution: Allow the poor people to pay the Department of Agriculture what they would ordinarily spend for food, and in return give them bonus stamps which are just as good as money for buying any U.S.-produced food in the stores. A scale had to be worked out arbitrarily to decide what people "ordinarily" spend, but the department had no trouble settling on a scale starting at $2 a head, with a maximum payment of $12 a month for the largest family with the lowest income. In exchange for the $12, the family would get $70 worth of tickets.

The assumption is that any adult breadwinner can manage to raise $2 for each member of his family once a month. For Congressman Jamie Whitten of Mississippi, chairman of the House Subcommittee for Agriculture Appropriations, this is more than an assumption; it is a certainty. Whitten is a powerful man in agriculture. Secretary of Agriculture Orville Freeman sometimes says, "I have two bosses. One is President Johnson. The other is Jamie Whitten." So when Freeman wants to clear something important, he takes it to Whitten.

Recently he went to Whitten for a private consultation on the idea of lowering the food stamp prices, maybe to 50 cents for people with no income. After all, there was a lot of rumbling in Mississippi. There were rumors, even, that some Negroes were so desperate they were contemplating breaking into Government warehouses. Well, what did Whitten think about it? "Nonsense," said Whitten. "There's nobody in Mississippi who can't raise $2 a month. If there is, just bring me a list of them and we'll take care of them." Freeman left the proposal at that.

If he ever gets around to making up the list—which should be about the longest noncensus list in history—Miss Marian Wright, Jackson attorney for the N.A.A.C.P., will be glad to give him her file of several hundred sworn paupers. Gene Roberts, head of the New York Times bureau in Atlanta, can probably add plenty of names. He recently wrote of one Locket Mayze, 59, who said "he could not remember when he last had a dollar in his pocket or when—with the exception of a hog's head given him by a friend—his wife and eight children had eaten anything other than surplus farm commodities." A couple of weeks ago Jim Hyatt told, in The Wall Street Journal, of meeting Richard Bogen, 62-year-old Negro farmhand, in an Arkansas plantation store, where he sat "with cap in hand and tears filling his eyes" because " 'Right now I've got just 2 pennies in my pocket.' " These people may be invisible to politicians, but any reporter who covers the South is constantly running into the Mayzes and the Bogens.

"Government administrators seem not to understand," Negro leader A. Philip Randolph told the National Advisory Commission on Rural Poverty, "that the poorest people simply don't have money." The South is thick with Negroes who live in a primitive world of barter. They work or they don't work, but when they do work it is for past debts or to establish future credit. No money changes hands. They wear cast-off clothes, they eat charity food. They buy nothing. The share-croppers wound up the season last October either in debt to their landlords or coming out of the cotton year with, say, $50—which promptly went to pay debts in town. Their pockets have been empty for six or seven months, at least. To them, $2 a head—or even 50 cents a head—for the stamp program might as well be $2,000 a head. They simply can't raise it. If they could raise it, it would only be by borrowing from their landlords, who charge up to 50 per cent interest.

The best proof of the nonexistence of money in some areas lies in the Agriculture Department's own file cabinets, where records show that in eight Mississippi counties that changed over from commodities to food ·stamps (the department won't permit both programs to operate in the same county because, with its usual optimism, it assumes a family getting cheap food doesn't need additional free food) the list of participants fell off by 21,000—which can be presumed to be the number who did not have the money to stay in. Although these two programs at present are social booby traps, with relatively minor adjustments they could be perfected and with even fewer changes could be spread. Agriculture officials concede that in the South there are 17.5 million people in poverty (nearly half the nation's total) but only two million are receiving Federal food.

Of the 283 poorest counties in 15 Southern and border states, 93 counties—the home of three million people considered poor by O.E.O. standards—have no form of food distribution whatever. In the other 190 counties live 7,100,367 poor people, but only 1,029,331 get food aid. There are several reasons the other six million may have been excluded: maybe they can't afford to pay for the stamps; maybe the commodities distribution center is too far from their home; maybe local welfare workers have not bothered to tell them about the programs or welfare officials have refused to qualify them for help. In some states it isn't easy to qualify. Department of Agriculture officials acknowledge, for example, that if a four-person family in South Carolina earns more than $1,400 a year it cannot qualify for the stamp program (the only aid available), although the O.E.O. rates nonfarm families of four as poor if they don't earn more than $2,250 a year.

Hard times aren't limited to the back country. Of the 310,000 persons living in Mobile County, Alabama, 99,000 are judged poor by Federal standards. None has access to either commodities or food stamps. Of the 67,000 poor in Pulaski County (Little Rock), Arkansas, only 3,483 get Federal food. In Harris County, Texas, location of the South's largest city, Houston, there are a quarter of a million poor people but only 20,000 get food aid, and only the commodities.

Unquestionably it is easier, however, to exist in the urban clumps. The odd job is easier to come by. Proximity helps—it is more convenient to send the children to a neighbor's table, or to borrow a dollar from a relative whose welfare check hasn't been held up. It is easier to wangle an Aid to Dependent Children check in urban counties because hunger is unsightly and the cities are more sensitive to esthetics these days.

The family living in the shanty on the "back 40" of the old plantation is out of sight, out of the county officials' minds, and therefore usually out of luck. In this respect, the forces squeezing the blacks out of the rural South and into the Northern cities may be nutritionally beneficial. The squeezing forces are fourfold: there's a cotton cutback in some areas; mechanization of many jobs is almost total; weed-killing chemicals are eliminating the need for a human being on the end of a hoe; and the $1-an-hour minimum wage that went into effect this year is re-hardening many a planter's heart. The same people who were considered "good ol' darkies" a few years ago are now considered deadwood, hardly worth keeping alive.

Nowhere are the faults and the promises of the Government's food distribution program seen better than in Mississippi, which has one of the most complete programs in America. Every county in the state participates in some form of Federal assistance, which is rare not merely by Southern standards but by national standards. Nowhere else in the Bible Belt are poor folks given anything like a comparable amount of assistance.

One-fourth of all Mississippians (about 470,000) are eating federally paid-for food, more even than New York's charity food population (440,000). The food comes via Washington, but at least Mississippi lets it in. By comparison, South Carolina won't let the commodities program into the state at all and permits the stamp program to operate in only 10 of 46 counties; in only three of the 20 poorest counties are the stamps sold, and on such a tight basis that only 10,900 of the 715,000 poor in these counties are assisted. Virginia has food programs for only 1.9 per cent of its impoverished people; Texas covers only 5.6 per cent; Louisiana, 7.9 per cent. In the Deep South no state but Mississippi allows more than 10.9 per cent of its poor people to participate in food programs—and Mississippi offers them to 42.3 per cent.

Yet Mississippi is a laboratory of hunger and of Federal fumbling. On the Delta—that northwestern bulge of the state that arches along the river from Memphis to Vicksburg—one can stand on a steaming summer day and be persuaded that God created the world simply to give Adam a cotton allotment. There is big money here. Delta plantation owners will take out of the soil more than a quarter of a billion dollars this year, most of it in tax-supported crops. In the same area, because of newly mechanized farming techniques, Government officials estimate there will be between 60,000 and 100,000 unemployed hands by this summer. And, since Mississippi has no general state or local welfare programs, these people must depend on Federal largesse.

Choose any shanty; only the number of bodies inside will vary. Here is a mother and six children, residents of Washington County, against the river. Four of the children are asleep on the floor. They sleep most of the day as well as all night. Their lips and legs are covered with scabs and open sores. The youngest has a distended stomach and from it the umbilical knot sticks out like a valve from an intertube. Some days they eat nothing. Most days they have one meal, of cornmeal. Washington County quit the commodities program in March and went on food stamps. Left over commodities are all this family has. Now, it is after 2 P.M. and they have eaten nothing, but the mother says she will cook "a little something" later on. She points to a bag on the floor by the stove; a couple of inches of meal are left of what has lasted them two weeks. When she runs out of cornmeal, she will borrow something from a neighbor. Yes, she nods, the neighbors are in bad shape, too. But she will get something.

This must be an extreme case, so drive on, northeast into the Delta's proudest county, Sunflower, home of Senator James O. ("Our Jim") Eastland, who operates a 5,800 acre plantation near Ruleville, which is also the home of Sunflower County's next best-known politician, Mrs. Fannie Lou Hamer, a leader of the Mississippi Freedom Democratic party. Mrs. Hamer used to be a sharecropper, but, like many thousands of others, she was chased off the land. Being well imbedded in the 32 million in this country officially designated as impoverished, Mrs. Hamer speaks empirically: "The main problem about bein' poor is that it only leaves you the choice between not eatin' at all and eatin' so bad you wonder if that is a improvement."

Although reared on a farm and now middle-aged, she has eaten turkey only twice in her life, once a couple of years ago when comedian

Dick Gregory shipped a batch of the birds to Mississippi Negroes and the other time when she bought a turkey on the installment plan and paid for it at the rate of 70 cents a week. When the conversation turns to food, Mrs. Hamer will always mention those two turkeys, because otherwise she has nothing to talk about except the customary meat that gets on her table—meat that is thinly attached to hog neckbones (she broke off a front tooth discovering just how thinly attached). She is a big woman, built out in rings of starch—rice and grits and more grits and flour—held together by bean proteins. Perhaps once a year she eats fruit, but only if a friend who has moved to the relatively luxurious welfare rolls of the North sends it. She cannot afford it herself.

Even the little towns of Mississippi, places like Indianola, county seat of Sunflower, have their slums and they are full of farm hands who no longer have a farm to work on and have come into town to do their starving. I met a boy in Indianola who had had nothing to eat that day but a plate of butterbeans; the day before it had been bread and butterbeans; the day before that, again just butterbeans. Sometimes, he said, it was bread alone. One-course diets are commonplace. Kenneth Dean, executive director of the Mississippi Council on Human Relations, who has moved among these people for many months, describes a typical hardship case:

"Breakfast will be grits, molasses and biscuit. For lunch, the adults will eat nothing, and the children who are at home will be given a piece of bread and a drink of Kool-Aid or water. The evening meal usually consists of boiled beans and cornbread." In the worst cases, which are not uncommon, "there is usually no table on which to eat, and what little food there is is eaten by hand out of a bowl or from a newspaper on the floor."

With hunger so abundant and easy to find, it might be anticipated that the Department of Agriculture would react to it in a dramatic fashion. But this has not been the case. Seventeen months ago, Congressman Joseph Resnick, Democrat of New York, made a tour of Mississippi and came back to Washington writing letters to all the appropriate Administration leaders about the "desperation point of . . . starving Negroes." Nothing happened.

A month later 35 Negroes invaded the abandoned Greenville, Miss., Air Force Base, and before a phalanx of troops was flown in to evict them they distributed leaflets explaining: "We are here because we are hungry and cold and we have no jobs or land." It made the front pages as a protest story, but their appeal for food somehow went astray. Last summer the Department of Agriculture's own Civil Rights Advisory Council held hearings in Jackson, Miss., and made confidential recommendations to Secretary Freeman that he act upon their "deep sense of urgency" that something must be done swiftly "before suffering, hopelessness and frustration make an evolutionary approach extremely difficult and infinitely more expensive, if not—for an interim—impossible." About the same time, across the Mississippi River, Arkansas State Welfare Director A. J. Moss was writing letters to Freeman, warning that thousands of families would soon be unemployed on the Arkansas Delta and that the food situation was critical. Neither warning disquieted the adamant Agriculture Department calm.

Then, in April, the Clark-Kennedy troupe hit Mississippi, accompanied by TV cameramen, journalistic jongleurs and the usual ballyhoo machinery. It made a difference. At this point Freeman began to move cautiously. He dispatched two of his aides—Howard Davis and William Seabron—to Mississippi for a confidential report. Davis and Seabron found, of course, what everyone else had been reporting for more than a year: many Mississippians are limp with malnutrition, many cannot afford to buy the food stamps, and some landlords are profiteering off the programs. Among the cases of suffering they cited a man in Winstonville, father of six, who got into the food stamp program only because "a New York A.B.C. newsman on assignment in Mississippi gave him $12 twice to buy food stamps. He does not know what he will do when his present commodities and stamp supplies are gone."

Another case: Mrs. Effie Mae Jackson of Billy May Plantation, mother of five, "has a problem of having the date to buy stamps come prior to receipt of her check from welfare. To meet this she borrows from her landlord the $22 each month, and when her check comes he charges her 50 cents on the dollar, which means she has to pay $33 for the stamps each month." This, plus her $10-a-month rent, means that she must pay $43 for food and rent out of the $55 she gets from welfare.

For some reason, the story Davis and Seabron brought back penetrated where others had failed. Freeman wrote Senator Clark that he was "deeply concerned about their findings" and that he might change the rules to make persons with no income pay only a fourth as much as at present. He said this before talking with Congressman Whitten. After the latest Whitten conversation, Freeman told Jack Conway, head of the Industrial Union Department of the A.F.L.-C.I.O. and unofficial boss of Walter Reuther's Citizens Crusade against Poverty, that he isn't going to try to cut the stamps' cost "until the department budget gets out of Whitten's committee."

And that is where reform of the program stands today. It hasn't started.

Civil rights leaders damn Freeman for not opening his ears until two winters had passed since he was first alerted to the predicament of the foodless Southern Negro. But Freeman is not his own man in this dispute. In many respects he is the prisoner of the Southerners who command the agriculture committees and the agriculture appropriations subcommittees in both houses of Congress. As human-support programs, neither the free commodities nor the food stamps are popular with these groups. A bill is now being pushed by some House Southerners that would kill the food stamp program by making it prohibitively costly for many states, particularly those states in Dixie with the highest concentration of Negroes. Many farm-oriented legislators have a hoary suspicion that any give-away program promotes shiftlessness among the menials.

Nowhere is this attitude better seen than in Alabama, where the distribution of Federal food is made inversely to need, and also inversely to the concentration of Negroes. The 30 richest counties, in the top half of the state, participate in the free-food program; the 37 poorest counties in the bottom do not. Although not notorious for pampering Negroes, the Alabama administration nevertheless encourages the acceptance of Federal surplus foods by the counties because it is a sure-fire way of "beating" Washington. For a very small expense—about one or two cents a day per recipient—the counties receive a cornucopia of food. Montgomery County, for example, would pay about $15,000 a year as the cost of distributing almost $1,000,000 in commodities to its people.

But Montgomery County won't enter the program. Neither will other counties where most of the state's Negroes live. Tallapoosa County, home of the State Welfare Commissioner, refuses to pay the $10,000 required to distribute $700,000 worth of surplus foods. The Negro leaders of Hale County have been trying for two years to get county officials to bring in a food program. First the officials said it was too expensive, but when Washington offered to bear the total cost, they still refused. Agriculture officials refuse to fight this kind of local obstinacy. Secretary Freeman promised a commodities program for Hale last August, but he hasn't delivered it yet.

Could the Federal Government just send the food in anyway, without local approval, and have Federal workers distribute it or let the poor people distribute it themselves? Yes; for 30 years the Secretary of Agriculture has had power to distribute food where emergencies exist. And, when pressed hard enough, he will. When Negroes in Dallas County, already warmed up by the Selma civil rights activities in 1965, began demonstrating loudly because they wanted food, Federal officials told Dallas County leaders the food was coming in, and if they wouldn't distribute it, civil rights leaders would. Dallas County surrendered and took the goods, but the scope of the victory is disputed. Some say it only hardened the will of surrounding counties to resist.

This kind of tugging and heaving reveals the great weakness of the food programs: commercial interests of the South use them for reprisal and coercion. They are the political and social weapons of a region. Free Federal food was valued by the Delta planters for many years because, by allowing their hired hands to live off it through the winter, it became a kind of subsidy for the farmers. (Free commodities were never given to Delta Negroes after spring plowing time, because a little hunger was expected to make them eager to earn $3 a day in the fields.)

But now that farming has become almost totally mechanized, field hands are, as one planter put it, "as useless as a mule." They and their shotgun shanties only clutter the landscape, chafing the consciences and the pocketbooks of the region. Get rid of them. And what better way than to shift to a food program they cannot afford? Half of the Delta counties have already dropped the commodities and put in food stamps. "What does that mean?" asked Amzie Moore, a Negro leader from Cleveland, Miss. "That means starve or go to Chicago. Well, we're not going to Chicago. We don't want the stamps unless it's a free stamp program."

The angry Negroes have some support. That faint thunder in the distance may develop into a real challenge. The U.S. Commission on Civil Rights has circulated a memo implying that Freeman has ignored his obvious powers to bring relief. The commission urges free food stamps for the penniless and both programs operating simultaneously in the poorest counties. The leaders of Reuther's Citizens Crusade want to strip Freeman of his role in distributing food and turn the whole job over to the Department of Health, Education, and Welfare—which was in fact Senator John Kennedy's proposal in 1959. The Crusade is putting out some pretty snappish statements about the preeminence of nutrition over profits. And now Senator Javits has asked the Senate Executive Reorganization Subcommittee to consider the "strip Freeman" proposal.

If impoverished Southerners are judged strictly as an economic factor, more food to keep them alive can be viewed skeptically as merely a temporary solution to the problem of making them profitable. But for them temporariness has always been a relative matter, and they would probably just as soon be fed even on that basis—for, as one high Citizens Crusade official pointed out: "We've been keeping them alive on a temporary basis for 300 years." Something more permanent, he felt, is not wholly impossible and is "limited only by the amount of money that American capitalism, with its Dixiecrat-dominated agriculture committees in Congress, is willing to spend to create a 20th century civilization in the South." The vagueness of the statement is important; here is a man who for a lifetime has been professionally concerned with labor and housing conditions of the Southern poor, and yet he has no specific plans to improve them, and the specific planners have not come much farther.

Many say that the salvation of the hungry Negro lies in modification of the agricultural South with industry. It is an old dream. Since the days of Gov. Hugh White's "Balance Agriculture with Industry" program a generation ago, Mississippi has been trying to bring in the smokestacks, and the same has been true for the South as a whole since the days of Henry Grady. Yet the skies over the South's vast boondocks are just about as blue and unsmudged as ever. Others, including such practical groups as the Southern Regional Council, are pushing for farm cooperatives to give the landed Negro independence from a repressive social structure. But this, too, though spottily successful, is something that has been tried off and on for years without more than denting the general poverty of the black farmer.

These efforts and failures are quite beside the point to the Negro who faces another one-meal, beans-only day. Very much to the point is the knowledge that his life can be changed, and immediately, by the simplest of Agriculture Department fiats.

If change does come, it will probably take some powerful motivating emotion to achieve it. But there is hope for that, too. When Robert Kennedy returned from his safari into Mississippi's shanty jungles, he told of seeing people who eat one meal every two days, but he described the results only as "extreme hunger." For politicians, "starvation" is a smut word. They don't like to come right out and say it exists in this country—so it becomes "hunger" or "malnutrition"—and even less do they like to see that which the taboo word describes; it embarrasses them. Testifying before a Senate group about swollen bellies and running sores and all the cottonpatch grotesqueries he had seen, Kennedy several times became so embarrassed he laughed. The last best hope of "extremely hungry" folks is that that discomfort will spread.

House of Representatives
RAT EXTERMINATION ACT OF 1967

MR. MATSUNAGA. ...Mr. Speaker, House Resolution 749 provides an open rule with 1 hour of general debate for consideration of

From *Congressional Record*, House of Representatives, July 20, 1967, pp. H9113–9120.

H.R. 11000 to provide Federal financial assistance to help cities and communities of the Nation develop and carry out intensive local programs of rat control and extermination. . . .

H.R. 11000 would authorize Federal assistance to cover two-thirds of the cost of 3-year local programs for rat extermination and control. The grants would be made to local governments, and the bill requires that the community have an approved workable program in order to be eligible for such aid. The Secretary of Housing and Urban Development, who would make the grants, would be required to cooperate and consult with other departments which have responsibilities related to the problem of rat control. Appropriations of $20 million would be authorized for each of the fiscal years 1968 and 1969 to make these grants. In view of the savings in property damages and the relief in human misery, which are sure to result, this legislation may be properly considered as a worthwhile investment.

Mr. Speaker, I urge the adoption of House Resolution 749 in order that H.R. 11000 may be considered.

MR. GROSS.   Mr. Speaker, will the gentleman yield?

MR. MATSUNAGA.   I yield to the gentleman from Iowa. . .

MR. GROSS.   The gentleman spoke of city rats. What about country rats?

MR. MATSUNAGA.   The country rats are being taken care of under existing programs.

MR. BARRETT.   Mr. Speaker, will the gentleman yield at that point?

MR. MATSUNAGA.   I yield to the gentleman from Pennsylvania.

MR. BARRETT.   I would like to tell the gentleman from Iowa, because he is so very enthusiastic about this type of program, they do have an agricultural program directed toward rat extermination, and there is also a program in the Department of the Interior. They are doing a fairly good job on this problem, but are not doing a consistent job.

Mr. Speaker, what we are after here is a continuity of rat control in the cities in order to exterminate the rats. . .

MR. HALEY.   Mr. Speaker, will the gentleman yield?

MR. MATSUNAGA.   I yield to the gentleman from Florida.

MR. HALEY.   Mr. Speaker, I wonder sometime if some of our distinguished committees that bring before us a monstrosity such as this, would just take into consideration the fact that we have a lot of cat lovers in the Nation, and why not just buy cats and turn them loose on the rats and thereby we could take care of this situation, without any $25 million from the Treasury of the United States. . .

MR. LATTA.   . . . I say to my colleagues, in view of the fiscal situation facing this country today, this is one program we can do without. This Congress has already raised the debt ceiling during this session in order to be able to meet its financial responsibilities. We are now to face the possibility of a surtax ranging from six percent to 10 percent. The President of the United States is going to send a surtax message to the Congress. He has been talking about it since the first of the year, and I wager that before the end of this Congress, it will be up here, and you and I will be faced with the question of saddling our constituents, the taxpayers of this country, if you please, with a new tax. . . .

Mr. Speaker, there is still some local responsibility remaining in this country and the killing of rats is one of them. This is not a national matter.

There is also some responsibility on the part of individual citizens. Certainly the Federal Government cannot, and should not, fulfill every need or wish of every one of its citizens. Our tax structure cannot stand it. The matter of putting out a little bit of rat poison should not be requested of the Federal Government. . . .

It seems to me, my colleagues, that here is a matter that could be laid aside until the fiscal situation in this country has brightened. Certainly when we are expending the billions of dollars that we are in Vietnam, we can lay this proposal aside. If there is any local responsibility on the part of local government remaining, this proposal can be laid aside. If the individual has any responsibility remaining, we can lay this matter aside. The individual does not want to pay for a new rat control program at this time with all of the costly new Federal employees to be employed to put out rat poison that the individual citizen could put out for himself. . .

MR. BROYHILL OF VIRGINIA.   Mr. Speaker, will the gentleman yield?

MR. LATTA.   I yield to the gentleman from Virginia.

MR. BROYHILL OF VIRGINIA.   Mr. Speaker, the gentleman made a very clear statement on how this rat bill discriminates against a lot of rats in this country. The committee report also shows that the bill discriminates against 97½ percent of the rats.

But I think the most profound statement the gentleman made is the fact that it does set up a new bureau and sets up possibly a commissioner on rats or an administrator of rats and a bunch of new bureaucrats on rats. There is no question but that there will be a great demand for a lot of rat patronage. I think by the time we get through taking care of all of the bureaucrats in this new rat bureau along with the waste and empire building, none of the $40 million will be left to take care of the 2½ percent of the rats who were supposed to be covered in the bill.

Mr. Speaker, I think the "rat smart thing" for us to do is to vote down this rat bill "rat now."

MR. LATTA.   I may say to the gentleman that when he raises the question of discriminating between city and country rats, it also discriminates against persons suffering from bites from other animals.

Forgetting about the rodents for a moment, it was mentioned by the gentleman from Hawaii that we have over 1,000 rat bite cases in the United States in a year's time.

How about the snake bite cases?

If we are going to start eradicating all the rats—how about the snakes in the West? How about bugs? You can go into homes and apartment buildings here in the city of Washington and find bugs galore. What are you going to do about the bugs? Are we to forget the people bitten by bugs? Should we start a bug corps? . . .

MRS. GRIFFITHS.   . . . Before this bill becomes too funny, I would like to say a few words for it. I am in support of this bill, Mr. Speaker. When I first came to this Congress I asked the Library of Congress how much this Nation had spent on defense in its history. They put some Ph.D.'s to work on the subject, and after 3 months replied that at that time—13 years ago—we had spent more than $1 trillion on defense. I observed the other day, when we had the Defense appropriation bill—which as I recall was for more than $75 billion—there was only one person who voted "No."

I would like to point out to those who may not be aware of it or to those who may have forgotten it, that rats are Johnny-come-latelys to recorded history. They were unknown in the ancient cities of the world. They came in out of the Arabian deserts about the 12th century, and from that day to this they have killed more human beings than all of the generals in the world combined. They have made Genghis Khan, Hitler, and all the other men look like pikers. Man has attempted to kill them and he has won a few battles, but he has lost the war.

The only enemy that has ever really killed rats is other rats.

For the benefit of those who may not know it, the average rat lives 3 years. It has a rootless tooth that grows 29½ inches in those 3 years. They have been known to cut through 4 feet of reinforced concrete.

All of the methods that one could possibly use cannot conceivably kill off more than 98 percent of the rats in one block. If there are left two males and 10 females, there will be 3,000 rats in 1 year to replace those that have been killed.

Perhaps Members think it does not make any real difference, and perhaps they think this is really a local problem, that it is a family problem, and why not get some rat poison and kill the rats in the household?

I should like to remind the Members who sit here in this body that they eat in restaurants night after night after night, and that all that can be done in this Capitol cannot control the rat population.

Rats are a living cargo of death. Their tails swish through sewers and over that food we eat. Their stomachs are filled with tularemia, amoebic dysentery. They carry the most deadly diseases, and some think it is funny. Some do not want to spend $40 million.

Mr. Speaker, if we are going to spend $79 billion to try to kill off a few Vietcong, believe me I would spend $40 million to kill off the most devastating enemy man has ever had. . . .

MR. DEVINE.   Mr. Speaker, I suppose this is another one of President Johnson's economy-in-Government schemes, although it is hard to try to label this as a reduction in domestic spending. In fact, it rings pretty hollow after the most recent gesture of L.B.J. when he "urged across the board cuts of 15 percent." How in the world does spending $40,000,000 chasing rats assist in trying to reduce the greatest deficit in history—now predicted at about $30 billion for fiscal 1968?

Some of us here in this body have been around long enough to remember when the American people were willing to exercise a little bit of initiative and personal resourcefulness and solve local problems on a local level. In fact they were frequently resolved on a personal basis, and Washington was not troubled with dotting every "i" and crossing every "t." The well-known television commercial, "Please, Mother, I would rather do it myself," was a source of pride and personal satisfaction. But, not if L.B.J. has his way.

The committee report claims "many children" are attacked, "maimed and even killed by rats, as an everyday occurrence." Come, now, let us have some supporting information. I am sure if rats were killing children every day, all of us would have heard something about it. The report goes on to say Philadelphia, St. Louis, and Cleveland have all recently averaged over 50 ratbites per year. Golly, almost one a week—so, spend $40 million. . . .

Inquiry through local dealers indicates rattraps—not mouse-traps—sell for $3.30 per dozen or about 28 cents each. A pretty fair brand of cheese costs 49 cents per pound and would bait 35 traps. So, for an extremely small personal investment, nearly every citizen could cooper-ate and eliminate this problem, and at the same time, save their Govern-ment $40 million. Would not this seem to be a wise step, particularly when the President and his advisers are calling on all Americans for more taxes to pay for the costs of Government?

Finally, one of our respected colleagues tells me he has about 23 cats in and around his barns, all of which he will make available to HUD, without charge. These feline ratcatchers are most effective, partic-ularly since they are led by a highly respected tomcat called Cotton that has earned a most enviable reputation in the ratcatching department.

Seriously, here is an excellent opportunity for the President, the administration, the Congress, to do more than pay lipservice to reducing Federal spending, and I urge my colleagues to vote against this bill known as H.R. 11000. . .

MR. BARRETT. . . . Mr. Speaker, I have noticed an unfortunate tendency among a number of people when this bill is discussed to indulge in jesting remarks, puns, and supposedly comical clichés. Let me assure my colleagues, Mr. Speaker, that in many of the areas of our cities this is no laughing or joking matter. It is a matter of the utmost serious-ness and gravity. Believe me, Mr. Speaker, there is nothing funny about rats and rat bites.

In the minority views of our committee report, the point is made that the funds authorized in this bill will be able to finance an intensified attack on rats in areas having a population of, and I quote, "only 5 million." I wish that the bill contained a larger authorization because the more money we authorize, the more rats we will exterminate. The $40 million authorized to cover 3-year programs was all we believed to be practically achievable. But let us not belittle a program that will offer the hope of ending the rat menace for 5 million human beings. Mr. Speaker, we should bear in mind that these 5 million people are the very millions who live in precisely the neighborhoods where the rat problem is most intense.

So, Mr. Speaker, I beseech and beg my colleagues from the bottom of my heart to vote overwhelmingly for this great, compassionate, and humane program for rat extermination which President Johnson recommended and which our committee endorsed. . . .

MR. MATSUNAGA. Mr. Speaker, I have no further requests for time. I move the previous question.

The previous question was ordered.

THE SPEAKER PRO TEMPORE (MR. ROONEY OF NEW YORK). The question is on the resolution.

MR. RHODES OF ARIZONA. Mr. Speaker, on that I demand the yeas and nays.

The yeas and nays were ordered.

The question was taken; and there were—yeas 176, nays 207, not voting 49. . . .

Earl R. Rolph
THE CASE FOR A NEGATIVE INCOME TAX DEVICE

The persistence in the United States of millions of people who are poor is a basic reason for the interest in what is often called negative income taxation. In a society which is supposedly the most affluent in the world, the presence of 30 to 35 million people described as poor, depending on one's definition of poverty, scarcely accords with the American dream. In the minds of some, it may raise nagging doubts about both the political structure and the economic system that generates such results. Strong supporters of the American system find it less embarrassing to diagnose poverty as a consequence of some deficiency in poor people, such as laziness, and enjoin them to reform their behavior. But such a diagnosis implies that people are poor out of choice, that they happen to have a strong preference for leisure. Such a diagnosis scarcely fits the evidence.

From "The Case for a Negative Income Tax Device," by Earl R. Rolph, *Industrial Relations*, Vol. 6, No. 2, February 1967. Reprinted by permission. Earl R. Rolph is Professor of Economics, University of California, Berkeley.

The reasons why millions of people have low incomes can be enumerated almost indefinitely. People's mental and physical characteristics differ in innumerable ways. Individual talents and inclinations for obtaining gain are subject, as well, to a wide dispersion. The main problem in explaining the income distribution observed in a complex society is not how to explain low incomes. Rather, it is how to explain why the distribution does not have normal statistical properties and in particular why the tail of the low end, including the range of negative incomes, does not have properties similar to those of the upper tail.

Welfare programs in the United States, insofar as they have any rationale, have been based on the theory that the "causes" of low income can be enumerated. Specific measures related to those causes can supposedly provide adequate assistance. Thus there are the categorical aid programs, unemployment insurance, and old age and survivors' insurance. Since the causes are not exhaustive, some cases of distress are inevitably left uncovered by public programs.

A welfare system aimed at alleviating poverty should adopt the premise that income dispersion, including negative income and small positive income, is normal and will not disappear next year or the year after. Since human productivity varies widely, as do other abilities, there are always some groups whose productivity will be low judged by some standard appropriate for "normal" people. If people of low productivity are to be employed in the absence of special subsidies, employers, to have an incentive to hire them, must be permitted to pay low wage rates. People's incomes from work will leave some of them and their dependents in poverty. To the extent they are denied the choice of working, by the establishment of minimum wages, their incomes will be even lower.

The income distribution as it naturally arises does not guarantee affluence for everyone in an affluent society. Government policy must be consistent with the fact that there are some able-bodied males who are not capable of earning as much as $3,000 a year or even $2,000 a year. Present welfare programs, geared as they are to various presumed causes of personal financial distress, presuppose that people not subject to special difficulties, such as ill health, old age, unemployment, etc., can earn adequate incomes and can bring up children who will develop into effective members of society. The presupposition is scarcely consistent with the facts. Mollie Orshansky found, for example, that 22.3 million people out of 27.9 million defined as poor were in families headed by a male. In addition: "Of the 15 million children counted poor in March 5.7 million were in the family of a worker who had a regular job in 1963 and was not out of work any time during the year." There are poor people who are unemployed or unemployable, but there are others who work and do so regularly. A wage structure that eliminates unemployment and underemployment of people with modest skills cannot be expected to end poverty levels of income, although such a pricing arrangement would result in a vast improvement for many presently disadvantaged groups. There is nothing in economic theory nor in the inherent charac teristics of human beings that precludes equilibrium wage rates of one dollar an hour or less for some types of labor services.

If, then, the premise is adopted that the dispersion of income, including low income, is a normal feature of economic affairs, what social measures are appropriate to obtain a socially acceptable level of income for everyone? Negative income tax devices are techniques to solve this problem.

POVERTY GAP APPROACH TO A NEGATIVE INCOME TAX

One approach to the problem is to define poverty as an amount of income less than some standard taken to be reasonably adequate, treat the difference between a person's actual income and the standard as the "poverty gap," calculate the number of dollars required to close the gap, and give each person the difference between his actual income and the standard. Poverty is then "cured" since by definition no one is left below the standard. Only few proponents embrace this position as stated in this bald manner. It is, however, a widely embraced basic premise both in and out of official circles.

Implementation would require legislation to define the standard, to provide for a definition of income as close to a person's total gain as is feasible, and to tax income obtained by the person from his own efforts at a rate of 100 per cent up to the poverty standard. Beyond this point, but not necessarily at it, the federal individual income tax may come into operation. We would then have two individual income taxes, possibly administered by different agencies—one for people with incomes below the standard and another for those above it.

The poverty gap approach to the negative income tax follows the philosophy of public assistance with some important modifications. Public assistance, as administered by states and localities, varies widely in the details of its administration. Common features of public assistance and a pure poverty gap negative income tax are a 100 per cent tax rate and, to a lesser degree, the use of income as the index of a person's or family's economic position. However, in public assistance and relief programs generally, financial aid is given only to those who apply, and then only if the applicants are deemed qualified according to the rules. The amounts of financial support provided typically fall well below the poverty level as defined by the Department of Health, Education, and Welfare.

Thus, a poverty gap negative tax would, if fully implemented at proposed levels, be a complete substitute for public assistance. This type of negative income taxation would differ, however, in the following ways from public assistance: (1) everyone whose income falls below the standard would receive assistance, thereby eliminating the need to make application; (2) reported income of those eligible would presumably be accepted as correct, subject to the same type of checking which now applies to income reported for federal income tax purposes; (3) the amount of assistance paid to an eligible family would be greater, in many cases several thousand dollars a year greater, than that under public assistance; and (4) the effective tax rate would not ordinarily exceed 100 per cent; under public assistance the rate for a person who takes a temporary job may be on occasion 200 per cent or even 1,000 per cent, depending on the rules applied to him, the difficulties he has returning to the relief rolls, and loss of free medical care for children. Rates in excess of 100 per cent mean that a person is punished for taking a job.

There are a number of difficulties with the poverty gap approach. A major one is that it is unfinanced. Billions of dollars would need to be disbursed to people with low incomes, and billions of dollars are not now presently lying around in the federal budget. In the happy event that the Viet Nam war is brought to a satisfactory conclusion, the funds used for it might be shifted to closing the poverty gap. Otherwise a major tax increase would be required. Such a tax increase would have to be over and above that presently needed for anti-inflationary purposes. In the absence of clear evidence of "progress" in the Viet Nam war, the poverty gap program may become financially feasible only some years hence, if at all.

The 100 per cent tax rate feature of the poverty gap approach is, of course, unworkable. Apart from other considerations, a 100 per cent tax rate means that people must work for nothing or else conceal their incomes. To enforce such a rate would probably require a return to the relief approach. Then a person who refuses a job may be disciplined by cutting him and his family off the rolls. Recognizing the unworkability of 100 per cent rates, poverty gap advocates have suggested lower rates, such as 80 per cent; few seem willing to go below 50 per cent.

This compromise of principle with practicality requires that the goal of closing the poverty gap be abandoned in favor of a more modest goal and that the non-poor be subsidized. If an income of $3,000 a year for a family of four is taken as the poverty line, and if for reasons of enforceability the tax rate is placed at 50 per cent, the goal of ending poverty would require an allowance of $3,000 a year to ensure that a family with a zero income would achieve a disposable income of $3,000. This technique would mean, however, that a family with an income of

$5,000 would get an allowance of $3,000, pay $2,500 in gross tax, and receive a net sum of $500 a year from the Treasury. Thus, people who are defined as non-poor would obtain a net subsidy if the allowance is placed at the poverty line with any tax rate below 100 per cent. To poverty gap thinkers, payments to those above the poverty line are viewed as inefficient or wasteful of public funds.

If, on the other hand, the allowance is placed below the poverty line, the goal of eliminating poverty is partially sacrificed. Instead of a disposable income of $3,000 for a family of four, a smaller allowance must be established. Obviously, the lower the credit, the greater will be the poverty gap remaining. The possible combinations of allowance size and tax rate are indefinitely large, but all would leave the poverty gap more or less unfilled.

There are numerous objections to the establishment of two federal income taxes, one for the poor and one for the non-poor. With two laws, means would have to be found to prevent some members of a family from successfully classifying themselves as poor by splitting off from the family for tax purposes. A large financial incentive would exist to divide the family into zero income units, leaving perhaps only the father to report positive income. The precise gain to a family would depend on the size of the allowance, the tax rate for low incomes, the tax rate for high incomes, and the definition of income. Rules might be devised to minimize family splitting for tax purposes. Effective rules have not, however, been devised for the present federal income tax law for families with property income. It remains feasible to give children assets, the income from which is taxed at lower rates than it would be if left in the names of the parents. The incentive to split income within the family arises from rate graduation under present law.

A further difficulty in a poverty gap design of a negative income tax is the treatment of people who, in a particular year, have a low income but are not poor. A person with assets of, say, $1,000,000, may in a particular year have an income of a negative amount or a small positive amount. He would, however, be classified as poor under a poverty gap system. A young engineer just completing his Ph.D. degree may have an income of $2,000 in one year, and hence be eligible for negative tax treatment, and have an income of $15,000 the following year. Given the fact that the income of some people fluctuates, there are certain to be people who are highly affluent, judged either by their net worth or by their average income over several years, but who have low incomes in particular years.

According to the usually accepted principles of income taxation, there is no objection to paying money to people who normally pay tax, but who, in a given year, happen to have low incomes. Under present law, for example, there are some modest averaging provisions, and persons in business who report negative incomes in a given year may be entitled to take advantage of loss carry-back and carry-forward provisions. In the case of loss carry-backs, people who so qualify are paid by the treasury for the year in which they suffer losses. In this aspect, the present law is a negative income tax. Provisions would be necessary to ascertain a person's negative or positive tax liability in the event he attains less than the poverty level income in a given year. To avoid hopeless confusion, the two income tax laws would have to be made consistent in their treatment of people with fluctuating incomes.

The above difficulties are a small sample of the actual difficulties likely to arise from having two federal individual income taxes. Until and unless the details of the laws are actually drafted, it is impossible to know all the problems that would emerge and what rules would be needed to prevent abuses. The one sure result is even greater complexity than now exists in income taxation in the United States.

CREDIT TAX APPROACH

There are many ways of designing a single federal individual income tax and a system of allowances. I shall set forth here a plan described as a credit income tax. The goals of this plan are: (1) to redistribute income systematically in the direction of reducing the present inequality, (2) to minimize incentive problems associated with high marginal rates, and (3) to reduce radically the complexity of the present federal income tax law.

The plan would reduce, and reduce substantially, the incidence of genuine poverty in the United States. However, the complete elimination of poverty would be at best a long-run target. As in other areas of economics, the critical issues are in the nature of more-or-less, rather than all-or-none. Poverty can never be totally eliminated unless society places those who are hopelessly incompetent in managing their own affairs in institutions and denies them their freedom.

The credit income tax suggested here has two main features: a system of flat-sum credits to which all residents of the United States would be entitled, and a general proportional income tax with zero exemptions. A person's or a family's net tax liability, plus or minus, is given by the formula, $T = Yr - Cu$, where T is the net tax liability, Y is taxable income, r is the tax rate, C is the size of the credit (assuming uniform per capita credits), and u is the number of credits for the unit (normally the family).

To illustrate, suppose the credit is $500 a person a year, and the tax rate is 30 per cent. Table 1 shows the tax liability for a family of four.

This combination of tax rate and credit would provide a net payment by the Treasury ranging from $2,000 for a person or family with an income of zero (ignoring truly negative income) to zero at a level slightly in excess of $6,000 of income.

The higher the credit, given the tax rate, the larger will be the net payments made to people with low incomes. On the other hand, the tax rate depends on the size of the credit. The rate also depends on the desired yield of the tax to the Treasury and the size of the tax base. To calculate the tax rate for the country as a whole, the following formula may be used: $r = \dfrac{\Sigma C + R}{Y}$ where ΣC is the sum of the credits, R is the desired yield, and Y is total taxable income. Taking the population in round figures to be 200 million, the credit to be $400 per capita, the desired yield to be $50 billion, and total taxable income to be $500 billion, we get:

$$r = \frac{\$80 \text{ billion} + 50 \text{ billion}}{500 \text{ billion}} = 26 \text{ per cent.}$$

In recent years, the yield of the federal individual income tax has been in the neighborhood of 9 to 10 per cent of personal income. If personal income were the tax base, a credit of $400 per capita would "cost" about 16 percentage points in the rate. This result does not mean that the average rate of tax would rise from 10 to 26 per cent of personal income. The effective or average rate would remain at 10 per cent. The extra percentage points become the "price" paid for redistribution, including redistribution to one's self.

To implement the credit income tax plan it would be necessary to redraft large parts of the present federal income tax law. It might seem rather drastic to suggest that the federal income tax should be radically changed in order to increase the incomes of people who presently have low incomes. In fact, however, a great part of this task would consist of simplifying the present law. Many of the complexities of the law as it now exists are a direct consequence of graduated rates. As Blum and Calvin have emphasized in this connection, much of the work of lawyers in the tax field arises from the simple fact that the tax rates vary, depending on how much income is reported for tax purposes in a given year. Among other things, all the complexities arising because of incentives that now exist to split income within the family would disappear. In addition, the inequities and the rules designed to deal with these inequities arising from the definition of the tax-paying unit would also disappear. Under a proportional tax the problem of averaging, a very serious problem under the present law, is solved automatically.

There are, from the point of view of tax design, large advantages to be gained by eliminating progressive rates. We ordinarily have thought in the past that it was necessary to have increasing rates of tax in order to have progressive taxation. This view turns out to be incorrect. It is possible to have proportional rates and progression by the device of a general credit, as illustrated by Table 1.

There would be social costs associated with the installation of a general credit income tax. For example, people who presently are not required to file would have to file to be eligible for the credit. This is about 10 per cent of the population. Although the group is relatively small, the compliance task would not be simple. Many of the nonfilers have rather complicated problems. Some are small-scale farmers who are

TABLE 1.   *The Credit Income Tax*[a]

Income	Net tax	Disposable income
0	— 2,000	2,000
1,000	— 1,700	2,700
2,000	— 1,400	3,400
4,000	— 800	4,800
6,000	— 200	6,200
8,000	+ 400	7,600
10,000	+ 1,000	9,000
20,000	+ 4,000	16,000
50,000	+ 13,000	37,000
100,000	+ 28,000	72,000
1,000,000	+298,000	702,000

[a] Assumes a tax rate of 30 per cent and credits of $500 a person for a family of four.

not accustomed to keeping books, some are occasional workers at odd jobs. Hence, an educational task of some magnitude would be in order.

From an economic point of view, however, the social costs of the credit income tax would be negative and would be negative by a large amount. Under the present system, many children are growing up without the advantages of proper food, shelter, clothing, medical care, and education. By increasing the financial means of parents, we would give offspring, on the average, higher levels of living. Society would gain in real terms in the form of greater productivity of the current generation of poor children when they become adults and of greater productivity of contemporary poor adults. Financial means are instrumental in obtaining work, when finding a job requires relocation away from depressed areas, proper dress to impress employers, and meeting living expenses while training. A credit income tax would not, to be sure, provide jobs for people with little skill; as already indicated, the legal and institutional restrictions on realistic wage rates for such people must be moderated as a necessary condition for achieving substantial progress in this area.

Closely related, and of much greater importance than an increase in the output of goods and services, is the effect of a credit income tax on the problems arising from concentrated pockets of city poverty. Although city poverty has been a feature of American life since the latter part of the nineteenth century, the current-day ghettos differ in two important respects from ethnic ghettos of the past: the hope of significant economic improvement within a generation has all but disappeared, and the city poor are no longer content to be poor.

Systematic redistribution in favor of lower income groups by a technique that carrys no stigma would immediately end the despair of many of the city poor. This change would be a large improvement. It would also improve the finances of cities by removing a substantial portion of the costs of relief from city budgets, permitting cities to finance measures to assist low income groups. Systematic redistribution would also tend to reduce the migration of the rural poor to the cities. These groups, as beneficiaries of a credit income tax, would find their position improved in their own communities and would, presumably, have little or no incentive to migrate. A city slum, however dismal, has held the only hope of improvement for many of the rural poor in the deep South. This is in part due to capricious methods of distributing relief (not limited to the South), including the practice of granting or withholding relief to "discipline" those whose behavior offends the politically dominant group. A credit income tax by contrast would afford no such power to local officials and would automatically give poor rural people greater economic and political security than they now enjoy.

Socially, the process of preparing people for working and living in metropolitan areas can be achieved at a lower cost in the hamlets of Alabama than in the ghettos of New York or Chicago. The large cities must be given the opportunity to take measures to improve the lot of the city poor without being handicapped by large numbers of newcomers out of the rural South.

CONCLUDING OBSERVATIONS

A credit income tax may appear to some to be a radical measure out of keeping with the American political tradition. Those who are inclined to take this view should weigh against it the large and expensive but inefficient programs that transfer goods and money to some groups at the expense of others. More of the same can be expected in the future in the absence of a program of systematic redistribution. With a credit income tax, any possible excuse for continuing agricultural price supports, for example, is removed. Subsidized public housing can be opposed without seeming to be ungenerous; low income groups, bolstered by the credit, may buy their own housing services in the market. From the point of view of high income groups, a credit income tax, if the credit is made modest in size, may be the less expensive alternative.

Those who like big government may find a credit income tax objectionable. No measure, to my knowledge, is a greater threat to the growth of nonmilitary government programs; the credit income tax undermines the most telling argument for many of these programs, namely, financial or real assistance to some group or groups.

A credit income tax can be installed in the near future without waiting for the end of the Viet Nam war. The Treasury and the Congress would need to redraft the Internal Revenue Code to include within the definition of Adjusted Gross Income many of the large classes of income presently fully or partially exempt from taxation, to reduce those deductions presently allowed for purposes other than to provide a more accurate definition of taxable income, and to simplify the code as a consequence of the adoption of a one-rate system. I do not wish to imply that such a change would be easy to achieve.

In the initial phase, the determination of the size of the credit may be accomplished by an estimation of the size of the tax base and the fixing of a rate deemed to be politically acceptable, perhaps 25 per cent, and then fixing the credit at the amount that would exhaust the difference between the potential yield and the desired yield of the income tax at that rate. If such a calculation permitted a credit of only $200 per capita a year in the first year, the automatic increase in the potential yield as income increased would permit the credit to be raised.

Once a credit income tax is established, the size of the credit and of the tax rate can be expected to become a political issue of some importance, with many people with persistent low incomes favoring a larger credit and many people with high incomes favoring a lower rate of tax. The political question of what the income distribution ought to be would then be clearly posed. Whatever the outcome over the years, at least a fundamental feature of economic life would become an explicit political question.

A credit income tax may be looked upon as a direct competitor with the Social Security program. A credit income tax, provided the size of the credit is not a trivial amount, would raise the level of incomes of those with low incomes; and, to the extent the Social Security program does likewise, as in the case of public assistance, aid to dependent children, and medicare, it is in fact competitive. But Social Security, unless the basic philosophy for its main programs—that it is an insurance program—is abandoned, cannot cope with large-scale poverty. An insurance approach implies that participants are "buying" insurance through the device called "contributions," meaning of course taxation, and only those who pay their way get benefits. No one would seriously hold that the radical income inequality found in the United States will be corrected by persuading everyone to acquire insurance against possible disasters. Social Security cannot, except by abandoning the insurance principle altogether, reach the genuine poor; many of these people are in a continuous state of disaster. Public assistance, one of the most unpopular and, for true believers in Social Security, one of the most embarrassing programs in the country, is direct testimony of the failure of the insurance principle. If a credit income tax eliminates public assistance, few tears need be shed. But if a credit income tax is installed and if, in another decade, the credit is made the equivalent of $1,000 a person a year, the entire Social Security program will need to be restudied to ascertain what features remain justified in a society in which poverty has been effectively eliminated as a social problem.

George Hildebrand
SECOND THOUGHTS ON THE NEGATIVE INCOME TAX

DISADVANTAGES OF THE TAX

NO FEASIBLE VERSION WOULD OBVIATE THE NEED FOR PUBLIC ASSISTANCE. Given the traditional American attitude toward public assistance and the extremely tight fiscal circumstances now prevailing and likely to prevail for some time to come, a 100 per cent guarantee plan is simply out of the question. This is to say nothing of the dubious social wisdom of having the federal government, to paraphrase Lampman, make the following declaration to every poor household: "We will pay you $3,000 a year if you promise not to work; and if you insist on working anyway, we will tax your earnings at a rate even higher than that applied to a multimillionaire." This is not the way to strengthen the position of the father in the family, nor to foster the still socially valuable ideal of self-support. But it is a way to establish politically a large dependent class, readily identifiable, fully subject to stigma, and well isolated from the rest of the community.

We are left, then, with an array of proposals for a fractional

From "Second Thoughts on the Negative Income Tax," by George H. Hildebrand, *Industrial Relations*, Vol. 6, No. 2, February 1967. Reprinted by permission. Mr. Hildebrand is Professor of Economics, Cornell University.

guarantee. Would any of them improve on payment levels now available under OASDHI and the categorical programs and serve as a more humane substitute? Table 1 suggests the answer, and it is largely negative.

With the sole exceptions of a single person or a couple at the minimum under OASDHI, Friedman's plan would do nothing for those now receiving some form of income maintenance and would seriously lower the positions of most of them. Tobin's version would also fall far short of present payments under assistance, except for G. A. Lampman's Version I which would be of real help to those at the OASDHI minima; but otherwise it lies well below present levels. If substituted, his Versions II-A through II-D would injure those now on Old Age Assistance, Medical Aid to the Aged, Aid to the Permanently and Totally Disabled, and Aid to the Blind; II-D would distinctly benefit families on Aid to Dependent Children and General Assistance, but II-A through II-C would not. All of these plans would aid poor households now excluded from any public income maintenance and supplementation—clearly a major gain on its own terms.

Assuming that any form of the negative income tax should make no poor household worse off than it is already, two conclusions became obvious. First, none of the plans can serve as an overall substitute for the existing categorical assistance program. And second, none of them would be an overall substitute for the present social insurances. In fact, all but Friedman's plan explicitly assume the retention of OASDHI and unemployment compensation. In consequence, these feasible versions of the negative income tax do not represent a unitary solution to the problem of income maintenance, either as a whole or for public assistance alone. Indeed, both Tobin and Lampman expect assistance to survive in some form. What we actually have proposed here, then, is one more addition to the present pluralistic system, an addition whose basic merit is that it would extend transfer payments at once to many millions now excluded from the system.

It is true that subsidies under these plans would be larger in some states than those now paid under the various assistance programs—in some instances much larger. But in the richer states the converse holds. The primary problem is how to make sure that supplementation by Treasury subsidies would be effective, not just *substitutes* for existing rates of payment under assistance. Since some form of assistance will continue to be needed even if the negative income tax were adopted, it is equally important to reform the old programs.

THE NEGATIVE INCOME TAX WOULD NOT DISPLACE THE MEANS TEST.   There are two reasons for this contention. The first is that public assistance will have to be retained. Since this is so, it will continue to be

TABLE 1. *Per Capita Benefits under Existing Income Maintenance Programs Compared with Those Payable under Various Fractional Guarantee Plans[a]*

(Annual Value)

| Existing programs | Current average per head | Friedman[b] | Tobin[c] | Payment per head under negative income tax for those with no other income | | | | | |
| | | | | I | Lampman[d] | | | | |
					II-A	II-B	II-C	II-D
Old Age Assistance (OAA)[e]	$ 941	$ 800	$ 400	$ 224	$ 375	$ 375	$ 188	$ 500
Medical Aid to the Aged (MAA)[e]	2,175							
Aid to the Permanently and Totally Disabled (APTD)	1,012	450–800	400	126	375	375	188	500
Aid to the Blind (AB)	1,105	450–800	400	126	375	375	188	500
Aid to Families with Dependent Children (ADC)	420	375	400	105	375	375	188	500
General Assistance (GA)	364	375	400	105	375	375	188	500
OASDHI:[f]								
Single person, minimum	528	800	528	752	528	528	528	528
Single person, maximum	2,016	800	2,016	2,240	2,016	2,016	2,016	2,016
Couple, minimum	396	750	400	606	396	396	396	396
Couple, maximum	1,512	750	1,542	1,712	1,512	1,512	1,512	1,512

Sources: Figures for payments under assistance programs from *Welfare in Review*, U.S. Department of Health, Education, and Welfare, Vol. IV (April, 1966); figures for OASDHI benefits from *Social Security Bulletin, Annual Statistical Supplement*, XXVIII (December, 1964), 25; values for subsidies estimated by the author.

[a] For OAA and MAA, subsidy under negative income tax assumes a single-person reporting unit. For ADC and G.A., subsidy is based on a four-person family reporting as a unit. All cases assume no other income besides subsidy, except, where applicable, OASDHI benefits. All assistance figures based on national averages.

[b] Assumes double exemption privilege is retained; OASDHI benefits excluded. Range shown for APTD and A.B. reflects possibility that recipient is under 65 or 65 and over.

[c] Tobin would exempt OASDHI beneficiaries from his plan, save that where such benefits fall below $400 the latter figure would become the minimum.

[d] Lampman would retain all OASDHI benefits; his Plan I retains double exemptions, meaning that subsidies would be added to OASDHI benefits, which are now excluded from other income. For versions II-A through II-D, his figures all apply to a family of four, converted here to per head equivalent.

[e] Present payments under these programs, assuming the same person was a recipient for a full year. Subsidies for both are calculated solely on the basis of income deficit. Actually, under the OAA and MAA programs, there is some possibility of overlap and a recipient may obtain payments from both programs.

[f] Assumes worker retires at 65 and that if there is a spouse, she, too, is 65 or over. Minimum and maximum are based on top and bottom monthly brackets under 1965 amendments, converted to annual values. Figures for couples are on a per capita basis. Figures for Lampman's plans II-A through II-D are for OASDHI benefits only. Subsidies may increase these, but the amounts could not be calculated.

necessary to audit the income and assets of claimants, both to fix net payment rates according to schedules and to police cases of gross fraud. Local communities would accept no less.

Second, if it could be a full substitute for existing public assistance, the negative income tax would still not displace the means test. Even in this optimal situation the most the device could do would be to introduce a self-administered means test, since every return must require a declaration of income. The returns filed by those claiming the subsidies would have to be checked, sampled, and audited—what else is this but a form of means test? In extreme cases, there would have to be prosecutions for fraud. And if the old principle of taxation still holds, that the higher the tax the greater the frequency of evasion, then surely the higher the prospective subsidy the greater will be the incidence of fraud—another, less welcome aspect of the symmetry concept.

IT WOULD BE DIFFICULT TO PROVIDE ADEQUATE, REGULAR, AND FREQUENT ASSISTANCE.   The basic principle of all modern public assistance is that transfer payments should be provided to help fill the unmet needs of poor households. To do this properly the degree of need must somehow be measured; payments must bear a reasonable relationship to need as determined; payments must continue to be made available in adequate amounts so long as the need lasts. How well would the negative income tax meet these criteria?

The use of some set of minimum income standards, with built-in adjustment for family size, is a simple and objective way to measure "need." The difficulties begin when one considers timing. If the subsidy is to be paid after the final return is filed, then the sum forthcoming will reflect "other" income already received and the size of the family at the time of filing. Under present practice, any qualified taxpayer can claim a lump-sum refund at this point. Is the subsidy to be treated in the same way? Is it to be paid over to the filer (say the male head), perhaps to be dissipated quickly, even though the household's need is a continuing one? If not, on what legal basis can the amount be parcelled out over the next 52 weeks? Suppose, further, that the household's capacity to earn other income or to get assistance payments is reduced in the year ahead, or that it suffers heavy medical expenses or acquires twins or an aged grandmother as new dependents. Any of these events will increase current need under the means test. But if the subsidy has been fixed on an ex post basis, it will have no reasonable relationship to actual need.

Suppose, instead, that income deficiency is calculated on an ex ante basis for the year ahead or, better, by quarterly declarations. I will pass over entirely the question of how to instruct perhaps ten million inexperienced prospective filers in the delicate art of preparing a tax return. I simply say that poor households will be no more able to avoid errors of optimism and pessimism in predicting other income than anyone else. If the family overstates its expected other income, it will receive a lump sum at the end of the period rather than at the time money was needed. If it understates income, it will have overdrawn the subsidy; it will have to settle up with the Treasury at that point—or accept a lower rate of payment for the next period. In either case, the consequence is the same: the subsidy ceases to bear any relationship to continuing current need. This difficulty seems inherent in any proposal to tie transfer payments to the mechanism of the income tax. I know of no way to get around it.

DOUBLE EXEMPTIONS AND EXCLUDABLE INCOME WOULD DISRUPT THE EQUITY OF THE SUBSIDIES. The premise of the negative income tax is that income deficiency is the best way to measure need—a proposition that I accept. As we have seen, there are two ways to calculate the deficiency: (1) fix a flat allowance per capita and set off other income at some rate, as Tobin and Schwartz would do, or (2) gauge deficiency by the value of unused deductions and exemptions (net of other income), as Friedman does and also Lampman in his Plan I. If this second method is used and if the subsidies are actually to reflect need as so measured, a major reconstruction of present tax law becomes necessary, as Lampman recognizes but Friedman does not. Otherwise, the amounts payable will depend on critical variables other than family size, i.e., the age of family members and the type of "other" income received. In other words, it will pay to be 65 years or over and it will pay to have income deriving from OASDHI benefits and tax-exempt bond interest. The reason is that double exemptions are now awarded to the elderly (and to the blind), while OASDHI benefits (for retirement, widowhood, or disability) and interest on certain securities need not now be counted in adjusted gross income for purposes of taxation.

Consider, for example, a pair of two-person families composed of man and wife. In the first, the couple is under 65; the husband earns $1,570 as an unskilled laborer; there is no other income. Exemptions and deductions total $1,600. Deducting "other" income, their deficiency is $30. Under Friedman's 50 per cent plan, their subsidy is a niggardly $15. Under Lampman's Plan I at 14 per cent, it is a microscopic $4.20.

Now take the second couple, both over 65 and receiving $1,570 from OASDHI, without other income. Double exemptions make their total exemptions and deductions worth $3,000. Retirement benefits need not be included as income. On Friedman's proposal, their subsidy would be $1,500, as against Lampman's $420. On the basis of final disposable income after subsidy, the first couple has only $1,585 under Friedman's plan, while the second gets $3,070, although household size and initial income are the same. The reason is that as the law now stands the subsidy would yield the elderly pair a 100:1 advantage over the working couple. Can it be seriously argued that their actual need is 100 times as great, especially with Medicare and MAA?

Looking at the matter in another way, under present law each child is "worth" $700 in exempt income, if one has the income in the first place, while each elderly person is worth either $1,500 or $1,600, depending on whether he or she files the return. Indeed, through the exclusion privilege, receipt of OASDHI benefits makes the aged person worth considerably more from the tax standpoint.

Justification for this differential treatment is not convincing, but to assault the tax privileges of the aged, many of whom are not poor on any standard, is no easier than an attack on motherhood. Yet, if equitable treatment is to be had under the negative income tax and the subsidies are to conform to the purposes of the proposal, then neither age nor type of other income should influence the size of the transfer. The problem is easily solved in principle. The real difficulty is political. It can be evaded simply by leaving tax privileges intact, as the price to be paid for getting more income into the hands of those poor who are now excluded from public assistance. However, this choice involves other encumbrances: the total cost of the new transfers might rise as much as 40 per cent, there would be substantial leakages to those who are not poor in terms of "all other income," benefits would not be geared strictly to number of dependents, and the self-supporting poor would receive grossly inequitable treatment.

Partly for these reasons, Tobin would exclude OASDHI beneficiaries and abolish single or double exemptions for those who are covered by his plan. Lampman, in all versions of his Plan II, would count OASDHI benefits as income and use a flat allowance in place of deductions and double or single exemptions for determining income deficiency. Obviously this is the preferred course if the intent of the negative income tax is to be served with full integrity. But to undertake it is to open up a political hornets' nest, sufficient probably to defeat the proposal itself.

CONCLUSION

The weaknesses of the negative income tax fall into two classes: those that are technical and those that turn on questions of cost and ideology. Some of the technical problems probably could be overcome. The level of minimum guarantee and the rate of offset could be high enough to replace most forms of public assistance. The means test feature cannot be eliminated and will continue as long as we have public assistance. Problems concerning the timing, adequacy, and frequency of payments will be much harder to resolve. Finally, it is theoretically possible to remove the tax privileges of the aged; to set up new controls to forestall induced splitting up of non-poor reporting units and to redefine the status of dependents; and to achieve a more general reform of the law, which now permits so many non-poor taxpayers to escape so much income taxation.

Questions of cost and ideology are quite another matter. Putting the poverty-income gap at about $12 billion in 1963, a new transfer program of at least $5 billion net would be required to accomplish anything significant, with OASDHI and assistance payments unchanged. Ignoring the question of whether the country can now afford even this much, the basic difficulty is to make sure that an adequate and equitable version could be had within this limit. With removal of double exemptions and excludable income, Friedman's plan would cost roughly $5 billion, *if* there were no disincentive effects. Lampman's II-D, to me his most attractive formulation, implies a minimum guarantee of $500 per head, and could involve a net cost of anything between $2 and $11 billion, depending on the extent of disincentive effects and reductions in public assistance. Thus neither Friedman's nor Lampman's plan assures a firm cost ceiling. Tobin's scheme is the most carefully drafted of all and has many attractive features. But on his estimate, it would cost at least $14 billion on 1962 data. As for the Schwartz and Theobald proposals, they would involve a net cost of over $25 billion and therefore are out of the question on this count alone.

I submit that the federal budget today cannot supply even $5 billion without substantial curtailment of other forms of expenditure. The one possibility would be to capture the needed revenue by all-out reform of the income tax law, including introduction of an equitable form of the negative income tax. I doubt that the needed reforms can be had, however, because they require the consent of the middle and upper income groups. The plea that the proceeds could be used to finance massive transfers to all of the poor, including the able-bodied, is likely to fall on deaf ears. Assistance by category is still a "categorical" imperative in our system of values. Although I prefer children's or family allowances—on a universal basis as a matter of right—to income maintenance through the income tax, I admit that they too suffer from the same political and fiscal handicaps.

If the above assessment stands up, then those of us who want to raise low incomes will have to settle for more modest immediate gains, deferring larger schemes for later and more appropriate times. This means we should concern ourselves now with reconstruction of public assistance.

Because of limited space, I venture into this subject only briefly, and even then somewhat timorously, because it is so complex. As a starting point, I take it for granted that some form of public assistance will always be needed, to fill out the interstices among the social insurances and also to supplement such benefits where they are too low. For the long term, it seems to me desirable to make need the sole criterion for eligibility, and where need is proved on clear standards, to make provision a matter of right. Incidentally, this is the most that the negative income tax itself would do. Both are simply alternative ways to provide universal transfer payments to the poor.

To put public assistance on these new foundations means that the categories must go and that all the onerous existing restrictions based on age, residence, length of residence, suitable home requirements, unemployability of either parent, total and permanent incapacitation, and relatives' responsibility must eventually be supplanted. It also means a greatly increased role for the federal government in setting standards and providing grants-in-aid.

These changes cannot be accomplished overnight. For one thing, they will cost a great deal of money—out of a population of 34 million poor persons in 1965, only 7.4 million were receiving public assistance, mostly at levels below those now being recommended. For another, these proposals would arouse militant opposition in Congress, whose members are responsible to local constituencies in which the traditional "Poor Law" approach finds expression in these very restrictions. Nonetheless, these objectives seem sound to me as long-term goals.

In the meantime, some practical changes can be made even in a regimen of tight budgets. The 2.1 million aged poor now on OAA might be transferred to OASDHI at corresponding benefit levels. It also may well be possible to drop MAA as Medicare and companion state programs under Title XIX get under way.

The main candidate for practical reform would be ADC, and I do not underrate the obstacles here. I estimate that it would cost about $500 million to raise the *minimum* payment rate per recipient to $50 monthly (the national average is now $35). If new federal standards could be imposed, desertion or divorce as a condition for eligibility could be ended (now imposed in 29 states). It would also be desirable to allow each ADC family to earn some minimum amount of other income— initially, say, $500—without deducting it from assistance payments. Coupling these changes to existing subventions to poor youngsters enrolled in the various job corps and training programs would achieve a substantial advance, at a net added cost of well less than $5 billion.

In counseling caution and delay regarding the negative income tax, I am not saying that it should be rejected out of hand. But I do contend that it is not demonstrably superior to a different kind of allowance system, entirely divorced from the income tax, or even to a major overhaul of public assistance. I also hold that it is a serious mistake to believe that all that the poor really need is a large-scale infusion of new money. They also require far more skilled social work as well as increased provision of other services in kind rather than in cash, for instance, education and vocational training.

Henry Hazlitt
THE COMING CRISIS IN WELFARE

The Negative Income Tax as proposed by Prof. Milton Friedman is essentially, with one modification, just one more form of the guaranteed annual income. So before discussing Prof. Friedman's defense of his specific proposal, let us begin by summing up the general case against the guaranteed income.

In the words of Mr. Robert Theobald, one of its principal sponsors, this proposal "would guarantee to every citizen of the United States . . . the right to an income from the Federal Government to enable him to live with dignity." This guarantee would be unconditional. Everybody would get it, regardless of whether or not he worked, could work, or was willing to work.

The recipients are to continue to get this guaranteed income, let me emphasize, not only if they resolutely refuse to seek or take a job, but if they throw the handout money away at the races, or spend it on prostitutes, or whisky, marijuana, or whatnot. They are to be given "sufficient to live in dignity," and it is apparently to be no business of the taxpayers if the recipient chooses nonetheless to live without dignity, and to devote his guaranteed leisure to gambling, dissipation, drunkenness, dope addiction, or a life of crime.

The first thing to be said about this scheme economically is that if it were put into effect it would not only be intolerably expensive to the taxpayers who were forced to support it, but that it would destroy the incentives to work and to produce on an unparalleled scale.

From "The Coming Crisis in Welfare," by Henry Hazlitt, *National Review*, April 18, 1967, pp. 416–418. Reprinted by permission. Mr. Hazlitt is a journalist and economist.

As even one of the contributors to Mr. Theobald's symposium, William Vogt, has remarked: "Those who believe that men will want to work whether they have to or not seem to have lived sheltered lives."

Who, in fact, would be willing to take the smelly jobs, or any low-paid job, once the guaranteed income program is in effect? The guaranteed-income sponsors propose to pay, say, $3,000 to a family without any income, but to families earning some income they would pay merely the supplementary sum necessary to bring the total up to $3,000.

Now suppose that you are a married man with two children, and your present income from some nasty and irregular work is $2,500 a year. The government would then send you a check for $500. But it would very soon occur to you that though you now had $3,000, you could have got this $3,000 without doing any work at all.

The scheme is not only economically but morally indefensible. If *"everybody* should receive a guaranteed income as a matter of right" (the words just quoted are Mr. Theobald's), who is to pay him that income?

NO FREE LUNCH

The truth is, of course, that the government has nothing to give to anybody that it doesn't first take from someone else. The whole guaranteed income proposal is a perfect modern example of the shrewd observation of the French economist Bastiat more than a century ago: "The state is the great fiction by which everybody tries to live at the expense of everybody else."

If you claim a "right" to "an income sufficient to live in dignity," whether you are willing to work or not, what you are really claiming is a right to part of *somebody else's* earned income. What you are asserting is that this other person has a duty to earn more than he needs or wants to live on so that the surplus may be seized from him and turned over to you to live on.

This is an absolutely immoral proposition.

The negative income tax (a misnomer for an income subsidy) suffers from most of the economic, political and moral vices of the guaranteed income. But it does have one important advantage over the guaranteed-income proposal in its cruder form: at least it would not destroy the incentive to work and produce to the same appalling extent.

Under the negative income tax, a man or a family would receive from the government a subsidy of 50 per cent, say, of the amount by which the family income fell below the so-called poverty-line in-come—let us say $3,000 a year. This means that if the family had no income at all it would receive a subsidy of $1,500. If it already had an earned income of $1,500, it would receive a government subsidy of $750, and so on.

Prof. Friedman, the distinguished author of this proposal, admits that, "like any other measures to alleviate poverty," his proposal would reduce "the incentives of those helped to help themselves"; but he goes on to argue, quite correctly, that it would not eliminate that incentive entirely, as the system of supplementing incomes up to some fixed minimum would. Under his plan an extra dollar earned would always mean more money available for expenditure.

I agree entirely that a subsidy calculated in this way—that is, one that would be reduced by only $1 for every $2 additional that the recipient was able to earn for himself—would not be nearly so destructive of incentives as the type of subsidy under which it would be pointless for the recipient to earn more on his own account.

In fact, some thirty years ago I put forward a similar proposal myself in an article in the *Annalist,* a weekly then published by the *New York Times.* What I suggested was a relief payment that would be reduced by only $1 for every $2 of self-earnings by the relief recipient. But this device solves only a marginal problem.

The negative income tax of Prof. Friedman, as put forward in 1962 in his book *Capitalism and Freedom,* was a comparatively modest proposal. He suggested that if a man had no income at all, he would receive a basic subsidy of $300. Once this idea got into practical politics, however, this basic sum would soon be denounced as utterly inadequate to allow a family of four to live in "decency and dignity." In fact, the humanitarian reformers would soon be demanding a basic subsidy of $3,000 or $4,000 to a family otherwise without income, and we would be back to the same starting point as the guaranteed income scheme.

Only—except for the fact that it would not destroy incentives as much—it would be even more expensive than the guaranteed income; because under it substantial subsidies would continue to be paid to people who were earning incomes of their own. If the basic subsidy to a family of no income were $3,000, families would continue to get some government subsidy until their incomes reached $6,000 a year!

Instead of a rigid ceiling, like the guaranteed income, the negative income tax would provide for a gradual tapering off. But otherwise it suffers from all the fatal flaws of the guaranteed-income proposal. Both would take money away from those who were earning it to turn it over both to those who could not earn it and those who refused to earn it. Money would be given to people whose incomes were low, without any regard to the reasons why those incomes were low. A person whose income was low or non-existent because he was a beatnik or a loafer or a drunk would get just as much, and no questions asked, as a person whose income was low or non-existent because he was blind or disabled or sick or the victim of some accident or circumstances beyond his control.

So far I have been summarizing arguments I have previously used against both the guaranteed income and the negative income tax. Prof. Friedman's reply to these in his March 7 article is peculiar. He applies a double standard: one standard is what is inherently desirable; the other is what is politically feasible. He defends his own proposals on the ground that they are desirable. He resents any suggestion that they would almost certainly never be adopted politically in the form he advocates. Yet he refuses to consider on their merits the alternatives suggested by his critics on the ground that they are not politically feasible. He argues that those who believe their adoption possible are living in "a dream world."

Friedman begins by telling his conservative and libertarian critics that they are foolish to object to the guaranteed income because we already "have a governmentally guaranteed income in substance though not in name." Even if his contention were true, it would be irrelevant to the merits of the case. If we already have a guaranteed income then the thing to do is to get rid of it.

Friedman then makes the undeniable statement that our present "grab-bag of relief and welfare measures" is "a mess." Precisely; and throwing the negative income tax on top of it would turn the mess into a nightmare.

But, Friedman insists, he is not proposing to throw his negative income tax on top of this mess; he is proposing to repeal all the existing relief and welfare measures and *substitute* his scheme for them.

Now who is living in a "dream world"? Does Friedman seriously believe that the veterans will quietly give up their pensions? That the farmers will calmly surrender their price supports and other subsidies? That the beneficiaries of subsidized public housing will cheerfully agree to pay a full economic rent? That we will soon hear the last of "free education" at the college level; of free school lunches; of food stamps? Will the workers give up unemployment compensation? Will the great mass of the voters give up any of their promised Social Security benefits? Will the elderly even give up the Medicare benefits they have just acquired?

Talk about living "in a dream world"!

Perhaps the worst evil in all these welfare, relief, and giveaway programs is that it is so fatally easy to get them adopted and so nearly impossible, once they have been adopted, to get rid of them, or to cut them back, or even to prevent their further cancerous growth and proliferation.

I have yet to hear of a single congressman, or even a handful of academic economists, who has endorsed Friedman's negative income tax exactly in the form he has proposed it—to wit, with a basic subsidy of only $300 a year, and as a complete substitute for our whole present "grab bag of relief and welfare measures."

Speaking for myself, I am not opposed to the negative income tax merely because I regard it as a political certainty that it would be far bigger than Friedman proposes and would simply be thrown on top of the immense welfare burden (in the neighborhood of $50 billion a year) that the American taxpayers already carry. I am opposed to it in principle. It is far inferior to the traditional methods of relief. Generations of experience with relief plans show that they will quickly get out of control and be subject to gross abuse, fraud, and chiseling, unless a means test is retained, unless there is some case-by-case and applicant-by-applicant examination—in brief, unless the recipients of unearned income from the government are subject to at least as much checking and investigation as income-tax payers. The advocates of the guaranteed income and the negative income tax think such a case-by-case check "humiliating" and administratively troublesome. Maybe so; but it is unfortunately unavoidable. There is no neat little mathematical gadget that will enable us to ignore and bypass this necessity.

The guaranteed income and the negative income tax schemes are wrong in principle because they would compel the self-supporting part of the population to support all the alleged "poor" without taking the trouble to find out *why* a particular individual is poor or even to make sure *whether* he is poor. They would treat precisely alike those who are poor through no moral fault of their own and those who are poor through their own gross delinquency.

LIMIT THE FRANCHISE?

We are confronted with a grave and immensely difficult problem, which we are bound to face candidly. Where any person, a child or an adult, is in fact helpless, or sick or disabled, or hungry, or jobless through no moral fault of his own, and where no private person or group is responsible for him, should "society," acting through government, make itself responsible?

The overwhelming majority of people would answer Yes. Since far back in history "society" has, in fact, assumed this responsibility. In England, the poor laws were enacted even before the reign of Elizabeth I.

The problem is, granted this responsibility, how can the government mitigate the penalties of failure and misfortune without undermining the incentives to effort and success? How can it prevent the abuse of relief and the ominous growth of an ever-bigger army of relief recipients?

I suspect that there is no perfect solution to this problem, but at best a least unsatisfactory solution.

But of one thing we can be reasonably certain. As long as those on relief have the vote while they remain on relief, politicans will continue to increase the burden of relief and welfare until it brings on hyper-inflation, insolvency, the wholesale destruction of incentives, or some other form of social and economic crisis.

Even Milton Friedman confesses political misgivings concerning what would happen to his tapered-off guaranteed income subsidy ("negative income tax") once it got into practical politics. He even quotes A. V. Dicey's question in 1914 whether it is wise to allow recipients of poor relief to retain the right to join in the election of a member of Parliament. But then he dismisses the "verdict of experience" as "mixed," and offers his proposal without suggesting any limitation of the franchise.

John Stuart Mill, writing in his *Representative Government* in 1861, did not equivocate: "I regard it as required by first principles that the receipt of parish relief should be a preemptory disqualification for the franchise. He who cannot by his labor suffice for his own support has no claim to the privilege of helping himself to the money of others."

Prof. Friedman may think that anyone who believes such a limitation of the franchise could be enacted in this generation is living "in a dream world." Perhaps. But does he himself believe that in the present political climate there is any possibility of his negative income tax being enacted in the modest form he proposes—and as a *substitute* for, instead of still another addition to, the present $50 billion worth of all other forms of relief and welfare now so solidly entrenched?

If he does believe that, he is really out on Cloud 9.

9
Civil Rights

In the decade immediately following the United States Supreme Court's desegregation decision, the issue of civil rights emerged as a national movement. While the movement had long-range goals, these goals were translated into immediate concerns—public school integration, desegregation of public facilities, equal employment opportunities, equal voting rights, and, to a lesser extent, open housing. In order to achieve these immediate goals, a variety of tactics was adopted. Pressure was exerted on all branches of the federal government, as well as on the general public, and, seemingly, major victories were won. The Supreme Court, at least through 1965, consistently ruled in favor of Negro claims. Congress passed new civil rights legislation, and the Executive branch issued new regulations aimed at eliminating racial discrimination in employment under federal contracts and banning such discrimination in the federally guaranteed housing market.

Some of these efforts had immediate pay-offs. For example, as a result of the Voting Rights Act of 1965, Negro voter registration in the eleven Southern states increased from 43 per cent in 1964 to 52 per cent in 1966. The increases were dramatic in such states as Alabama, where the 1966 registration rose to 51 per cent—the 1964 level was 23 per cent—and in Mississippi, where the increase was from 7 per cent to 33 per cent. In the 1966 fall elections Negro candidates were more successful than at any time since the Reconstruction Era.

However, by the middle of the 1960s it became increasingly

obvious that the relative position of the Negro had shown little improvement. The 1964 Civil Rights Act did bring about a sudden increase in school desegregation in the South. In the spring of 1967, 16 per cent of Negro public school students were enrolled in desegregated schools. In the spring of 1966, the comparable figure had been 6 per cent. Nonetheless, thirteen years after the Supreme Court's desegregation decision, the vast majority of American children attended schools that were largely segregated. Indeed, school segregation increased during this period throughout the North and West. The sit-in demonstrations of the 1950s and early 1960s, along with the Public Accommodations sections of the 1964 legislation, did result in desegregating many public facilities. On the other hand, for the past fifteen years, the per cent of Negro unemployment has continued to be twice that of white unemployment. The median Negro family income in 1949 was 51.8 per cent of the median white family income. By 1964 the relative position of Negro family income to white family income had increased to only 55.8 per cent.

The tactics adopted by the movement, placing, as it did, heavy emphasis on governmental support, fell far short of achieving the broader goal of improving the lot of the Negro in America. The instruments of government can make promises, but the gap between a promise and its fulfillment is frequently dependent upon the pressures of private groups. This is not to discount the importance of such promises as public pressures on the status quo, but simply a recognition of their limited value.

The civil rights movement has invested considerable time, money, and effort in supporting public school integration. The Coleman report, however, gives rise to a number of serious questions about the possible impact or lack of impact of school integration on Negro children. Indeed, prior to the Coleman report, some advocates of "black power" were already taking the position that the issue of school integration was irrelevant to the broader goals of the civil rights movement. The Coleman Report suggests that, generally, the home background of pupils is the most important single variable contributing to pupil achievement. On the other hand, the Report also indicates that minority group children show some improvement in achievement in integrated learning situations. The Report could imply that more energy should be channeled into improving minority schools rather than simply working for school integration.

It may well be that the cohesiveness of the original civil rights movement has been dissipated by a series of events. The war in Viet Nam has captured a considerable portion of the public attention that had been previously devoted to the civil rights movement. The destructive riots in such cities as Los Angeles, Newark, and Detroit have given rise to the issue of "white backlash." And, finally, the minimal change in the relative position of the Negro in America during this past decade may be leading people to question the efficacy of the tactics adopted by the early civil rights movement. It seems apparent that the civil rights movement is beginning a search for new tactics and perhaps a broader strategy in order to achieve the goal of justice and equality for the American Negro. It is in this context that the discussion of black power has been taking place.

The Moynihan Report
THE NEGRO FAMILY

At the heart of the deterioration of the fabric of Negro society is the deterioration of the Negro family. It is the fundamental source of the weakness of the Negro community at the present time. There is probably no single fact of Negro American life so little understood by whites. The Negro situation is commonly perceived by whites in terms of the visible manifestations of discrimination and poverty, in part because Negro protest is directed against such obstacles, and in part, no doubt, because these are facts which involve the actions and attitudes of the white community as well. It is more difficult, however, for whites to perceive the effect that three centuries of exploitation have had on the fabric of Negro society itself. Here the consequences of the historic injustices done to Negro Americans are silent and hidden from view. But here is where the true injury has occurred: unless this damage is repaired, all the effort to end discrimination and poverty and injustice will come to little.

The role of the family in shaping character and ability is so pervasive as to be easily overlooked. The family is the basic social unit of American life; it is the basic socializing unit. By and large, adult conduct in society is learned as a child. A fundamental insight of psychoanalytic theory, for example, is that the child learns a way of looking at life in his early years through which all later experience is viewed and which profoundly shapes his adult conduct. It may be hazarded that the reason family structure does not loom larger in public discussion of social issues

Condensed from "The Negro Family: The Case for National Action," United States Department of Labor, Office of Policy Planning and Research, March 1965. This report is known as the Moynihan Report after its principal author, Daniel P. Moynihan, formerly Assistant Secretary of Labor.

is that people tend to assume that the nature of family life is about the same throughout American society. The mass media and the development of suburbia have created an image of the American family as a highly standardized phenomenon. It is therefore easy to assume that whatever it is that makes for differences among individuals or groups of individuals, it is not a different family structure.

*   *   *

But there is one truly great discontinuity in family structure in the United States at the present time: that between the white world in general and that of the Negro American. The white family has achieved a high degree of stability and is maintaining that stability. By contrast, the family structure of lower class Negroes is highly unstable, and in many urban centers is approaching complete breakdown.

There is considerable evidence that the Negro community is in fact dividing between a stable middle-class group that is steadily growing stronger and more successful, and an increasingly disorganized and disadvantaged lower-class group. There are indications, for example, that the middle-class Negro family puts a higher premium on family stability and the conserving of family resources than does the white middle-class family. . . .

There are two points to be noted in this context. First, the emergence and increasing visibility of a Negro middle-class may beguile the nation into supposing that the circumstances of the remainder of the Negro community are equally prosperous, whereas just the opposite is true at present, and is likely to continue so. Second, the lumping of all Negroes together in one statistical measurement very probably conceals the extent of the disorganization among the lower-class group. If conditions are improving for one and deteriorating for the other, the resultant statistical averages might show no change. Further, the statistics on the Negro family and most other subjects treated in this paper refer only to a specific point in time. They are a vertical measure of the situation at a given moment. They do not measure the experience of individuals over time. Thus the average monthly unemployment rate for Negro males for 1964 is recorded as 9 percent. But during 1964, some 29 percent of Negro males were unemployed at one time or another. Similarly, for example, if 36 percent of Negro children are living in broken homes at any specific moment, it is likely that a far higher proportion of Negro children find themselves in that situation at one time or another in their lives.

Nearly a quarter of Negro women living in cities who have ever married are divorced, separated, or are living apart from their husbands. The rates are highest in the urban Northeast where 26 percent of Negro women ever married are either divorced, separated, or have their husbands absent. On the urban frontier, the proportion of husbands absent is even higher. In New York City in 1960, it was 30.2 percent, not including divorces. Among ever-married nonwhite women in the nation, the proportion with husbands present declined in every age group over the decade 1950–1960. . . .

Both white and Negro illegitimacy rates have been increasing, although from dramatically different bases. The white rate was 2 percent in 1940; it was 3.07 percent in 1963. In that period, the Negro rate went from 16.8 percent to 23.6 percent. The number of illegitimate children per 1,000 live births increased by 11 among whites in the period 1940–63, but by 68 among nonwhites. There are, of course, limits to the dependability of these statistics. There are almost certainly a considerable number of Negro children who, although technically illegitimate, are in fact the offspring of stable unions. On the other hand, it may be assumed that many births that are in fact illegitimate are recorded otherwise. Probably the two opposite effects cancel each other out.

On the urban frontier, the nonwhite illegitimacy rates are usually higher than the national average, and the increase of late has been drastic. In the District of Columbia, the illegitimacy rate for nonwhites grew from 21.8 percent in 1950 to 29.5 percent in 1964. A similar picture of disintegrating Negro marriages emerges from the divorce statistics. Divorces have increased of late for both whites and nonwhites, but at a much greater rate for the latter. In 1940 both groups had a divorce rate of 2.2 percent. By 1964 the white rate had risen to 3.6 percent, but the nonwhite rate had reached 5.1 percent—40 percent greater than the formerly equal white rate.

As a direct result of this high rate of divorce, separation, and desertion, a very large percent of Negro families are headed by females. While the percentage of such families among whites has been dropping since 1940, it has been rising among Negroes. The percent of nonwhite families headed by a female is more than double the percent for whites. Fatherless nonwhite families increased by a sixth between 1950 and 1960, but held constant for white families. It has been estimated that only a minority of Negro children reach the age of 18 having lived all their lives with both their parents. Once again, this measure of family disorganization is found to be diminishing among white families and increasing among Negro families.

The majority of Negro children receive public assistance under the AFDC program at one point or another in their childhood. At present, 14 percent of Negro children are receiving AFDC assistance, as against 2 percent of white children. Eight percent of white children receive such assistance at some time, as against 56 percent of nonwhites, according to an extrapolation based on HEW data. (Let it be noted, however, that out of a total of 1.8 million nonwhite illegitimate children in the nation in 1961, 1.3 million were not receiving aid under the AFDC program, although a substantial number have, or will, receive aid at some time in their lives.) Again, the situation may be said to be worsening. The AFDC program, deriving from the long established Mothers' Aid programs, was established in 1935 principally to care for widows and orphans, although the legislation covered all children in homes deprived of parental support because one or both of their parents are absent or incapacitated.

In the beginning, the number of AFDC families in which the father was absent because of desertion was less than a third of the total. Today it is two-thirds. HEW estimates "that between two-thirds and three-fourths of the 50 percent increase from 1948 to 1955 in the number of absent-father families receiving ADC may be explained by an increase in broken homes in the population."

✿   ✿   ✿

That the Negro American has survived at all is extraordinary—a lesser people might simply have died out, as indeed others have. That the Negro community has not only survived, but in this political generation has entered national affairs as a moderate, humane, and constructive national force is the highest testament to the healing powers of the democratic ideal and the creative vitality of the Negro people. But it may not be supposed that the Negro American community has not paid a fearful price for the incredible mistreatment to which it has been subjected over the past three centuries.

In essence, the Negro community has been forced into a matriarchal structure which, because it is so out of line with the rest of the American society, seriously retards the progress of the group as a whole, and imposes a crushing burden on the Negro male and, in consequence, on a great many Negro women as well.

U.S. Department of Labor
THE NEGROES IN THE UNITED STATES: THEIR ECONOMIC AND SOCIAL SITUATION

In March 1966, nonwhite workers constituted about 11 percent of the civilian labor force of the United States, but accounted for over 21

Condensed from United States Department of Labor, *Bulletin* No. 1511, June 1966.

percent of the unemployed and 25 percent of the long-term unemployed. Throughout the period since World War II, nonwhite unemployment rates have consistently exceeded the rates for white workers, but the gap varies with the business cycle. In the most recent full year of the current upswing, when unemployment rates for white workers averaged 4.1 percent, the rate for nonwhites was twice as high—8.3 percent. . . .

Differences between the composition of the nonwhite segment of the labor force and the white segment help to explain why overall unemployment within the two groups responds differently to changes in economic conditions. There is a higher proportion of women in the nonwhite force, and a smaller proportion of adult men, but the same proportion of teenagers. Similarly, their greater need for income keeps a higher proportion of nonwhite workers engaged in the search for work, even when conditions are not favorable for finding it. Nonwhite women are much more likely than are white women to be heads of their families. And in families with husbands at their head (the usual situation), nonwhite women tend to participate in the labor force at higher rates than white women, regardless of income.

✻   ✻   ✻

Global averages of family and individual income, and simple ratios of Negro to white income, reveal a wide gap between Negro and white income, and a small improvement recently. But they do not tell the whole story.

Negro family incomes were about 56 percent of white incomes in 1964, compared with 53 percent in 1961–63. The ratios have been consistently much higher in the North and the West (70 percent or more) and in metropolitan areas, and much lower in the South (less than 50 percent). In rural areas in 1960, they were below 40 percent. The ratio tends to be highest among young people (who usually have more formal schooling than their elders). Among the occupations, there is little or no gap in public employment (as for mail carriers, postal clerks, firemen, and policemen), or in jobs such as nonfarm labor and private household work where there is negligible competition with whites, or among young professional and clerical workers in the North and West.

The income gap is less between nonwhite and white workers who work full time throughout the year. Yet, even for year-round, full-time work, the median yearly earnings of nonwhite men in 1964 were only a little over $4,000 and the median for nonwhite women was less than $3,000.

Negro earnings are so low that, regardless of whether Negroes are employed, unemployed, or out of the labor force, their incomes fall within a narrow range at a low level. On the other hand, the factor of employment causes a great widening of the range and level of white incomes.

In 1964, 37 percent of Negro families had incomes below $3,000, compared with only 15 percent of white families. In the North and the West, about one-fourth of the Negro families had incomes below $3,000 in 1964, compared with about half of such families in the South. Non-white farm families had less than half the income of white farm families in 1964. Nonwhite families off the farm averaged higher than white families.

* * *

The extensive effort of the Negro family to ensure its security meets not only discriminatory hiring practices, but also the situation that many of the occupations and industries in which Negroes are numerous have a large degree of seasonality and high unemployment, even in good times. A larger proportion of Negroes than white workers are not covered by collective bargaining agreements, minimum wage laws, and social security; this is especially true among the older workers. Those Negroes who are covered by union contracts are likely to be newer employees than their white coworkers and thus have less seniority and other forms of security.

About 40 percent of nonwhite families, compared to 12 percent of white families, were judged poor in 1964. Although there has been more improvement among them since 1959, the incidence of nonwhite poverty remains very great, particularly in the family types especially prone to poverty—those with very young household heads, those headed by women or by the elderly, and those with many dependents.

Families headed by women are particularly vulnerable to poverty because of women's low earnings and the number of children they support. In the 1960's, women have headed about 23 percent of all nonwhite families, compared to about 9 percent of the white families. About 8 in 10 of the nonwhite families headed by women included children. Regardless of marital status (widowed, divorced, single, or separated), nonwhite women who are heads of households are more prone to poverty than white women who head households—about 7 in 10 as compared to 3 in 10.

* * *

The Negro urban consumer has about the same spending pattern as the white urban consumer at the same income level. According to the 1960–61 consumer expenditures survey of the Bureau of Labor Statistics, most Negro and white urban consumers fell into a large middle-income group—$3,000 to $7,500. However, almost all of the remaining Negroes had less than $3,000 to spend, whereas the remainder of the whites tended to have $7,500 or more.

The most notable differences between Negro and white consumers were the degrees to which they went into debt, saved, and bought durable goods. Relatively low-income Negroes ($3,000 to $4,999) averaged less debt than white consumers of the same income group. Middle-income Negroes ($5,000–$7,499) averaged larger net increases in savings than middle-income whites. For the same income groups, Negro and white consumers averaged about the same amount of personal insurance, but fewer Negroes than whites, proportionately, bought automobiles or were homeowners. These findings may possibly reflect a differential in the availibility and cost of credit, regardless of collateral or other assets. They may reflect also family size and responsibility. Negro families, in general, had more persons in the family at each income level than white families. Because they more often have more than one earner, job-related expenses have to be budgeted.

Home ownership presents special problems for Negroes. They generally buy in a highly restricted market. The limitations on Negro home ownership make one of the most serious imbalances of supply and demand in the economy.

The urge toward home ownership is amply demonstrated by nonwhite families. Although about half of all nonwhite families were poor in 1960 and many were in very large cities where apartment living is usual, 38 percent were homeowners. This is far lower than the 64 percent for white families. Moreover, about half the nonwhite homeowners owned their houses free and clear, compared with a little more than 40 percent of the white homeowners.

Of the homeowners with mortgages in 1960, the nonwhites were much less likely to have received FHA or VA assistance than the whites or to have bought a new house. In addition, nonwhite homeowners in 1960 were more than twice as likely as white homeowners to be spending 30 percent or more of their income on housing and over three times as likely to be paying over 6 percent interest on a first mortgage.

*   *   *

The Negroes' struggle for equality is taking many forms, as are the programs supporting this struggle. The foregoing pages reveal in part to what extent the Negro is gaining.

The Negro household presents a picture of substantial effort to insure and sustain security, through multiple workers, multiple jobs per worker, high labor force participation, plus substantial increases in school enrollment and educational attainment.

As Negroes persevere and surmount longstanding hurdles, as the spotlight on discrimination in American society probes wider and deeper, and as civil rights and antipoverty legislation penetrate further and are widely implemented, the strides will lengthen.

In the meantime, Negroes still hold a disproportionately large number of manual and lowpaying jobs; their children are more likely to attend inferior schools; they have limited choice of residence; and they suffer discrimination and prejudice.

The changes taking place in American institutions could bring about the most important condition of all—that of equality among Americans of varying color, origin, or creed. The only conclusion the facts permit is that the measures taken and the changes they have made so far are not nearly enough.

The Coleman Report
EQUALITY OF EDUCATIONAL OPPORTUNITY

SEGREGATION IN THE PUBLIC SCHOOLS

The great majority of American children attend schools that are largely segregated—that is, where almost all of their fellow students are of the same racial background as they are. Among minority groups, Negroes are by far the most segregated. Taking all groups, however, white children are most segregated. Almost 80 percent of all white pupils in 1st grade and 12th grade attend schools that are from 90 percent to 100 percent white. And 97 percent at grade 1, and 99 percent at grade 12, attend schools that are 50 percent or more white.

For Negro pupils, segregation is more nearly complete in the South (as it is for whites also), but it is extensive also in all the other regions where the Negro population is concentrated: the urban North, Midwest, and West.

More than 65 percent of all Negro pupils in the 1st grade attend schools that are between 90 and 100 percent Negro. And 87 percent at grade 1, and 66 percent at grade 12, attend schools that are 50 percent

Condensed from *Equality of Educational Opportunity*, U.S. Department of Health, Education, and Welfare, Office of Education, 1966. Government Printing Office. Dr. Coleman is Professor of Sociology at Johns Hopkins University.

or more Negro. In the South, most students attend schools that are 100 percent white or Negro.

The same pattern of segregation holds, though not quite so strongly, for the teachers of Negro and white students. For the Nation as a whole the average Negro elementary pupil attends a school in which 65 percent of the teachers are Negro; the average white elementary pupil attends a school in which 97 percent of the teachers are white. White teachers are more predominant at the secondary level, where the corresponding figures are 59 and 97 percent. The racial matching of teachers is most pronounced in the South, where by tradition it has been complete. On a nationwide basis, in cases where the races of pupils and teachers are not matched, the trend is all in one direction: white teachers teach Negro children but Negro teachers seldom teach white children; just as, in the schools, integration consists primarily of a minority of Negro pupils in predominantly white schools but almost never of a few whites in largely Negro schools.

In its desegregation decision of 1954, the Supreme Court held that separate schools for Negro and white children are inherently unequal. This survey finds that, when measured by that yardstick, American public education remains largely unequal in most regions of the country, including all those where Negroes form any significant proportion of the population. Obviously, however, that is not the only yardstick. The next section of the summary describes other characteristics by means of which equality of educational opportunity may be appraised.

THE SCHOOLS AND THEIR CHARACTERISTICS

The school environment of a child consists of many elements, ranging from the desk he sits at to the child who sits next to him, and including the teacher who stands at the front of his class. A statistical survey can give only fragmentary evidence of this environment.

Great collections of numbers such as are found in these pages— totals and averages and percentages—blur and obscure rather than sharpen and illuminate the range of variation they represent. If one reads, for example, that the average annual income per person in the State of Maryland is $3,000, there is a tendency to picture an average person living in moderate circumstances in a middle-class nieghborhood holding an ordinary job. But that number represents at the upper end millionaires, and at the lower end the unemployed, the pensioners, the charwomen. Thus the $3,000 average income should somehow bring to mind the tycoon and the tramp, the showcase and the shack, as well as the average man in the average house.

So, too, in reading these statistics on education, one must picture the child whose school has every conceivable facility that is believed to enhance the educational process, whose teachers may be particularly gifted and well educated, and whose home and total neighborhood are themselves powerful contributors to his education and growth. And one must picture the child in a dismal tenement area who may come hungry to an ancient, dirty building that is badly ventilated, poorly lighted, overcrowded, understaffed, and without sufficient textbooks.

Statistics, too, must deal with one thing at a time, and cumulative effects tend to be lost in them. Having a teacher without a college degree indicates an element of disadvantage, but in the concrete situation, a child may be taught by a teacher who is not only without a degree but who has grown up and received his schooling in the local community, who has never been out of the State, who has a 10th grade vocabulary, and who shares the local community's attitudes.

One must also be aware of the relative importance of a certain kind of thing to a certain kind of person. Just as a loaf of bread means more to a starving man than to a sated one, so one very fine textbook or, better, one very able teacher, may mean far more to a deprived child than to one who already has several of both.

Finally, it should be borne in mind that in cases where Negroes in the South receive unequal treatment, the significance in terms of actual numbers of individuals involved is very great, since 54 percent of the Negro population of school-going age, or approximately 3,200,000 children, live in that region.

All of the findings reported in this section of the summary are based on responses to questionnaires filled out by public school teachers, principals, district school superintendents, and pupils. The data were gathered in September and October of 1965 from 4,000 public schools. All teachers, principals, and district superintendents in these schools participated, as did all pupils in the 3d, 6th, 9th, and 12th grades. First grade pupils in half the schools participated. More than 645,000 pupils in all were involved in the survey. About 30 percent of the schools selected for the survey did not participate; an analysis of the nonparticipating schools indicated that their inclusion would not have significantly altered the results of the survey. The participation rates were: in the metropolitan North and West 72 percent, metropolitan South and Southwest 65 percent, nonmetropolitan North and West 82 percent, nonmetropolitan South and Southwest 61 percent.

All the statistics on the physical facilities of the schools and the academic and extracurricular programs are based on information provided by the teachers and administrators. They also provided information about their own education, experience, and philosophy of education, and described as they see them the socioeconomic characteristics of the neighborhoods served by their schools.

The statistics having to do with the pupils' personal socioeconomic background, level of education of their parents, and certain items in their homes (such as encyclopedias, daily newspapers, etc.) are based on pupil responses to questionnaires. The pupils also answered questions about their academic aspirations and their attitudes toward staying in school.

All personal and school data were confidential and for statistical purposes only; the questionnaires were collected without the names or other personal identification of the respondents.

Data for Negro and white children are classified by whether the schools are in metropolitan areas or not. The definition of a metropolitan area is the one commonly used by Government agencies: a city of over 50,000 inhabitants including its suburbs. All other schools in small cities, towns, or rural areas are referred to as nonmetropolitan schools....

ACHIEVEMENT IN THE PUBLIC SCHOOLS

The schools bear many responsibilities. Among the most important is the teaching of certain intellectual skills such as reading, writing, calculating, and problem-solving. One way of assessing the educational opportunity offered by the schools is to measure how well they perform this task. Standard achievement tests are available to measure these skills, and several such tests were administered in this survey to pupils at grades 1, 3, 6, 9, and 12.

These tests do not measure intelligence, nor attitudes, nor qualities of character. Furthermore, they are not, nor are they intended to be, "culture-free." Quite the reverse: they are culture-bound. What they measure are the skills which are among the most important in our society for getting a good job and moving up to a better one, and for full participation in an increasingly technical world. Consequently, a pupil's test results at the end of public school provide a good measure of the range of opportunities open to him as he finishes school—a wide range of choice of jobs or colleges if these skills are very high; a very narrow range that includes only the most menial jobs if these skills are very low.

Table 6 gives an overall illustration of the test results for the various groups by tabulating nationwide median scores (the score which divides the group in half) for 1st-grade and 12th-grade pupils on the tests used in those grades. For example, half of the white 12th-grade pupils had scores above 52 on the nonverbal test and half had scores below 52. (Scores on each test at each grade level were standardized so that the average over the national sample equaled 50 and the standard

TABLE 1. *Percent (Except Where Average Specified) of Pupils in Elementary Schools Having the School Characteristic Named at Left*

| Characteristic | Whole Nation | | | | | | Nonmetropolitan | | | | | | Metropolitan | | | | | | | | | |
| | M–A | PR | I–A | O–A | Neg | Maj | North and West | | South | | Southwest | | Northeast | | Midwest | | South | | Southwest | | West | |
							Neg	Maj	Neg	Maj	Neg	Maj	Neg	Maj	Neg	Maj	Neg	Maj	Neg	Maj	Neg	Maj
Age of main building:																						
Less than 20 yrs	59	57	66	61	63	60	48	54	72	34	73	40	31	59	28	63	77	75	52	89	76	80
20 to 40 yrs	18	18	20	20	17	20	35	13	21	43	17	28	23	23	18	18	11	20	27	10	14	9
At least 40 yrs	22	24	13	18	18	18	17	32	4	20	9	29	43	18	53	18	12	4	21	1	7	7
Average pupils per room	33	31	30	33	32	29	25	28	34	26	21	31	33	30	34	30	30	31	39	26	37	31
Auditorium	20	31	18	21	27	19	3	5	16	40	14	19	56	40	27	10	20	21	11	1	47	12
Cafeteria	39	43	38	30	38	37	41	33	46	64	47	54	41	45	24	22	34	32	48	38	34	14
Gymnasium	19	27	20	14	15	21	9	8	15	31	15	21	46	49	36	19	6	5	13	17	0	8
Infirmary	59	62	64	77	71	68	52	52	49	44	38	39	74	90	74	79	81	76	59	48	93	96
Full-time librarian	22	31	22	24	30	22	4	13	32	22	5	11	46	43	22	15	38	50	11	12	19	13
Free textbooks	80	82	80	85	84	75	73	56	70	73	99	98	100	98	72	54	84	82	83	65	98	100
School has sufficient number of textbooks	90	87	91	93	84	96	97	99	76	94	97	96	90	97	97	99	74	98	82	84	95	90
Texts under 4 yrs. old	66	68	60	52	67	61	66	51	60	60	47	85	57	56	67	59	71	91	76	53	77	77
Central school library	69	71	72	83	73	72	44	58	74	77	48	75	83	89	57	70	79	69	59	33	81	95
Free lunch program	64	73	66	52	74	59	61	50	87	94	83	70	50	43	42	48	90	85	74	82	65	47

TABLE 2. *Percent of Pupils in Elementary Schools Having the Characteristic Named at Left*

Characteristic	Whole Nation						Nonmetropolitan						Metropolitan									
							North and West		South		Southwest		Northeast		Midwest		South		Southwest		West	
	M-A	PR	I-A	O-A	Neg	Maj	Neg	Maj	Neg	Maj	Neg	Maj	Neg	Maj	Neg	Maj	Neg	Maj	Neg	Maj	Neg	Maj
Regionally accredited schools	21	27	25	22	27	28	38	29	16	22	59	39	34	24	52	49	21	35	42	23	22	9
Music teacher	31	34	41	33	24	35	22	43	26	17	37	42	34	49	38	32	21	17	23	61	9	13
Remedial reading teacher	41	45	35	41	39	39	37	46	15	11	12	26	73	58	60	17	28	31	18	29	66	70
Accelerated curriculum	34	32	42	37	29	40	47	26	28	24	32	13	34	47	21	28	19	41	34	76	43	73
Low IQ classes	43	44	44	56	54	48	54	48	30	29	47	25	60	51	73	45	48	33	63	66	77	75
Speech impairment classes	41	44	42	58	41	51	34	49	13	11	27	22	59	73	86	67	20	41	34	23	86	82
Use of intelligence test	93	77	90	95	88	95	85	93	80	91	92	90	73	91	97	99	92	100	97	98	98	99
Assignment practice other than area or open	6	11	9	5	12	6	6	1	27	20	26	2	7	4	1	2	12	22	0	0	4	1
Use of tracking	37	47	40	34	44	36	36	28	38	25	38	23	66	50	40	38	45	35	50	48	36	40
Teachers having tenure	68	68	69	79	70	64	70	64	34	49	7	36	100	98	94	76	51	58	64	39	92	90
Principal salary $9,000 and above	51	52	56	69	51	51	45	34	12	12	22	36	95	86	92	72	30	26	35	14	98	99
School newspaper	23	29	35	37	28	29	39	43	25	26	8	6	28	22	31	24	29	27	22	11	31	31
Boys interscholastic athletics	55	44	51	47	41	43	71	62	51	51	59	72	22	22	31	46	38	22	43	54	34	22
Girls interscholastic athletics	35	29	36	32	26	26	37	35	39	38	40	44	19	14	17	17	2	6	29	43	25	18
Band	71	63	64	76	66	72	82	81	39	40	54	76	67	73	77	86	66	85	52	33	95	94
Drama club	26	37	32	33	38	29	43	33	50	31	25	25	34	32	36	29	35	23	33	2	37	36
Debate team	6	4	4	7	5	4	0	3	14	6	10	6	1	3	0	0	3	6	16	8	0	2

TABLE 3. *For the Elementary Schools Attended by the Average White and Minority Pupil—Percent of Teachers with Characteristic Named at Left*

Characteristic	Whole Nation						Nonmetropolitan						Metropolitan										
							North and West		South		Southwest		Northeast		Midwest		South		Southwest		West	
	M-A	PR	I-A	O-A	Neg	Maj	Neg	Maj	Neg	Maj	Neg	Maj	Neg	Maj	Neg	Maj	Neg	Maj	Neg	Maj	Neg	Maj
Percent teachers who spent most of life in present city, town, or county	37	54	35	39	53	40	34	40	54	55	40	31	64	51	55	39	69	37	35	18	24	24
Average teacher verbal score	22	22	22	23	20	23	23	24	17	22	20	22	22	23	22	23	19	23	21	24	22	24
Percent teachers majored in academic subjects	19	18	17	21	17	16	16	18	12	14	16	22	19	17	17	15	18	16	9	7	23	22
Percent teachers who attended college not offering graduate degrees	39	41	37	32	53	37	48	38	63	47	44	30	45	38	39	40	72	46	44	26	22	21
Percent teachers who attended college with white students enrolled	79	70	85	83	39	97	81	99	9	97	28	93	73	97	75	97	7	95	43	98	82	96
Average education level of teacher's mother (score)	3.7	3.5	3.7	3.8	3.5	3.7	3.4	3.5	2.9	3.5	3.6	3.7	3.6	3.7	3.7	3.6	3.5	4.2	3.8	3.8	4.1	4.2
Average highest degree earned	3.1	3.1	3.1	3.1	3.2	3.0	2.8	2.8	3.1	3.0	3.4	3.3	3.2	3.1	3.1	3.0	3.2	3.0	3.5	3.2	3.3	3.1
Average teacher years experience	13	12	12	12	13	12	12	13	14	16	14	13	11	11	11	11	14	10	13	11	11	10
Average teacher salary ($1,000's)	5.9	6.0	6.1	6.6	6.0	6.0	5.8	5.7	4.7	5.0	5.5	5.4	7.2	7.1	7.0	6.5	5.2	5.0	5.9	5.1	7.8	7.3
Average pupils per teacher	30	30	30	28	20	28	26	25	32	27	23	26	27	26	29	28	28	30	30	42	30	31
Percent teachers would not choose to move to another school	58	57	59	59	55	65	56	60	49	73	57	64	53	64	49	63	61	76	63	59	55	66
Percent teachers plan to continue until retirement	44	42	41	39	45	37	42	35	50	51	57	55	31	32	34	31	51	34	48	46	41	34
Percent teachers prefer white pupils	27	21	26	20	7	37	22	32	6	57	10	45	8	18	12	37	1	57	12	48	8	31
Percent teachers approved compensatory education	56	59	56	64	61	56	53	56	55	47	53	44	69	66	65	55	59	49	56	54	73	66

TABLE 4. *For the Average Minority or White Pupil, the Percent of Fellow Pupils with the Specified Characteristics*

Characteristic	Whole Nation						Nonmetropolitan						Metropolitan									
							North and West		South		Southwest		Northeast		Midwest		South		Southwest		West	
	M-A	PR	I-A	O-A	Neg	Maj	Neg	Maj	Neg	Maj	Neg	Maj	Neg	Maj	Neg	Maj	Neg	Maj	Neg	Maj	Neg	Maj
Elementary schools:																						
Mostly white classmates last year	59	52	66	63	19	89	59	91	17	91	19	72	33	87	26	91	7	91	27	91	20	86
All white teachers last year	75	68	77	74	53	88	71	89	53	87	57	84	60	89	52	88	49	89	51	89	52	85
Encyclopedia in home	62	57	64	70	54	75	62	72	36	65	48	64	71	84	60	80	51	80	57	72	64	83
Secondary schools:																						
Mostly white classmates last year	72	56	72	57	10	91	77	96	12	94	23	88	41	90	40	89	4	95	14	96	35	81
All white teachers last year	73	57	75	57	25	89	79	93	11	93	23	90	44	84	45	88	3	92	16	95	46	79
Encyclopedia in home	77	76	75	82	69	82	76	78	52	75	66	75	82	87	80	86	67	88	73	83	78	83
Mother high school graduate or more	49	47	50	53	40	58	51	58	23	45	44	48	51	63	49	63	37	58	41	49	53	65
Taking college preparatory course	36	38	35	41	32	41	29	35	22	33	28	32	39	53	43	55	34	44	29	31	34	46
Taking some vocational course	27	30	28	32	27	23	22	24	23	20	25	20	30	20	28	25	27	16	37	38	35	30
2½ yrs. or more of science	36	38	38	38	39	42	41	41	41	38	47	39	30	55	32	38	43	43	42	38	26	34
1½ yrs. or more of language	37	41	35	43	35	40	29	30	25	26	19	23	43	60	36	44	43	44	34	23	31	50
3½ yrs. or more of English	77	73	80	76	69	83	68	78	66	89	75	84	79	91	73	79	67	89	71	87	62	72
2½ yrs. or more of math	47	45	44	47	44	49	40	39	43	46	50	52	47	63	41	50	46	55	58	45	37	47

TABLE 5. *For the Average Minority or White Pupil, the Percent of Fellow Pupils with the Specified Characteristics*

Characteristics	Whole Nation						Nonmetropolitan						Metropolitan									
							North and West		South		Southwest		Northeast		Midwest		South		Southwest		West	
	M-A	PR	I-A	O-A	Neg	Maj	Neg	Maj	Neg	Maj	Neg	Maj	Neg	Maj	Neg	Maj	Neg	Maj	Neg	Maj	Neg	Maj
Mother not reared in city	45	33	44	33	45	42	58	50	64	65	53	61	25	19	35	32	45	42	48	60	34	33
Real father at home	77	71	75	84	64	83	80	84	65	84	64	85	67	83	70	84	58	84	55	84	62	74
Real mother at home	90	88	90	89	85	92	90	92	82	93	82	94	88	92	90	92	83	92	83	94	86	88
5 or more brothers and sisters	28	27	30	27	44	20	30	24	56	23	54	23	25	15	34	19	48	13	47	17	36	21
Mother expects best in class	48	49	45	42	62	43	47	39	71	55	67	54	50	41	49	38	69	49	71	51	53	41
Parents daily discuss school	47	46	44	42	49	47	44	44	51	51	52	54	50	52	44	45	53	53	51	43	43	44
Father expects at least college graduation	38	34	35	37	38	37	36	32	33	37	39	44	33	39	36	38	39	44	45	45	37	40
Mother expects at least college graduation	41	39	39	41	44	41	41	35	42	40	48	45	38	42	43	41	48	45	52	50	43	44
Parents attend PTA	36	38	34	37	51	37	36	40	59	37	50	34	43	37	45	36	61	44	42	26	36	30
Parents read to child regularly before he started school	25	28	24	24	30	26	26	24	30	25	32	23	32	31	27	27	33	29	31	21	26	27

deviation equaled 10. This means that for all pupils in the Nation, about 16 percent would score below 40 and about 16 percent above 60.)

With some exceptions—notably Oriental Americans—the average minority pupil scores distinctly lower on these tests at every level than the average white pupil. The minority pupils' scores are as much as one standard deviation below the majority pupils' scores in the first grade. At the 12th grade, results of tests in the same verbal and nonverbal skills show that, in every case, the minority scores are *farther below* the majority than are the 1st graders. For some groups, the relative decline is negligible; for others, it is large.

Futhermore, a constant difference in standard deviations over

TABLE 6. *Nationwide Median Test Scores for First- and Twelfth-Grade Pupils*

Test	Racial or ethnic group					
	Puerto Ricans	Indian-Americans	Mexican-Americans	Oriental-Americans	Negro	Majority
First grade:						
Nonverbal	45.8	53.0	50.1	56.6	43.4	54.1
Verbal	44.9	47.8	46.5	51.6	45.4	53.2
Twelfth grade:						
Nonverbal	43.3	47.1	45.0	51.6	40.9	52.0
Verbal	43.1	43.7	43.8	49.6	40.9	52.1
Reading	42.6	44.3	44.2	48.8	42.2	51.9
Mathematics	43.7	45.9	45.5	51.3	41.8	51.8
General information	41.7	44.7	43.3	49.0	40.6	52.2
Average of the 5 tests	43.1	45.1	44.4	50.1	41.1	52.0

the various grades represents an increasing difference in grade level gap. For example, Negroes in the metropolitan Northeast are about 1.1 standard deviations below whites in the same region at grades 6, 9, and 12. But at grade 6 this represents 1.6 years behind, at grade 9, 2.4 years, and at grade 12, 3.3 years. Thus, by this measure, the deficiency in achievement is progressively greater for the minority pupils at progressively higher grade levels.

For most minority groups, then, and most particularly the Negro, schools provide no opportunity at all for them to overcome this initial deficiency; in fact, they fall farther behind the white majority in the development of several skills which are critical to making a living and participating fully in modern society. Whatever may be the combination of nonschool factors—poverty, community attitudes, low educational level of parents—which put minority children at a disadvantage in verbal and nonverbal skills when they enter the first grade, the fact is the schools have not overcome it.

Some points should be borne in mind in reading the table. First, the differences shown should not obscure the fact that some minority children perform better than many white children. A difference of one standard deviation in median scores means that about 84 percent of the children in the lower group are below the median of the majority students—but 50 percent of the white children are themselves below that median as well.

A second point of qualification concerns regional differences. By grade 12, both white and Negro students in the South score below their counterparts—white and Negro—in the North. In addition, Southern Negroes score farther below Southern whites than Northern Negroes score below Northern whites. The consequences of this pattern can be illustrated by the fact that the 12th grade Negro in the nonmetropolitan South is 0.8 standard deviation below—or in terms of years, 1.9 years behind—the Negro in the metropolitan Northeast, though at grade 1 there is no such regional difference.

Finally, the test scores at grade 12 obviously do not take account of those pupils who have left school before reaching the senior year. In the metropolitan North and West, 20 percent of the Negroes of ages 16 and 17 are not enrolled in school, a higher dropout percentage than in either the metropolitan or nonmetropolitan South. If it is the case that some or many of the Northern dropouts performed poorly when they were in school, the Negro achievement in the North may be artificially elevated because some of those who achieved more poorly have left school.

RELATION OF ACHIEVEMENT TO SCHOOL CHARACTERISTICS

If 100 students within a school take a certain test, there is likely to be great variation in their scores. One student may score 97 percent, another 13; several may score 78 percent. This represents variability in achievement *within* the particular school.

It is possible, however, to compute the average of the scores made by the students within that school and to compare it with the average score, or achievement, of pupils within another school, or many other schools. These comparisons then represent variations *between schools*.

When one sees that the average score on a verbal achievement test in School X is 55 and in School Y is 72, the natural question to ask is: What accounts for the difference?

There are many factors that in combination account for the difference. This analysis concentrates on one cluster of those factors. It attempts to describe what relationship the school's characteristics themselves (libraries, for example, and teachers and laboratories and so on) seem to have to the achievement of majority and minority groups (separately for each group on a nationwide basis, and also for Negro and white pupils in the North and South).

The first finding is that the schools are remarkably similar in the effect they have on the achievement of their pupils when the socioeconomic background of the students is taken into account. It is known that socioeconomic factors bear a strong relation to academic achievement. When these factors are statistically controlled, however, it appears that differences between schools account for only a small fraction of differences in pupil achievement.

The schools *do* differ, however, in the degree of impact they have on the various racial and ethnic groups. The average white student's achievement is less affected by the strength or weakness of his school's facilities, curricula, and teachers than is the average minority pupil's. To put it another way, the achievement of minority pupils depends more on the schools they attend than does the achievement of majority pupils. Thus, 20 percent of the achievement of Negroes in the South is associated with the particular schools they go to, whereas only 10 percent of the achievement of whites in the South is. Except for Oriental Americans, this general result is found for all minorities.

The conclusion can then be drawn that improving the school of a minority pupil will increase his achievement more than will improving the school of a white child increase his. Similarly, the average minority pupil's achievement will suffer more in a school of low quality than will the average white pupil's. In short, whites, and to a lesser extent Oriental Americans, are less affected one way or the other by the quality of their schools than are minority pupils. This indicates that it is for the most disadvantaged children that improvements in school quality will make the most difference in achievement.

All of these results suggest the next question: What are the school characteristics that account for most variation in achievement? In other words, what factors in the school are most important in affecting achievement?

It appears that variations in the facilities and curriculums of the schools account for relatively little variation in pupil achievement insofar as this is measured by standard tests. Again, it is for majority whites that the variations make the least difference; for minorities, they make somewhat more difference. Among the facilities that show some relationship to achievement are several for which minority pupils' schools are less well equipped relative to whites. For example, the existence of science laboratories showed a small but consistent relationship to achievement, and table 2 shows that minorities, especially Negroes, are in schools with fewer of these laboratories.

The quality of teachers shows a stronger relationship to pupil achievement. Futhermore, it is progressively greater at higher grades, indicating a cumulative impact of the qualities of teachers in a school on the pupils' achievement. Again, teacher quality is more important for minority pupil achievement than for that of the majority.

It should be noted that many characteristics of teachers were not measured in this survey; therefore, the results are not at all conclusive regarding the specific characteristics of teachers that are most important. Among those measured in the survey, however, those that bear the highest relationship to pupil achievement are first, the teacher's score on the verbal skills test, and then his educational background—both his own level of education and that of his parents. On both of these measures, the level of teachers of minority students, especially Negroes, is lower.

Finally, it appears that a pupil's achievement is strongly related to the educational backgrounds and aspirations of the other students in the school. Only crude measures of these variables were used (principally the proportion of pupils with encyclopedias in the home and the proportion planning to go to college). Analysis indicates, however, that children from a given family background, when put in schools of different social composition, will achieve at quite different levels. This effect is again less for white pupils than for any minority group other than Orientals. Thus, if a white pupil from a home that is strongly and effectively supportive of education is put in a school where most pupils do not come from such homes, his achievement will be little different than if he were in a school composed of others like himself. But if a minority pupil from a home without much educational strength is put with schoolmates with strong educational backgrounds, his achievement is likely to increase.

This general result, taken together with the earlier examinations of school differences, has important implications for equality of educational opportunity. For the earlier tables show that the principal way in which the school environments of Negroes and whites differ is in the composition of their student bodies, and it turns out that the composition of the student bodies has a strong relationship to the achievement of Negro and other minority pupils.

*   *   *

This analysis has concentrated on the educational opportunities offered by the schools in terms of their student body composition, facilities, curriculums, and teachers. This emphasis, while entirely appropriate as a response to the legislation calling for the survey, nevertheless neglects important factors in the variability between individual pupils within the same school; this variability is roughly four times as large as the variability between schools. For example, a pupil attitude factor, which appears to have a stronger relationship to achievement than do all the "school" factors together, is the extent to which an individual feels that he has some control over his own destiny. Data on items related to this attitude are shown in table 10 along with data on other attitudes and aspirations. The responses of pupils to questions in the survey show that minority pupils, except for Orientals, have far less conviction than whites that they can affect their own environments and futures. When they do, however, their achievement is higher than that of whites who lack that conviction.

Futhermore, while this characteristic shows little relationship to most school factors, it is related, for Negroes, to the proportion of whites in the schools. Those Negroes in schools with a higher proportion of whites have a greater sense of control. Thus such attitudes, which are largely a consequence of a person's experience in the larger society, are not independent of his experience in school.

EFFECTS OF INTEGRATION ON ACHIEVEMENT

An education in integrated schools can be expected to have major effects on attitudes toward members of other racial groups. At its best, it can develop attitudes appropriate to the integrated society these students will live in; at its worst, it can create hostile camps of Negroes and whites in the same school. Thus there is more to "school integration" than merely putting Negroes and whites in the same building, and there may be more important consequences of integration than its effect on achievement.

Yet the anlaysis of school effects described earlier suggests that in the long run, integration should be expected to have a positive effect on Negro achievement as well. An analysis was carried out to examine the effects on achievement which might appear in the short run. This analysis of the test performance of Negro children in integrated schools indicates positive effects of integration, though rather small ones. Results for grades 6, 9, and 12 are given in table 7 for Negro pupils classified by

TABLE 7. *Average Test Scores of Negro Pupils*

Grade	Region	Reading comprehension, proportion of white classmates last year				Math achievement, proportion of white classmates last year			
		None	Less than half	Half	More than half	None	Less than half	Half	More than half
12	Metropolitan Northeast	46.0	43.7	44.5	47.5	41.5	40.6	41.1	44.5
12	Metropolitan Midwest	46.4	43.2	44.0	46.7	43.8	42.6	42.9	44.8
9	Metropolitan Northeast	44.2	44.8	44.8	47.1	43.1	43.5	43.7	47.2
9	Metropolitan Midwest	45.3	45.2	45.3	46.4	44.4	44.3	44.1	46.6
6	Metropolitan Northeast	46.0	45.4	45.8	46.6	44.0	43.4	43.6	45.6
6	Metropolitan Midwest	46.0	44.7	44.9	45.1	43.8	42.8	42.9	44.1

TABLE 8.   *Average Test Scores of Negro Pupils*

Grade	Region	First grade with majority pupils	Proportion of majority classmates last year				Total
			None	Less than half	Half	More than half	
9	Metropolitan Northeast	1, 2 or 3	45.9	46.7	46.9	48.1	46.8
		4, 5 or 6	45.2	43.3	44.4	44.4	44.8
		7, 8 or 9	43.5	42.9	44.6	45.0	44.0
		Never	43.2				43.2
9	Metropolitan Midwest	1, 2 or 3	45.4	46.6	46.4	48.6	46.7
		4, 5 or 6	44.4	44.1	45.3	46.7	44.5
		7, 8 or 9	44.4	43.4	43.3	45.2	43.7
		Never	46.5				46.5
12	Metropolitan Northeast	1, 2 or 3	40.8	43.6	45.2	48.6	46.2
		4, 5 or 6	46.7	45.1	44.9	46.7	45.6
		7, 8 or 9	42.2	43.5	43.8	49.7	48.2
		10, 11 or 12	42.2	41.1	43.2	46.6	44.1
		Never	40.9				40.9
12	Metropolitan Midwest	1, 2 or 3	47.4	44.3	45.6	48.3	46.7
		4, 5 or 6	46.1	43.0	43.5	46.4	45.4
		7, 8 or 9	46.6	40.8	42.3	45.6	45.3
		10, 11 or 12	44.8	39.5	43.5	44.9	44.3
		Never	47.2				47.2

the proportion of their classmates the previous year who were white. Comparing the averages in each row, in every case but one the highest average score is recorded for the Negro pupils where more than half of their classmates were white. But in reading the rows from left to right, the increase is small and often those Negro pupils in classes with only a few whites score lower than those in totally segregated classes.

Table 8 was constructed to observe whether there is any tendency for Negro pupils who have spent more years in integrated schools to exhibit higher average achievement. Those pupils who first entered integrated schools in the early grades record consistently higher scores than the other groups, although the differences are again small.

No account is taken in these tabulations of the fact that the various groups of pupils may have come from different backgrounds. When such account is taken by simple cross-tabulations on indicators of socioeconomic status, the performance in integrated schools and in schools integrated longer remains higher. Thus although the differences are small, and although the degree of integration within the school is not known, there is evident even in the short run an effect of school integration on the reading and mathematics achievement of Negro pupils.

Tabulations of this kind are, of course, the simplest possible devices for seeking such effects. It is possible that more elaborate analyses looking more carefully at the special characteristics of the Negro pupils, and at different degrees of integration within schools that have similar racial composition, may reveal a more definite effect. Such analyses are among those that will be presented in subsequent reports.

Randolph Blackwell and Stokely Carmichael
BLACK POWER: THE WIDENING DIALOGUE

Q.   Malcolm X was a man whom I knew very well. And one of the philosophies that he continued to insist upon was that inevitably all the so-called civil rights movements must come to the point where they must part ways with their white supporters. It was Malcolm's thesis, and I quote him here, that "you can't trip a man when he is helping you." And it was his feeling that the white supporters of the civil rights movement would go along with the civil rights movement insofar as they themselves were being benefitted directly or indirectly, and that when the going really got tough, you could not rely on them either for moral or financial support. Is this the point to which SNCC has come now? Or is it the philosophy which SNCC is now following?

MR. CARMICHAEL.   It seems to me that . . . one of the things that upset me is the fact that all the white supporters of the civil rights movement want to rid the black community of racism when it does not in fact exist, and that they are afraid to go into their own community and rid it of the racism where it really does exist. So one of the things that we have to do is to tell them to get into their own community and rid it of racism. They want to make the black community nonviolent, when they are afraid to go into their own community and preach nonviolence where it belongs. I'm always appalled at the fact that the Quakers are always trying to make me nonviolent and never worrying about Jim Clark. It seems to me Jim Clark is the one that needs to be nonviolent, not me. And of course it also has to do with the problem of color. . . . it is a problem of color because the white people in this country who are alienated by this society now find themselves working in the black community. There is no place for them to go within the white society. It

Condensed from, New South, Vol. 21, No. 3, Summer 1966, Southern Regional Council, Inc. Reprinted by permission. Mr. Carmichael is past chairman of the Student Nonviolent Coordinating Committee. Mr. Blackwell is Director of the Citizen Crusade against Poverty, Southern Rural Development Project.

seems to me if they talked about developing a real movement in this country, they would have to start working in the poor white community and not polarizing the races as they now do by working in the black community. I think that Malcolm X had certain valid points—that white society just because they give us money can't dictate to us what we are going to do. That what they could do is try to understand people like LeRoi Jones and understand they can no longer condemn him, and let it stand at that. As a matter of fact, their condemnation of him might make us run to him. And the best they can do is try to understand him. I think that he did have valid points and black people in this country have to move to a position of psychological equality and that is very, very important. And they can't do that with white people getting everything for them. They have to confront the white power structure themselves, so that means that white allies will have to be pushed aside; we can no longer have white people getting poverty money for you—you have to get it yourself so that you know that black people can do those things on their own—so that they don't always need somebody white to do it for them. The tutorial programs will have to be done by black people so that black children can identify with black people and realize there are black people like themselves who can do it. I think that what happens is that white allies further white supremacy, without the whites involved in those projects realizing it; but what it is saying is that there are no black people who can do this and we have to come and help you again.

Q. Mr. Blackwell, in reading the press reports of Dr. King's speech in Chicago on Sunday, he seemed to be talking "tougher" than I have read him in many a month. Is Dr. King moving over to a so-called "tougher" position?

MR. BLACKWELL. I don't think there is any substantial change in Dr. King's position. It is as it has always been pretty much as it was set forth in Chicago. Certainly events of recent days have compelled him to articulate more specifically his position on certain questions. But had these questions been raised a year ago, I think perhaps the answer would have been substantially the same. We indulge the notion that Martin Luther King is a pretty militant person, and yet it would appear that he is *the* conservative of social change, 1966. I rather suspect that it is a matter of the proper question, the precise question, having not been raised earlier.

Q. What do you consider that precise question?

MR. BLACKWELL. Oh, well, much of the discussion of recent days has hovered around the issue of Black Power. Perhaps it sounds like he has changed—I don't know if there is anything unique about the whole discussion of Black Power, *per se.* Certainly this is the kind of thing that Frederick Douglass was talking about; it's not substantially different from what Dr. DuBois talked about for some 50 years; it's not substantially different from what Edgar Brown of a different school and period talked about, or the National Negro Youth Congress of a different period talked about, or the Universal Improvement Association of a different period talked about. I think it is very important for us to recognize that Black Power as it is presently being journalistically abused is not anything particularly new or unique. I think it does need to be talked about and certainly when it is raised, it invites one to be specific in what he is talking about, and one of the tragedies of it is that invitation has not gone forward often enough to clear the air precisely as to what we are saying when we say Black Power.

Q.   Since you associate that power with persons like Frederick Douglass, etc., and you say it has been around for some length of time, are you also saying now that the SCLC can endorse or will endorse . . .

MR. BLACKWELL.   It isn't a matter of endorsing; we have never had any difficulty with the proposition that Negro people have the right to self-determination. It seems to me the unfortunate thing about Black Power as it is presently being used is that it tends to suggest that this is the sole concern of Negro people in the civil rights movement. It might very well be that this is the sole concern of certain organizations and this does not trouble us. It happens that SCLC believes that the 20th century civilization is infinitely more complicated than just the race problem and because of that we have to be concerned with advancing technology; we have to be concerned with expanding population; we have to be concerned with a number of social forces that we feel are colliding and compelling decisions that cannot be answered purely by viewing our concern as just one of the positions of the Negro people.

MR. CARMICHAEL.   I just think that for six years, black people in this country have demonstrated, and that they demonstrated from a point of weakness, that they marched and they were the ones that got their heads beaten, got shot, with white allies, and what they were saying to the country was, "Look, you guys are supposed to be nice guys, and we are only going to do what we are supposed to—why are you going to beat us up? Why don't you straighten yourselves out?" Six years later we are at the same point. I think you can't speak from a point of weakness any more. What you do is organize yourself and you go see a man and you say, "Look, baby, I got 5,000 votes. We need a street paved. Either you get it or we get a boy for our votes." You know, that's it—no question about it being right any more. You're going to continue bombing Vietnam; that's clear to me. When you finish there, you're going to Santo Domingo, and that's clear to me. I don't want to be a part of that. So all I am saying to you is just let me have my road and my school, and you go on. I don't want to be a part of you. I don't want any part of that until you get people in your country who want to stop that and then you can sit down and talk to me; and while you are talking all that nonsense I don't want [any] part of you. The world is still the same; we just want to get the things that belong to us and you can go on and bomb. You can build you better bombs. And it seems to me this is what you have to talk about—that we can't be expected any more to march and get our heads broken to say to you that you are nice guys. You are not nice guys. We have found you out. You are rotten through and through—that's what we're saying. And, Alexander the Great was really Alexander the Barbaric. And that's what we are going to start from.

Q.   You talk about Black Power, and yet around the country in places like Chicago with Mr. Dawson, in New York with Mr. Powell, in Los Angeles with Mr. Hawkins, and Detroit now we do see Negro politicians, but I take it that these aren't the people you mean when you say Black Power.

MR. CARMICHAEL.   Black Power doesn't mean black faces to SNCC. It never has meant that, and if the press ever asks us for a definition without attaching the fears of white America to it, we would have clarified it in one fell swoop. Black Power is the coming together of black people and electing representatives and forcing those representatives to speak to their needs. That's all Black Power ever has been as far as the Student Nonviolent Coordinating Committee is concerned.

Q.   Do the present Negro politicians and congressmen speak to the needs of the Negro?

MR. CARMICHAEL.   No, sir, they do not, because Black Power is going to contradict American politics. Because Black Power is going to mean that the representatives speak to the needs of the people and it seems to me that black people in this country have two dilemmas. Number one, they are black. Number two, they are in the state of poverty. The solutions thrown to the people in the past have been integration—which speaks very despicably of their blackness but never speaks of the poverty the black people find themselves in. So when you talk about integration you talk about a Morehouse student who graduates; you don't talk about a black person in Vine City who drinks wine.

You don't talk about a cotton picker who makes $3 a day. They are not going to integrate because, well, what integration really says is like the Bible "only through me"—only through my schools will you have better education; only through my neighborhoods will you have better housing, never through your own. It seems to me it has nothing to do with the question of poverty. And that black people will force those politicians to speak to the question of poverty. And that's why Black Power must be distorted by the American press. It has to be. Because people are more interested in building better schools than bombing the hell out of Vietnam. I am willing to wager that across the country, even if they are white, I still think they'd rather build better schools rather than bomb Vietnam.

Q.   What would happen in Lowndes County . . . What about the white minority?

MR. CARMICHAEL.   What about them?

Q.   What happens to them? When the black majority runs Lowndes County, will the minority have as much right . . . to speak their views?

MR. CARMICHAEL.   That seems to me to be speaking to your own fears, to what white people have done to black people in this country when they had the power. Now just historically, and I've been across Africa and I swear by Almighty God that there is no reason why Africans shouldn't have killed every white person in their country. But after they received independence I've seen no "black" and "white" signs in Africa. I've seen no oppression of white people in Africa. Let me go one step further. The workers, you know, in the 1930's organized themselves and their cry [was] "workers of the world unite, because we need power to stop the exploitation." Now, when they organized, they didn't take over the factories. They just wanted to stop the oppression. Now I said at the very beginning that black people as far as I see do not want to take over this country. They just want to get white people off their backs. Now, if in fact, getting white people off your back means stopping the exploitation and the easy way in which they live, then that speaks to white people and not to black people.

Q.   Does that mean separation between white and black?

MR. CARMICHAEL.   There is separation now in Lowndes County, my dear.

Q. I know that.

MR. CARMICHAEL. The white people separated us.

Q. I know, but what are they fighting for, what . . .

MR. CARMICHAEL. I don't know what you're fighting for. SNCC is fighting to get black people the things they should have. That's all. And then they can decide if they want to accept the white people in Lowndes County who've brutalized them lo, these many, many years when no white person in this country raised a voice against it . . . You know in Africa, we had the land. When the missionaries left, we had the Bible, and they had the land . . .

Q. I'd like to ask Mr. Carmichael what he thinks black people need to do who're being asked to serve in the military forces of this country and who're being asked to pay taxes to support the foreign policy of this country. How do you cut out of this system?

MR. CARMICHAEL. I don't think we have enough strength to say no. Some of us do. SNCC people tell them no every day . . . But we have to develop within our communities the right to say no. See, this country has to integrate for this country's sake. Johnson can't fight a war for freedom, democracy, peace, integration, without black people. So they have to integrate—they must integrate on the fields of Vietnam so that it's brotherly nation fighting against these bad Communist people, see. But that's why the country has to integrate. I don't think black people have to integrate. I just think they have to get power to get the things they need.

Q. Mr. Blackwell, SCLC took a position on this problem—what is that position?

MR. BLACKWELL. Ours is basically a moral position. It is not likely to change. We believe that all war is evil; we don't believe in killing, period. We would be opposed to Vietnam and we would be opposed to any war that you could describe basically because we do not believe that war is the way to solve differences . . .

Q. One of the points of disagreement . . . comes out in Randy's statement concerning the fact that the poor have common needs that make it possible for them to be organized regardless of race; this is the SCLC understanding of the situation and I'd like to know how Stokely responds to that kind of thing. Why can't black and white people be organized together? Number two—one of the points of view that, I take it, Stokely and others have been making about nonviolence is that a violent and immoral country has been very happy to have the Negroes act nonviolent and moral because it didn't cost them very much, and Stokely is saying we're through with that kind of business—that if this country is going to be violent and immoral, we're not going to let them put us on. Now I wonder how Mr. Blackwell responds to that kind of statement about what has been going on in the last six years. Is this actually the case, and what do you think about Stokely's response to it?

MR. CARMICHAEL. Well, I don't want to get involved in that question; that's academic to me. On the question of organizing ..., I don't know of any civil rights organization that's been working in the white community, with the exception of SNCC. We've tried several times and failed, but maybe now we're making some headway—maybe only now. But I don't know any other organization that tried to organize poor whites. And the reality of it is that poor whites are very racist, because the country is racist, and that to go into a poor white community in Mississippi or Alabama and talk about integration is to invite suicide upon one's self. And everybody in the country knows that. So to talk about bringing black and white together is purely academic. You have developed within the black community of this country a movement that can sustain itself on its own momentum. That is not now done in the white community. As a matter of fact, the poor white community is becoming more hostile because they see everybody running to the black community, and nobody coming to them. And, when people talk this nonsense to me I dismiss them with a wave of the hand, because they're not willing to go to the white community and work where they belong—where they should be doing the work—because they want to be like the "Pepsi" generation—where the action is.

MR. BLACKWELL. Well, you know there is a real difference of opinion here. The opinion that I hold, and the opinion that the SCLC tends to hold, is not one that is popularly accepted. I think it's one that needs to be turned up, over and over, and examined. We're not satisfied in our own minds that the poor white community *is* the most racist segment of the white community. We're not sure. We have not been able to be certain that much of the violence that comes from the poor white community is not the product of ignorance rather than deep-seated racial prejudice. I think that one could allow themselves to reach the conclusion that a person is more racist because he is capable of a violent act, whereas, the bank president who would never do anything violent might sit perfectly still and say, "I'll never change, I'll never change, I'll never change." Now, that doesn't mean that he's going to go out and shoot anybody. I think that racism in the South has been nurtured to a very great extent by the public media—radio, the press, and other units of this sort—and poor white people don't own these institutions. So that one needs, I think, to be a little hesitant about how quickly they arrive at the conclusion that poor whites are the most racist. If you'll pardon the personal reference, back in 1947 I came down to Georgia to work on a voter registration drive as a college student and found in the back woods of Dawson, Georgia a very broken down, extremely rural, white congregation that had over its pulpit—and to get some picture of how poor the church was, they had split a bed sheet and had made two signs— something about the supremacy of God and the brotherhood of mankind without regard to race. I'm talking about an extremely rural part of Georgia in 1947, so that I approach the conclusion that the poor white South is the most racist with some degree of trepidation, because I don't think there is sufficient evidence to support the conclusion . . . What I am saying is that . . . it seems to me that there is a segment of the population now that is prepared to give up on American society and its capacity to change. It would appear to me that we're just full of change.

Q.   I'd like to echo what has been said in the way of having antagonism against poor whites and letting some of the wealthier whites or more prosperous whites off the hook. If you know anything about economics at all, we know that industrial business interests have used whites and Negroes—to place them against each other at the very first level. Negroes are scabs over and over again, and, of course, it's the poor whites that are the victims of the results. And, if at the time the Supreme Court decided that the schools should be integrated, had the rich whites come out unequivocally and tried to lead people in the proper direction, there is no telling what would have happened. As we said, the poor whites are kept in a dismal ignorance by people who are themselves anxious to keep whatever there is stirred up, because it means power to them.

MR. CARMICHAEL.   I've worked on the assumption that this country from top to bottom, from right to left, is racist. And when I said when you talk about the poor white community . . . talk about hooking up with them—the poor people—to bring about changes—what I'm saying is that I don't see how you can hook up with them, how black people can hook up with them, when they're right now fighting those same black people—whether they're less racist, more racist, or what have you. Somebody has to organize them. Now, if a black person went into that kind of community he has to organize them to two things—(1) that he's not poor, and (2) that the black man is his equal. . . .

I think one of the tragedies of the Movement is that within the growing militancy of young black people in the ghettos that there isn't an organization which can in fact speak to them. And that is a tragedy.

Q.   What about CORE?

MR. CARMICHAEL.   The Congress of Racial Equality does not speak to them. It is just now trying to address itself to them. There isn't one civil rights . . . there was a riot in Chicago last night, there was a riot in Bedford Stuyvesant last night, there was a riot in Philadelphia last night, and I dare say that there was not one leader, so-called leader, who could go into those communities and talk to those people and have them listen to him.

Q.   Why is that so?

MR. CARMICHAEL.   I think that's so because the civil rights movement up until this time has been talking to white liberals. Its attitudes have been geared to white liberals, and I think the greatest thing about Black Power is for once black people are going to use the slogan that they want to use; they don't give a damn who likes it. And that's very important, because the white press is trying to stop the use of that word, Black Power. And the black people are going to legitimize it and we're going to see how the white press is going to start addressing itself to us, rather than we addressing ourselves to them. It seems to me that one of the jobs of an organization is to speak to this country in the tone of its community. Not to be a buffer zone but to speak in the tone of that community and we intend to do that.

Q.   Mr. Blackwell, do you want to speak to that?

MR. BLACKWELL.   It seems we are oversimplifying this particular thing. I would be willing to say that perhaps the reason why we do not speak instantly and effectively to people in the segment of the Negro population is . . . because we have not defined what we would say to them. I think that the philosophy of nonviolence, for example, is one that has not been refined completely. I don't know how successful we will be when we have refined it but we are working on it constantly. I'm not sure that we have anything that would be meaningful to say in any of the organizations . . .

Q. I would like to ask Carmichael what role does integration play in the work that his group is doing today? ... How does integration work with Black Power or do you believe, as LeRoi Jones, that black and white should be totally separate?

MR. CARMICHAEL.   I think it depends upon what you mean by integration. If you mean that white people from Beverly Hills are going to move into Watts and live with us and send their kids to the schools in the black community, if you talk about white people in Lowndes County sending their kids to Lowndes County Freedom Organizations, or if you're talking about us sending some of our children to their schools then I'm for that—that's integration. But if you're talking about draining the energies of my neighborhood and sending it to your neighborhood—and telling me that because they go through there they are better—and the rest of us are still bad because we haven't been through there—then you can have your supremacy. Because that's all it is.

Q. What is your attitude towards the Watts revolt, and what is your attitude toward the same tendency that is manifesting itself in the ghetto today?

MR. BLACKWELL.   We believe that an understanding of the civil rights movement from our point of view would require that you understand that the movement is much broader than so many public accommodations, so many school classrooms desegregated, or what have you. We say this—that we are engaged in the business of causing people to pick up their souls—or, as a philosophy student would say it—causing people to say I am a man of dignity and worth, and you cannot treat me this way. So that we do not find ourselves alienated from the people in Watts, because we are, in a sense, engaged in creating a kind of climate that could conceivably go off into a Watts, as we cause people to pick up their souls, or as we cause people to say I am a person of worth and dignity. This saddles us with a particular responsibility. As we cause people to stand and say I am of worth and dignity, and I will not be treated this way, there comes the accompanying responsibility to cause them to know that there are ways to right the wrongs without burning down the town.

MR. CARMICHAEL.   You see the people I blame for Watts are Martin Luther King and the Student Nonviolent Coordinating Committee, and the mass media of this country. Because you see I think that every time they saw Martin get slapped, they got mad. And every time they saw four little black kids get bombed, they got madder. And when nothing happened, boy, they were steaming. Because they knew that the reason, and the only reason that those people got hit was because they were black. The only reason we are depressed in the country is because we are black. I was very discouraged because of the news publications—you see those cats are out to make money, so they started out talking about the extremist elements in the black community. Again, the oppressor shifts the blame to the oppressed, you see. I didn't think that their remarks were extreme. As a matter of fact, the people who forced them to live in those conditions are the extremists. And, those are the people we've got to talk to. Now, it's funny to me that they couldn't even talk to those people—they couldn't even talk to those extremists—those reactionaries—and the only answer that those reactionaries had were more guns, more policemen, mow them down, we must have law and order. I've had so much law and order, I swear before God I want some chaos! I want some chaos so bad I can taste it on the tip of my lips, because all I see is law and order, everywhere I go, law and order: from Canton, Mississippi to Watts, Los Angeles, to Harlem to Chicago—nothing but law and order. The tragedy of that situation was that there wasn't one black person of any significance in this country who was willing to use those riots to get something for black people. All of them started to condemn it as soon as it happened—they were condemning the savages and the beasts, and they said, "they must find other ways." And I'm sure they must find them. What's happening is that Watts is now in the same place, the very same place, as it was a year ago. And what you have now is the mass media writing stories about "Let's get Whitey," so that they can develop the whole framework in which law and order must be maintained. And that's all those articles do—they're developing a whole spectrum, so that if anything happens in Watts again, law and order can be maintained because they say, the folks in Watts are saying, "Let's get Whitey." But all the folks in Watts are saying is, "Get off my back, let me have the things I'm supposed to have." That's all they're saying. They don't care about· getting Whitey. Whitey is irrelevant to them, man; they just want a decent house, a job, a decent way of life, that's all they want. And this country won't speak to that. They evade the issue every time by raising irrelevant questions about violence, black power, black supremacy, black nationalism, anti-whites. Those are the same things they throw at you every time you talk about a decent way of life. That's because they're not willing to give in, because it's going to shake the economic foundations of this country if black people get a decent way of life. And they're going to force that confrontation, not black people because they don't control the press; they don't even control their own lives. And this is what people are going to have to be willing to do. When they want to talk to me about a decent way of life, then I'm going to sit down and talk to them—but don't talk to me about nonviolence unless you want to be nonviolent in Vietnam. And don't tell me that you can't hate anybody, because I want to know how many Americans love the Vietnamese they shoot. Just don't talk to me about that nonsense. And I'm just saying that the country is evading the issue—and that's the issue in Watts—that's the issue all over. In Omaha, Nebraska 200 Negroes got to riot before the mayor says, "My goodness, what a shame, they don't have jobs." And, at that, he came off his liberal position that it wasn't a race riot, it was just a disturbance. Just some juveniles rioting. And what does it take for black people to force this country to address itself to those problems—what does it take? And when it takes those things, why do white people get up and start blasting them instead of blasting themselves? The question philosophically is the question that Camus and Sartre raise, "Can a man condemn himself?" Can white society, white liberals, specifically, who hook up with white America condemn themselves—*condemn themselves* for what's been going on in white America? And, the rhetorical answer is, of course, no. They can't do it. So that the only people left to do it are the black people.

MR. BLACKWELL.   I'd like to inject that we, I mean SCLC, don't believe that we can separate today from yesterday nor can you separate today from tomorrow. And because we feel they cannot be separated, we are particularly concerned with using today the most ideal democratic, moralistic methods possible to effect the change because we believe that today is a part of tomorrow, and that if we would establish an ideal democratic or moralistic tomorrow we must employ these techniques today.

Q.   I have a question for Stokely in regards to shaking the economic foundation. It seems that the Negro, of course, does aggrandize Nkhrumah, who is an avowed Marxist, a socialist. You also mentioned a few moments ago that you were not anti-Semitic, but anti-exploitation. We had James Forman here earlier, and questions presented to him in regard to this economic thing—he said there needs to be a reallocation of money. Is this idea altogether socialist? Is this your particular stand—socialism? Is the capitalistic system outdated?

MR. CARMICHAEL.   Well, I don't know about socialism, because God knows I hear so much about those proletariat, chauvinistic, intellectual masturbations, that I don't even know what it means any more. I think that when you talk about realistic coalitions . . . How can a white liberal who supports the civil rights movement, who can afford to fly from New York and march free, then fly back home to a suburban area,

can he form an economic coalition with a black person in Mississippi that
he is trying to help who makes $3 a day? Can he do it? Now that's the
question we raise in SNCC, and it seems to me that you just can't talk
about coalition unless that man is willing to give up half his salary to a
black family. And that's what we've got to talk about. Now it seems to me
that the stock bonds are closed, that the frontiers are closed, and what's
left for black people, in order to move and to gain property—because we
are a propertyless people in this country—and this country does not
function on morality and love and nonviolence, but on power, both
political and economic—we ain't got neither of them in this country. The
only thing left open for us is the political arena. So, we have to grasp
that, and then use that to speak for economic arenas. Now, I don't know
how you do that. Because the question is going to be in Lowndes
County, where 86 families own 90 per cent of the land. Eighty-six
families own 90 per cent of the land. What are those black people going
to do? That's the question. What type of work are they going to do, and
where are they going to get the money from? And, that's the question
nobody wants to talk about, because holding hands and singing black
and white together is so much nicer.

Q.   Do you want to talk about it?

MR. CARMICHAEL.   I most certainly do. I've been trying to.

Q.   You just said how is the political power going to be used to
achieve economic power.

MR. CARMICHAEL.   That's precisely what I said.

Q.   Can you answer that, or at least make some remarks about
that.

MR. CARMICHAEL.   Yes, well, we have a lot of workshops around
that which I don't want to talk about. What I'd like to see is the country
start talking about those things—stop talking about black nationalism,
anti-white, and "Let's get Whitey." These things I think happen to be
very irrelevant. And is Black Power going to take over, and are the Mau
Maus going to come up in the white suburbs at night and burn me
out—because that's all it means. I mean, that's what their reactions mean
to me. That the Mau Maus are coming so we're going to stop them. Or
they chide, "Don't forget you are only 20 per cent of the population; if
you get too smart we'll really wipe you out." . . . It seems to me that one
of the things that you can do with the political system is that you can use

the power to tax the way it's supposed to be used in this country. And if you use the power to tax in Lowndes County, you can get you some good schools and some good roads. But you have to control that government before you can get the right to tax the folks to be taxed. You have to control, and that's all there is to it, and there isn't any question in my mind. I don't know about other people's minds—if they've got questions in their minds just come visit me in Lowndes County in the shacks where I've been living for a year and a half, and eat the food I've been eating. Then they'll see that there is no question except control of that government and use the power to tax the way it's supposed to be used. Now that's one of the ways I think the political spectrum can speak to the economic spectrum. That's the way the people get robbed all the time. There's a difference between the farmers' program and the welfare program. The biggest recipient group in this country are farmers. They sit home and get money for doing nothing. The difference is they own land, and they are property speaking, and they control the programs because they sit home and they send their lobbyists to Washington and say get me a hundred dollars for not planting anything on this acre of land. And welfare mothers don't control their programs, because if they did they'd give each of them $125 for each child, which is what they deserve. That's the difference. It is who controls. And the black people, it seems to me, are saying this day, that we want the right to control.

Q. Mr. Carmichael, you spoke of the United States as being morally bankrupt and stated a desire to disassociate yourself from that nation and that people . . . [and said] you have seen no white man who is eligible for this group, and that you are willing to take every Negro along with you. Now, I don't see the white community as black, or the black community as white as you do. Are you talking about moral—about a conclave of rectitude, or Black Power, or what's the relationship between the two?

MR. CARMICHAEL. Well, it seems to me when you talk about oppressors against oppressed, you talk about the oppressed ridding itself of the oppressors, and the oppressed deciding how to rid themselves of the oppressors, not in fact the oppressors telling the oppressed how to rid himself of the oppressor. Now, that makes *good* sense in *my* mind. I don't know about in *your* mind. For me, it is very simple to differentiate. I am oppressed for one reason in this country whether I was born in Lowndes County, Alabama, or whether I was born in Harlem, New York. 'Cause I'm black. It is crystal clear to me—that is the only reason we are suppressed. Not because we are ignorant, not because we are supposed to be lazy, not because we're dull and stupid and got good rhythm, but because we're black. So, it seems to me, whether I like it or not, I have a common ally with fellow black people who are oppressed because they're black. And I need them to rid myself of the oppressors. So, I have to get them with me. Now, that is not to say, young man, that there are not white people who see things the same way I do. But it is to say that those are the people I speak to *first* because they are oppressed, and they are the ones I address myself to primarily, not to the friends from the oppressing group, who call themselves friends, who in the past have caused us to worry about their friendship, which is a reality that you must speak to. But I speak first and primarily to the oppressed group, and . . . we decide what they want to use as a tactic to rid ourselves of the oppressor. That's what's complicated in the philosophy of this country. The *lies* that they've told about us. You know, I used to sit down and think about that junk, man. Cats used to say how lazy Negroes were. I mean, I used to ride the Delta in Mississippi, baby, and I used to see black people picking cotton. You ever pick cotton in the hot sun? Try it some time, brother—for $3 a day; and white folk riding up and down in air conditioned cars, and they got the nerve to call me lazy! They got the *nerve* to call *me* lazy! And then they talk about hard work and sweat—"if you work hard, you'll succeed." If that were true black people would own this country! My mother used to get up at 5 o'clock in the morning and fix me breakfast and then go across town and fix breakfast for "Miss Ann." And "Miss Ann" was a liberal. Yes, she was a liberal. She was going to give me money to go through college. She didn't understand that she was taking my mother from me when I needed her most, and for me to speak to my mother and tell her to stop this and tell Miss Ann she would have to clean her dirty kitchen, and her dirty children herself. And that's a problem that white people are not ready to speak to in this country. Because a hell of a lot of them got maids, and they are paying their maids $30–$40 a week, and help their children go to college. And they are part of the family. Well, baby, my mother was part of *my* family—I needed her home with me. Just like "Miss Ann" was part of her family, and she stayed at home with her children. To say that is to be racist, isn't it? And to say that is to be anti-white, isn't it? Well, those are questions that white America has to deal with—I'm through dealing with it—that's your problem, you solve it—I'm not going to take care of your problems and mine, too. You want to start talking about it; *you* made those problems in your community. You go to the liberal state of California, the *liberal* state of California, whey they voted for *segregated housing*—and you go to the suburbs and you open up freedom schools, 'cause God knows, they need it. That's where you stay, and that's where you work. Don't come and tell me about I need freedom schools, baby, 'cause I don't need to know nothing about it, I am just trying to get something. But you talk to them white folk in California; you sit down in those rich, suburban areas with those kids who are very racist and you explain to them the point of view from which they must work, and don't talk to me about Negro history, 'cause I know ... was the man who invented the first telephone in this country, and that he was black. That doesn't give me dignity; just speaks to the lies you've been telling me, and hiding from me. I need to know about LeRoi Jones in this day and age; I need to know about Mrs. Fannie Lou Hamer in this day and age; I need to know who John Hulett is; I need to know who Lerone Bennett is—and I need to connect that now, today. So that there is another subterfuge—"we must give them Negro history." Don't take me back to the past, baby—bring me to the future—let me know about Nkhrumah. Let me know about those cats—let me know about Lumumba. I want to know about the present day and where we're going and it seems to me that we have to develop that ourselves. *We* have to do it because white people just *can't*—they just aren't going to do it. Cause you are going to run from Berkeley and come to Mississippi and tell me what I need to do, and I'll tell you, baby, look at your Berkeley. Look at your Robert Scheer who is a great liberal who is trying to coalesce black, poor people with college students who are economically secure—what kind of coalition is that? A coalition based on integration, love, peace and nonviolence ain't got nothing to do with food. He's talking about coalescing economically secure college students with ghetto people who are unemployed. And they are going to fight for the same thing? Be serious. Those college kids are fighting for the right to wear a beard and smoke pot ... I'm not talking about everybody on the college campus now. The only university movement of any significance was the free speech movement under Mario Savio who got his inclination of fighting from SNCC. And what happened is that they fell through ... and in fact they didn't even know what they were fighting for when they came to the confrontation.

Q.   I don't understand the symbolism; "Miss Ann," is it objectionable?

MR. CARMICHAEL.   Did your father work as a butler or a maid for "Miss Ann?"

Q.   I mean, it's the title.

MR. CARMICHAEL.   It's all three—it's a combination. The combination is that you see, I came home late in the afternoon, my mother wasn't there because she was taking care of "Miss Ann's" children. She was giving her attention to "Miss Ann's" children, not to me, so I developed a hatred for "Miss Ann's" children. They told me that's unnatural; ok. The second thing is the type of work my mother was doing. She was a maid.

Q. Well, there are white people—

MR. CARMICHAEL. There may be white people, but more black people that are maids, and that's what's common to us—that's the type of work we do—that's what the poverty program is now doing in Mississippi—training people to be maids and digging ditches—that's the poverty program.

Q. It's hard to get one now.

MR. CARMICHAEL. Oh, yes, it is awfully hard to get a maid; I'd just as soon they weren't maids. It is also the money she was being paid. If Miss Ann was making $125 a week, she was paying my mother $30 a week and giving her old clothes from the children and promised to help send me to college. I don't know what made her think I was going to use any of *her* money to send me to college. And when I resented it she couldn't understand it, but be that as it may.

Q. Can't y'all do something about getting the wages up?

MR. CARMICHAEL. No, we can do something about making Miss Ann our maid. Is that racist? *That's right.* I want Miss Ann to be *my* maid. Now, let's see how it feels on the other foot, see, 'cause this country doesn't know what equality is, baby. Now, let Miss Ann come to my home and clean up my house and don't see her children, and I'll be *glad* to send her children to college, 'cause she is letting my wife go out and make some more money. I'll be glad to help give her back ten per cent of her earnings—I'd be more than happy to give her child a full scholarship to any school in the country, send her to Smith—she's letting my wife go out and make all that money . . .

Samuel DuBois Cook
THE TRAGIC MYTH OF BLACK POWER

Man is, among other things, a myth-making creature. Indeed, the almost infinite capacity to create and perpetuate illusions is one of man's most generous and massive endowments. Myths, of course, serve a variety of functions in the human economy, and may be harmless, creative or destructive. Profoundly destructive and self-defeating is the myth of "Black Power." It is a dangerous romantic illusion. It is an illusion of power, but we should not underestimate the power of the illusion.

Social movements have a peculiar way of breeding internal rebels and of generating purposes and qualities quite different from, and at variance with, their initial character, direction, and moral tone. So, ironically, an important sector of the civil rights movement is beginning to wave the ominous flag of black nationalism and, in voices and style reminiscent of the demonic racism which has informed and inspired so much of the southern political process, shout incantations of "Black Power." Quite a reversal of meaning, value and aspiration.

What is the meaning of the slogan "Black Power"? The answer depends not only on who is defining the term but also the place, time, and atmosphere. Its chief proponents display a remarkable absence of consistency and specificity of meaning. One of the great hazards of the slogan is its ambiguity, complexity, and mystical quality. It not only means many things to many people but also, judging from the record, many things to the same people.

Shorn of pretensions, hypocrisy, and intellectual dishonesty, the slogan "Black Power" does have, when words, context, and program are combined, a generic or core meaning, and that meaning is racist. It is anti-white. It is separatist and isolationist. Make no mistake about it: Vigorous denials under pressure notwithstanding, the unique dimension of the Black Power myth is racism. "If there is anything new in the slogan," Les Dunbar properly noted, "it is racism."

The racist character of the myth of Black Power is expressed in

From *New South*, Vol. 21, No. 3, Summer 1966, Southern Regional Council, Inc. Reprinted by permission. Dr. Cook is Professor of Political Science, Duke University.

many ways: counsel to exclude whites from positions of leadership and influence in the civil rights movement, advocacy of independent all-Negro third parties, the symbol of the Black Panther, the call for a "black takeover of political and economic power," the declaration of the irrelevance of integration and the issue of violence, self-righteous and glib assertions of the moral decadence of white America, and the general ventilation of anti-white frustrations, emotions and bitterness. "Black Power" is meaningful only in the context of "white power." Thus an appeal to Black Power is necessarily an appeal against white power: hence, an anti-white mentality and strategy. Why is the slogan so dear to the hearts of its exponents? It is calculated not only to "develop" pride and self-confidence in "black people," but also to serve as a catharsis and to exploit anti-white resentment, frustration, bitterness, and sentiments.

Imitating the dishonesty and corporate hypocrisy of the substance of southern history (and much of northern history as well) on the score of race relations, the proponents of Black Power, for the most part, piously renounce any claim to racism. But no one should be deceived.

SOURCES OF THE MYTH OF BLACK POWER

There are several reasons for the escape from the world of reality to the world of fantasy—called Black Power. First, there is the experience of bitter disappointment, disgust, and despair over the pace, scope and quality of social change. Some civil rights workers, especially the young ones with all their idealism, activism, unselfish commitment, and great enthusiasm, were, at first, excessively optimistic about the immediacy and completeness of basic changes in the structure of American society. Failing to recognize the ultimate dimensions and depth of racism in the mind and institutions of the country, they were supremely confident that they could re-make and democratize the country and eradicate racism in swift and short order. They had great and overwhelming visions of the millenium. Excessive hopes and extravagant expectations breed disillusionment, despair, and cynicism. Pessimism is the child of inordinate optimism.

Lacking a sense of history and a sane appreciation of the stubborn and brute realities of power and life, the excessive optimists were, when history did not conform to their preconceptions and expectations, cut off from the saving fresh water of a sober philosophy of social and historical change. They lost perspective, balance, and faith. Initially, they were blind to the persistence and power of the vested interests of the *status quo;* they are now blind to the ideals and richness of the beloved community. They forgot the difficulties of achieving a fully integrated society, and they now proclaim, with a gnawing and brooding sense of treason to past goals, the irrelevance of integration. Morris R. Cohen was right. History is, among other things, "the cemetery of human hopes."

A second source of the myth of Black Power was the prolonged and direct encounter of certain civil rights workers—especially those connected with SNCC and CORE—with the grim and aching realities, the dark and brute actions and deceptions of certain sections of the Deep South. They were exposed to the worst parts of Georgia, Alabama, Mississippi, and Louisiana. Their existence rocked and reeled against harsh oppressions and wretched evils. The scars and bruises of constant battle against violence, fear, intimidation, and perversions of governmental institutions operated to enlighten and to blind.

Close, direct and continuous contact with, and immediate and concrete involvement in the harsh brutalities of life often is a double-edged experience: a source of light and darkness, insight and blindness, confusion and clarity, wisdom and foolishness. It can cause us to lose perspective, balance and sound judgment and to oversimplify and distort, to forget the larger universe and deeper dimension, and to identify the part with the whole. So, Carmichael, facing an angry, jeering, sneering, cursing, and rock-throwing mob saw in it not the worst but the best there is in white America. Again, he could find no white allies in Lowndes County, Alabama, but then went on not only to organize Negroes there (which was his only choice) but to commit the supreme fallacy of identifying the whole structure, process and character of Lowndes County with the whole of America. That county became his model. What was necessary in Lowndes County is, to him, necessary in every political system and situation in the United States.

The myth of Black Power was, perhaps, also prompted by an attempt to capture the following of Malcolm X, with his black nationalism creed, as well as by the immediate and dramatic popularity of the slogan. It makes crowds roar, conversations sparkle, and television cameras click. It wins headlines. After all, it made Stokely Carmichael a national figure overnight.

FOUR FALLACIES OF BLACK POWER

The myth of Black Power is pragmatic nonsense, strategically self-defeating, anthropologically illusionary, and ethically destructive. It is impossible to divorce racism politics from other institutions and processes of culture. Bipolarity in politics means the polarization of the total culture on racial lines. Forms of power are integrally related. Racism in politics, as southern history clearly demonstrates, means racism in the socio-economic and other institutions of life. Splendid isolation and separatism in the political process mean splendid isolation and separatism in the whole web of culture.

A. PRAGMATIC NONSENSE.   Like so much of the political history of the white South divorced from reality, the myth of Black Power is a tragic exercise in futility. It is political mysticism, superstition, alchemy or astrology. The Negro must form alliances and coalitions with liberal, progressive, and moderate whites. Since he is a clear minority, constituting only about 10.5 per cent of the total population, sheer arithmetic is against the success of any isolated program of action. There is no possibility of any black takeover of power. The Negro, therefore, must have allies and friends. In pragmatic terms, Black Power, or domination, is a dangerous myth and self-defeating illusion. It can only produce frustration, disappointment, heartache, bitterness, and disaster for the Negro. Because of both quantitative and qualitative considerations, polarization of politics on a white-versus-black basis would be, for Negroes, the height of folly and would mean political suicide.

Demographic factors will not be nullified by emotional outbursts and the incantations of political witchdoctors and magicians. In no state do Negroes constitute a majority (Mississippi, which is 42.0% Negro, has the highest ratio) and hence cannot hope to control such a primary center of power. Because of the great tide of migration, the ratio of Negroes to whites in the South has been declining for decades; it dropped from 30% to 20% from 1950 to 1960. In 1900, for example, Negroes constituted 44% of the population of Florida, 47% of the population of Louisiana, and 58% of the population of South Carolina, but in 1960, those percentages had dropped, respectively, to 17.8, 31.9, and 34.8. During the 1950's, the Negro ratio of the population declined more than 10% in more than half of the counties in the South (569), while it increased by 10% in only 134.

If the Black Power argument has any validity and meaningful possibility and applicability, it must be in the context of those Black Belt counties in which Negroes constitute a majority of the population. But, here again, demographic factors are instructive and sobering. Counties with Negro majorities have declined dramatically in recent generations and decades. Between 1900 and 1960, for example, counties with Negro majorities in Virginia went from 36 to 15, parishes in Louisiana with Negro majorities dropped from 31 to 10.

In 1960, Negroes constituted a majority in only 12 of 67 counties in Alabama, 28 of 82 in Mississippi, 34 of 159 in Georgia, 15 of 46 in South Carolina, 8 of 100 in North Carolina, 2 of 95 in Virginia, 2 of 67 in Florida, and 3 of 254 in Texas. Of the 11 states of the Old South, Negroes, in 1960, had majorities in only 134 of 984. This is, in the total framework, not much potential power. In terms of the crucial matter of registered voters, Negroes have majorities in only a handful of the 134 counties in which they have numerical majorities.

Besides, the Black Power philosophy, in the very nature of the case, can have no strategy or program in counties where Negroes are a distinct minority. This doctrinaire concept would place Negro power in a strait jacket and political ghetto of the worst kind. If it were successful in the counties with Negro majorities, it would be, for that very reason, a supreme failure in that vast region in which Negroes are in the minority. Because of political retaliation, it would do havoc with the movement for racial justice and paralyze the civil rights movement. It would gain an inch but lose miles and miles.

It also should be noted that counties are simply creatures of state governments and hence at their mercy. They can be shifted, altered, merged or liquidated at will. White majorities, therefore, through control of state machinery, could manipulate, control, and starve counties with Negro majorities—assuming, of course, that white-dominated federal courts and national political institutions go along. It is worth remembering that the counties with Negro majorities are the poorest economically, educationally, and otherwise in the poorest section of the country. Getting control of them, in view of the poverty and continuous migration, would be governing ghost towns or cemeteries.

Negro voting power, even when maximized, will generally only be able to hold the balance of power in close elections. Ten thousand votes will not be effective against 100,000. History reminds us that, at the end of Reconstruction, the Negro was eliminated from participation in the southern political process precisely because he held the balance of power in interparty contests. To achieve his objective, the Negro has to work with others in the totality of American institutions.

It is, of course, true that alliances presuppose allies and in some local situations such as Lowndes County where Negroes have no present allies, Negroes will have to "go it alone" until some emerge. Negroes, however, must encourage, not discourage, the emergence of allies, and always extend the hand of political friendship and cooperation. The Black Power slogan is no more a way to encourage the cooperation of whites than the white supremacy slogan is to solicit the support of Negroes. The Black Panther symbol militates against collaboration and the democratization of the political process.

B. STRATEGY AND TACTIC. If the Negro had a cosmic enemy who had seized control of the department of strategy and tactics of the civil rights movement, he could not invent a more disastrous political methodology. The mind shudders in disbelief. The slogan of "Black Power" is a terrible political tactic for a number of reasons. First, it facilitates division and warfare within the civil rights movement when so much needs to be done and solidarity is so much needed. Consider the time and energy lost in trying to define, clarify, and defend the slogan. Consider how it promotes misunderstanding and ill-will within the Movement. It pits leader against leader and organization against organization.

Second, the myth of Black Power gives moderate and even liberal whites a ready-made excuse to discontinue support of the Negro's struggle. It gives them an easy out. Third, it unnecessarily plays on the historic fears of many whites who think in terms of "black domination." It revives their myths of Reconstruction and assists their rationalization of the historic exclusion and alienation of the Negro from full partnership in the structure and process of power. It reinforces the irrational and fanatical fears of those whites who think that Negroes are interested in cheap retribution and bitter revenge. Fourth, the tactic of Black Power fosters racial polarization of the political process and thereby aggravates the brutally racist politics of so much of white America. Whites will organize more intensely against Negroes, and in cases of minority versus majority in this country the outcome is a foregone conclusion.

Above all, the myth of Black Power is politically self-defeating. Getting control of a few rural, poverty-stricken counties in the South will not solve any of the Negro's problems. In order to solve the great issues of housing, education, employment, political alienation, poverty, slumism, etc., the Negro desperately needs much more, rather than much less, support from the white community. He has to have wider and deeper public support if his miseries and frustrations are not to increase. To get new civil rights and other needed legislation, to win more elective and appointive positions, and to overcome his historic alienation from the public institutions of the country, the Negro must have allies. Once more, Black Power, when arrayed against white power, is a dangerous and self-defeating illusion.

C. MAN AND BLACK POWER.   Powerless individuals, and groups, while not necessarily dangerous, can be as self-righteous as powerful ones. The weak can be as vain and self-deceptive as the strong. Negroes have witnessed and suffered long and much from the way in which whites have used power. Some Negroes are on the brink of making the fateful assumption of moral superiority, of thinking that Negroes with power are better than whites with power, of asserting that the uses of power are a function of race.

But race has nothing whatever to do with the exercise of power. Negroes are equal members of the human estate. They share all the defects as well as the virtues, all the misery as well as the dignity, all the tragedy as well as the glory, all the strengths as well as the weaknesses, and all the curses as well as the blessings of a common humanity. Negroes with power are as destructive and creative, as egoistic and altruistic, and as dangerous and self-serving as whites with power. Like whites, they are subject to all the temptations, perversions, tyrannies, pretensions, and abuses of power. Like whites, their possession of power is likely to make them indifferent, insensitive, arrogant, vain, self-seeking, morally complacent, and deaf to the cries of the suffering and disabled. Negro politicians are as bad and as good as white politicians. Their organizations are as corrupt and as noble, comparatively speaking, as their white counterparts.

Public life, therefore, might not be more blessed and creative under "Black Power." History and current experience demonstrate that Negro politicians are politicians first and Negroes second and, like white politicians, they are generally more concerned with getting elected and re-elected than with the promotion of racial justice. Reflect upon Congressmen Dawson and Powell as well as a host of lesser figures. Indeed, some of the worst enemies of racial progress are Negro public officials, some of whom were elected by Negro constituencies. If it is argued that they are that way because they are members of the "establishment" or "power structure," we might agree, but we would also add that men of power, whatever their breed or creed, have a way of creating their own "establishments" and power structures. It will be so of "Black Power."

In addition to Negro politicians, consider the rivalries and jealousies of certain civil rights leaders and organizations. Men will use the very slogan Black Power for selfish purposes—both personal and organizational. At the recent ceremony in Jackson, Mississippi, culminating the famous "Meredith March," one civil rights leader called for racial solidarity when, the previous night, he had voted to deny the NAACP the opportunity to participate in the program. Consider, too, the petty empires of tyranny and authoritarianism as well as the prominence of self-serving "leaders" of the Negro community—churches, schools, social and fraternal groups, and other organizations and institutions. They are a grim reminder that the psychology and evils of power are the common property of all humanity.

There should be no illusions about men of power—whatever their race. The myth of Black Power raises tragically false hopes and expectations. It promotes excessive optimism which, if not checked and sobered by a realistic appreciation of human nature, will reap a bitter harvest of disappointment, disillusionment, pessimism, frustration, cynicism, and despair.

D. PHILOSOPHICAL AND ETHICAL DIMENSION. The ultimate argument against the myth of "Black Power" is ethical, the vision of the good, and the higher possibilities of human history, the quality of public life that ought to be created and conserved. It is the same simple and ancient argument against "white supremacy," "Nordic superiority," and every other form of racism and tribalism making a particular group the center of meaning and value: our common humanity and the need to create the Good Life, the beloved community. Black Power for what? How will it be used? To what end? Will it be used for the tragically self-defeating purpose of revenge and retribution, to substitute one system of injustice for another? Mankind has suffered enough from the irrationalism and incubus of racism. Somehow, somewhere, the vicious circle must be broken.

The kind of political and social order needed is one in which race is value-free: neither a curse nor a blessing, nor defect nor virtue, nor special privilege nor handicap. The goal must be the creation of the beloved community—a free, open, and pluralistic society whose very structure of being, whose very processes of existence, reflect the solidarity of the human family. Essential is a philosophy which unites rather than separates men, which makes men humble, not arrogant; free, not in new chains. The vision must be inclusive, not exclusive; universal, not particularistic; healing, not devouring.

The method must always be one that promotes the reconciliation of Negroes and whites, binds wounds, repairs torn social tissues, and makes the society morally healthy and whole in its fullest dimensions and highest possibilities.

Love, said Paul Tillich, means re-union of the separated. That, too, is the ultimate character of justice. Justice is the restoration of the harmony and ultimate glory of the social order—the coming together again, after a long night of tragic estrangement, of races and classes that have been fragmented and stunted by false doctrines, corrupt systems and ideologies, corporate evils, and perverted visions and institutions.

Negroes ought to use their expanding political power, therefore, to enlarge and deepen the good of history, to destroy wretched wrongs, to eliminate the cancer of racism, to usher in the Good Life, to create the beloved community, to re-unite the separated.

How?

10
Foreign Policy

The war in Viet Nam, which underwent dramatic escalation almost immediately after President Johnson's assumption of the Presidency in his own right, hangs like a miasma over the American landscape. It distracts and exhausts officialdom. It threatens to frustrate the political priorities—to abolish poverty, ignorance, and racial injustice in our time—enunciated by Mr. Johnson in his election campaign of 1964. It cruelly destroys thousands of our young men and, thereby, blights forever the lives of their families. It habituates us to violence and destruction and, thereby, coarsens our humanity. It frets and impairs our relations with many of our oldest European allies. It blocks the efforts, so recently begun, to come to more livable terms with the Soviet Union. It weakens our moral authority within the world community, and it brings us closer to a direct confrontation with China.

Yet, perhaps the most ominous of the war's consequences, barring only the cost in human lives, is the severe distemper it produces inside our own society. The symptoms of distemper range from a vague uneasiness about our course in Viet Nam all the way to snarling, venomous hatred of the President, hatred that reaches beyond the President, indeed, to the whole apparatus of governance and authority.

While conservative critics of Mr. Johnson were inclined in 1964 to accuse him of following a "no win" policy, criticism from that quarter and on those grounds has been muted since the President began to bomb North Viet Nam in early 1965. On the contrary, what drives many critics of the war to the very border of frenzy is the realization that in 1964 they voted for and worked for Mr. Johnson, who as campaigner successfully portrayed Mr. Goldwater as the warrior-adventurer, the Cato of American politics, and as a man insensitive to the risks of nuclear holocaust. Mr. Johnson came on as the man of peace, restraint, forbearance, and limited American commitment. When Mr. Johnson, then, so swiftly "let slip the dogs of war," it seemed to these critics to be not only a betrayal of his campaign pledges, but also a reversal of the unmistakeable verdict of the electorate in 1964. This reversal of form produced the first crack in what has come to be called the "credibility gap" and, no doubt, has contributed to some people's tendency to express antipathy to the war in terms of a virulent personal hostility toward the President.

Most of the protest against the war comes from what, with some simplification, we can call the Left. In print it is expressed mostly in the liberal and radical journals of opinion and in the literary reviews. The campuses of the better universities are another focus of protest, though undoubtedly a majority of the college students accept, with varying degrees of enthusiasm, the President's stipulation that the war is a melancholy necessity we must somehow endure. The alienated young are another conspicuous source of vehement protest. It is not clear whether the war turns the young persons against the society and its leadership or these youths see the war as the final dramatic evidence of their prior conviction that the society is hopelessly degenerate and vicious. The relationships are tangles, but as these youthful critics see it, the moralizing school principal, the policeman routing teeny-boppers on the Sunset Strip, the philandering businessman slumped over his pre-prandial martini, and the brutal Sheriff siccing the dogs on marching Negroes are all one with the American pilot dropping napalm on a suspected Viet Cong village.

Abhorrence of violence is a major theme of the Viet Nam protests. Much of the expression of this does, indeed, come from persons and groups long identified with forms of pacifism. What seems clear, however, is that while much of the expression of protest is couched in terms of a general horror of violence, the real target is the violence employed by the United States in the particular case of Viet Nam. Again, when protesters attack the United States because it is "interfering in the internal affairs of Viet Nam," it is not clear whether the critics are attacking all interventions, everywhere, or only this particular intervention by the United States. The point here is that there is a distinct moral flavor to much of the criticism. Such criticism tends to be sweeping and absolute and its terms to be hyperbolic. Such critics become inflamed when the Administration spokesmen respond in the terms of "American commitments," "strategic necessity," "containment of communism," or "punishing aggression." The morally outraged tend to have a simple solution or prescription. It is swift and, if necessary, unilateral American cessation of military action as a prelude to full American withdrawal.

Though President Johnson tends to identify all criticism of our course in Viet Nam with this absolute protest—he invariably directs his defense against "Nervous Nellies," or the "cussers and flag-burners"—there is another, more important line of criticism of the policy in Viet Nam. It is represented here by Professor Morgenthau and the Democratic Senators. Here the language is less apocalyptic, and moral judgments are eschewed. Professor Morgenthau addresses himself to a strategic perspective of which he has long been critical. We cannot, he argues, maintain an open-ended commitment to defend every nation everywhere against violation of its territorial integrity. We cannot rush to defend all nations that are threatened, from within or without, by communist pressure. We must protect our interests when they are threatened. But we must protect them with intent and means that are proportionate to the interests involved. We must not jeopardize our real and vital interests for the sake of interests that are marginal or chimerical. Professor Morgenthau is not convinced that our real and vital interests are equally threatened each time a nation goes communist. Professor Morgenthau, one of the most visible and articulate of the critics of the war in Viet Nam, consistently argues that the costs of our intervention there are all out of proportion to the threat to our vital interests, and, hence, the more we up the costs through escalation, the more irrational our policy becomes.

Senator George McGovern (Dem., S.D.) is one of the more outspoken and articulate of a band of Senatorial "doves," most of whom, gallingly enough for Mr. Johnson, are Democrats. Senator McGovern, neither cusser nor flagburner, clearly has moral objections to the war, but most of his speech fits into a policy context, and he takes off from a strategic perspective that he shares with Professor Morgenthau.

McGeorge Bundy, a formidable old debating opponent of Professor Morgenthau and one of the architects of our Viet Nam policy, clearly disdains the febrile rhetoric of the Cold War 1950s, just as he disdains a simple "free world *vs* slave world" strategic vision. His strategic vision, nevertheless, differs from Professor Morgenthau's, and from it he derives a defense of our course in the Far East as both necessary and just.

Mr. Bundy recognizes that there must be places where American writ does not run and its power does not reach. This does not distress him unduly. But he has learned well the lessons taught to the West by its sad experiences with Fascist aggression in the 1930s. For him, the United States will continue to be involved, sometimes painfully, in the fates of far-flung peoples. There is also implicit in Mr. Bundy's statement the sense of an American mission, the sense that our power and our traditions thrust upon us an obligation to act in defense of others beyond the hard calculation of our own interests.

Secretary Rusk, armed with the strategic vision of Mr. Bundy, makes a head-on defense of our conduct in Viet Nam. Taking off from the Department of State's *White Paper* of 1965, the Secretary argues that the Viet Cong are nothing less than the chosen instrument of the Hanoi regime's aggressive designs on South Viet Nam and that, in any case, the Hanoi regime now attacks openly in the South with its own forces. We have made a military intervention first of all to forestall the direct military conquest of South Viet Nam. Having successfully prevented the direct military conquest, we now press the war to North Viet Nam in the hope that Hanoi will come to recognize the futility of its aggressive design, desist in it, and come to the peace table for discussion, among all interested parties, of the future of the region.

McGeorge Bundy
THE END OF EITHER/OR

II

It has not been easy for us to accept the complexity of the world. The revolution in our foreign affairs which dates from the Fall of France made demands that were met only at the price of great oversimplification. For twenty years from 1940 to 1960 the standard pattern of discussion on foreign policy was that of *either/or:* Isolation or Intervention, Europe or Asia, Wallace or Byrnes, Marshall Plan or Bust, SEATO or Neutralism, the U.N. or Power Politics, and always, insistently, anti-Communism or accommodation with Communists. The drama of these debates, the sweeping generalities which were used repeatedly by political leaders from Roosevelt through Eisenhower, and the excess of certainty which infected every Secretary of State from Hull through Dulles—all these forces served to push into the background the fact that the world is not simple. . . .

We need not be self-righteous in criticizing the simplifications

From "The End of Either/Or" by McGeorge Bundy. Excerpted by special permission from *Foreign Affairs,* Vol. 45, January 1967. Copyright by the Council on Foreign Relations, Inc., New York. Mr. Bundy is President of the Ford Foundation.

that were popular in the generation that joined the world. If we are old enough, the odds are overwhelming that we shared in them. Time after time, simplification was the prerequisite of decision and action, and what is most important about this twenty years is that most of the great decisions were right. If the acceptance of complexity was somewhat delayed, and if the political cost of the first great encounters with failure (in China), and stalemate (in Korea) was high, still there is no major nation whose record in that period is half as good.

But in the 1950s the balance of advantage shifted against black-and-white thinking. It was the tragedy of the Eisenhower Administration that the President, who understood in his bones the need for generosity and accommodation, was served by a Secretary of State who combined great subtlety—even deviousness—of tactics with a deep internal need for arbitrary moral certainty. Where there really were still clear-cut issues (as in Berlin or the Formosa Straits) the Eisenhower Administration was capable of a careful firmness that many of us underrated at the time. But where it was not simple—which was most of the time in most countries—the record was disappointing.

The day of *either/or* may have ended with the death of John Foster Dulles, for black-and-white was never the instinctive mode of General Eisenhower. But with John F. Kennedy we enter a new age. Obviously there had been much recognition of complexity in the years before 1961, but Kennedy was the first American President to make a habit of it. Over and over he insisted on the double assertion of policies which stood in surface contradiction with each other: resistance to tyranny and relentless pursuit of accommodation; reinforcement of defense and new leadership for disarmament; counter-insurgency and the Peace Corps; openings to the left but no closed doors to the reasonable right; an Alliance for Progress and unremitting opposition to Castro; in sum, the olive branch and the arrows. He argued that the surface contradictions were unreal, and by the 1960s the country was ready to agree. In the Presidency of Lyndon Johnson this view has persisted. Like Theodore Roosevelt, and for similar reasons, Mr. Johnson often prefers the poster to the etching, but those upset by language too vivid for their own tastes have too often overlooked the equally vivid language that asserts with equal conviction the countervailing and complementary doctrine. Under the last two Presidents at least, the recognition of complexity has been the first law of policy.

A closely related lesson has been the demonstration that what happens in the world is not determined by Americans alone. (Others with an exaggerated sense of their own importance have had to learn this lesson still more painfully than we—Moscow and Peking are consoling instances—but this essay is about our troubles, not theirs.) Already in the last years of the Truman Administration the painful experiences with China and Korea were turning the minds of perceptive men to the problem of the limits of American influence, and the message was preached in a series of sensible books by men who left office with Mr. Acheson. But in the 1950s Washington did not speak in the rhetoric of restraint, and later events have had to teach us as a nation what a few learned earlier from harsh, direct experience. . . .

We have confirmed our acceptance of continuing engagement in the world's affairs, while no longer needing the somewhat artificial encouragement of a belief that we are both all-righteous and all-powerful. We no longer doubt that we should have extensive policies—and take extensive actions—in Europe, in South America, in Asia and in all the oceans. (We still have doubts about Africa, and they are reflected both in the too low priority which we tend to give to the problems of that continent and in the somewhat jerky quality of what we have done in places like the Congo.) We no longer expect these undertakings to produce final results by fixed dates. We have accepted involvement in the real world, and we see that world more nearly as it is. . . .

We also have two decades now of hard experience in the practice of international affairs, and the day has passed when any other nation could claim the advantage of experience and exposure in comparison with us. In particular areas and for particular purposes, others still have special skills that we cannot match. But taken as a whole, the stock of American experience, understanding, sympathy and simple knowledge is now much the most impressive in the world.

These assertions are comforting, however, only in a comparative sense. It does not follow at all that we have all the power and skill we need. Complexity increases; the threat of aggression persists; and so does the menace of nuclear weapons to the future of all mankind. The demands upon American strength and good sense do not decrease. We cannot ensure peace or progress anywhere alone. But there is no safety yet for free men anywhere without us, and it is the relation between this astonishing proposition and the complexities of each part of the world that makes the conduct of our foreign affairs such an overwhelming task.

III

The great present case, of course, is Viet Nam. Nothing about it is simple. Indeed what has made debate so easy, and action so hard, in Viet Nam is that the debater can defend the propositions he likes from a great pile of evidence in which there is plenty to support every view. In our actions, however, we have to live with the whole. The truth in Viet Nam is that there is both aggression from the North and civil conflict in the South, both corruption and self-sacrifice, both strong anti-Communist feeling and a weary lack of affection for much of the present anti-Communist leadership. The political base for an effective non-Communist state is still weak—but it does exist. The Vietnamese do not think of the Americans as they thought of the French—but they do retain a stubborn insistence on doing things in their own way.

The internal complexities are matched internationally. Viet Nam is indeed a test of Communist revolutionary doctrine, and what happens there will affect what happens elsewhere; but victory for Ho would not mean automatic communization of all Asia, and the defeat of aggression would not mean an end to the pervasive—if sometimes exaggerated—threat of China. The lines of influence and concern stretch out in all directions, but almost never in simple and straightforward terms. There is no simple unity among either Communists or non-Communists on Viet Nam. Those who support our view do so for reasons that vary, and many of those who are critical would be more critical still if we were now to back out. On the international scene, as inside Viet Nam, the only general proposition that seems valid is that sweeping and simple views are useful only for those who do not have responsibility.

This is not the place for a study of the long line of decisions that has brought us where we are in Viet Nam. The continuing conviction, through twelve years, has been that we should be ready to do our full share to help prevent the Communists from taking South Viet Nam by force and terror. This conviction has led to decisions that few foresaw in the early 1950s. Those decisions have enlarged the costs and raised the stakes of both success and failure. The most conspicuous increase in our effort has been military, and more than once decisions have been made just in time. It seems almost certain that without the military commitments made by President Kennedy and President Johnson in late 1961 and early 1965—in each case after the most prayerful consideration of the consequences of both action and inaction—South Viet Nam would have been delivered to the tender care of Hanoi and the chances for peaceful progress in many Pacific nations would have been heavily reduced. My own belief is that these great decisions, with all their costs, have been right, and that it is right to persevere—in the interest of the Vietnamese, in our own interest and in the wider interest of peace and progress in the Pacific.

The political requirements, less dramatic but equally essential, have also grown with time, and at the end of 1966 performance in this field has still not matched the encouraging successes of the armed forces. In part, of course, the difficulty here is simply that without general and sustained military superiority in a given area it is hard even to begin on political action. Beyond that, the job is much more unfamiliar to us all.

Finally, unlike the direct campaign against major Communist military units, the political effort, in all its forms, can take effect only as it engages the energies and convictions of the Vietnamese people themselves. So we must not be surprised that real pacification is hard to get in the Vietnamese countryside. It is, after all, the one thing above all others that the Communists are determined to block by whatever means they can. That this work remains slow and hard, less than two years after the days of highest Communist hope, is not astonishing. But it is also no ground for complacency, and it remains right for both Saigon and Washington to give the highest possible priority to this part of their work.

Viet Nam is thus both military and political. It is also an example of another kind of double imperative: the requirement for *both* action *and* restraint. It is necessary to act, but it is also necessary to keep that action within limits. What makes this rule a matter of life and death in military matters is of course the ghastly spectre of nuclear exchanges—anywhere with anyone. But there are other reasons for restraint. Even without the ultimate weapons, we would want no war with China. Even without China we would go badly wrong to commit ourselves, by word or by act, to the destruction of the régime in Hanoi. We simply are not in the business of destroying Communist states by force (a proposition confirmed in a most painful way at the Bay of Pigs).

The most debated of our military actions in Viet Nam is of course the bombing of the North. In a measure this debate is less an argument between the Government and its critics than a conflict between two schools of thought, both of which the Government opposes. Given their quite opposite politics and military prejudgments, it is natural that there should be a sharp divergence between single-minded advocates of air power and equally single-minded believers that all forms of bombing are both immoral and ineffective. Those who choose to believe that Hanoi is the aggrieved party in Viet Nam will have still stronger feelings. So debaters here and abroad have naturally made the bombing a central topic, and the tactical advantage of this emphasis for Communists is obvious.

But the truth is that the bombing of the North has never been more than one military instrument among many—an instrument made legitimate by previous hostile actions, made necessary by the critical dangers of 1965, and justified still by its value in hampering the work of infiltration and supply. All bombing carries risks of error and of civilian damage. The bombing of the North has been the most accurate and the most restrained in modern warfare. Those who have watched the President and his Secretary of Defense in action on this subject can testify that it is wholly wrong to charge them with recklessness, or with abdication of their responsibility. What they deserve instead is the understanding support of those who want restraint, as they continue to resist pressures from the few who do believe in greatly widening the war as a means to ending it.

Here, indeed, is the precise and persisting difference on which the country ruled by its vote in 1964. The real choice is not between "doves" and "hawks." It is between those who would keep close and careful civilian control over a difficult and demanding contest, and those who would use whatever force is thought necessary by any military leader in any service.

There is also a decisive difference between raising the cost of aggression and trying to "win" by "defeating" Hanoi. To attempt such a "victory" would be terribly wrong on three counts: (1) it would carry great risk of war with China and the Soviet Union; (2) it would engage us in a new and terrible contest for which we have no taste or need—a contest for the future of North Viet Nam; (3) it would not settle the issue in the South. What three administrations have always understood is still true: the decisive area of our interest in Viet Nam is in the South. It is there that our military and political actions can and should be intensified. It is there that we can also give massive support for relief, for rehabilitation and for economic and social advances—always behind the shield of growing military and political strength and self-confidence.

The contest in Viet Nam is not likely to be short, though its major combat phase may end well before the long hard work of real pacification and rebuilding. Fortunately the American people have demonstrated that their staying power in this effort is much greater than either friend or foe expected. In the face of repeated disappointments and in spite of the confusion of angry debate and imperfect understanding on all sides, our people have shown great resilience of spirit. They have accepted the stress of this effort, and they have refused to give support to easy wrong answers at either extreme. Open opposition has flourished. There has been less jingoism than in any previous war in our history. The nation has endured the special demands of an uncensored war—one which has been freely reported from our side of the lines by a number of men who clearly doubt its value. This is also the first war with daily television from the field. I think it is good, on balance, that the war is brought into our living rooms, but it remains a striking fact that this time we get our dose of "The Naked and the Dead" not afterward, but instantly.

The ability of the people of the United States to keep their balance in this unprecedented situation is profoundly encouraging. Whatever criticism may be current abroad, it is just this sturdy temper that all our friends have needed before and may need again in future. The true value of the United States as an ally and friend rests not on the language of treaties which always have escape clauses, and not on mechanical notions of cause and consequence, but rather upon the fact that this is a nation which sees things through and tries to see them straight.

The prospect in Viet Nam, then, is for more struggle and sacrifice. Of course it is always possible that the Communists may give up their opposition to negotiations, and certainly it is essential that we ourselves should be ready and eager for such a change in their position. There is every reason for the openness and responsiveness that the President and the Secretary of State have repeatedly shown, not only in their words but in public and private diplomacy. The passionate sincerity of this commitment will be proven to all doubters on the day that their offer is accepted. But it would be wrong to count on any early Communist response. Communists, like other men, negotiate when they think it helps them to achieve an objective, and up to now the clear Communist objective has been to take over South Viet Nam. The Communists are quite right in supposing that our own firm purpose in any negotiation will be very different from theirs. Moreover, the struggle will necessarily continue during any negotiations until acceptable terms for an armistice are worked out, and in these circumstances a prolonged negotiation could easily undermine the confidence of Communists in the South. For these reasons it is unlikely that the men in Hanoi will agree to negotiations until our purpose or theirs has changed. Even then the prospect for a negotiated settlement may be weak, for if the Communists do decide that their present purposes exceed their capacity, may they not prefer a private decision to a public admission? This is what happened in Greece, and it is as likely an ending in Viet Nam as a peace by formal agreement. Actions leading to reciprocal actions may be the eventual path away from open warfare—and it was right for the United States to make it plain again in September, through Ambassador Goldberg, that the United States is ready to take this road too.

It is not pleasant to have to write of the prospects for accommodation with Vietnamese Communists in these stark terms. A number of talented and honorable writers have pinned their faith to very different notions of what may be practicable. But they have produced little evidence to back their faith. It would be agreeable if there were a real prospect of a peaceful coalition with Communist participation and non-Communist control; but this picture, drawn from the unusual experience of France and Italy in the 1940s, seems irrelevant to the realities of Viet Nam. It would be good also if there were a serious prospect of inducing the Communists as an organized force to accept a political contest divorced from force and terror, in a securely neutralized and guaranteed state; but the evidence of past Communist behavior in Viet

Nam does not support this hope. My own unhappy conclusion is that many of those who write about this kind of solution are really engaged in concealing—perhaps even from themselves—their willingness to let South Viet Nam go to the Communists rather than face the trials of a continued struggle. In this respect they simply do not speak for their country, and it is of great importance that Communists everywhere should come to understand that fact.

IV

Viet Nam is our most immediate foreign business, but even Viet Nam should not let us forget the strength which permits and the interest which requires our active effort elsewhere. As in South Viet Nam itself, so in relating Viet Nam to other concerns, the right choice is not either/or; it is both/and.

First, we need *both* military *and* economic action. Our stake in Viet Nam, and our larger stake in Asia, will not end as aggression subsides. We have an abiding national interest in the progress of the people across the Pacific. This interest has been magisterially reaffirmed in the President's trip to Asia. It is part and parcel of the still wider American interest in enlightened help to those who are helping themselves. The level of our economic aid is too low today to serve our own interests, and the fight for a strong and responsive program next year may be the most urgent single cause in foreign affairs for men of good will to back.

Second, we are *both* an Atlantic *and* a Pacific partner. Our interest in the future of Europe has not weakened merely because the most active danger today is in Asia. Since the missile crisis of 1962 Europe has known four years of continental quiet that are unmatched in the last half-century. Not all Europeans have taken full advantage of this quiet to work for harmony beyond their present borders, and we ourselves have been a little slow, until recently, in moving out from successful defense toward wider settlement. We face a serious test now in working both against nuclear spread and for Atlantic partnership, but it is a test we can meet. Certainly it is wrong to suppose that our effort in Viet Nam changes or weakens our interest in Europe. We must put troops where they are most needed, but we can and will sustain the great Atlantic commitment we have honored steadily for twenty-five years. . . .

Hans J. Morgenthau
TO INTERVENE OR NOT TO INTERVENE

. . . What follows from this condition of intervention in our time for the foreign policies of the United States? Four basic conclusions can be drawn: the futility of the search for abstract principles, the error of anti-communist intervention per se, the self-defeating character of anti-revolutionary intervention per se, and the requirement of prudence.

First, it is futile to search for an abstract principle which would allow us to distinguish in a concrete case between legitimate and illegitimate intervention. This was so even in the nineteenth century when intervention for the purpose of colonial expansion was generally regarded to be legitimate and when the active players on the political stage were relatively self-sufficient nation-states, which not only were not in need of intervention but actually were opposed to it as a threat to their existence. If this was so then, it stands to reason that in an age where large segments of whole continents must choose between anarchy and intervention, intervention cannot be limited by abstract principles, let alone effectively outlawed by a United Nations resolution.

Let us suppose that nation A intervenes on behalf of the government of nation B by giving it military, economic and technical aid on the latter's request, and that the government of B becomes so completely dependent upon A as to act as the latter's satellite. Let us further suppose that the local opposition calls upon country C for support against the agents of a foreign oppressor and that C heeds that call. Which one of these interventions is legitimate? Country A will of course say that its own is and C's is not, and vice versa, and the ideologues on both sides will be kept busy justifying the one and damning the other. This ideological shadowboxing cannot affect the incidence of interventions. All nations will continue to be guided in their decisions to intervene and their choice of the means of intervention by what they regard as their respective national interests. There is indeed an urgent need for the

From "To Intervene or Not to Intervene," by Hans J. Morgenthau. Excerpted by special permission from *Foreign Affairs*, Vol. 45, April 1967. Copyright by the Council on Foreign Relations, Inc., New York. Hans J. Morgenthau is Professor of Political Science at the University of Chicago.

governments of the great powers to abide by certain rules according to which the game of intervention is to be played. But these rules must be deduced not from abstract principles which are incapable of controlling the actions of governments, but from the interests of the nations concerned and from their practice of foreign policy reflecting those interests.

The failure to understand this distinction between abstract principles and national interests as guidance for a policy of intervention was in good measure responsible for the fiasco of the Bay of Pigs in 1961. The United States was resolved to intervene on behalf of its interests, but it was also resolved to intervene in such a way as not openly to violate the principle of nonintervention. Both resolutions were legitimate in terms of American interests. The United States had an interest in eliminating the political and military power of the Soviet Union, which used Cuba as a base from which to threaten the security interests of the United States in the Western Hemisphere. The United States also had an interest in avoiding whatever would jeopardize its standing in the new and emerging nations. The United States failed to assign priorities to these two interests. In order to minimize the loss of prestige, the United States jeopardized the success of the intervention. Instead of using concern for prestige as a datum among others in the political equation—that is, as an interest among others—it submitted to it as though it were an abstract principle imposing absolute limits upon the actions necessary to achieve success. In consequence, the United States failed thrice. The intervention did not succeed; in the attempt we suffered the temporary impairment of our standing among the new and emerging nations; and we lost much prestige as a great nation able to use its power successfully on behalf of its interests.

Had the United States approached the problem of intervening in Cuba in a rational fashion, it would have asked itself which was more important: to succeed in the intervention or to prevent a temporary loss of prestige among the new and emerging nations. Had it settled upon the latter alternative, it would have refrained from intervening altogether; had it chosen the former alternative, it would have taken all the measures necessary to make the intervention a success, regardless of unfavorable reactions in the rest of the world. Instead, it sought the best of both worlds and got the worst.

The Soviet Union's intervention in Hungary in 1956 is instructive in this respect. The Soviet Union put the success of the intervention above all other considerations, and succeeded. Its prestige throughout the world suffered drastically in consequence. But Hungary is today a communist state within the orbit of the Soviet Union, and Soviet prestige recovered quickly from the damage it suffered in 1956.

The interventions of the United States in Cuba, the Dominican

Republic and Viet Nam, as well as others less spectacular, have been justified as reactions to communist intervention. This argument derives from the assumption that communism everywhere in the world is not only morally unacceptable and philosophically hostile to the United States, but is also detrimental to the national interests of the United States and must therefore be opposed on political as well as moral and philosophic grounds. I shall assume for the purposes of this discussion that, as a matter of fact, communist intervention actually preceded ours in all these instances, and shall raise the question as to whether our national interest required our counter-intervention.

Ten or twenty years ago, this question could have been answered in the positive without further examination. For then communism anywhere in the world was a mere extension of Soviet power, controlled and used for the purposes of that power. Since we were committed to the containment of the Soviet Union, we were also committed to the containment of communism anywhere in the world. However, today we are faced not with one monolithic communist bloc controlled and used by the Soviet Union, but with a variety of communisms, whose relations with the Soviet Union and China change from country to country and from time to time and whose bearing upon the interests of the United States requires empirical examination in each concrete instance. Communism has become polycentric, that is to say, each communist government and movement, to a greater or lesser extent, pursues its own national interests within the common framework of communist ideology and institutions. The bearing which the pursuit of those interests has upon the interests of the United States must be determined in terms not of communist ideology but of the compatibility of those interests with the interests of the United States.

Subjecting our interventions in Cuba, the Dominican Republic and Viet Nam to this empirical test, one realizes the inadequacy of the simple slogan "stop communism" as the rationale of our interventions. While this slogan is popular at home and makes but minimal demands upon discriminating judgment, it inspires policies which do either too much or too little in opposing communism and can provide no yardstick for a policy which measures the degree of its opposition by the degree of the communist threat. Thus on the one hand, as part of the settlement of the missile crisis of 1962, we pledged ourselves not to intervene in Cuba, which is today a military and political outpost of the Soviet Union and the fountainhead of subversion and military intervention in the Western Hemisphere, and as such directly affects the interests of the United States. On the other hand, we have intervened massively in Viet Nam, even at the risk of a major war, although the communist threat to American interests from Viet Nam is at best remote and in any event is infinitely more remote than the communist threat emanating from Cuba.

As concerns the intervention in the Dominican Republic, even if one takes at face value the official assessment that the revolution of April 1965 was controlled by Cuban communists, it appears incongruous that we intervened massively in the Dominican Republic, whose revolution was, according to our government's assessment of the facts, a mere symptom of the disease, while the disease itself—that is, Cuban communism—is exempt from effective intervention altogether.

This type of intervention against communism per se naturally tends to blend into intervention against revolution per se. Thus we tend to intervene against all radical revolutionary movements because we are afraid lest they be taken over by communists, and conversely we tend to intervene on behalf of all governments and movements which are opposed to radical revolution, because they are also opposed to communism. Such a policy of intervention is unsound on intellectual grounds for the reasons mentioned in our discussion of contemporary communism; it is also bound to fail in practice.

Many nations of Asia, Africa and Latin America are today in a pre-revolutionary stage, and it is likely to be only a matter of time until actual revolution will break out in one or another of these nations. The revolutionary movements which will then come to the fore are bound to have, to a greater or lesser degree, a communist component; that is, they risk being taken over by communism. Nothing is simpler, both in terms of intellectual effort and, at least initially, practical execution, than to trace all these revolutions to a common conspiratorial source, to equate all revolutionary movements with world communism, and to oppose them with indiscriminate fervor as uniformly hostile to our interests. The United States would then be forced to intervene against revolutions throughout the world because of the ever-present threat of a communist take-over, and would transform itself, in spite of its better insight and intentions, into an anti-revolutionary power per se.

Such a policy of intervention might succeed if it had to deal with nothing more than isolated revolutionary movements which could be smothered by force of arms. But it cannot succeed, since it is faced with revolutionary situations all over the world; for even the militarily most powerful nation does not have sufficient usable resources to deal simultaneously with a number of acute revolutions. Such a policy of indiscriminate intervention against revolution is bound to fail not only with regard to the individual revolution to which it is applied but also in terms of its own indiscriminate anti-communism. For the very logic which would make us appear as the anti-revolutionary power per se would surrender to communism the sponsorship of revolution everywhere. Thus anti-communist intervention achieves what it aims to prevent: the exploitation of the revolutions of the age by communism.

In truth, the choice before us is not between the status quo and revolution or even between communist and non-communist revolution, but between a revolution hostile to the interests of the United States and a revolution which is not hostile to these interests. The United States, far from intervening against revolutions per se, has therefore to intervene in competition with the main instigators of revolution—the Soviet Union, Communist China and Cuba—on behalf of revolution. This intervention should serve two alternative aims: first, to protect the revolution from a communist take-over, and second, if we should fail in this, to prevent such a communist revolution from turning against the interests of the United States. Such a policy, substituting the yardstick of the American national interest for that of anti-communism, would obviously form a complete reversal of the positions which we have taken in recent years and of which our interventions in Viet Nam and the Dominican Republic are the recent prime examples.

If this analysis of our policy of intervention is correct, then we have intervened not wisely but too well. Our policy of intervention has been under the ideological spell of our opposition to communism and potentially communist-led revolutions. Yet while this ideological orientation has continued to determine our policy of intervention, the Soviet Union has continued to pay lip service to support for "wars of national liberation" but has in practice relegated these wars to a secondary place in the struggle for the world. This softening of the Soviet ideological position has become one of the points of contention in the ideological dispute between the Soviet Union and China. In a statement of June 14, 1963, the Chinese Communist Party declared that "the whole cause of the international proletarian revolution hinges on the outcome of revolutionary struggles" in the "vast areas of Asia, Africa and Latin America" that are today the "storm centers of world revolution dealing direct blows at imperialism." In their reply of July 14 of the same year, the Soviet leaders opposed the "'new theory' according to which the decisive force in the struggle against imperialism . . . is not the world system of socialism, not the struggle of the international working class, but . . . the national liberation movement." The Soviet Union's recent practice of restraint in fomenting and supporting revolution has matched this theoretical position. This ideological "revisionism" has of course not prevented the Soviet Union from intervening, as in Syria and Somalia, when its national interest appeared to require intervention.

One factor which cannot have failed to influence the Soviet Union in toning down its ideological commitment to intervention has been the relative failure of ideological intervention. The United States, China and Cuba have joined the Soviet Union in the experience of that failure. The new and emerging nations have been eager to reap the benefits of intervention, but have also been very anxious not to be tied with ideological strings to the intervening nation. After making great efforts, expending considerable resources and running serious risks, the participants in this worldwide ideological competition are still approximately at the point from which they started: measured against their ambitions and expectations, the uncommitted third of the world is still by and large an ideological no-man's-land.

This experience of failure is particularly painful, and ought to be particularly instructive, for the United States. For we have intervened in the political, military and economic affairs of other countries to the tune of far in excess of $100 billion, and we are at present involved in a costly and risky war in order to build a nation in South Viet Nam. Only the enemies of the United States will question the generosity of these efforts, which have no parallel in history. But have these efforts been wise? Have the commitments made and risks taken been commensurate with the results to be expected and actually achieved? The answer must be in the negative. Our economic aid has been successful in supporting economies which were already in the process of development; it has been by and large unsuccessful in creating economic development where none existed before, largely because the moral and rational preconditions for such development were lacking. Learning from this failure, we have established the theoretical principle of concentrating aid upon the few nations which can use it rather than giving it to the many who need it. While this principle of selectivity is sound in theory, its consistent practical application has been thwarted by the harsh political and military realities which may require economic aid which is economically not justified, as well as by political and military considerations derived from the ideological concerns discussed above.

This principle of selectivity must be extended to the political and military sphere as well. We have come to overrate enormously what a nation can do for another nation by intervening in its affairs—even with the latter's consent. This overestimation of our power to intervene is a corollary of our ideological commitment, which by its very nature has no limit. Committed to intervening against communist aggression and subversion anywhere, we have come to assume that we have the power to do so successfully. But in truth, both the need for intervention and the chances for successful intervention are much more limited than we have been led to believe. Intervene we must where our national interest requires it and where our power gives us a chance to succeed. The choice of these occasions will be determined not by sweeping ideological commitments nor by blind reliance upon American power but by a careful calculation of the interests involved and the power available. If the United States applies this standard, it will intervene less and succeed more.

Dean Rusk and Paul Niven
A CONVERSATION WITH DEAN RUSK

MR. NIVEN. Whether deliberately or not, the last few weeks have brought an escalation of the war in Viet-Nam. Whether it was deliberate or not remains a matter of semantic argument between the administration and its critics. There is no doubt, however, that criticism of and dissent from the war has escalated both in depth and in breadth.

Viet-Nam is not the only issue of the hour, even if it is the towering one. Indeed, one of the themes of the critics is that the war is deflecting high officials here in Washington from other and larger issues. Despite Viet-Nam there has been a considerable relaxation of tension between East and West, as symbolized by the consular and space treaties and our continuing talks on antimissile defense and the spread of nuclear weapons.

The spirit of *détente* was symbolized also by the arrival in this country of the daughter of Joseph Stalin with no outburst of chauvinistic exultation on our part, no public anguish on the part of the Kremlin, and a civilized demeanor on the part of the lady involved.

Even as the United States and the Soviet Union pull closer together, China pulls farther and farther apart from both. In Western Europe new issues and old issues are at hand and recently took Vice President Humphrey on an important and not uneventful tour of the capitals of some of our NATO allies.

Substantive questions give rise anew on Capitol Hill and elsewhere to larger questions concerning the overall American commitment all over the world, about its moral validity, and about its practicability in terms of our power in the world.

It seems a very appropriate time, all in all, to talk with a man

From "A Conversation with Dean Rusk," *Department of State Bulletin*, Vol. LVI, May 22, 1967. Mr. Rusk is Secretary of State and Mr. Niven is Washington correspondent of the National Educational Television Network.

who for 6 years and 3 months now has been the principal foreign policy adviser to Presidents Kennedy and Johnson. Here we are then in the State Department to talk to Secretary Dean Rusk.

Mr. Secretary, I don't think we've had polls in the last 3 or 4 weeks to see whether opposition to the war in Viet-Nam is actually increasing among the country as a whole. But certainly there has been an increase in the intensity and depth of public manifestations of opposition. How do you and other officials of the administration who have spent so many hours trying to put your case and explain it to so many people account for this increase in public opposition?

SECRETARY RUSK.   Well, we have seen some highly organized demonstrations of minorities here and there in the country. But the people of the United States elect a President and a Congress to make these great decisions of national policy.

And it is my impression that the ordinary men and women around the country understand what is involved in Viet-Nam. Now, we understand that many of them are impatient and want to see the steps taken to finish this war. Because after all that has happened since 1945, it is tragic that once again we should have to use force to resist an aggression because we have learned a lot of lessons of what happens when aggression occurs.

MR. NIVEN.   When you say that these are highly organized demonstrations, obviously the Communists are not uninterested in doing this in this country and elsewhere—but do you suggest that even among the organizers of this opposition the Communists are anything like the Majority?

SECRETARY RUSK.   Oh, I am not trying to establish any sense of numbers in this matter. I think there are different groups. The Communist apparatus is busy all over the world, and it is busy in this country. Others who are genuine pacifists, conscientious objectors, people with strong religious convictions on this point—for them I have the greatest respect. There are others who, for one reason or another, doubt that Viet-Nam is our problem. There is a variety of reasons why people object. But particular demonstrations are pretty highly organized.

THE DILEMMA OF DISSENT

MR. NIVEN.   Well, you and General [William C.] Westmoreland and others have pointed out that such demonstrations are bound to raise questions on the other side about our will to continue. On the other hand, isn't there a great danger that in trying to stifle dissent we create new problems?

SECRETARY RUSK. Well, Mr. Niven, there has never been any effort to stifle dissent. We have a dilemma in this respect, because two things are true.

The one is that in our kind of free society there must be complete freedom of expression, the opportunity for dissent, the right lawfully and peacefully to register one's difference of view. Now, that is fundamental to our system, and there has never been any effort to stifle that.

The other thing that is equally as true is that Hanoi undoubtedly is watching this debate and is drawing some conclusions from it. Now, if we were to see 100,000 people marching in Hanoi calling for peace we would think the war was over. Now, it requires a good deal of sophistication on the part of Hanoi to understand that this is not the way we make decisions in this country—that there are a President and a Congress who are elected by the people and that the President and the Congress are supported by the great majority of the American people in these great decisions.

MR. NIVEN. Senator [Thruston B.] Morton suggested the other day that—quoting General Westmoreland—when someone speaks of irresponsible acts at home without distinguishing between the genuinely irresponsible burners of draft cards and people who lay down in front of trains and so forth and the really idealistic citizens who have strong reservations about the war, he only encourages the irresponsible elements among the dissenters. Don't you think there is something to that?

SECRETARY RUSK. Well, I wouldn't know how to judge something of that sort. I think all of us, whether we are official or private citizens, have a responsibility for all of the consequences of our acts and what we say. And when people elect to go into these matters and make their opinions known they should take into account what the total effect will be.

But, again, in our society there must be full opportunity for free expression and there must be a debate in this country. And when differences exist we couldn't have our kind of free society without it.

MR. NIVEN. It would be perhaps too much to expect for the North Vietnamese to understand that these demonstrations are a minority. But surely their Soviet allies are sophisticated enough at this stage of the game to understand this and to tell them that what is more important is the polls showing 70 percent of the people—

SECRETARY RUSK.   Oh, I think there are those in the Communist world who understand this better than Hanoi might. I think the Soviet Union undoubtedly has more experience with us and they have a closer familiarity with our institutions and the way we operate. I think there is more understanding in Moscow on this point than there is in Hanoi.

MR. NIVEN.   Mr. Secretary, the war itself—are we now in such a position that any substantial deescalation unilaterally would be almost as disastrous as pulling out?

SECRETARY RUSK.   Well, let me point out that partial deescalation on our side seems to be uninteresting to Hanoi. For example, they object to the idea of a pause in the bombing, the suspicion of bombing. We have tried that seriously three times, and then there were two holiday truces in addition, a total of five times when there was no bombing. And before that we went through 5 years of increasing North Vietnamese attacks upon South Viet-Nam without any bombing in North Viet-Nam on our part.

They are saying now that we must stop the bombing permanently and unconditionally and at the same time are refusing to undertake the slightest military step which they would take on their side to draw back on their part of the war.

Now, let me illustrate what this means. If we were to say that we would negotiate only if they stopped all of their violence in South Viet-Nam while we continued to bomb North Viet-Nam, most people would say we were crazy. Now, why is what is crazy for us reasonable to some people when exactly the same proposition is put by the other side? What we need to have is some tangible step toward peace. And they have had many, many opportunities to register a willingness to engage in serious talks, to take some de facto practical steps to move this matter toward a peaceful solution.

MR. NIVEN.   Well, you have got just one interpretation of their attitude. Max Frankel of the Sunday Times magazine did the same thing. But he also said that the President's letter to Ho Chi Minh said in effect "We will stop the bombing if you will leave your quarter of a million Communist forces in South Viet-Nam unreplenished and unsupplied against a million troops on our side." Now, is that not a fair representation?

SECRETARY RUSK.   Well, we said that we will stop the bombing if you will stop the infiltration and if you stop the infiltration we will stop the further augmentation of our forces.

MR. NIVEN. Would they not hold that our forces at this point are so augmented and so well supplied that they could not leave their forces?

SECRETARY RUSK. They may, but their forces are where they have no right to be. They have no business being there. They have no right to try to seize South Viet-Nam by force. We are entitled under the SEATO treaty, as well as under the individual and collective security— self-defense arrangements of the U.N. Charter, to come to the assistance of South Viet-Nam upon their request when they are subjected to this kind of aggression.

Now, we are not referring to something as though there is no difference between the two sides here. North Viet-Nam is trying to seize South Viet-Nam by force. If tomorrow morning they were to say that "This is not our purpose," we could have peace by tomorrow night. Now, it is just as simple as that, Mr. Niven. They are trying to impose a political solution upon South Viet-Nam by force from the North. Now, it can be peace if they hold their hands. And I don't see how there can be peace as long as they continue in that effort.

HANOI'S DEMAND FOR CESSATION OF BOMBING

MR. NIVEN. Is the principal objection to a cessation of bombing for the fourth time that we would incur more and more odium in the world were it renewed if they didn't come to the conference table, or is it purely military?

SECRETARY RUSK. Well, the principal problem is that, as I indicated, a suspension in the bombing would be rejected by Hanoi as an ultimatum. They say that we must guarantee that this suspension would be permanent and unconditional. Now, that means stopping half the war without knowing what will happen with the other half of the war. And the President has said that we will be glad to hear from them on almost anything they would do on the military side in order to take a step toward peace in the situation.

At the moment there are three or four divisions up in the so-called demilitarized zone, in that general area, North Vietnamese troops. No one is able to whisper to us behind his hand that if we stop the bombing those divisions will not attack our Marines who are 3 or 4 miles away. Now, we can't be children about this. We can't be foolish. We need to know what the military effect would be if we stopped the bombing in North Viet-Nam on a permanent and unconditional basis.

And no one is able or willing to give us the slightest information as to what the result would be.

MR. NIVEN.   It seems to me that the great weakness in the case of your critics, including the highly placed ones in this country, is that they are forever looking for evidence of unwillingness to negotiate on the part of the administration without examining the question, "Is there any willingness to negotiate on the other side?" But isn't it fair to say, Mr. Secretary, that over the years the willingness of either side to negotiate and consequently the terms on which it was willing to negotiate has varied according to its appraisal of the military and political situation, where the advantage lay at the moment?

SECRETARY RUSK.   Not really. It depends upon what result would be brought into being.

Now, for example, in 1962, on the basis of an agreement between Chairman Khrushchev and President Kennedy in Vienna in June 1961, we went to Geneva. We made substantial concessions in order to get an agreement on Laos. That was signed in July 1962. Among the concessions we made, for example, was to accept the nominee of the Soviet Union to be Prime Minister of Laos, Prince Souvanna Phouma.

Now, we did not get performance by Hanoi on any one of the four principal elements in that agreement. They did not withdraw their North Vietnamese forces from Laos. They did not stop using Laos as an infiltration route into South Viet-Nam. They did not permit the coalition government to function in the Communist-held areas of Laos. And they did not permit the International Control Commission to function in the Communist held areas of Laos.

That agreement was based upon a major effort on our part to take a giant step toward peace in Southeast Asia. It didn't derive from any close-in, narrow view of what the military situation would be. Now, from that time forward we have been probing in every way that we could think of to try to find a peaceful basis to bring this war to a conclusion in South Viet-Nam.

Now, we can't bring it to a conclusion by giving them South Viet-Nam. We have major commitments there.

U.S. WILL TALK WITHOUT, OR ABOUT, CONDITIONS

MR. NIVEN.   Weren't our conditions for talking a year ago, during the bombing pause in January '66, a little more unconditional than they are this time? Did we then not make it clear that we were willing to sit down and negotiate and continue the bombing pause?

SECRETARY RUSK. Well, there was a temporary suspension of the bombing, and we had been told before that pause started that a somewhat longer pause than the 5-day pause which we had had earlier might make it possible for something constructive to open up. We had been told that by some of the Communist countries. As a matter of fact they said, some of them, that if you stop 15 or 20 days that might open up some possibilities. Well, we stopped for twice as long as they suggested. But on the 34th day of that pause Hanoi came back and said that you must stop your bombing permanently and unconditionally and only then can there be any talks. And at that time they said you must take the four points of Hanoi and you must accept the Liberation Front as the sole spokesman for South Viet-Nam. In other words, they were demanding that, in effect, we surrender South Viet-Nam to the North.

MR. NIVEN. We have, however, as a result of that experience perhaps, upped the ante, have we not, this time, where we have said that we demand the cessation of infiltration of men—

SECRETARY RUSK. We will talk to these people without conditions of any sort. Now, they have raised a major condition, the stoppage of the bombing on a permanent basis. So we have said all right, we will talk to you about conditions, we will talk to you about that condition, we will talk about other things—what you should do on your side, as a preliminary to negotiation, if you wish, you see.

So we will talk to them either way, without conditions or about conditions. Now, it shouldn't be all that difficult for contacts to explore the possibilities of peace even while the fighting is going on. We negotiated on the Berlin blockade while Berlin was under blockade. We talked about Korea while the shooting was going on.

MR. NIVEN. You can talk while the bombing and infiltration continues.

SECRETARY RUSK. Yes. Indeed, in Korea we took more casualties after the talks started than we did before the talks started. And in the case of the Cuban missile crisis, we negotiated that question with the Soviet Union while they were building their missile sites just as fast as they could, you see. So there is nothing in our statements that means that if there is any real interest in peace that contracts and explorations cannot occur, either about the settlement or about the first steps toward peace and deescalating the violence, either one of them.

MR. NIVEN. Their position for 2 years now, of course, has been the bombing must stop. But if they were to abandon that and Ho Chi

Minh cabled the President and said, "I will meet you in New Delhi 2 weeks from now without conditions, let the war go on," the President would go?

SECRETARY RUSK. Well, we will be in touch with them at the first opportunity that there will be a representative of Hanoi somewhere to talk about peace. We will be there.

MR. NIVEN. Publicly or privately?

SECRETARY RUSK. Well, I think it is very likely that the most profitable contacts initially would be private. But we have asked for a conference of—of the Geneva conference of '54 or the Geneva conference of '62 or an all-Asian peace conference or a meeting between North Viet-Nam and South Viet-Nam in the demilitarized zone; or we have suggested the two cochairmen [of the Geneva conferences] might be in touch with the two parties to do something about it, that is, Britain and the Soviet Union; or we would be glad to see the three members of the International Control Commission—India, Canada, and Poland— undertake this role. Public or private, direct or indirect—it makes no difference to us.

MR. NIVEN. Through your own knowledge, would you expect to end the war with negotiations or with a fizzling out, notably of the cessation of infiltration?

SECRETARY RUSK. It is very hard to say. The Greek guerrilla operations fizzled out. There were systematic discussions preceding that. I think we ought to keep both doors open. And we have said to the other side on more than one occasion that if you don't want to come into a conference, if that is complicated, if you don't want to get into formal negotiations, then let's start doing some things on the ground of which each one of us can take note and to which we can respond, let's begin some de facto deescalation of this situation. And that hasn't produced any results either.

GENEVA ACCORDS A BASIS FOR SERIOUS TALKS

MR. NIVEN. Apart from the question of how to get into negotiations, what really is there to negotiate about, Mr. Secretary? As long as Hanoi is not willing to represent—to accept the South Vietnamese government or the emerging South Vietnamese government as the principal political structure of South Viet-Nam, as long as we are unwilling to accept the National Liberation Front as the principal political structure there, what really is there for the United States and North Viet-Nam to talk about?

SECRETARY RUSK. Well, I think that they and the Soviet Union continue to talk in terms of the Geneva accords of 1954 and 1962. The Warsaw Pact countries in their meeting in Bucharest last year put out a statement in which they called upon us to comply completely with those accords. We said fine, let's get going. When we took this matter to the Security Council of the United Nations, the Soviet representatives said, "No, the United Nations is not the proper forum, the Geneva machinery is the proper forum." So Ambassador Goldberg said, "All right, if that is your view, then let's get going with the Geneva machinery."

I think if there is to be serious talk it is likely to be on the basis of the 1954 and 1962 agreements which were signed by the other side. We signed the 1962 agreements, although we did not sign the 1954 agreements. But we accepted both of these agreements as an adequate basis for peace in Southeast Asia.

MR. NIVEN. The President has said he would be happy to accept the outcome of free elections throughout Viet-Nam.

SECRETARY RUSK. That is correct.

MR. NIVEN. Mr. [Henry Cabot] Lodge last week said it was unthinkable that we let the Viet Cong into the democratic structure of South Viet-Nam.

SECRETARY RUSK. I think what he perhaps meant was that we don't see any indication that the South Vietnamese under genuinely free elections would elect the Liberation Front or the Viet Cong. Now, you have many groups in South Viet-Nam, the Buddhists and the Catholics, the Montagnards, the million ethnic Cambodians who have been living there for a long time, the million refugees who came down from Hanoi in 1955, that period. They disagree among themselves on a number of points. But the point that they seem to have in common is that they do not want the Liberation Front. So we would not expect that the South Vietnamese would elect the Viet Cong if there were free elections.

PROGRAM OF RECONCILIATION

MR. NIVEN. But what kind of a settlement would filter down to the village and end the situation in which the Viet Cong and the present agents of South Viet-Nam are struggling for control of that village? What would end the guerrilla war?

SECRETARY RUSK.   Oh, I think in the first place a decision by Hanoi to abandon the effort to seize South Viet-Nam by force. This is by all means by all odds the most important single decision that could affect that result. I think that the rapid increase in the rate of defections from the Viet Cong, the growing disillusionment in the countryside, as one can sense it, with the Viet Cong and their very severe impositions upon the villagers, are having an effect without that decision by Hanoi. But this is a simple problem of an attempt by Hanoi to do something in the South. If they would abandon that, I am quite sure the South Vietnamese, including the Viet Cong, would come to terms among themselves.

Very recently the South Vietnamese Government announced a program of reconciliation in which they said that they would accept back into the body politic those genuine southerners who had gone over to the Viet Cong and would like to return. There would be amnesty. They would not be mistreated. They could resume their place in society. And indeed some of the defectors from the Viet Cong, the so-called returnees, have been candidates in village elections in the last three Sundays. And some of them have been elected.

So I have no real doubt that the southerners, if left alone, would resolve these problems among themselves. They can't do it so long as the North is insisting upon keeping this pressure going against the South by military means.

MR. NIVEN.   With the continuing pressure are you confident that the emerging democratic apparatus is going to survive and that the generals won't say "No" at the last minute?

SECRETARY RUSK.   Well, I think the military leadership is very strongly committed to the constitutional process, because in January of last year they themselves took the initiative to start this process going. Now, when it came to the meeting at Honolulu, they repeated that and we indicated that we were in favor of it, and this process has been going on ever since. But I think the military leadership is strongly committed to this constitutional process which they initiated and which has been picked up by the people in electing a constituent assembly, which has promulgated a constitution, and with elections that are anticipated this September.

MR. NIVEN.   To return for just a moment to the question of bombing, Mr. Secretary, there is a projected lull of a day or two on the

Buddhist birthday later this month. Is there any possibility that that will be attended by a flurry of diplomatic activity and be extended?

SECRETARY RUSK.   The Government of South Viet-Nam has again said that they would be glad to meet with the Government of North Viet-Nam in the demilitarized zone to talk about an extension of that truce. Now, the short period of cessation of the bombing is not the kind of cessation that North Viet-Nam has described as a prerequisite for serious negotiations. Now, if between now and then there was some indication that they were prepared to talk without that condition or about that condition, then of course that would be of some interest. But we have no indication that that is coming.

MR. NIVEN.   Wouldn't this perhaps be a face-saving means of getting something going on both sides?

SECRETARY RUSK.   Well, if they wish to raise the question further to extend that pause they can do so with Saigon, or they can communicate in other respects if they would be interested in some such arrangement. The problem has been that they don't seem to think very much of any temporary arrangement.

HANOI TAKES ADVANTAGE OF TRUCE PERIODS

MR. NIVEN.   Well, suppose they proposed to suggest it be extended a week or so. Would that inevitably bring the reply from us "What will you do by way of reciprocation to reduce—"

SECRETARY RUSK.   Well, these are matters that need to be discussed. That is why Saigon has offered to meet them in the demilitarized zone to talk about it—because an extended pause without something serious going on simply means that they have an opportunity to resupply and move their people about and to load all the sampans in North Viet-Nam with supplies for the guerrilla troops and get everything all set for a fresh lunge, you see, when it is over.

During the Tet pause, when the hour arrived for the Tet truce to begin, hundreds of ships, boats, barges, trucks, suddenly raced for the South. They were there at the starter's gate like horses on a racetrack, and they just rushed pellmell to the South with thousands of tons of supplies to reequip their forces and resupply them. But the important thing is that, although they knew that suspension was coming and they knew that we were interested in talking seriously during that suspension, they didn't have a diplomat at the starting gate. They were not willing to talk seriously about a settlement of the problem or about prolonging the arrangements or have some mutual deescalation of the violence during that Tet truce.

MR. NIVEN.   It has been argued that the military advantage to us, in terms of infiltration, of continuing the bombing may be outweighed by the unifying effect of the population of North Viet-Nam, may actually increase their will to continue the war. What is your appraisal of that?

SECRETARY RUSK.   Well, no one likes bombing. People get mad under bombing. But there are some very important operational questions there. I mentioned those three divisions in the demilitarized zone. These North Vietnamese forces are just a few miles away from our Marines. Are we going to say to our Marines, "You must wait until those fellows get 2 miles away before you shoot at them, but don't shoot at them when they are 9 miles away because that would be too rude—that is over on the other side of the border"? If we see a truck column of 40 trucks coming down just north of the demilitarized zone, are we going to leave them alone and then have them use that ammunition against our men the next day? You can't do that. Let's have some peace.

We can have peace literally within 24 hours if Hanoi is willing to take seriously the 1954 and 1962 agreements, abandon its effort to seize South Viet-Nam by force, and join in mutual steps to turn down this violence and get to the conference table.

MR. NIVEN.   Mr. Secretary, will you turn to East-West relations as a whole? Up to a year or so ago it seemed to be the position of the Soviet Union until Viet-Nam was settled nothing could be settled. Now, we never agreed to that. The proliferation of talks and treaties since then suggests that the Russians have now turned away and are quite anxious to continue, and expand if possible, the *détente* in spite of Viet-Nam. Is that a fair appraisal?

EFFECT OF VIET-NAM ON EAST-WEST RELATIONS

SECRETARY RUSK.   Well, undoubtedly the Viet-Nam question injects a serious problem of tension, and on both sides. For example, there are many people in this country who have serious questions about whether we should ourselves open the door to expanding trade with Eastern Europe while the Viet-Nam situation is still going on. And I have no doubt they have some problems on their side in the same direction. However, we were glad to see that despite Viet-Nam it was possible to proceed with the space treaty, and we have been working hard on the nonproliferation treaty despite Viet-Nam. So as far as we are concerned, we are prepared to continue to work at these individual questions, small or large, if the other side is willing to do so. But there are tensions there that complicate the question on both sides, and I wouldn't want to deny that.

MR. NIVEN.   You brought up a political question I would like to ask you—would like to pursue with you. Some of the people on the Hill opposed to the administration's policy in Viet-Nam have said when you send people around the country, military officers or others, as they put it, talking the language of the cold war and whipping up passions about the war in Viet-Nam, you create a body of public opinion in this country which makes it difficult to get the consular treaty, to get through an increased East-West trade, and so forth. Is this true?

SECRETARY RUSK.   Well, I cannot generalize about that. Our general view is that we have to do what is necessary in Viet-Nam because of our commitments and because of its relation with the general problem of organizing a durable peace in the world. But on the other hand we ought to be ready to try to resolve other questions, large or small, if we can.

Now, that's difficult. And it is not easy for all of our people to understand why it's important. But I think the central question in front of us all is the question of organizing a peace. And every policy needs to be weighed in terms of whether it will contribute toward that objective or not.

Now, we send out a thousand cables a day out of this Department. My guess is that most of the people would approve of most of those cables and that those who object to one particular part of the policy would support much of the rest. But the object of the entire effort is to organize a global peace, because we are in a situation—and have been for over a decade—where the organization of a peace is necessary to the survival of the human race, in very simple terms. . . .

George McGovern
THE LESSONS OF VIET NAM

. . . Before we take any further steps toward a larger war—and I notice in the press that our commander is said to be asking for considera-

Senator George McGovern, a Democrat, is the junior Senator from South Dakota. This speech, given on April 25, 1967, is reprinted from the *Congressional Record* for that date.

bly more troops in Vietnam—or before we undertake any new ventures of this kind elsewhere in the world, I would hope that we will reexamine the assumptions which have involved us in what I believe to be a mistaken course. . . .

To assist in stimulating such a re-examination, I make the following indictments of our Vietnam policy:

First. Our Vietnam policymakers have distorted history to justify our intervention in a civil conflict supposedly to defend a free nation against external aggression from another nation; actually we are backing a dictatorial group in Saigon against a competing group backed by a dictatorial regime from the north.

Second. Our Vietnam policymakers are unwittingly advancing the cause of communism while seeking to contain it. . . .

Third. While orally calling for negotiations, we are practicing military escalation and diplomatic rigidity in such a fashion as to foreclose negotiations.

Fourth. Our policymakers have frequently misled the American public, the result being a serious loss of credibility for the U.S. Government.

Fifth. We are wasting human and material resources needed for the revitalization of our society.

Sixth. We are jeopardizing essential U.S. foreign policy interests, including a promising improvement in East-West relations.

Seventh. We bypassed the United Nations until the 11th hour and have disregarded the opinion and the sensibilities of the international community.

Eighth. We are weakening America's moral position and beclouding American idealism.

Ninth. We are creating at home a climate of intimidation designed to silence dissent and meaningful discussion of policy.

This is a grave indictment. I will summarize briefly the facts and arguments which substantiate these charges.

First. The historical rationalization of our Vietnam intervention is based on the Munich analogy or "the domino theory." At Munich in 1938 the Western allies failed to stand up to Hitler's demand for a piece of Czechoslovakia. The result of this surrender was a series of aggressions leading to World War II. In Vietnam—so the theory goes—we are faced with another Hitler in the form of Ho Chi Minh, or perhaps Moscow or Peking working through Ho Chi Minh. If only Ho or his backers can be stopped in Vietnam, we will have averted another Munich and saved mankind from world war III.

As one of our soldiers was reported to have said, according to a newspaper in my State:

We are fighting in Vietnam so we won't have to have foxholes and barbed wire entanglements on the Main Street of Aberdeen, South Dakota.

It is said that if we do not crush Ho, his control of Vietnam will topple such other dominoes as Laos, Thailand, Cambodia, Burma, the Philippines, and perhaps India, Pakistan, Australia, and Japan, and then on to Hawaii and San Francisco. We are left to wonder how a flotilla of Vietnamese or Chinese junks is going to get by the 7th Fleet en route to San Francisco.

This, I think, is a piece of historical nonsense. There is no analogy between Munich and Vietnam, and countries are not dominoes.

Hitler was a madman commanding the world's mightiest military machine—a machine with the mobility, the offensive power, and the assigned mission of leaping across national frontiers until the world was conquered. At Munich, he directly threatened Czechoslovakia, a highly developed democratic state that was ready to fight for its survival with any indication of Western support.

Ho Chi Minh, doubtless guilty of many sins, has nevertheless devoted most of his public life to winning independence for his country. A confirmed Marxist, he is more significantly an ardent nationalist, bound less by the claims of international communism than by Vietnamese nationalism. He is far less interested in what Peking or Moscow want, than he is in what he wants for his own country.

During World War II he stood with the United States against the Japanese and assisted American flyers shot down over Japanese-held jungle areas. With the end of World War II, he resisted French efforts to regain colonial control of his people. After 8 years of fighting, he defeated the French and emerged a national hero. At the Geneva Conference of 1954, he agreed to end the fighting, withdraw his forces north of a temporary cease-fire line at the 17th parallel, and await an election 2 years hence that doubtless would have led to his election as leader of a united Vietnam. President Eisenhower has written that in 1954 after expelling the French, Ho had the support of at least 80 percent of the Vietnamese people, both north and south.

But the promised elections were blocked by Premier Ngo Dinh Diem whom we were instrumental in installing in South Vietnam. Of equal significance—and this is sometimes lost sight of—Diem cut off all trade and other relationships with North Vietnam and ruthlessly suppressed his internal opposition.

I remember that the late Bernard Fall, whom I referred to a while ago, said that the cutting off of trade between the north and south had as much to do in causing the conflict that eventually developed as anything else.

This was the background for the Vietcong revolt in the south, aided by Ho Chi Minh from the north. Although marked by bloodshed and violence, it is scarcely analogous to Hilter's attempted global conquest in moving against international frontiers with a mighty military machine. The insurrection in Vietnam grew out of local conditions which pitted one group of Vietnamese against another. Even if there had never been such a country as China, the probability is that that revolt would have taken place.

Ho Chi Minh heads one of the smallest and most impoverished states in the world. Neither in capacity nor by inclination can he be seriously seen as a Hitler-type conquerer threatening the security of America and the world.

As for the falling dominoes that are said to be marked for "wars of liberation" elsewhere in Asia and therefore seems to be the rationalization for the enormous commitment we are making there—it is clear that the challenge to them is not a Hitler or a Ho from the outside, but their own domestic political, economic, and social problems. A country that builds a government responsive to the needs of the citizenry—that faces up to the internal problems of misrule, injustice, and human misery need have little fear of falling victim to a "war of liberation." A government that ignores these fundamental concerns of its people as the dictators of South Vietnam have done is headed for trouble and does not deserve to be saved—indeed, it probably cannot be saved—by American soldiers. . . .

Second. To contain Communist Chinese influence and power in Asia, we have set up a series of unpopular dictators in Saigon. Ignoring Vietnam's deep-seated historic opposition to China, we have assumed that since Ho Chi Minh was a Communist, he must therefore be a tool of Peking or Moscow.

Mr. President, it is an uncontested historical fact that for a thousand years the people of southeast Asia have resisted the Chinese more than any other outside power.

Actually, the most powerful force moving in Vietnam as elsewhere in Asia is nationalism—not international communism. Ho Chi Minh left to his own devices might have united the Vietnamese as an effective buffer against Chinese penetration of southeast Asia. U.S. policy, far from containing Peking or Moscow, is most likely to draw outside Communist power and influence into southeast Asia. It may even reunite the feuding Communist world. . . .

The destruction of South Vietnamese villages by American bombers and the growing occupation of city and countryside by American forces raises the unpopular specter of a Western-style occupation again and plays into the hands of Communist propagandists all over Asia. In the north, American bombers are pounding away at the North Vietnamese economic and industrial strength. The resulting chaos or vacuum is hardly calculated to provide a formidable barrier to Chinese penetration.

Third. Our diplomacy before, during and after the Geneva Conference of 1954 has been narrow and self-defeating. For years we made no effort to negotiate or even offer to negotiate an end to the violence. When Ho Chi Minh indicated in 1964 to the Secretary General of the United Nations, U Thant, that he was ready to talk about a settlement, we rejected this opportunity as we rebuffed other peace feelers before and since. The Johnson administration has insisted it is prepared to embark on "unconditional discussions." Thus, on April 27, 1967, President Johnson said:

> I will talk to any government, anywhere, any time *without any conditions,* and if they doubt our sincerity, let them test us.

When tested, however, as it has been on a number of occasions, the administration has insisted on conditions—and pretty harsh ones at that. Some of the conditions would, in effect, virtually require the prior capitulation of the other side. This was the central fact that emerged from President Johnson's celebrated letter to Ho Chi Minh in February, a letter which far from representing a new and more moderate approach to peacemaking was, in fact, a hardening of our previous position in terms of the conditions we demanded of Hanoi.

Fourth. The American people have been given in the past decade a bewildering array of false assurances, contradictory interpretations, and mistaken predictions about Vietnam. We were assured that our role would be limited to an advisory function—that this was a war which the Vietnamese people must win or lose. Time after time, top administration officials contended that this was basically a political struggle that could be decided in Saigon's favor only if the government there could draw together enough grassroots support to offset the guerrillas. We were repeatedly assured that American troops and bombers could not solve that problem and in fact would make it worse. For example, speaking on June 12, 1966, just a few days before the first bombing of Hanoi and Haiphong, the U.S. Army Chief of Staff, Gen. Harold K. Johnson, said:

> It would be foolish to expand the war and destroy North Vietnam's economic and military capabilities since this would only double the price of the war because the United States would have to ultimately rebuild what it destroyed.

Yet, only days later, we began doing exactly what General Johnson had said it would be foolish to do. Repeatedly, administration spokesmen have explained in vigorous terms the limits of our policy and our operations in Vietnam only to have those limits abruptly exceeded before the previous words had died away. Defense Secretary Robert S. McNamara and Secretary of State Dean Rusk's major pronouncements on the war have been marked by one consistent quality—they have all proved to be wrong.

In the 1964 presidential campaign, millions of Americans rejected Senator Goldwater's prescription for victory in Vietnam through bombing, jungle defoliation, and a major escalation of American forces. President Johnson and his top Cabinet officers built a convincing case against bombing and the escalation of American ground forces. "We seek no wider war" was the winning slogan of 1964.

Yet, the mandate for peace of 1964 has been translated into the Goldwater prescription on the installment plan. Little wonder that the administration is faced with a credibility gap as wide as the Grand Canyon.

If one were to attempt a balance sheet on the costs and benefits of our Vietnam venture, high on the cost side would be the planting of doubt and resentment leading to a loss of faith in Government on the part of many of our people, especially the youth. One of the invaluable sources of national strength is the capacity to enlist the enthusiastic support of the young for essential national interests. To blunt that enthusiasm and vital faith in the reliability and fundamental honesty of our Government is a grievous blow to a democratic society.

Fifth. There are other incalculable costs to America and to the world that stem from Vietnam. We are now pumping Federal funds into the war effort at a rate of over $2 billion monthly. This is a serious drain on our balance of payments, our dollar, and our fiscal health. It represents money urgently needed to rebuild our decaying, explosive, riot-ridden city slums; to strengthen educational, recreational, and employment opportunities in rural America; to clean up our polluted rivers and streams. It would be ironic, indeed, if we devote so heavy a proportion of our resources to the pacification of Vietnam that we are unable to pacify Los Angeles, Chicago, and Harlem.

Sixth. It may be that the greatest cost of our Vietnam involvement is its regrettable impact on other vital foreign policy interests of the United States. The improved relations with the Soviet Union that followed the sobering Cuban missile crisis of 1962 gave promise of a detente between the world's two great nuclear powers. Likewise, the fragmentation of the international Communist bloc opened the way for new U.S. initiatives. The reaction against heavy-handed Chinese interference in

Africa, Indonesia, and elsewhere suggested further opportunities for a sensitive, flexible U.S. policy. In eastern Europe, the so-called Soviet satellites have seemed to beckon for better relations with the West. Progress toward nuclear control was promised by the limited test ban treaty of 1963.

All of these hopeful and challenging foreign policy opportunities have been threatened or thwarted by the fast-deepening, U.S. preoccupation with the war in Vietnam. Our policy planners, the Congress, and the American people are devoting so much energy and attention to one tiny corner of southeast Asia that we tend to lose sight of the fast-changing global panorama that is unfolding before our eyes.

Seventh. The United States was founded by men who declared our national independence with "a decent respect for the opinions of mankind." Our Nation 170 years later, took the lead in establishing the United Nations to preserve the peace. On several occasions we worked through United Nations channels to meet international crises—the Arab-Israel conflict, the Suez crisis, Korea, the Congo, Cyprus, Kashmir, and Yemen. But in Vietnam, we have plunged in alone with only a belated reference to the United Nations.

The United Nations Charter commits us to seek the settlement of disputes through the international machinery of that organization. Our SEATO treaty commits us only to confer with the other treaty signatories on possible action. Yet, in the name of a vague international commitment we fight on in Vietnam with no backing from the United Nations, no broad SEATO support, and, indeed, little support from any source other than a few small states heavily dependent upon our favor. The only important power publicly backing our Vietnam course is Britain which is dependent upon American support for maintenance of the pound. Even in this instance, Prime Minister Harold Wilson has disassociated his government from our bombing of Haiphong and Hanoi.

Eighth. America's greatest asset in the world has been our democratic tradition, our concept of human dignity, and a humane society devoted to peace. But Vietnam presents a different view of America. Here the world sees America intervening with massive military power—napalm, artillery, and bombing—on a scale heretofore used only against Nazi Germany and Tojo's Japan in the 1940's. American actions in Vietnam, however well intentioned, do not square with the image of America that the world has traditionally admired.

In November of 1965, I visited a civilian casualty hospital in Danang near the site of one of our largest airbases in Vietnam. The poorly equipped wards were jammed with terribly burned, broken and torn men, women and children, innocent victims of our bombs, napalm and artillery. They lay silently—two persons on each cot—their pained eyes following me as I walked from bed to bed. I wondered that day, as I do now, if this great Nation of ours has the right to make so costly a decision on behalf of another people who have already suffered so grievously.

Ninth. Our course in Vietnam does not square with the conscience of the judgment of many thoughtful Americans. But as the tempo of the battle increases and the martial spirit rises, the dissenter will need to draw deeply on his courage. Our official spokesmen have demonstrated a growing resentment toward the doubter and the dissenter. The impression is being created that while freedom of conscience and expression are desirable theoretical principles, they are too dangerous to practice in wartime. Even when the claims of top level officials prove to be groundless or contradictory, the pressure is on to accept the next pronouncement without question. To challenge the soundness of our policy judgments is more and more being equated with "letting down the boys in Vietnam" or giving aid to Hanoi. It is almost as though we are fighting so intently to secure freedom in Vietnam that we are willing to sacrifice it in America. It is still a regrettable truism that truth is the first casualty in wartime. Yet, it is in times of national crisis and conflict that America most urgently needs men who will speak out with maximum candor.

For my own part, I reject the assumptions that lie behind our involvement, and I regret each new step toward a deeper involvement. Before we take those fateful additional steps that may lead to Armageddon, I recommend now as I have in the past, but with a new urgency and a deeper concern, that we:

Stop the bombing, north and south, end search and destroy offensive sweeps, and confine our military action to holding operations on the ground. Bombing the north has failed to halt or seriously check the flow of troops to the south and may, in fact, have prompted a much greater war effort by Hanoi. Secretary McNamara himself told a Senate committee:

> I don't believe that the bombing . . . has significantly reduced (nor would reduce) the actual flow of men and material to the South.

In the south, our bombs have killed or maimed countless numbers of innocent people and alienated others whose support we covet. A defensive holding action in the south as advocated by Generals Gavin and Ridgway could be pursued while determined efforts are being made to negotiate a ceasefire. It is the bombing of North Vietnam that presents the greatest obstacle to a settlement and greatest danger of involving Russia or China in the war.

We should clearly state our willingness to negotiate directly with the Vietcong with some recognition that they will play a significant role in any provisional government resulting from a ceasefire and a negotiated settlement.

We should use what influence we have to encourage a more broadly based civilian government in Saigon—a government willing to start discussions with the other side looking toward arrangements to end the war.

We should advocate an international presence to police a ceasefire, supervise elections, provide an umbrella for the resettlement of Vietnamese concerned about their safety, and arrange for the withdrawal of all outside forces and the conversion of military bases to peacetime uses.

The path to sanity and peace in south-east Asia will not be easy. The way to a larger war is enticing and simple. But before we make that choice, let us recall the words of Virgil:

> Easy is the descent to Hell; night and day the gates stand open; but to reclimb the slope and escape to the outer air, this indeed is a task.

But if we can accomplish that task, we should use the Vietnam experience as a guide to future policy. The enormous destruction of life and property in Vietnam, both American and Vietnamese, will have served no useful purpose unless we learn well the lessons that this tragic conflict can teach us. Those lessons, I believe, include the following:

First, conflicts of this kind have historical dimensions which are essentially political, economic, and psychological; they do not respond readily to military force from the outside. Surely, the military might of the United States can subdue little Vietnam, south and north.

But is this what the struggle is all about? I think not. We are confronted in Vietnam with an indigenous guerrilla force that has enjoyed the sympathy or the complicity of much of the local peasantry. The ineffective and unpopular regimes of Saigon have not earned the confidence of their subjects. Urgent priorities, of which land reform is probably the most important, have been ignored. Thus, the destruction of the military power of the guerrillas and of North Vietnam leaves fundamental political and economic problems still festering to set the stage for future conflict or continued tyranny and injustice.

Second, in the future the United States should avoid committing its power to internal struggles of this kind. The factors involved are so complex and confusing that it is beyond the capacity of an outside nation to know which group deserves support and which opposition. In spite of the administration's strenuous efforts to picture the situation as a war of aggression from the north, it is essentially a civil conflict among various groups of Vietnamese. The Vietcong control is strongest in the delta country of the south a thousand miles from North Vietnam and that control is exercised by indigenous forces who enjoy the cooperation of the local peasantry.

Such internal disputes should be fought out by the competing groups without outside interference, or be referred to the United Nations. We have no obligation to play policeman for the world and especially in Asia, which is so sensitive to heavy-handed interference by even well-meaning white men.

Third, unpopular, corrupt regimes of the kind we have been allied with in Saigon do not deserve to be saved by the blood of American boys. Local governments that have done a good job usually have the confidence of the local citizens. They ordinarily do not have a guerrilla problem and when they do, their own people are loyal enough to the Government to take care of the guerrillas instead of depending on us to do that for them.

Even if one assumes that we are faced with a battle for power between Ho Chi Minh of the north and Marshal Ky of the south, there is no clear issue here of black and white or tyranny and freedom. Ho is a Communist tyrant, but does Marshal Ky with his admiration for Adolf Hitler represent the kind of ideals and morality that American men should die for?

I have never regretted my service as a bomber pilot in World War II when we stopped the madmen Hitler, Mussolini, and Tojo. But I do not believe that Vietnam is that kind of testing ground of freedom and free world security. It is a confusing civil conflict with no real certainty as to the issues at stake. I do not want to see my son or other boys die in that kind of doubtful struggle.

Fourth, those who believe that American military power has an important role to play in the Pacific should return to the once-accepted doctrine of our best generals that we should avoid committing American soldiers to the jungles of Asia. Our power in the Pacific is in naval and air strength as a deterrent against aggression. Local governments must deal with their own guerrilla problems.

Fifth, Congress must never again surrender its power under our constitutional system by permitting an ill-advised, undeclared war of this kind. Our involvement in South Vietnam came about through a series of moves by the executive branch—each one seemingly restrained and yet each one setting the stage for a deeper commitment. The complex of administration moves involving the State Department, the CIA, the Pentagon, AID, and various private interests—all of these have played a greater role than has Congress. Congress cannot be very proud of its function in the dreary history of this steadily widening war. That function has been very largely one of acquiescence in little-understood administration efforts. The surveillance, the debate, and the dissent since 1965, while courageous and admirable, came too late in the day to head off the unwise course charted by our policymakers. . . .